1453

MICHAEL KINNEAR

Cartography by the author

THE BRITISH VOTER

An Atlas and Survey since 1885

BATSFORD ACADEMIC AND EDUCATIONAL LTD LONDON

© Michael Kinnear 1981
First Published 1968
Second edition 1981
All rights reserved. No part of this publication
may be reproduced, in any form or by any means,
without the permission from the Publisher

Typeset by Keyspools Ltd, Golborne, Lancs
and printed and bound in Great Britain by
The Anchor Press Ltd,
Tiptree, Essex
for the publishers
Batsford Academic and Educational Ltd
An imprint of B. T. Batsford Ltd
4 Fitzhardinge Street
London W1H 0AH

ISBN 0 7134 3482 1 (cased)

Acknowledgment

I should like to thank Mr Maurice Shock and Professor Geoffrey Lambert, who made many valuable comments on the manuscript. Mr Peter Hayden and Professor Keith Robbins both made several useful suggestions about the Nonconformist vote. Mr and Mrs Robert Purcell were very hospitable to me when I stayed with them in London. The Social Sciences and Humanities Research Council of Canada and the Faculty of Graduate Studies of the University of Manitoba were both helpful to me. Finally, I wish to thank my wife, Mary.

Winnipeg, Canada,
5 June, 1980

Contents

Section IV

Section V

Section VI

Introduction

The study of politics considers economic and social forces, just as it considers national issues and intellectual developments. This does not imply that issues and ideas are unimportant or even secondary; on the contrary, it implies that the study of economic and social forces helps explain their significance. This book examines the social, economic and organisation background of British politics on a nationwide scale, over the period since 1885.

The study of the economic and social background to politics, and the extensive use of maps in such a study, has had a long history. In 1913 André Siegfried published his pioneering work on politics in Western France.[1] Siegfried's book contained numerous maps and charts illustrating such things as seats won by parties, and the relation between clericalism and royalism. Other French political scientists carried on Siegfried's work, although it was not until 1951 that François Goguel published an electoral geography of France as a whole.[2] By 1957, French psephological techniques had become very sophisticated, as was indicated by the publication of a joint work on the 1956 French elections.[3] That book examined in detail the influence of social, economic and other factors on the election results. It did not ignore political issues but described politics in the round, instead of only one aspect, such as the events of the election campaign.

British historians and political scientists have long recognised the importance of economic and social factors in the politics of other countries, and they have used social statistics extensively in their work. For instance, Williams and Zeldin have both used maps and similar material in their books on French politics, while Carr and Macartney have used maps and graphs extensively in their standard histories of Spain and Hungary.[4] However, until the 1970s, there were few books about the relationship between social and economic factors in British elections. There were numerous studies of individual constituencies, but, apart from *The British Voter*, none of the country as a whole during the 20th century. The articles by Michael Steed in the most recent Nuffield studies of current British elections have gone far to correct this; as have the articles by Ivor Crewe in the *Times Guides to the House of Commons. The Economist* has also had a great many articles of high quality covering many aspects of regional variation.

There were three main reasons for the apparent lack of interest until the 1970s in the social background of politics in Britain. First, until 1966, census figures were not available by constituency; secondly, election results even now are not available by polling division; third, and perhaps most important, before 1970, the notion that British politics were 'national' was prevalent to such an extent that there was little recognition of local and regional variations.

Because the census figures were not available by constituency until 1966, it was not possible to correlate them with election results without long and arduous work on each census. One may contrast this with Germany, France and Italy, where such correlations were possible.[5] In *The British Voter*, the author provided constituency-based census returns for the first time, on the Census of 1921. This year was chosen because it was mid-way between the first election covered in the book, and the last. There is some arbitrary allocation of census figures in a few of the smaller rural districts; but the net effect of this on the figures presented here is very small, and does not affect any significant conclusions.

One drawback to the use of any census figures is that until 1918, the electorate was not the same as the population enumerated in the census. There was no way of determining from the figures alone whether a high or a low proportion of, say, the miners in a given constituency had the vote. The only way to do this would be to examine the electoral register for a given election in that constituency. It would be a large task to do this for one election in one constituency; and larger still for a dozen elections in hundreds of constituencies, assuming all the records were kept.

The maps on pp. 117-127 of this book show the location of certain occupational groups in the country in 1921 and 1966. The census figures are most accurate when applied to the inter-war and post-1966 elections; but if one extrapolates and compares the two sets of figures, one can use them for the intervening period as well.

With the publication of census figures by constituency after 1966, scholars have been able to compare them with election results much more easily. One good example of this is the work by Crewe and Payne on the 1970 election.[6] Crewe and Payne used several mathematical techniques to produce a formula by which one could say that the swing, or other voting pattern in a given constituency or region was exceptional. Thus the role of individual candidates and regional differences could be demonstrated much more clearly than before.

A second drawback to the study of the social background of British politics is that election results are available only by constituency, and most constituencies do not have homogeneous populations. Some constituencies are more nearly homogeneous than others, especially in the cases of mining, slum and agricultural seats. However, such seats were and are a minority, and even they are not completely homogeneous. In some countries election results are available by polling divisions, and these figures can be examined in greater detail than figures

1 Siegfried, *Tableau politique de la France de l'Oeust sous la Troisième République* (1913, reissued in 1964)
2 Goguel, *Géographie des éléctions françaises* (1951)
3 Duverger, et. al., *Les éléctions du 2 Janvier 1956* (1957)
4 P. M. Williams, *Politics in Postwar France* (1954; reissued in 1964 as *Crisis and Compromise*); T. Zeldin's 2-volume history of 19th century France was issued in 1973

and 1977; A.R.M.Carr, *Spain, 1808–1939* (1966) and C.A.Macartney, *Hungary and Her Successors* (1965 ed.)
5 e.g., Chassériaud, *le parti démocrate chrétien en Italie*, 126-216; Fink, *Die NPD bei der Bayerischen Landtagswahl 1966*, 51-87; Milatz, *Wähler und Wahlen in der Weimarer Republik*, passim; Goguel, op. cit.
6 Butler and Pinto-Duschinsky, *The British General Election of 1970*, 416-436.

for Britain. For example, if figures are available for polling divisions, it is generally possible to find a number of such divisions which contain few people apart from miners. By examining the political allegiance of such places, one can make useful conclusions about the political allegiance of the mining vote in general. On the other hand, if election results are available only by constituency, one cannot make such firm conclusions about the mining vote. But election results are available, even if not by polling division. It is thus possible to devise rough guides about the voting of mining and other constituencies, so long as one takes into account the qualifying factors mentioned.

The third and most important reason for the relative lack of interest in the social background of British politics is that the study of British elections is a recent development. While psephology had developed in France before the First World War, it was not until 1947 that a book appeared on a British election,[1] and it was not until the 1950s that British psephology got off the ground. Consequently, the three elections of 1951, 1955 and 1959 greatly influenced the development of election-studies in Britain; and these elections had hardly any regional trends which differed markedly from national trends. The intensive study of these three elections therefore gave credence to the notion that British politics is more 'national' than, say, French politics. However, the three elections were historically unusual. Most past elections in Britain had shown wider variations than any of the three, as even the most cursory glance shows. For instance, in 1945 the swing to Labour had ranged from 2·5% in Glasgow to 22% in North-west Kent; while in 1950 the swing to the Conservatives had ranged from 2·3% in mining seats in Wales to 8·8% in North Lancashire.[2] Such wide variations were not found in the elections of 1951, 1955 and 1959. These three elections also differed from those held after 1964, when regional variations once more became apparent; and even more so in the 1970s, when third and fourth party votes averaged 20·4% of the total compared with only 4·7% for the elections of 1951-59. The high percentages for Liberal and Nationalist candidates in the 1974 elections make it difficult even to speak of a uniform national trend, as distinct from numerous contradictory regional ones.[3]

It must be admitted that with the exception of the Nationalist vote in Scotland and Wales in the 1970s, and apart from Ulster, electoral variations in Britain have been less marked than in some European countries. However, the variations have existed, and it would be misleading to play them down.

Some regional studies exist, the best-known of which are Morgan's account of Welsh politics between 1868 and 1922; and Rose's work on Ulster in the 1960s. As well, two volumes on the mid-1920s, by C. P. Cook and the author of this book, examine the social background to elections. There is also a brief account of Scottish politics in the 1960s.[4] Studies have also appeared on the mining and farming communities, but most have been written from the economic viewpoint, with little attempt to relate it to politics.[5] So important regions have not been examined in detail,

though recently books have appeared on London, Lancashire, and Liverpool for part of the period covered by this book.[6]

Another gap has been that the influence of religion on politics in the twentieth century has been little examined. Although Morgan has dissected the significance of religion in Wales, little has yet been written about its importance in England or Scotland. Yet Nonconformity had considerable importance in politics in England, at least during the first two decades of this century, while Roman Catholicism may have had an even longer period of political significance. The main drawback to the study of the political significance of religion is that only one reliable census was taken of religious groups, in 1851. Although unofficial 'censuses' and surveys were taken of some areas in later years, they were invariably taken by a group interested in presenting statistics favourable to one religious group or another, for use as political ammunition.

As an alternative to such biassed and unofficial surveys, one must rely on the statistics provided by the religious groups themselves. These statistics, though more reliable than the surveys, are only a rough guide, because of the different methods used in compiling them. The Roman Catholic statistics define as a Roman Catholic anyone baptised as such; while the Nonconformist statistics define as a Nonconformist only an active member of a chapel. Anglican statistics consider only those persons who took Communion on Easter Sunday. It is possible to make a reasonable estimate of the Roman Catholic and Nonconformist populations using the statistics provided by the religious groups. The Nonconformist figures are more nearly accurate than the Roman Catholic ones, because they can be applied directly to electoral divisions, while the Roman Catholic ones can be applied only indirectly.[7] In this book the distribution of Nonconformists and Roman Catholics has been calculated for 1922 for two reasons: first, it was not possible to determine what proportion of the members of the religious groups had the vote before 1918; and second, because of the great importance attached by Nonconformists to their numbers in pre-war debates on education, Nonconformist statistics for the pre-war period may have been inflated. By 1922 the Nonconformists had less cause to inflate their figures, and their statistics were probably more reliable. The 1922 figures are for the closest peacetime election to the pre-war period.

The statistical and other material in this book may be helpful in examining a wide variety of topics. For instance, it is possible to trace connections between the middle-class, the agricultural, the Nonconformist and other votes, with the political affiliation of constituencies and districts. It is also possible to determine what exactly were the regions in British politics. In many respects the administrative divisions of Britain into counties did not correspond to social divisions, and it is often possible to identify regions which overlapped county boundaries. The material in this book cannot solve some very important problems. For instance, one can make a tentative conclusion about the middle class that it appears to have been more variable in political allegiance than certain other groups. This is to some extent confirmed by public opinion polls.[8]

1 R. B. McCallum and A. Readman, *The British General Election of 1945* (1947 reissued in 1964)

2 Fuller tables of the swing are given in map, General Election of 1945 p. 57, and in map, General Election of 1950, p. 59.

3 The term 'region' has been variously defined. For the purposes of this book it is interpreted loosely as meaning an area of the country which differed politically in some respect from other areas.

4 K. O. Morgan, *Wales in British Politics, 1868-1922* (1963); Richard Rose, *Governing Without Consensus* (1971); C. P. Cook, *The Age of Alignment* (1975); M. Kinnear, *The Fall of Lloyd George: the political crisis of 1922* (1973); I. Budge and D. W. Urwin,

Scottish Political Behaviour (1966)

5 *R. G. Gregory, The Miners and British Politics, 1906-14 is an exception.*

6 Thompson, *Socialists, Liberals and Labour: The struggle for London, 1885-1914* (1967); Clarke, *Lancashire and the New Liberalism* (1971); Lawton and Cunningham, *Merseyside* (1970)

7 The maps on pp. 127 and 131 describe the method of calculating the figures for the distribution of Nonconformists in England and of the Roman Catholics in Scotland for 1922

8 See maps, General Elections of 1964 and 1966, pp. 67 and 69

However, the opinion polls were not taken with the end in view of answering this question, and in any case, they were not always reliable.

Another question to which this book can give only a partial answer is the very important one of minority groups. Some evidence in this book indicates that minorities were more cohesive where they were strong than where they were weak. For instance, speakers of Gaelic and Welsh tended to retain their languages more where they were an overwhelming majority than where they were a minority.[1] It is, however, an open question whether this cohesion was found in other groups and, if so, whether it has a political significance. Budge and Urwin found, for instance, that in a Scottish constituency where the Roman Catholics formed a large portion of the electorate, both middle-class and working-class Roman Catholics tended to vote Labour.[2] On the other hand, two surveys of constituencies where Roman Catholics were a small proportion of the electorate found no significant correlation between middle-class Roman Catholics and Labour voters.[3] The sample of middle-class Roman Catholics in each of these surveys was too small for firm conclusions to be drawn. However, the Roman Catholics examined by Budge and Urwin may well have acted with their working-class co-religionists because of a feeling of cohesion caused by the presence of a large community of Roman Catholics. Before any final conclusion could be made about this, an intensive study would be required of several hundred middle-class Roman Catholics, in places with varying proportions of Roman Catholics. The normal opinion poll is of 1,000-4,000 people in the whole country, only a few of whom would be middle-class Roman Catholics. Such a sample would be too small to provide realistic conclusions about the question posed here.

This question, whether minority groups are more cohesive when strong than when weak, is of great importance, but it cannot be answered by examining election results. Consequently, it cannot be answered for the past. However, the material in this book points out where some minorities were strong, and in that way it can help students of political behaviour in future elections.

British politics since 1885 may be divided into four distinct periods. From 1885 to 1918, the Liberal and Conservative parties predominated; while from 1935 to about 1965 the Labour and Conservative parties predominated. However, in the 1920s all three major parties were strong. For this reason, this book examines the 1920s in some detail. The years after about 1965 saw a gradual increase in Liberal and minor party support; but at the moment it is too soon to tell whether this was a psephological watershed, or merely a short-term dissatisfaction with the two major parties.

Pages 82-115 of this book, which examine party strength and organisation, deal primarily with the 1920s, for two reasons. First, in the early 1920s two party organisations were established virtually from scratch. These were the local Labour organisations and the local Lloyd George Liberal organisations. An examination of the way these two organisations were set up gives some insight into the mechanics of party structure. The second reason for studying the 1920s in detail is that in the first years of the decade there were serious divisions in all three major parties. Much material is available for the study of these divisions. Of course, there have been many divisions within one party or another in

modern times: for example, the division within the Liberals over Home Rule in 1885-7[4]; within the Conservatives over tariffs in 1904-6[5]; and within Labour over Bevan in 1950-51. However, there was no other period in recent times when all major parties have been divided simultaneously; and this gives special interest to a study of the 1920s.

Some features emerge from this study of the 1920s, such as the difficulty of Labour in expanding in working-class districts where the Liberals were strong. This was noticeable in East Lancashire, the textile district of West Yorkshire and the mining area of Derbyshire, among other places.[6] Another aspect of the period was that, while the Liberal and Conservative areas overlapped, and while Liberal and Labour areas also overlapped, Labour and Conservative areas did not overlap very much. One might conclude that the Liberals appealed to a wider range of voters than either the Conservatives or Labour.[7] This is confirmed by most opinion polls taken since the Second World War. Such polls have found that Liberal support has been distributed fairly evenly among the classes, while Conservative and Labour support has been drawn disproportionately from one class or another.[8] This wide appeal of the Liberals may have been one of the major reasons for their decline: since they did not speak for any one group, the Liberals could not rely on any group for solid support.

The most important conclusion reached in this study of the 1920s is that the situation was unclear, that political alignments were not so predetermined as often suggested, and that although certain probable trends could be discerned at the beginning of the 1920s, there was nothing to indicate that those trends were inevitable. The period was more confused and uncertain than sometimes realised, and this book can point out only part of the confusion. It is hoped that the detailed studies of the three main parties which are at present in progress will make this clearer.

This book does not, and because of the nature of the evidence cannot, say why voters made up their minds. However, certain tentative conclusions can be drawn. Widespread and rapid fluctuations followed the two major expansions of the electorate in this period, in 1884 and 1918. In each case there was a decade of fluctuation in party fortunes, which was followed by a period of relative stability. Such fluctuations in party fortunes were not prominent except after enfranchisements.[9] Although other oscillations occurred, they generally took the form of expansions or contractions of parties in areas they had previously held. One may therefore conclude, first, that newly-enfranchised voters shopped around before making their choice of parties; and second, that once such voters had made their decision, most of them kept to it. Many factors influenced their choice, primarily the social class of the voters concerned, their religion, and party policies. It is improbable that these influences accounted for all the decisions, although they probably accounted for most. Some voters based their decisions on the personalities of individual candidates or on the influence of notable persons in their districts. For instance, the personal influence of Joseph Chamberlain may have been partly decisive in transferring Birmingham from the Liberal to the Conservative camp. Probably the influence of individuals was greatest in the periods of flux following expansions of the electorate. In more settled periods such personal influences no doubt counted for less.

---

1 This is examined in the maps, Scotland and Wales, pp. 131 and 135
2 Budge and Urwin, op.cit., 63
3 R. S. Milne and H. C. Mackenzie, Marginal Seat, 1955, 65; and Bealey et al., op.cit., 173
4 Examined in M. Hurst, Joseph Chamberlain and Liberal Reunion (1967)
5 See map, Unionist Free Traders in 1904, p. 101

6 See maps, General Elections of 1918 to 1929, pp. 39-49
7 See maps, Liberal, Conservative and Labour seats, 1918-1929, pp. 85, 107 and 113
8 See maps, General Elections of 1964 and 1966, pp. 67 and 69 for opinion polls showing the relation between social class and party affiliations
9 It should be noted that the period of fluctuation in 1929-31 followed a minor expansion of the electorate

Two types of map may be used to illustrate social and political distribution, the cartogram map and the map showing land areas. There are several varieties of cartogram, which may be described as the 'pie', the 'square' and the 'continuous area'. The 'pie' chart shows land areas, and within each land area has a circle, from which pie-like sections are cut, indicating the proportion of votes going to each party.[1] The 'square' has a number of squares of equal size, which each represent one constituency[2]; while the 'continuous area cartogram' is a combination of the 'square' and the ordinary map showing land areas. It has thousands of small squares, each constituency having an equal number. These squares are arranged so that the approximate shape of each constituency is preserved, while constituencies with large land areas do not dominate the map to the virtual exclusion of constituencies with small land areas.[3]

The area cartogram has one advantage only over the ordinary map showing land areas; that is, it does not give greater weight to places with large than to places with small areas. For instance, between the wars the constituency of Caithness and Sutherland had over 1·7 million acres, while the constituency of the City of London had less than 1,000 acres. On a normal map the one member from Caithness and Sutherland would therefore be represented by 1,700 times as much space as the two members from the City of London. An area cartogram does away with this difficulty.

However, all three types of map create more problems than they solve. The basis of such maps is that they attempt to show people, not land areas. Yet constituencies have never had the same number of electors. For example, in 1966 the constituencies ranged from 113,645 in North Antrim to 22,823 in the Western Isles. In other periods variations in the size of constituency have been even more marked.[4] Consequently, if the maps have equal-sized squares, pies or anything else, they do not represent the true distribution of population or of votes. A second drawback to the use of such maps is that they cannot be compared if the redistribution took place. If a new seat was set up in a redistribution, a square or a pie would have to be created, and it would be difficult to say exactly where the new square or pie came in. On a regular map, showing land areas, the boundaries of the new and old seats could be compared readily.

The most important drawback to the use of area cartograms is that they do not accomplish what they set out to do. A map of elections is intended to clarify problems; that is, it is supposed to indicate where things happened. A graph or chart indicates far better than a cartogram who won an election. For instance, if one wished to know the number of Labour M.P.s returned in a given election, it would be simpler to look up the figure in a table than to make a rough guess by examining such a map. Even area cartograms are less helpful in this respect than tables. On the other hand, a straightforward map of land areas indicates far better which areas voted which way.

The second major category of electoral map is the normal one showing land areas. This sort of map has only one serious drawback, that it exaggerates the significance of constituencies with large land areas. In recent British elections the Conservatives have won a strong majority of seats with large land areas; hence a quick glance at ordinary maps of these elections may make one think that the Conservatives won overwhelming victories in the country as a whole. Such impressions can be corrected by including with the main maps a series of enlarged maps of the major urban complexes. Labour usually has done better in such complexes than elsewhere, and the enlarged maps therefore counteract the distortion due to Conservative wins in seats with large land areas. In examining the maps in this book, the reader is advised to base his impressions on the whole map, including the smaller maps of urban areas. In that way, it is hoped that the chief fault of land-area maps can be overcome.[5]

Few maps in this book show the percentage of votes won by parties in individual elections. Many such maps were prepared as background material for the book, but most were not included, for several reasons. First, most elections before 1945 had large numbers of unopposed candidates. Therefore, there would be no way of indicating the distribution of votes in constituencies without contests. A second reason for excluding most of the percentage maps is that until 1931 many complex local matters affected the outcome of elections. The most important of these was local party alignments. In some constituencies one candidate had the support of two parties out of three; in others a candidate may have had the support of only one party; occasionally a candidate had the support of all parties. Unless one knew the local situation, one might be misled into thinking that a particular seat was, say, a Liberal stronghold because the Liberal vote was high. Much of the high Liberal vote might have been due to Labour or Conservative support, and the seat in question could have had fewer Liberal voters than another seat with a lower Liberal vote, but where the Liberal candidate faced candidates of both other major parties. Maps which show simply which party won each seat avoid both pitfalls; while maps showing the winners of seats over an extended period indicate the effective areas of party strength.

Southern Ireland is not illustrated in the maps in this book, because it was only a part of the country up to 1922, and nearly all the maps in this book would therefore not apply to it. Also, Southern Ireland was virtually a political monolith from 1885 to 1922. Nearly every seat there voted Nationalist or Sinn Fein, and the few exceptions have been mentioned in the comments on the elections. The only significant split in Southern Ireland came in the 1892 and 1895 elections, when the Parnellites won several seats. The distribution of the Parnellites in the two elections has been examined in the commentary.

Finally, it should be remembered that most hypotheses raised in this book are tentative. Given the nature of the evidence available, they could be nothing else. It is important to remember also that election results cannot tell one the precise effect of a particular factor. Election results may be compared with an equation having several variables, in which the exact significance of each variable is unknown. Even the closest examination of election results cannot provide a final answer to such a question as the effect of Liberal withdrawals on the Labour and Conservative vote. It may be said that an intensive examination of the results yields many probable answers to such problems, but never final ones.

---

1 Such 'pie' maps have been used in a study of Belgian elections prepared by de Smet and Evalenko, *Les élections belges* (1956)

2 Such 'square' maps have been used in Butler and King, *The British General Election of 1964* and *The British General Election of 1966*

3 Such 'compromise' maps have been used in *The Times Guide to the House of Commons, 1964,* and in *The Times,* 4 April, 1966

4 In 1915 the population of constituencies varied from 312,804 in Romford to 13,112 in Kilkenny

5 There is also a third type of map, the 'isodemographic', which eliminates county and constituency boundaries. While such maps can give useful general impressions, they have little value in showing the statistical data for individual areas.

General Election of 1885

Overall results

party	total votes	% of total
Conservative	1,935,216	44·1
Liberal, Labour, Independent Liberal, Radical, Crofter, etc.	2,156,952	49·0
Nationalist	299,784	6·9
Total	**4,391,952**	**100·0**

Seats won by area

area	Cons.	Lib.	Ind. Lib.	Crofter	Lab.	Irish Nat.	total
England	214	233	4	—	4	1	456
Wales	4	29	—	—	1	—	34
Scotland	8	58	—	4	—	—	70
N. Ireland*	16	—	—	—	—	8	24
S. Ireland	—	—	—	—	—	77	77
Universities	8	1	—	—	—	—	9
Total	**250**	**321**	**4**	**4**	**5**	**86**	**670**

Unopposed returns by area

area	Cons.	Lib.	Ind. Lib. etc.	Irish Nat.	total
England	1	3	—	—	4
Wales	—	4	—	—	4
Scotland	—	5	—	—	5
N. Ireland*	2	—	—	—	2
S. Ireland	—	—	—	17	17
Universities	7	1	—	—	8
Total	**10**	**13**	**—**	**17**	**40**

* 'Northern Ireland' was the portion of Ireland which remained in the U.K. after 1922. 'Southern Ireland' was the portion of Ireland which formed the Irish Free State after 1922, and Newry, a borough disfranchised in 1918

Comments

The general election of 1885 was the first in which a majority of the adult male population was eligible to vote. The Reform Act of 1867 had extended the vote to most householders in borough constituencies, but had discriminated against many householders in county constituencies. While the Reform Act of 1884 did not grant universal suffrage, at least it eliminated this discrimination. As a result, the electorate rose from 3 million to $5\frac{3}{4}$ million, or approximately 59% of the adult male population.[1] The election of 1885 was also the first to be fought on the revised boundaries, in which 140 borough seats disappeared, mostly in the South of England.[2] The chief increases in representation occurred in London, Lancashire, Yorkshire and the North-east. By this redistribution, the North of England attained its maximum influence in the Commons.[3] In

previous distributions the South had many more seats, as it was to have in later distributions. This tendency has remained until the present, because of the more rapid increase of population in the South. The increasing disparity between the North and South of England can be seen from the following table:

number of seats	1831 election	1880 election	1885 redist	1922 redist	1954 redist	1969 redist
South of England	417	355	315	330	351	366
Rest of Britain & N. Ire.	121	215	269	273	279	269
lead of South over rest	**296**	**140**	**46**	**57**	**72**	**97**

The chief beneficiaries of this redistribution were the Liberals, whose strongholds were Wales, Scotland and the North of England.[4] The Conservatives were the chief beneficiaries of later redistributions.[5] The Liberals also benefited from the fact that no redistribution was carried out in the 33 years between 1885 and 1918; and consequently they did not risk losing seats in areas of declining population such as the Scottish Highlands and rural Wales.

The most notable thing about the election of 1885 is that the Liberals very nearly won a majority of the whole House. If one counts the Crofters, Radicals and various Independent Liberals in with the more orthodox supporters of Gladstone, the Liberals had 334 seats, while the combined Irish Nationalists and Conservatives had 336, a lead of only 2 over the Liberals. In Great Britain and Northern Ireland there were 334 Liberals to 259 Conservatives and Irish Nationalists. The fact that the Liberals were in a minority of 2 in the whole House was caused by the activities of Irish Nationalists in British seats. Parnell had advised his supporters to vote Conservative if there were no Irish Nationalists running. Because of this, the Conservatives gained several seats. Herbert Gladstone estimated that the number of seats lost by the Liberals in this way was 20.[6] It is almost certain that the Nationalists caused the loss of at least 5, and perhaps 7, more. The Liberals gained several seats in 1886 which had substantial Roman Catholic or Irish electorates, and they had probably gone Conservative in 1885 because of Parnell's instructions.[7]

Irish Nationalist activities probably did not cause the Conservative victory in West Lancashire. Although West Lancashire was in 1885 an area of strong Roman Catholicism (and of even stronger Protestantism), it is likely that most of the Roman Catholics did not have the vote. Most Roman Catholics were immigrant Irish, who were not in the more prosperous, or voting, half of society. Nevertheless, they had a considerable influence on the result of some elections in West Lancashire by an indirect means. For some

1 As estimated by N. Blewett, 'The Franchise in the United Kingdom, 1885-1918', *Past & Present*, Dec. 1965, 31
2 C. O'Leary, *The Elimination of Corrupt Practices in British Elections, 1868-1911*, 182
3 In this discussion 'south' is defined as those English counties south of Yorkshire and Lancashire.
4 See map, Liberal Seats 1885–December 1910, p. 83
5 See, for example, map, Effect to the 1918 Redistribution on the December 1910 Results, p. 71
6 Morley, *Gladstone*, 11, 498

7 The seats were: Cockermouth, Lanark North-West, Liverpool-Exchange, Manchester North and South-west, and possibly Lancaster and Scarborough. See map, Changes, 1885-1886, p. 21. D. C. Savage says that the Irish vote possibly accounted for the Unionist victories in Govan, Lanark North-west and Kirkcudbright, where the Unionist majorities in 1885 were small. He discounts this, however, by mentioning that only Lanark North-west returned to the Liberals in 1886. (Savage, 'Scottish Politics, 1885-6', *Scottish Historical Review*, April 1961, 128)

time the Irish had supported the Liberals; and since the majority of the population was Protestant, this led to increased Protestant support for the Conservatives. The brief Nationalist–Conservative flirtation of 1885 was not long enough to affect this very much. The political significance of the Protestant–Conservative tie can be seen from the following table. The Roman Catholic percentage refers to 1851, and changes may have taken place between 1851 and 1885. However, no such comprehensive religious census has been taken in Britain since 1851, and Roman Catholic diocesan and other figures are not very reliable. The table shows that places with many Roman Catholics in 1851 had few successful Liberal candidates in 1885. One may conclude that where there were many Roman Catholics, the Liberals lost more electoral support than they gained, because of Protestant revolts.

West Lancashire	% RC, 1851	Vote, 1885[1]
Liverpool	43·7	Cons.
Chorley	38·7	Cons.
Preston	36·4	Cons.
Prescot (Widnes)	30·5	Cons.
Garstang	30·2	Cons.
West Derby	29·3	Cons.
Wigan	29·1	Cons.
Ormskirk	22·7	Cons.
Warrington	19·9	Cons.
Fylde	16·8	Cons.
Lancaster	10·8	Cons.

East Lancashire	% RC, 1851	Vote, 1885[1]
Manchester	35·4	Cons.
Clitheroe	25·7	Lib.
Salford	15·5	Lib.
Leigh	11·8	Lib.
Blackburn	8·9	Cons.
Bolton	8·1	Cons.
Ashton	7·6	Cons.
Bury	5·2	Lib.
Oldham	4·8	Lib.
Burnley	4·8	Lib.
Rochdale	3·1	Lib.
Rossendale	2·2	Lib.

Expressed in another way, in areas with over 15% Roman Catholics in 1851, 4 Liberals and 25 Conservatives were successful in 1885; in areas with under 15% Roman Catholics, 11 Liberals and 4 Conservatives won. Probably the Roman Catholics were normally Liberal (if they had the vote); and the more Roman Catholics there were, the stronger was the Protestant–Conservative reaction to them. The constituency of Lancaster was an exception. In 1885, Lancaster voted Conservative, but from 1886 to 1910, it was normally Liberal. Lancaster had many Nonconformists as well as many Roman Catholics,[2] and some Nonconformists probably backed the Liberals there despite the Liberals' Roman Catholic tie.

The division between West Lancashire, with its Protestant–Roman Catholic split and numerous Conservative M.P.s, and East Lancashire, with fewer Roman Catholics and fewer Conservative M.P.s, was a feature of elections in Lancashire until 1924. As late as the election of 1923, there was a clear division between the two areas.[3] Even the seats in West Lancashire which had a tendency to go Liberal were unusual. While Protestantism in most of West Lancashire tended to be Anglican, in a few seats there were also many Nonconformists, notably in Lancaster, Southport

and Blackpool. Before 1918 Blackpool was not a separate constituency and was politically submerged in the surrounding rural areas. However, both Southport and Lancaster exhibited a more marked tendency to Liberalism than other nearby seats. One may conclude that the Nonconformists in West Lancashire were more willing than the Anglicans to come to terms with the Irish.

Areas of Conservative strength in this election were West Lancashire and Northern Ireland, where religion played a prominent part in politics; London and the South-east; and three agricultural areas around York, Grantham and Exeter. The Conservatives did not do well in areas of heavy industry, except in Liverpool and Manchester. In Birmingham, for instance, the Conservatives came close in only one of the 7 seats: in many industrial parts of London they fared little better.

In the rest of London and the South-east the Conservatives dominated until 1945. Sometimes the Conservatives won more seats in London, but only when they swept the country as a whole. The political geography of London thus remained stable in comparison with that of many other areas. This was partly caused by the subdivision of London into well-defined working-class and other areas. In smaller cities, with perhaps only 6 or 7 seats, there were normally few seats with a clear working-class majority or a clear middle-class majority in the electorate. In London the city was so large, and the working- and middle-class regions so large as well, that individual constituencies were more homogeneous than in smaller cities. On the edges of the working- and middle-class areas were many heterogeneous constituencies of shifting allegiance.[4]

Two boroughs stood out in the South-east as pockets of Liberal strength in an otherwise solidly Conservative area. These were Hythe and Hastings. In Hythe, the Liberal ran as a semi-independent, and there was no Conservative candidate. Both seats were areas of relative Nonconformist strength, as well as of Liberal strength.[5] Several other single-membered boroughs stood out from their surrounding county seats in 1885. Grantham and Boston were Liberal seats in a predominantly Conservative rural area; while the Denbigh District, Durham and Wakefield were Conservative in predominantly Liberal rural areas. Many factors may have been involved in producing these results. One might have been the personal influence of the candidates on what was in most cases a small electorate in a small town. Grantham, for example, had an electorate of only 3,000 in a population of 18,000. Durham had an electorate of 2,600 in a population of 15,000 in 1911.

It is interesting that more small boroughs did not differ from their surroundings. The Conservative Sir Michael Hicks-Beach felt that the Liberals tended to do best in small boroughs. He thought it advisable to lump groups of those boroughs together in single constituencies, rather than include them in county divisions, where they would add to Liberal strength, and make the county constituencies more marginal.[6] Such grouping took place only in Wales and Scotland. In England some of the very small boroughs remained, and it is apparent from the map that in fact they did not usually form noticeable centres of Liberalism contrasting with neighbouring county seats. In fact, the Conservatives won slightly over half the small, scattered, single-member boroughs which are listed beneath insets 15 and 16.[7]

1 Source: *Religious Census of 1851*, 92-8. Not all areas of Lancashire are covered in these tables. They were not listed separately in the religious census of 1851 because their population was too small. In Blackburn a Liberal and a Labour candidate ran against two Conservatives; the result is therefore not comparable to other seats with Liberal–Conservative straight fights
2 See map, Distribution of Nonconformists in England in 1922, p. 127
3 See map, General Election of 1923, p. 45
4 See map, Liberal Seats 1885–December 1910, p. 83; map, Labour Seats 1918-1929,

p. 113, and map, Labour Seats 1955-1966, p. 115. One must remember, in comparing these maps, that the working- and middle-class areas changed over the years, with the working-class areas gradually growing larger
5 See map, Distribution of Nonconformists in England in 1922, p. 127
6 Lady V. Hicks-Beach, *Life of Sir Michael Hicks-Beach*, 217-20
7 The figures were: Conservatives 24, Liberals 15, Independent Liberals 2. Many other single-membered boroughs were really parts of larger urban complexes e.g. Dudley or Aston Manor.

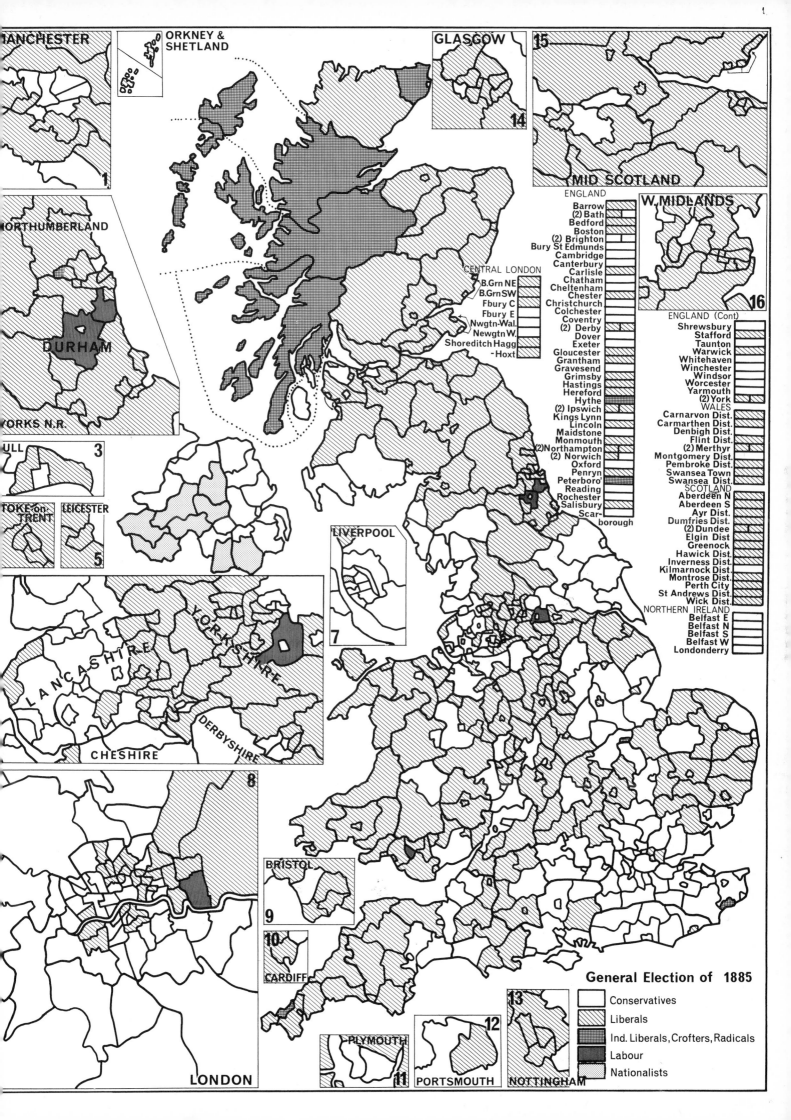

General Election of 1885

Areas of Liberal strength included most agricultural seats in England, the industrial areas of West Yorkshire and East Lancashire, the more industrialised English boroughs, and practically all Scotland and Wales. The great Liberal victories in Scotland and Wales were not founded on small majorities: the Liberal percentages in Scotland and Wales were 64 and 61 respectively. In Northern Scotland four 'Crofters' defeated orthodox Liberal candidates. These 'Crofters' were relics of the Highland clearances, and they sat with the Liberals in Parliament. The 'Crofters' were successful in the same areas with 'Land League – Labour' candidates in the 1918 election.[1] One of these seats, Inverness, had over 90% Gaelic speakers.[2] It also had a large proportion of indigenous Roman Catholics, in some of the southern islands of the Outer Hebrides. This seat went Labour in 1935, although it was predominantly rural, and it has remained Labour ever since.[3]

The only part of Scotland which did not vote Liberal was the extreme South-west, Kirkcudbright and Wigtown, and Bute; and the two Clyde constituencies of Dumbartonshire and West Renfrew. These 5 constituencies had either large Roman Catholic populations or numerous Irish immigrants[4] or both. In these seats, as in West Lancashire, the Protestant reaction probably helped the Conservatives. In Kilmarnock there was a Liberal split, and in North-west Lanark a large proportion of immigrant Irish swung the seat to the Conservatives. Inverness did not go Conservative even though it had many Roman Catholics, probably because those Roman Catholics were isolated on individual islands. Consequently their presence had little effect on Protestants on other islands in the constituency. In any case, most Catholics in Inverness were not Irish but indigenous.

Another area of Liberal strength was the agricultural and semi-agricultural district lying just south of a line drawn from the Wash to the mouth of the Severn and thence to Cornwall. This area was one of the most marginal in the country between 1885 and 1923. In the elections of 1885, 1892, 1906 and 1923 it voted strongly Liberal; in those of 1886, 1895, 1900 and 1918 it voted strongly Conservative; while in the two elections of 1910, and in 1922, it was divided fairly evenly. Few other parts of the country have shown such consistent marginality over so long a period, apart from certain areas of London. In 1885 the Liberals did well in this area because of the enfranchisement of many rural voters.

Although the Liberals did well in working-class constituencies, they did not win all working-class areas. They had considerable strength even in the most solidly Conservative industrial centres, such as Liverpool; but their appeal was insufficient to do them any effective good in that city, or in several others. Only in the West Riding of Yorkshire was there a large region in which the division between Liberal and Conservative seats was clearly along class lines. If one compares the results of the 1885 election with the results of post-Second World War elections, one notices that the Liberals in 1885 won almost precisely the areas won by Labour.[5] In Sheffield, for instance, the Liberals won the east, and the Conservatives the west, of the city; the division was identical in 1964 between Conservative and Labour. In other parts of England such neat divisions did not occur, because of the influence of religion, as in West Lancashire and West Scotland; or for various other reasons. The percentage of Roman Catholics in West Yorkshire was small. It was also an area with few Irish immigrants in 1891. In most large centres of West Yorkshire in 1891, only about 2% of the population had been born in Ireland. On the other hand, up to 7% had been born in Ireland in parts of West Lancashire.

The final area of Liberal strength was the West Midlands, the 'Grand Duchy' of which the 'Grand Duke' was Joseph Chamberlain. This area left Liberalism in 1886 with Chamberlain, never to return, even in the great Liberal triumph of 1906. The only parts of the West Midlands which showed Liberal strength thereafter were the Potteries, and also the Black Country just west of Birmingham.

---

1 In 1918, 'Highland Land League' candidates ran in Inverness and the Western Isles. Although they had the support of the Labour Party they campaigned on a land reform platform, rather than on a Socialist one. *Highland News* (Inverness), 7 and 14 Dec. 1918
2 See map, Gaelic Speakers in Scotland in 1921, p. 131
3 In the 1885 redistribution the islands were in Inverness constituency; after 1918 they formed a new constituency, the Western Isles, along with a part of the former Ross and Cromarty constituency. The Crofters are discussed in D. W. Crowley,

'The "Crofters Party", 1885-1892', *Scottish Historical Review,* April 1956, 110-26. Crowley states (116-9) that Crofters won in Caithness and Ross and Cromarty; while 'Independent Crofters' won Argyll, Inverness and Wick District. *The Constitutional Year Book, 1917,* 316-27, on which the map is based, does not list Wick District as a 'Crofters' victory, although it does list both Argyll and Inverness
4 See Jackson, *Irish in Britain,* map on p. 16
5 See map, Election of 1964, p. 67

General Election of 1886

Overall results

party	total votes	% of total
Conservative	1,037,779	37·5
Liberal Unionist	385,986	14·0
Total Unionist	**1,423,765**	**51·5**
Liberal	1,241,357	44·9
Irish Nationalist	99,774	3·6
Total	**2,764,896**	**100·0**

Seats won by area

area	Cons.	Lib. Unionist	Lib.	Irish Nat.	total
England	277	55	123	1	456
Wales	6	4	24	—	34
Scotland	10	17	43	—	70
N. Ireland	15	2	—	7	24
S. Ireland	—	—	—	77	77
Universities	8	1	—	—	9
Total	**316**	**79**	**190**	**85**	**670**

Unopposed returns by area

area	Cons.	Lib. Unionist	Lib.	Irish Nat.	total
England	81	24	25	—	130
Wales	—	3	8	—	11
Scotland	—	2	7	—	9
N. Ireland	3	—	—	1	4
S. Ireland	—	—	—	65	65
Universities	4	—	—	—	4
Total	**88**	**29**	**40**	**66**	**223**

Comments

The Liberals had a net loss of 144 seats in the election of 1886,[1] more than they lost in any subsequent election. Although this was smaller than the Unionist net loss of 245 seats in 1906, it was still a marked defeat for the Liberals. Areas remaining Liberal included West Yorkshire, rural Wales and Eastern Scotland. Elsewhere, in both seats and votes, there was a landslide against the Liberals.

Two issues affecting the outcome of the 1886 election were Home Rule and Joseph Chamberlain.[2] Many Liberals left their party, at least ostensibly, over Irish Home Rule, and even some of those remaining had doubts about the wisdom of granting Home Rule.[3] The Liberals also lost some radical support, since many radicals felt that Joseph Chamberlain was at least as good a guarantor of the radical tradition as Gladstone. Although these two things were important, they were not the only influence at work in 1886. Another influence of considerable significance was the activity of individual Liberal M.P.s.

The importance of individual M.P.s and candidates is at a zenith in a period of political uncertainty, for bewildered voters are likely to prefer someone who seems competent to deal with the situation, rather than someone who seems as bewildered as the electorate. Such periods of political uncertainty have been rare in Britain in the past 100 years, because in most elections party lines and policies have been drawn long before the elections. However, in two elections party lines were very unclear, and policies were apparently undecided. Consequently candidates who could cast light on those lines and policies were more likely to win support than candidates who could not. These elections were held in 1886 and 1922. In each, party alignments changed just before the election, and there was marked confusion of party platforms and alliances during the election campaigns. The election of 1886 was less confused than that of 1922, but it was much more confused than other elections held between 1885 and 1966.

The notion that the influence of candidates is greatest in times of confusion is a hypothesis which cannot be proven, because of the vagueness of the term 'influence'. However, personal influences probably accounted for some of the more unusual results in 1886. In some places where Liberal M.P.s were strong Home Rulers, they maintained their majorities, even though Liberal M.P.s in neighbouring seats lost much support. For instance, John Morley kept practically all his 1885 support in Newcastle, although nearby Liberal seats had swings of up to 10% to the Unionists. Morley was a strong Home Ruler. On the other hand, Sir Henry James was a strong opponent of Home Rule. Because of his vigorous defence of his position James was able to head off a rebellion in his constituency Liberal Party in Bury and was returned unopposed in 1886.[4]

Some other candidates in 1886 clearly had a strong personal following. For example, the Marquis of Hartington held Rossendale in 1885 and 1886 with majorities of 2,000, although he changed sides between the elections. In 1892, after Hartington had succeeded as Duke of Devonshire, the Liberals regained Rossendale, and held it in all elections before 1918 with majorities ranging from 1,000 to 2,000. Apparently, much of the 1886 vote for Hartington was a personal vote. An even more striking example could be found in the Totnes division of Devon. There F. B. Mildmay had won 52·5% of the vote in 1885, as a Liberal. In 1886 he won 80·2% as a Liberal Unionist; this was a direct swing of 37·5% against the Liberals. In the adjacent seat of Ashburton, C. Seale-Hayne had won 58·1% in 1885 as a Liberal, and 53·1% in 1886, also as a Liberal. This was a swing of only 5% against the Liberals, and it was a strong indication of the importance of the activities of individual Liberal M.P.s at that time.

The relation between the Irish vote and the Protestant reaction against the Liberals was confused in both Lancashire and Scotland, the two chief areas of Irish immigration. In Scotland most areas of heavy Irish immigration voted Unionist, while those where there

1 'Liberals' in 1885 include Crofters, Labour and Independent Liberals in this calculation
2 Scottish Disestablishment had faded out as an issue by 1886, though it had been important in 1885. (D. C. Savage, 'Scottish Politics, 1885-6', *Scottish Historical Review*, 1961, 129-30)
3 For example, Samuel Smith. See S. Smith, *My Life Work*, 231
4 Askwith, *Lord James of Hereford*, 165-78

were fewer Irish tended to vote Liberal. However, there were several exceptions to this general tendency. In most instances they occurred in seats where the Liberal M.P. ran in 1886 as a Liberal Unionist. In Scotland there were 27 seats where over 9% of the adult male population was born in Ireland. In 1886 the Unionists won 17 of those seats, and the Liberals 10. In the 43 remaining Scottish seats, with under 9% Irish, the Unionists won 9 and the Liberals 34. In the 9 Unionist victories in the latter group, 6 had Liberal M.P.s choosing to run as Unionists. Presumably they brought some personal followers with them.

In the Scottish constituencies with many Irish, there was a swing against the Liberals in most of them, but that swing was greatest where there were from 3% to 10% Irish-born. Where there were more Irish-born, the Liberals gained voters from Irishmen which cancelled the lost votes of those who disliked the Irish. However, where there were only 3% to 10% Irish, there were enough to bring on a reaction against the Liberals, but not enough to do the Liberals any good electorally. Where there were under 3% Irish-born, the Liberals did not generally suffer much from reaction against the presence of Irish. This is only a general tendency, and many constituencies behaved differently because of a wide variety of factors.

In England the connection between the percentages of Irish and the reaction against the Liberals was even more complex than in Scotland. It is difficult to justify sweeping statements about the effect of the Irish vote in England, because the results were affected in many seats by such things as the influence of local M.P.s. Probably, however, the swing against the Liberals was not as great in English constituencies with many Irish as it was in Scottish constituencies with many Irish. However, the anti-Irish reaction was politically more significant in Scotland than in England, because the Conservatives had won most of the English seats with many Irish in 1885, and a reaction in favour of the Conservatives helped them only slightly. In Scotland the Liberals had won most of the areas of Irish concentration, and they lost many seats in those places in 1886, 11 in all. One may conclude, therefore, that the Irish issue helped the Unionists in 1886 in Scotland more than in England, in seats and votes.

A second influence in 1886 was the radicalism of Chamberlain and of his colleagues such as Jesse Collings. It is not possible to calculate the precise electoral importance of Chamberlain, or of Liberal Unionism in general. According to one estimate the Liberal Unionists amounted to little outside Birmingham and some other large towns.[1] Some evidence can be found to sustain this view in the performance of Liberal Unionists in the three constituencies where there were three-way fights between Liberals, Liberal Unionists and Conservatives. In all three the Liberal Unionist came third, winning 4·4% in Newmarket, 4·6% in Camberwell North and 19·6% in Romford. These results are the only ones which indicate the electoral strength of the Liberal Unionist party when considered as a separate force from the Conservatives. In other constituencies the Liberal Unionist vote included almost all of the Conservative vote of 1885.[2] However, it would be misleading to say that the results in these 3 constituencies represented the total importance of the Liberal Unionism. In many constituencies the Liberal Unionist candidates had substantial local followings. The cases of James, Hartington and Mildmay have already been mentioned. The case of Joseph Chamberlain is also fairly obvious, though it is impossible to say how many votes he shifted in Bir-

mingham in 1885-6, since 5 of the 7 Birmingham seats were unopposed Liberal Unionist victories in 1886, while the sixth was not contested by the Liberal Unionists, but by a Conservative. In the seventh Jesse Collings defeated a Liberal by 4,475 to 1,040, with most of the Conservatives apparently abstaining.[3] The importance of the Liberal Unionists was two-fold. In some places they may have been strong enough to win on their own; in many more they provided the extra support without which the Unionist could not have been elected.

Despite Hamilton's estimate that the Liberal Unionists amounted to little outside Birmingham and other large towns, it is fairly evident from the map that the Liberal Unionists did best in the rural, not the urban, areas. Birmingham was the only city which elected an appreciable number of Liberal Unionists, apart from Glasgow, which elected 2. Under half the Liberal Unionists came from borough constituencies. The chief Liberal Unionist areas in 1886 were Birmingham, rural Scotland and the group of agricultural constituencies just south of the line drawn from the Wash to the Severn and thence to Cornwall. This group of constituencies has already been mentioned in connection with the election of 1885. Many of these rural constituencies might have gone Unionist in any case, but the presence of Chamberlain and Collings, two of the most prominent reformers, on the Unionist side, aided the Unionists. A much more important factor aiding the Liberal Unionists in agricultural seats was Whig influence. Most Liberal Unionist M.P.s from agricultural seats were Whig followers of Hartington. Their desertion of the Liberal Party left the Liberals leaderless in many places. The map makes clear the virtual elimination of the Liberals from English agricultural seats. Practically the only ones they retained were Nonconformist strongholds,[4] along with a scattering of other seats.

Unionist strength in this election was very great; but they did not win everywhere. Rural Wales, some Nonconformist strongholds in England, West Yorkshire and Eastern Scotland remained faithful to the Liberals. These areas represented the bedrock of Liberal strength, as can be seen by examining the maps on pp. 83 and 85. Although the Liberals retained most of their seats in the North-east mining and shipbuilding districts, their strength was rather illusory. Apart from rural constituencies, there were 21 seats in the North-east, which elected 23 M.P.s. The Liberals won ten of these seats without a contest. In the 11 contested seats they won only 5 (representing 7 M.P.s). In 3 of the 5 seats they won, there was a very large swing against the Liberals in comparison with 1885: in Darlington the swing was 10·6%; in Tyneside 11·9%. In Sunderland it is not possible to calculate the exact swing, as there was only one Conservative candidate in 1885, and only one Unionist (a Liberal Unionist) in 1886, fighting two Liberals. In the fourth constituency won by the Liberals, Newcastle, John Morley retained most of his vote of 1885. In the fifth, Wansbeck, the Liberal candidate had a swing in his favour of 7%. The Liberal was C. B. Fenwick, a local resident, and one of the first miners elected to Parliament. This illustrates once more the importance of the individual candidates. In the final seat won by the Liberals, Stockton, there was little change between 1885 and 1886 in the percentage vote. Thus although the Liberals kept most of their seats in the North-east they could have fared much worse if they had fought all of them. In 1895 and 1900, when they had to fight more, they lost more.[5]

1 Lord George Hamilton, as qu. by M. Hurst, *Joseph Chamberlain and Liberal Reunion*, 43
2 Except in Torquay, where there was a straight fight between a Liberal Unionist and a Conservative. The Liberal Unionist, the former Liberal M.P., won 49·5%, representing a swing against him of 3·0% since 1885

3 In Birmingham the Liberal Association remained unsplit until 1888. (M. Hurst, 'Joseph Chamberlain, the Conservatives, and the succession to John Bright, 1886-9', *Historical Journal*, vol. 7, no. 1, 90)
4 See map, Distribution of Nonconformists in England in 1922, p. 127
5 See maps, General Elections of 1895 and 1900, pp. 25 and 27

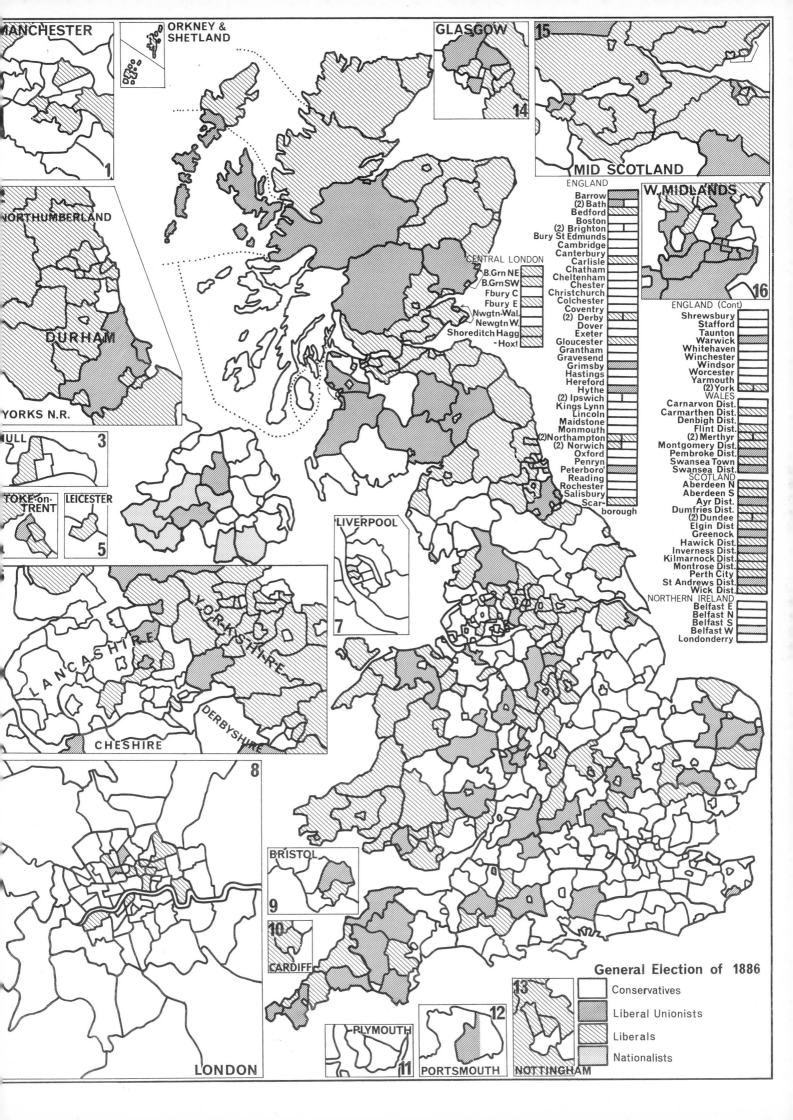

Party Gains in 1886

Summary of gains and losses

area	Cons. gains	Cons. losses	Lib. Unionist* gains	Lib. Unionist* losses	Lib. gains	Lib. losses	Irish Nat. gains	Irish Nat. losses
England	73	10	55	6	10	128	—	—
Wales	3	1	4	2	1	7	—	—
Scotland	4	2	17	6	2	21	—	—
N. Ireland	—	1	2	—	—	—	1	2
S. Ireland	—	—	—	—	—	—	—	—
Universities	—	—	1	—	—	1	—	—
Total	**80**	**14**	**79**	**14**	**13**	**157**	**1**	**2**

* All Liberal Unionist victories in 1886 were gains since 1885, because there was no Liberal Unionist group in the 1885 election. Liberal Unionist 'losses' in 1886 were only those seats where a Liberal Unionist who had sat in the 1885-6 Parliament was defeated, in each case by a Gladstonian Liberal. In this table 'Liberals' in 1885 include Crofters, Radicals, Labour, etc.

In 1885, the Irish Nationalists had instructed their followers to vote Conservative where there was no Irish Nationalist candidate. In 1886 they instructed their followers to vote Liberal. Since the Liberals gained 12 seats in 1886, against the national tide in favour of the Unionists, it is tempting to attribute those gains to the influence of the change in the Irish vote. However, in several seats this was probably not the case. It is difficult to determine exactly what the Irish vote was, or how strong it was. Figures given in the Census of 1891 for the distribution of Irish-born are incomplete and also misleading. They are incomplete in that they do not give the distribution of Irish-born except by county or by urban sanitary districts with a population of 50,000 or more. Many constituencies were smaller than this, and therefore are not listed separately in the census. In such cases the only course is to take the county total of Irish-born and divide it by the number of seats in the county. While this may be an overestimate of the Irish vote in some places, in others it is certainly an underestimate. For instance, in Cumberland the Irish vote was concentrated in the coastal seats of Cockermouth, Egremont and Whitehaven.

The second drawback of the available statistics is that they are for all persons born in Ireland, whether they were 2 years of age or 62, whether they were Protestant or Roman Catholic. The Irish Nationalist vote was therefore smaller than the total of Irish-born persons. Most of the Irish-born were of voting age,[1] and most were also Roman Catholic; but it is impossible to say exactly what the proportions were.

Despite the incomplete statistics, it is possible to estimate whether or not some constituencies turned Liberal in 1886 because of the Irish vote. If the number of Irish-born in an area was very much greater than the number of votes the Liberals gained in 1886,[2] then the Irish vote was probably decisive. If, on the other hand, the number of Irish was about the same as, or less than, the number of votes gained by the Liberals, the Irish vote was probably not decisive. For instance, in Manchester the Liberals gained 2 seats in 1886. The average number of Irish-born per constituency in Manchester was 1,750. The number of voters who swung to the Liberals in their 2 gains was 535 in one constituency and 284 in the other. Therefore, the Irish vote was probably decisive in both seats. On the other hand, in Wolverhampton there was an average of only 178 Irish-born in each of the 3 seats. In Wolverhampton West the number of voters changing sides from 1885 to 1886 was 138. In Wolverhampton West it is unlikely that the Irish vote was decisive. For it to have been decisive, nearly 100% of the Irish would have had to turn out (assuming that they were all registered voters, that they were all over 21 and that they were all Roman Catholic), nearly 100% would have had to vote for the Unionists in 1885 and nearly 100% for the Liberals in 1886. Because none of these was likely, in Wolverhampton West the Irish vote was almost certainly not decisive in 1886. The following table shows the estimated Irish vote in 1891, and its probable effect in 1886:

seat	Lib. gain, votes 1885-1886	estimated Irish vote	effect of Irish vote
Buckrose	148	100-200	nil
Cockermouth	507	1000	Liberal gain
Lanark North-west	717	4000	Liberal gain
Lancaster	526	2000	Possible Lib. gain
Leeds East	728	700-750	nil
Liverpool–Exchange	95	2500	Liberal gain
Manchester North	535	1750	Liberal gain
Manchester South-west	284	1750	Liberal gain
Montgomery District	128	50	nil
Scarborough	120	300	Possible Lib. gain
Wednesbury	428	175	nil
Wolverhampton West	138	175	nil

It is probable that the Irish vote accounted for the change in 5 seats, and in perhaps 2 more, and that it did not bring about the change in 5 remaining seats. In Kilmarnock the change was caused by the elimination of the 1885 Liberal split. The Irish vote may also have helped the Liberals retain some seats where they had very small majorities.

All Liberal Unionist victories in 1886 were gains, since there had been no Liberal Unionist group in the 1885 election. Most Liberal Unionist seats were those where Liberal Unionist M.P.s chose to run after the split in the Liberal Party. 66 of the 79 Liberal Unionist wins were in this category. In a further 3 seats Liberal Unionist candidates defeated Gladstonian Liberal candidates where neither had sat in the 1885-6 Parliament.[3] Liberal Unionists won 2 seats in Northern Ireland where there was a small swing against the Nationalists.[4] Another Liberal Unionist victory in a seat not held by a Liberal Unionist at dissolution was in Birmingham.[5] In only 6 seats did Liberal Unionists defeat sitting Liberal M.P.s.[6] On the

1 In Scotland, where the total number of Irish-born males and the number over 20 were both given, 88·32% were over 20. (*Census of Scotland 1891*, 278)
2 Calculated by averaging the Conservative majority in 1885 and the Liberal majority in 1886
3 Falkirk District, Newcastle-under-Lyme and Glasgow–St. Rollox

4 Londonderry County South and Tyrone South
5 Bordesley, won by Jesse Collings, who had been unseated at Ipswich
6 North Bedfordshire, Peebles and Selkirk, Cheshire–Northwich, West Yorkshire–Skipton, Ayrshire South and Pembroke District

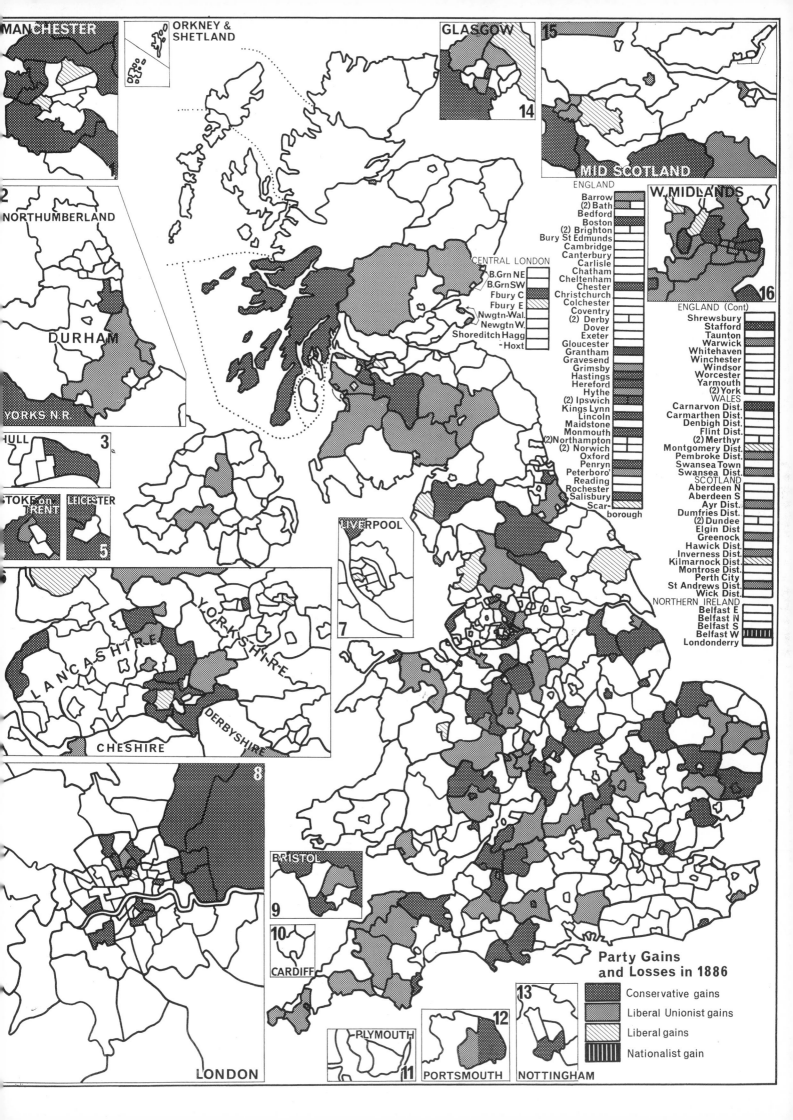

Party Gains and Losses in 1886

other hand, Liberals defeated 12 sitting Liberal Unionists,[1] although in almost every case there was a strong swing towards the Unionists. It is therefore evident that retiring M.P.s had a significant advantage over their rival Liberal or Liberal Unionist opponents.

In no area did the Conservatives make all the gains, and the Liberal Unionists none, in 1886; nor did the Liberal Unionists make all the gains, and the Conservatives none, in any area. However, the Conservatives made most of the gains in London, East Lancashire and in the smaller English boroughs. The Liberal Unionists were strongest in Western Scotland, Devon and Cornwall, the West Midlands, East Anglia, and in Glasgow. All the areas supporting the Liberal Unionists in 1886 showed above average support for the Lloyd George Coalition at the Carlton Club Meeting in 1922.[2]

1 Nottingham West, Tyneside and Blackfriars; Cardiganshire and Carmarthen District in Wales; Otley and Osgoldcross in West Yorkshire; East Fife, Edinburgh

Central and East, Elgin and Nairn, and Hawick District in East Scotland
2 See map, Carlton Club Meeting, p. 105

General Election of 1892

Overall results

party	total votes	% of total
Unionist	2,056,737	47·3
Liberal	1,921,614	44·2
Nationalist	242,293	5·5
Parnell Nationalist	69,194	1·6
Labour	59,940	1·4
Total	**4,349,778**	**100·0**

Seats won by area

area	Cons.	Lib. Unionist	Lib.	Lab.	Parnell Nat.	Nat.	total
England	231	31	189	4	—	1	456
Wales	3	—	31	—	—	—	34
Scotland	9	11	50	—	—	—	70
N. Ireland	16	3	—	—	—	5	24
S. Ireland	1	1	—	—	9	66	77
Universities	8	1	—	—	—	—	9
Total	**268**	**47**	**270**	**4**	**9**	**72**	**670**

Unopposed returns by area

area	Cons.	Lib. Unionist	Lib.	Lab.	Parnell Nat.	Nat.	total
England	17	6	9	—	—	—	32
Wales	—	—	4	—	—	—	4
Scotland	—	—	—	—	—	—	—
N. Ireland	11	—	—	—	—	—	11
S. Ireland	—	—	—	—	—	10	10
Universities	6	1	—	—	—	—	7
Total	**34**	**7**	**13**	**—**	**—**	**10**	**64**

1 J. L. Garvin, *Chamberlain*, II, 545, said the Liberals had anticipated a majority of 100 in 1892
2 Lichfield elected a Liberal Unionist in 1892, a Conservative in 1924, and a 'National' candidate in 1931. In all other elections from 1885 to 1966 it elected a Liberal (to 1923) or a Labour candidate (1929-66)
3 The Liberal Unionists had not taken office in the Salisbury Government of 1886-92, while the Lloyd George Liberals took many important offices in the Coalition Government up to 1922. This meant that the Liberal Unionists had been able to dissociate themselves from unpopular parts of the Salisbury record, while the Lloyd George

Comments

In 1892 the Liberals hoped to recover much ground lost in 1886.[1] Though they made considerable headway in London, Wales, North-east Lancashire and the agricultural districts of the South Midlands and South-west, they did not regain many seats in Scotland or in the West Midlands. In the West Midlands they recovered only 6 of the 26 they had lost in 1886, and they lost one, Lichfield, which they had won in 1886.[2] The Liberal failure to recover lost ground in the West Midlands or in Scotland was the most striking thing about the election of 1892. In each place the Liberal Unionists were the predominant partner in the Unionist alliance, and it seems likely that the split in the Liberal Party was what prevented its recovery. The Liberal Unionists won 47 seats in all, or about two-thirds of the seats they had won in 1886. Their relative success may be contrasted with the great decline of another Liberal breakaway group in similar circumstance. In 1922 the Lloyd George Liberals lost three-quarters of their seats.[3]

Because of the limited extent of the Liberal recovery in 1892, the Liberals formed only an unstable minority government, dependent on Irish Nationalist support. The Irish Nationalists were divided among themselves over the issue of Parnell. Of the successful Nationalists 9 were Parnellites, who won 4 seats near Galway and 4 more near Dublin.[4] Partly because of the instability of their Irish support, the Liberals fell in 1895 and were routed in the election of that year.

Liberals could not dissociate themselves from unpopular parts of the Coalition record. On the other hand, the Liberal Unionists could maintain with some justification that they had put pressure on Salisbury to introduce measure of social reform such as the Allotments Bill of 1887 and the abolition in 1891 of fees in primary schools.
4 The Parnellite seats near Galway were: Clare East, Clare West, North Galway, Roscommon South. Their seats in and near Dublin were: Dublin County North, Dublin Town – St. Patricks, – Harbour, and – College Green. The Parnellites also won Waterford.

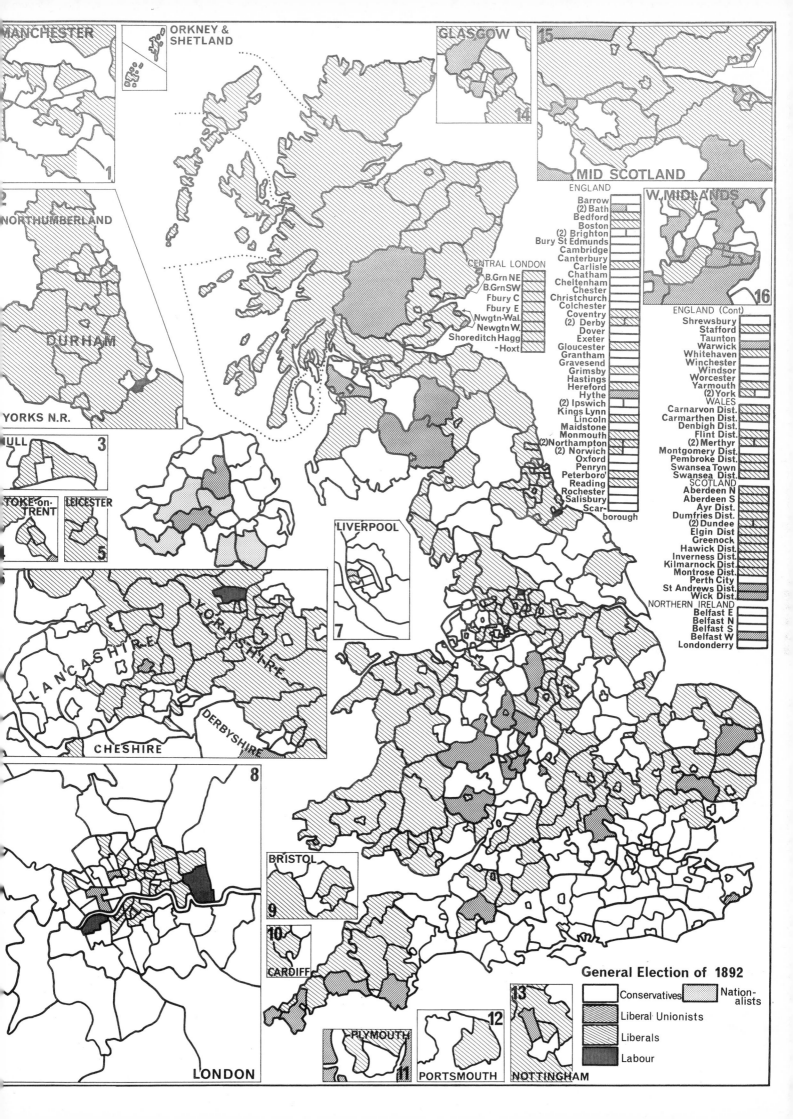

MANCHESTER

ORKNEY & SHETLAND

GLASGOW

15

1

14

NORTHUMBERLAND

MID SCOTLAND

W. MIDLANDS

2

16

DURHAM

YORKS N.R.

CENTRAL LONDON

B.Grn NE
B.Grn SW
Fbury C
Fbury E
Nwgtn-Wal.
Newgtn W.
Shoreditch Hagg
-Hoxt

HULL

3

STOKE-on-TRENT

LEICESTER

5

LANCASHIRE

YORKSHIRE

LIVERPOOL

7

DERBYSHIRE

CHESHIRE

8

BRISTOL

9

LONDON

10

CARDIFF

13

12

PLYMOUTH

11

PORTSMOUTH

NOTTINGHAM

ENGLAND

Barrow
(2) Bath
Bedford
Boston
(2) Brighton
Bury St Edmunds
Cambridge
Canterbury
Carlisle
Chatham
Cheltenham
Chester
Christchurch
Colchester
Coventry
(2) Derby
Dover
Exeter
Gloucester
Grantham
Gravesend
Grimsby
Hastings
Hereford
Hythe
(2) Ipswich
Kings Lynn
Lincoln
Maidstone
Monmouth
(2)Northampton
(2) Norwich
Oxford
Penryn
Peterboro'
Reading
Rochester
Salisbury
Scar-
borough

ENGLAND (Cont)

Shrewsbury
Stafford
Taunton
Warwick
Whitehaven
Winchester
Windsor
Worcester
Yarmouth
(2) York
WALES
Carnarvon Dist.
Carmarthen Dist.
Denbigh Dist.
Flint Dist.
(2) Merthyr
Montgomery Dist.
Pembroke Dist.
Swansea Town
Swansea Dist.
SCOTLAND
Aberdeen N
Aberdeen S
Ayr Dist.
Dumfries Dist.
(2) Dundee
Elgin Dist
Greenock
Hawick Dist.
Inverness Dist.
Kilmarnock Dist.
Montrose Dist.
Perth City
St Andrews Dist.
Wick Dist.
NORTHERN IRELAND
Belfast E
Belfast N
Belfast S
Belfast W
Londonderry

General Election of 1892

Conservatives	Nationalists
Liberal Unionists	
Liberals	
Labour	

General Election of 1895

Overall results

party	total votes	% of total
Unionist	1,780,753	49·2
Liberal	1,657,856	45·8
Labour	40,389	1·1
Nationalist	95,208	2·6
Parnell Nationalist	48,017	1·3
Total	3,622,223	100·0

Seats won by area

area	Cons.	Lib. Unionist	Lib.	Lab.	Parnell Nat.	Nat.	total
England	293	50	112	—	—	1	456
Wales	8	1	25	—	—	—	34
Scotland	17	14	39	—	—	—	70
N. Ireland	14	3	1	—	—	6	24
S. Ireland	1	1	—	—	12	63	77
Universities	8	1	—	—	—	—	9
Total	341	70	177	—	12	70	670

Unopposed returns by area

area	Cons.	Lib. Unionist	Lib.	Lab.	Parnell Nat.	Nat.	total
England	91	14	8	—	—	—	113
Wales	—	—	2	—	—	—	2
Scotland	2	1	1	—	—	—	4
N. Ireland	12	1	—	—	—	—	13
S. Ireland	—	—	—	—	4	40	44
Universities	8	1	—	—	—	—	9
Total	113	17	11	—	4	40	185

Comments

In 1895 Liberals and Labour lost on balance 97 seats. The Unionist lead in votes over the Liberals remained what it had been in 1892, that is 3%. However, this figure is misleading because there were 89 more unopposed Unionists in 1895 than in 1892, mostly in safe Unionist seats. In Wales and Scotland, where most seats were contested in both elections, the swing against the Liberals was 7% and 2½% respectively. If all seats had been contested in England, the average swing against the Liberals probably would have been at least as great. The tide against the Liberals was noticeable in all parts of the country, especially in Wales, Scotland, London and the agricultural seats of the South Midlands and South-west. In the last two places the Liberals lost 21 of the 34 seats they had gained in 1892. The heavy Liberal losses in agricultural seats may be compared with their equally heavy losses in such seats in the election of 1924. In each case the election followed a period of exceptional Liberal weakness in Parliament. In 1895 the Liberals had the added drawback that, although they were the Government, and although they were dependent on agricultural areas, they failed to solve the crisis in farm prices, which had declined from 87 to 74 between 1892 and 1895.[1]

Though the tide was against them, the Liberals gained a few seats, notably Lanark North-west and Tyrone North. Their victory in Lanark North-west was unremarkable, since the seat voted for the loser in every election from 1885 to 1906.[2] Their victory in Tyrone North was of more interest. There the Liberal association had been split in 1885, and had not put up a candidate. The Conservatives won in 1885, 1886 and 1892. By 1895 the Liberals were ready to put up a candidate. This candidate won nearly all the Nationalist vote, along with a few hundred votes which had formerly gone to the Conservatives.[3]

The Irish Nationalists gained only one seat, Londonderry, on a turnover of 33 votes. The changes in Ireland were primarily Parnellite gains, although the Parnellites lost 2 county divisions, Clare West and Galway North. The Parnellite gains were concentrated in boroughs and in county divisions near Dublin. After the 1895 elections, the Parnellites therefore held 6 seats in or near Dublin, 3 borough seats elsewhere, and only 3 other county divisions. The orthodox Nationalists held only 3 borough seats in Southern Ireland, including Newry. Possibly the Parnellites were stronger in urban areas than in rural ones because weaker clerical influence in urban areas meant that clerical condemnation of Parnell was ineffective there.

The Liberal Unionists recovered much lost ground in 1895, though this was more apparent than real. At least 7 Liberal Unionist seats won in 1895 were really Conservative strongholds. They were Marylebone West, Holland, Manchester South, Wakefield, Heywood, Lincoln and Lonsdale. In several other seats, such as Lambeth North and Liverpool – Exchange, the specifically Liberal Unionist vote was probably small. Consequently, although the Liberal Unionists won 70 seats in 1895, at least a tenth were not won because of Liberal Unionist strength in them. In North-east Lancashire the Liberal Unionists won only one seat, compared with 3 in 1886. Their weakness was actually greater than that, as the two leading Liberal Unionists in the area in 1886 had become peers, and were no longer as active in elections in the district as they had been. Thus the Liberal Unionists either declined, or were absorbed into the regular Conservative organisation, except in their strongholds of 1892, Scotland the West Midlands and a few scattered seats in the South-west.

In both West Yorkshire and the North-east the division between Unionist and Liberal areas resembled the division between Conservative and Labour areas in 1924. As in 1886 nearly all the mining seats in West Yorkshire and the North-east voted against the Conservatives, as did the woollen districts and slums in West Yorkshire. It is fairly clear that in these two areas at any rate, there was a closer connection between the Liberal vote than in many other parts of the country.

1 Rousseaux Price Indices, qu. by Mitchell and Deane, *British Historical Statistics*, 472-3. 100 is the average of 1865 and 1885
2 In the 1910 elections the seat went Liberal, although the swing in the country was against them
3 See D. C. Savage, 'The Origins of the Ulster Unionist Party, 1885-1886', *Irish Historical Studies*, March 1961, 189

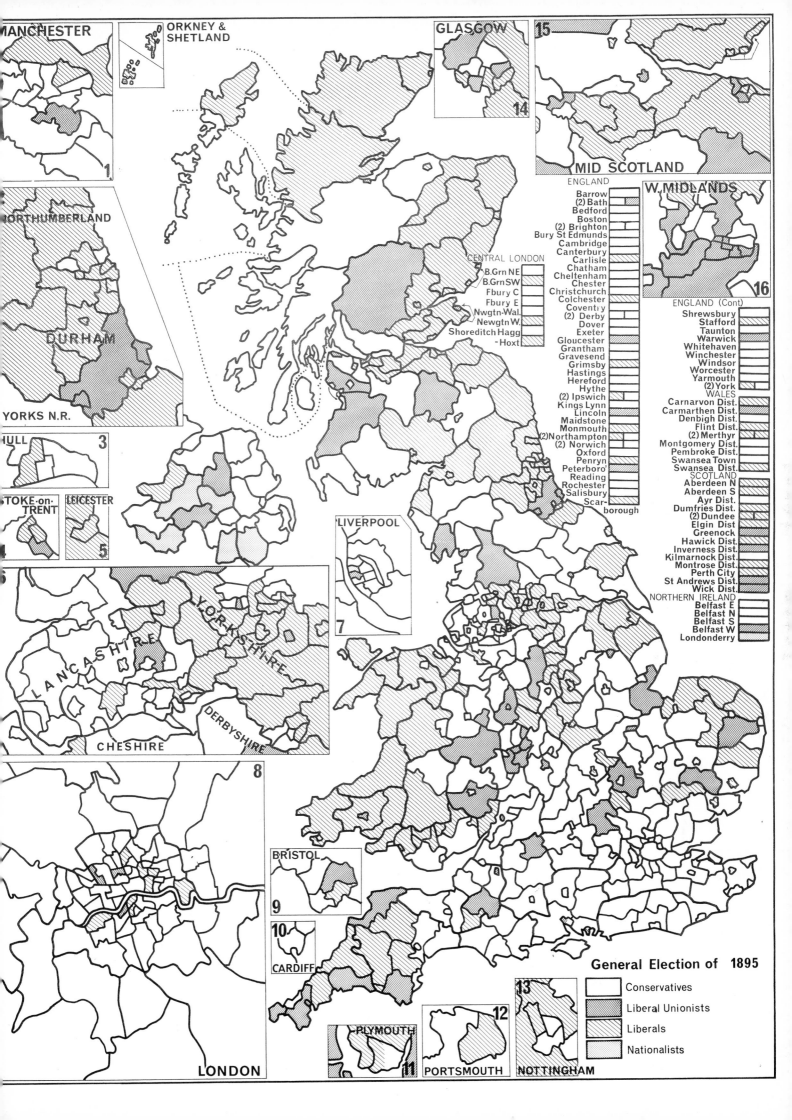

General Election of 1895

- Conservatives
- Liberal Unionists
- Liberals
- Nationalists

MANCHESTER **1**

ORKNEY & SHETLAND

NORTHUMBERLAND

DURHAM

YORKS N.R.

HULL **3**

STOKE-on-TRENT **4**

LEICESTER **5**

LIVERPOOL **7**

LANCASHIRE

YORKSHIRE

DERBYSHIRE

CHESHIRE

8

BRISTOL **9**

CARDIFF **10**

PLYMOUTH **11**

PORTSMOUTH **12**

NOTTINGHAM **13**

LONDON

GLASGOW **14**

15 MID SCOTLAND

W. MIDLANDS **16**

ENGLAND
- Barrow
- (2) Bath
- Bedford
- Boston
- (2) Brighton
- Bury St Edmunds
- Cambridge
- Canterbury
- Carlisle
- Chatham
- Cheltenham
- Chester
- Christchurch
- Colchester
- Coventry
- (2) Derby
- Dover
- Exeter
- Gloucester
- Grantham
- Gravesend
- Grimsby
- Hastings
- Hereford
- Hythe
- (2) Ipswich
- Kings Lynn
- Lincoln
- Maidstone
- Monmouth
- (2) Northampton
- (2) Norwich
- Oxford
- Penryn
- Peterboro'
- Reading
- Rochester
- Salisbury
- Scarborough

CENTRAL LONDON
- B.Grn NE
- B.Grn SW
- Fbury C
- Fbury E
- Nwgtn-Wal.
- Newgtn W.
- Shoreditch Hagg
- Hoxt

ENGLAND (Cont)
- Shrewsbury
- Stafford
- Taunton
- Warwick
- Whitehaven
- Winchester
- Windsor
- Worcester
- Yarmouth
- (2) York

WALES
- Carnarvon Dist.
- Carmarthen Dist.
- Denbigh Dist.
- Flint Dist.
- (2) Merthyr
- Montgomery Dist.
- Pembroke Dist.
- Swansea Town
- Swansea Dist.

SCOTLAND
- Aberdeen N
- Aberdeen S
- Ayr Dist.
- Dumfries Dist.
- (2) Dundee
- Elgin Dist
- Greenock
- Hawick Dist.
- Inverness Dist.
- Kilmarnock Dist.
- Montrose Dist.
- Perth City
- St Andrews Dist.
- Wick Dist.

NORTHERN IRELAND
- Belfast E
- Belfast N
- Belfast S
- Belfast W
- Londonderry

General Election of 1900

Overall results

party	total votes	% of total
Unionist	1,676,020	51·1
Liberal	1,503,652	45·9
Labour	16,633	0·5
Nationalist	82,578	2·5
Total	**3,278,883**	**100·0**

Seats won by area

area	Cons.	Lib. Unionist	Lib.	Lib.–Lab. and Lab.	Nat.	total
England	287	45	123	—	1	456
Wales	6	—	26	2	—	34
Scotland	19	17	34	—	—	70
N. Ireland	15	3	1	—	5	24
S. Ireland	1	—	—	—	76	77
Universities	6	3	—	—	—	9
Total	**334**	**68**	**184**	**2**	**82**	**670**

Unopposed returns by area

area	Cons.	Lib. Unionist	Lib.	Lib.–Lab. and Lab.	Nat.	total
England	117	23	10	—	—	150
Wales	—	—	10	—	—	10
Scotland	3	—	—	—	—	3
N. Ireland	9	2	—	—	2	13
S. Ireland	—	—	—	—	56	56
Universities	6	3	—	—	—	9
Total	**135**	**28**	**20**	**—**	**58**	**241**

Comments

The overall results of the 1900 election showed a net gain of 9 seats for the Liberals and Labour. In reality the Liberals lost some ground in this election. Their gains came primarily in relatively safe seats which they had lost in 1895 in English agricultural seats and in Wales. They also made a slight comeback in working-class seats in London. Though they gained only 2 seats in London while losing 2 others, they made slight percentage gains in 13 seats, 12 of which were working-class. These limited gains in Liberal strongholds were offset by Unionist gains in some seats with a long Liberal tradition. For example, the Unionists won Brightside, a Sheffield

seat which had elected Liberals from 1885 to 1895, and which continued to elect them from 1906 to 1922. The Unionists won control of Scotland for the first time since 1832, and also won all 3 seats in the Potteries, a feat they did not duplicate in any other election between 1885 and 1979.

Several Unionist gains may be ascribed to war hysteria or to prosperity induced by the war. These were: seats in Orkney and Shetland, Portsmouth and Plymouth, all naval centres; ship-building seats and ports in the industrial North-east such as Tynemouth, Middlesbrough, Stockton and Sunderland; and the heavy industrial seat of Brightside. All these seats presumably did well out of the Boer War, and all voted Unionist. The Unionists did well in Glasgow, reducing the Liberals to one seat in the city and suburbs;[1] however, the Unionists did well in Scotland as a whole, especially in the Western half. This East–West split was not along the lines of industrial–rural Scotland. The Unionists did well in large towns throughout Great Britain, and won a majority of seats in every major city. The result in Manchester and Salford is noteworthy. There, although no seats changed hands, there was a marked swing to the Unionists. In the surrounding districts, the Liberals recaptured 3 seats. In the second 'khaki' election, in 1918, the same trend was noticeable: there was a much stronger swing to the Unionists in Manchester and Salford than in surrounding seats.

In Wales the Liberals regained most of the ground they had lost in 1895. Although the activities of Lloyd George against the Boer War attracted much attention at the time, Morgan[2] estimates that most Welsh Liberal candidates were either pro-war or neutral in 1900, and that the Liberal success there was not due primarily to fellow-feeling of one 'oppressed nation' for another. Even so, anti-war sentiment probably helped the Liberals, though one cannot say how much. The Liberals also regained several agricultural seats in 1900, perhaps because the agricultural prosperity some rural voters had expected from Chamberlain had not matured.[3] Other places showing slight swings to the Liberals were the most heavily working-class seats of London. There the Liberals had swings favourable to them in 12 seats.[4] There was a swing favourable to the Liberals in only one middle-class seat in London, Chelsea.[5] Apparently there was more enthusiasm for the war in the middle-class than in the working-class London seats.

---

1 Govan
2 Morgan, *Wales in British Politics,* 178 and 180-1
3 The Rousseaux price index for agricultural produce fell from 91 to 81 in the 1890s; although there was a slight increase in the late 90s, agriculture was still badly off. (Mitchell and Deane, *British Historical Statistics,* 472-3)

4 Battersea, Camberwell, North Bermondsey, Finsbury Central, Haggerston, Kensington North, Limehouse, Poplar, Rotherhithe, St. Pancras South, Southwark West, Whitechapel
5 Even Chelsea had a working-class area, the detached part in Kensal Town

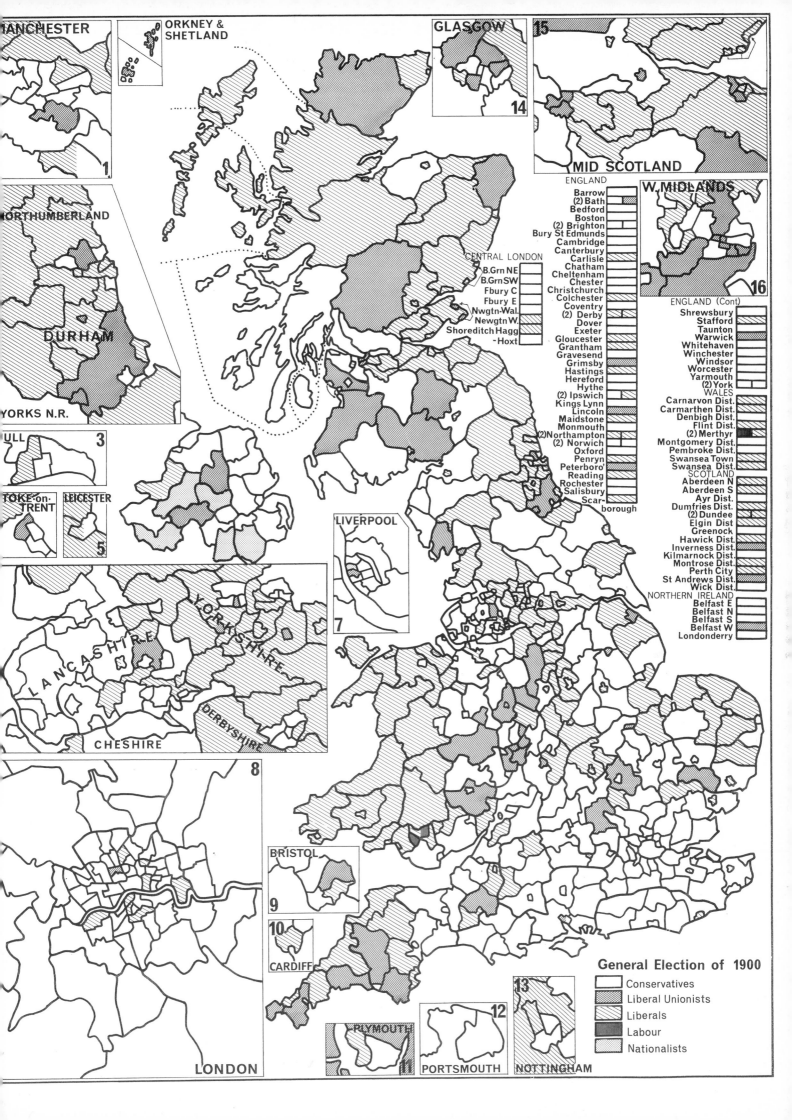

General Election of 1906

Overall results

party	total votes	% of total
Unionist	2,463,606	43·7
Liberal	2,583,132	45·9
Labour	528,797	9·4
Nationalist	35,109	0·6
Others*	21,557	0·4
Total	**5,632,201**	**100·0**

* includes Russellites

Seats won by area

area	Cons.	Lib. Unionist	Lib.	Lib.–Lab. and Lab.	Nat.	total
England	105	16	287	47	1	456
Wales	—	—	29	5	—	34
Scotland	6	4	58	2	—	70
N. Ireland	14	1	3*	—	6	24
S. Ireland	1	—	—	—	76	77
Universities	7	2	—	—	—	9
Total	**133**	**23**	**377**	**54**	**83**	**670**

* includes Russellites

Unopposed returns by area

area	Cons.	Lib. Unionist	Lib.	Lib.–Lab. and Lab.	Nat.	total
England	3	—	13	1	—	17
Wales	—	—	10	2	—	12
Scotland	—	—	1	—	—	1
N. Ireland	6	—	—	—	3	9
S. Ireland	—	—	—	—	71	71
Universities	3	1	—	—	—	4
Total	**12**	**1**	**24**	**3**	**74**	**114**

Unionist seats won by Free Traders, Balfourites and Tariff Reformers

	1905	1906
Tariff Reformers	172	102
Balfourites:		
Preferentialists 73 ⎫	171	36
Retaliationists 98 ⎭		
Free Traders	27	16
Others	4	3
Total	**374**	**157**

Source: P. Fraser, 'Unionism and Tariff Reform: the Crisis of 1906', *Historical Journal*, 1962, 155

Comments

In 1906 most factors favoured the Liberals, as they had favoured the Unionists in 1895 and 1900. None of these elections indicated the real distribution of party strength in the country: for that, one must examine the results of the two elections of 1910, and that of 1892. However, the elections of 1895, 1900 and 1906 show what were the bedrock areas of Liberalism and Unionism before 1914. Seats remaining Liberal in 1895 and 1900, and seats remaining Unionist in 1906 could be considered 'safe'.

It is unlikely that many floating voters in 1906 chose the Unionists. The only substantial areas of Unionist strength were the urban areas of West Lancashire, Birmingham and Sheffield. In the Unionist stronghold of the South-east the Liberals gained many seats. The issues which drove the floating voters to the Liberals are familiar: 'Chinese slavery', the Education Act of 1902 and, most important, the internal conflict of the Unionists over tariffs.[1] In 1905, before the election, Balfour handed over the government to the Liberals, hoping for a Liberal fight over the offices to be distributed. There was a short quarrel but the election followed the transfer of power almost immediately. The results demonstrated that the few voters who thought ill of the Liberals for fighting over jobs were greatly outnumbered by those who felt Balfour had thrown in the sponge.

The Unionists lost 250 seats in this election and gained 5, in comparison with the 1900 results. Although this was the biggest loss in seats any party has suffered between 1832 and 1979, it was at first glance not a great landslide in votes. A straightforward comparison of the percentage of total vote going Unionist in 1900 and in 1906 indicates that the Unionists lost 7%. A second method of comparison, using figures for the average percentage obtained by opposed candidates, indicates that the Unionists lost 8·4%.[2] These are the only precise figures which can be obtained for the 1906 election, but they are misleading. In 1906 13 Unionists were returned without a contest; but in 1900 no fewer than 163 Unionists had been unopposed. Most of the unopposed victories were in safe seats. This means that the average Unionist percentage obtained per opposed candidate in 1900 was lower than if all the safe seats had been contested, as they were in 1906. Consequently, the average percentage obtained by each opposed Unionist in 1900 would probably have been considerably higher than the 52·5% they did obtain. Perhaps it would have been 60%, and almost certainly it would have been at least 55%. In either case the Unionist drop from 1900 to 1906 would have been higher than that indicated by comparison of either percentages of the total vote or percentages obtained per opposed candidate. The Unionist percentage loss was not 7 or 8·4%, but 10%, and possibly 15%. The latter figure is similar to the 14% drop in the Conservative vote between 1935 and 1945, when the Conservatives and allies lost 219 seats.[3]

Though there was a big swing away from them, in seats as well as in votes, the Unionists remained an electoral force of considerable strength. The 44% they won in 1906 was 6% more than they got in 1922, when they won the election with a substantial majority. The difference was that their opponents were divided in 1922,

1 On the Unionist split, see map, Unionist Free Traders, 1904, p. 101; P. Fraser 'Unionism and Tariff Reform: The Crisis of 1906', *Historical Journal*, 1962, 149-66; and A. K. Russell, *Liberal Landslide: The General Election of 1906* (1973); and Rempel, *Unionists Divided* (1972)
2 The figures for average percentages obtained by opposed Unionists in 1900 and 1906 have been obtained from D. Butler, *British Political Facts*, 122. Figures for overall percentages have been calculated from results given in the *Constitutional Year Book, 1908*, 225-6
3 The Labour loss of 7% in 1931 was accompanied by a loss of 236 seats

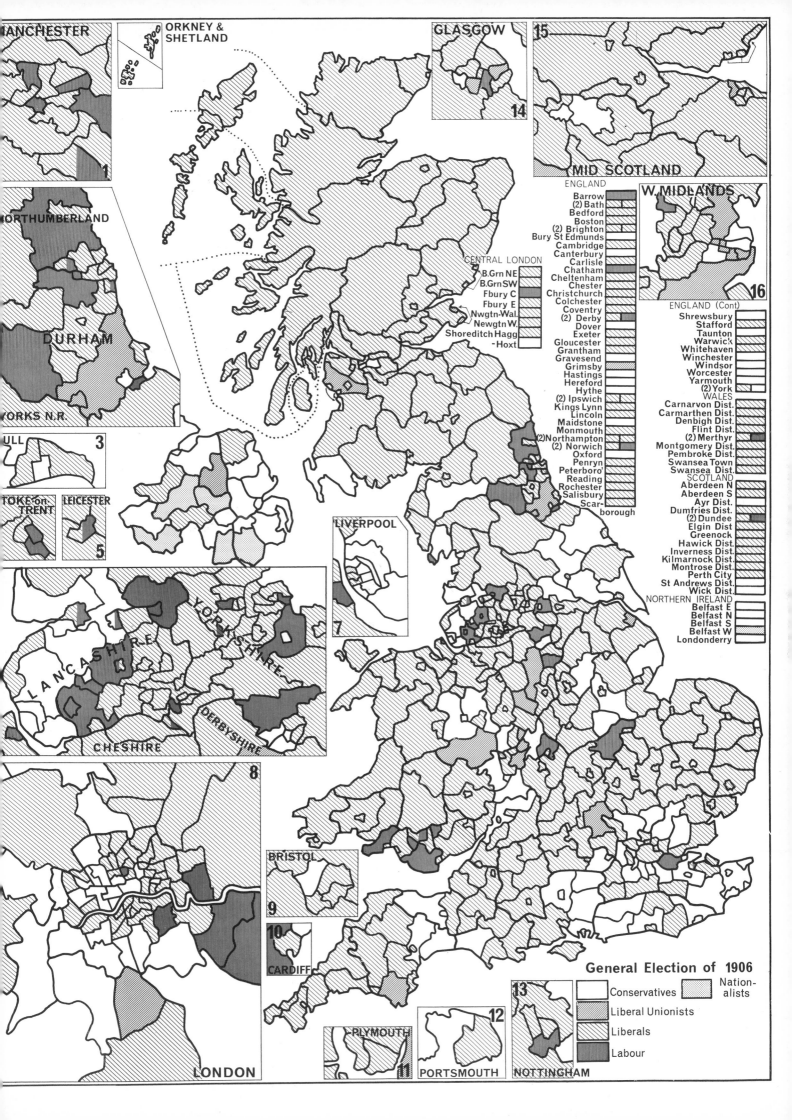

MANCHESTER
1

ORKNEY & SHETLAND

GLASGOW
14

15

MID SCOTLAND

W.MIDLANDS
16

NORTHUMBERLAND

DURHAM

YORKS N.R.

HULL
3

STOKE-on-TRENT

LEICESTER
5

CENTRAL LONDON
B.Grn NE
B.Grn SW
Fbury C
Fbury E
Nwgtn-Wal.
Newgtn W.
Shoreditch Hagg
-Hoxt

ENGLAND
Barrow
(2) Bath
Bedford
Boston
(2) Brighton
Bury St Edmunds
Cambridge
Canterbury
Carlisle
Chatham
Cheltenham
Chester
Christchurch
Colchester
Coventry
(2) Derby
Dover
Exeter
Gloucester
Grantham
Gravesend
Grimsby
Hastings
Hereford
Hythe
(2) Ipswich
Kings Lynn
Lincoln
Maidstone
Monmouth
(2)Northampton
(2) Norwich
Oxford
Penryn
Peterboro'
Reading
Rochester
Salisbury
Scar-
borough

ENGLAND (Cont)
Shrewsbury
Stafford
Taunton
Warwick
Whitehaven
Winchester
Windsor
Worcester
Yarmouth
(2) York

WALES
Carnarvon Dist.
Carmarthen Dist.
Denbigh Dist.
Flint Dist.
(2) Merthyr
Montgomery Dist.
Pembroke Dist.
Swansea Town
Swansea Dist.

SCOTLAND
Aberdeen N
Aberdeen S
Ayr Dist.
Dumfries Dist.
(2) Dundee
Elgin Dist
Greenock
Hawick Dist.
Inverness Dist.
Kilmarnock Dist.
Montrose Dist.
Perth City
St Andrews Dist.
Wick Dist.

NORTHERN IRELAND
Belfast E
Belfast N
Belfast S
Belfast W
Londonderry

LIVERPOOL
7

LANCASHIRE
YORKSHIRE
CHESHIRE
DERBYSHIRE
8

BRISTOL
9

10
CARDIFF

13
NOTTINGHAM

LONDON

PLYMOUTH
12
11
PORTSMOUTH

General Election of 1906

☐ Conservatives	▨ Nationalists
	▥ Liberal Unionists
	▧ Liberals
	■ Labour

whereas they were relatively united in 1906. Only 3 places remained strongly Unionist, West Lancashire, Sheffield and Birmingham. Elsewhere the Liberals won even such safe seats as Brentford and Enfield in Middlesex. In West Lancashire much Unionist strength was probably due to continuing anti-Irish feeling. In Sheffield and Birmingham their campaign for Tariff Reform probably helped the Unionists. In both Sheffield and Birmingham there was increasing awareness of vulnerability of local industries to foreign competition. It is notable that in East Lancashire and in the western part of West Yorkshire, both textile areas which did not much fear foreign competition, the Unionists lost 29 of the 30 seats they had won in 1900.[1] On balance, the tariff reform issue damaged the Unionists most where the Unionists themselves could not make up their minds about it: although the Unionist Free Traders and Tariff Reformers each lost 40% of their M.P.s, the group which backed Balfour's course of 'fiscal agnosticism' lost 79% of its M.P.s.

In the countryside few large areas remained Unionist. Those which did included most of the seats in the South-east, 6 more in the South-west, some partly agricultural seats in the West Midlands, and a few more in rural Yorkshire and Lincolnshire. Few seats remaining Unionist had an appreciable number of Nonconformists,[2] and in the seats where the Unionists won despite the presence of numerous Nonconformists, there was an above average swing against them. For example, the Unionists retained 2 seats in rural Lincolnshire, Horncastle, with about 15% Nonconformists, and Stamford, with about 5%. The swing against the Unionists in Horncastle was 8·4%, while that in Stamford was only 3·2%.

The Unionists regained 5 seats they had lost in 1900. Three of these 5 gains were caused by split votes. In Lanark North-west and Govan the anti-Unionist vote was split in 1906; while in Dublin County South the Unionist vote had been split in 1900, while it was united in 1906. The other 2 Unionist gains, Maidstone and Hastings, are less easy to explain. Both seats had above average

proportions of Nonconformists in 1851, but they also had even greater proportions of Anglicans. It is possible that the religious issue in 1906 harmed the Liberals more than it helped them in these seats.[3] However, local factors may have caused the Liberal defeat.

In most areas where it was to dominate after the First World War, Labour showed appreciable strength in 1906, because all but 4 Labour victories were in seats where there was a pact between Liberals and Labour.[4] In Scotland, where there was no such pact between the 2 parties, Labour was less successful than in England and Wales. The 12 Labour candidates in Scotland polled an average of 2,809 votes each, but only 2 were elected. In only 4 other seats in Scotland is it likely that Labour intervention caused Liberal defeats.[5]

The places where Labour and Liberal–Labour candidates won in 1906 consisted of 4 main groups of seats: 2-membered constituencies where one Liberal and one Labour candidate ran together (11 seats, including the 2 adjacent single-membered seats of Rochester and Chatham);[6] mining seats (16);[7] slums in major cities (10);[8] and seats where Liberals had never won in the period 1885-1900, and where there was a large working-class vote (5).[9] In these last 5 seats, co-operation between Liberals and Labour lasted into the 1920s, although it did not last so long in other parts of the country. Outside the groups mentioned, Labour won only 13 other seats.

For the first and last time since 1885 the Liberals won a majority of the seats in England. They also won overwhelming victories in Scotland and Wales, and they even won 3 seats in Northern Ireland. In their Northern Irish victories local factors were involved. They had previously held North Tyrone on the basis of the Irish Nationalist vote and a small number of Liberal Unionist votes. Their 2 gains, in Antrim North and Tyrone South, were not victories for Home Rule, but for a Liberal splinter group known as the 'Russellites'. The Russellites were not at first in favour of Home Rule, although they later became Home Rulers. It is doubtful that they would have won in 1906 if they had made Home Rule their goal.[10]

---

1 In the election of 1923, which was also fought in part on the issue of tariffs, the Unionists lost 11 of the 24 seats they held in the same areas. In the period 1900-5, exports of iron, steel, cutlery and machinery rose by 8·6%. These goods were the basis of much industry in Sheffield and Birmingham. However, in the same period, exports of cotton and wool rose by 28·7%, or at least three times the rate of iron, cutlery and machinery. East Lancashire and the Western part of West Yorkshire largely depended on production of cotton and woollen goods. The figures:

Year	Export of iron, etc.	Exports of cotton and woollen goods
1900	54·8	90·0
1903	54·5	93·7
1905	59·5	115·8

Source: Mitchell and Deane, *British Historical Statistics*, 305. Figures are £millions at current prices
2 See map, Distribution of Nonconformists in 1922, p. 127
3 In 1851, 18·0% of the population in Maidstone was Anglican, and 11·2% was Nonconformist; in Hastings the relative figures were 18·5% and 7·5%. (*Religious Census of 1851*, cclxiii and 17). Pelling (*Social Geography*, 1980) suggests that electoral corruption may have been involved in Maidstone in 1900–6
4 The English and Welsh seats in which Labour won against Liberal opposition were Chester-le-Street, Merthyr Tydfil (one seat), Bradford West and Deptford.

The pact in England and Wales is examined carefully in F. Bealey and H. Pelling, *Labour and Politics, 1900–1906*, which lists Labour candidates in 1900 and 1906. It does not list Liberal-Labour Candidates. There was no pact between Liberals and Labour in Scotland. As late as 1910 the Scottish Liberals showed their dislike of the Labour party by supporting the Osborne judgement, which forbade a compulsory trade union levy for political purposes. (*Minutes of the Scottish Liberal Association*, 22 Oct. 1910)
5 Labour won Blackfriars and one seat in Dundee, and probably caused Liberal defeats in North Ayrshire, Lanark–Govan, Lanark North-west and Camlachie
6 Blackburn, Bolton, Chatham, Derby, Halifax, Leicester, Newcastle-on-Tyne, Norwich, Preston, Stockport and Sunderland
7 Chesterfield, Barnard Castle and Chester-le-Street, Gower, Rhondda, South Glamorganshire, St. Helens, Ince, Newton, Westhoughton, Monmouthshire West, Hallamshire, Normanton, Merthyr Tydfil (one seat), and the partly mining seat of Leeds East
8 Four seats in Manchester and Salford; 2 in the Potteries; one in Wolverhampton; one in Glasgow; one in Bradford; and one in London (apart from those listed in the next category)
9 Birkenhead, Deptford, Preston (one seat), West Ham South, Woolwich
10 The Russellites, followers of T. W. Russell, are examined critically in St. J. Ervine, *Craigavon: Ulsterman*, 99–103; Reginald Lucas, *Col. Saunderson, M.P.*, 231–2, 310–1.

General Election of January 1910

Overall results

party	total votes	% of total
Unionist	3,127,887	46·9
Liberal	2,873,251	43·1
Labour	532,807	8·0
Nationalist	126,647	1·9
Others	6,812	0·1
Total	**6,667,404**	**100·0**

Seats won by area

area	Cons.	Lib. Unionist	Lib.	Lib.–Lab. and Lab.	Nat.	total
England	210	24	188	33	1	456
Wales	2	—	27	5	—	34
Scotland	7	2	59	2	—	70
N. Ireland	16	2	1	—	5	24
S. Ireland	1	—	—	—	76	77
Universities	6	3	—	—	—	9
Total	**242**	**31**	**275**	**40**	**82**	**670**

Unopposed returns by area

area	Cons.	Lib. Unionist	Lib.	Lib.–Lab. and Lab.	Nat.	total
England	2	1	1	—	—	4
Wales	—	—	—	—	—	—
Scotland	—	—	—	—	—	—
N. Ireland	8	—	—	—	1	9
S. Ireland	—	—	—	—	54	54
Universities	6	2	—	—	—	8
Total	**16**	**3**	**1**	**—**	**55**	**75**

Comments

The recovery between 1906 and January 1910 was chiefly confined to the Conservative wing of the Unionist coalition. The Conservatives rose from 134 seats to 242, a gain of 108, while the Liberal Unionists rose from 23 to 31, a gain of only 8. As in other elections after 1892, many Liberal Unionist victories were primarily Conservative victories, and the Liberal Unionists' contribution was significant only in about two-thirds of the seats they won. For example, the Liberal Unionist victory in Durham City was really a Conservative victory. The Liberal Unionist winner had run successfully in 1906 as a Tariff Reform Conservative, when he had defeated a Liberal Unionist Free Trader. He probably adopted the Liberal Unionist label in January 1910 merely as an electoral aid. In January 1910, more than in most other elections from 1886 to 1906, Liberal Unionism was confined to the West Midlands, with few other areas electing more than one or two Liberal Unionists each. Even in the West Midlands the Liberal Unionists lost ground relative to the Conservatives.

Unionist gains in January 1910 were restricted to 3 broad groups of seats. They were agricultural seats in the South Midlands; London and the South-east; and the Black Country West of Birmingham. The Unionists made no net gains in Scotland or Wales, in votes or seats; nor did they recover many seats in the textile areas of East Lancashire and West Yorkshire. The continued Unionist emphasis on tariff reform probably harmed them in all 4 areas. In the North-east the Unionists lost 3, and gained 2, seats. Their losses were caused by adjustments among their opponents, rather than by significant swings against the Unionists;[1] however, the area remained strongly anti-Unionist.

The Unionists regained most English agricultural seats they had lost in 1906, though they were weaker in Cornwall than they had been in 1900. Their Cornish losses may be attributed to continued Nonconformist anxiety about education.[2] In the nearby seat of Devon–Tavistock the Unionist loss meant little in electoral terms, as their majority in 1900 had been only 15 votes. Elsewhere in England, the Unionists regained most agricultural seats they had held in 1900, perhaps because of the appeals of tariffs to a protectionist industry. If there had not been a slight agricultural boom, in comparison with 1906,[3] the Unionists probably would have won several more agricultural seats.

The Unionists failed to recover several mining seats they had lost in West Lancashire for the first time between 1885 and 1906. These seats[4] remained Labour strongholds throughout the period 1906-66, and 3 stayed Labour even in 1931. In another West Lancashire seat, Preston, the Unionists recovered a 1906 loss. Preston had returned one Liberal and one Labour candidate in 1906, but in January 1910 there were 2 Liberal candidates and one Labour. This split contributed substantially to the Unionist recovery in Preston. Another factor aiding the Unionists was that one Liberal candidate, J. E. Gorst, had formerly been a Conservative junior minister. Many Liberal voters were apparently unenthusiastic about him. Between 1918 and 1945 there was an alliance between Liberals and Labour in Preston in several elections. The only 2 elections in which the Conservatives won both seats were those of 1931 and 1935, that is, in Conservative landslides.

The Liberals retained nearly all their seats in Wales and Scotland. In both Wales and Scotland the results of the elections of 1906 and 1910 marked a return to the pattern noticeable in 1885. In Wales the Liberals were actually stronger in January 1910 than they had been in 1885, since they won 61% of the vote in 1885 and 70% in January 1910. In Wales the Unionists had never come close to equality with the Liberals, but in Scotland, between 1886 and 1900, the Scottish Liberals had not had a substantial majority over their opponents.

---

1 In South-east Durham the Unionist had been unopposed in 1906. In January 1910 a Liberal defeated him. In Darlington a Labour candidate had failed to dislodge a Liberal Unionist in 1906, but a Liberal did so in January 1910. In Stockton there had been a split between Liberals and Labour in 1906, but this had been overcome by 1910, when only a Liberal ran
2 See map, Distribution of Nonconformists in England in 1922, p. 127. The 3 Cornish seats were Bodmin, St. Ives and Truro

3 The Rousseaux price index of agricultural produce in 1906 was 83, and was 94 in 1910; the same index for industrial products was 103 in 1906, and 100 in 1910. There was therefore a relative as well as an absolute improvement in farm prices between 1906 and 1910 (Mitchell and Deane, *British Historical Statistics*, 473). It should also be noted that the 1911 census was the only one after 1851 which showed an increase in the number of persons engaged in agriculture. (*ibid.*, 60-1)
4 St. Helens, Wigan, Ince, Westhoughton, Newton. Westhoughton, Wigan and Ince remained Labour in 1931

In 1906, and again in the 2 elections of 1910, the Scottish Liberals recovered their 1885 position. Counting Labour and Liberals together, they won 64% in 1885 and 63% in January 1910. The recovery of Liberal fortunes in Scotland in 3 successive elections indicates that the significance of the split over Home Rule was gradually declining. This was further emphasised by the virtual disappearance of the Liberal Unionist M.P.s from Scotland. They declined from 4 in 1906 to 2 in January 1910.

The Liberals also kept most working-class seats they had won in 1906 in London and suburbs, though they lost such seats as Harrow, Guildford, Chelsea and Chertsey, in which the working-class electorate was relatively small. In 1900 Liberals and Labour had won only 8 seats shown in Inset 8; in 1906 they won 50 in the same area, of which they retained 30 in January 1910. It is likely that social reform was a key factor in keeping many of these working-class seats Liberal in January 1910.

General Election of December 1910

Overall results

party	total votes	% of total
Unionist	2,426,635	46·4
Liberal	2,290,020	43·8
Labour	374,409	7·1
Nationalist	131,720	2·5
Other (inc.Soc.)	11,509	0·2
Total	**5,234,293**	**100·0**

Seats won by area

area	Cons.	Lib. Unionist	Lib.	Lib.–Lab. and Lab.	Nat.	total
England	210	26	185	34	1	456
Wales	3	—	26	5	—	34
Scotland	6	3	58	3	—	70
N. Ireland	15	2	1	—	6	24
S. Ireland	—	—	—	—	77	77
Universities	6	3	—	—	—	9
Total	**240**	**34**	**270**	**42**	**84**	**670**

Unopposed returns by area

area	Cons.	Lib. Unionist	Lib.	Lib.–Lab. and Lab.	Nat.	total
England	46	8	14	2	—	70
Wales	—	—	10	1	—	11
Scotland	1	—	11	—	—	12
N. Ireland	9	—	—	—	1	10
S. Ireland	—	—	—	—	52	52
Universities	6	2	—	—	—	8
Total	**62**	**10**	**35**	**3**	**53**	**163**

Comments

An examination of the areas where seats changed hands between 1892 and 1910 indicates the direction British politics had been taking in those years. Although the swing to the Liberals and Labour was not large,[1] many events in Britain between 1892 and 1910 could well have led to major changes in the electoral map. Among these events were the disappearance of most party leaders of 1892; increased emphasis on tariffs and on social reform; and the rise of Labour from a small fragment to a third party of respectable size. There had also been 3 landslide elections in a row, which had disturbed the electoral pattern at least temporarily. Despite these things, the electoral map of Britain in December 1910 closely resembled that of 1892. Some seats changed, but they were far less numerous than those which stayed the same.[2]

Few places turned to the Unionists between 1892 and December 1910; among them were 4 seats in Plymouth and Portsmouth, and some small boroughs and English agricultural seats. Places turning Liberal or Labour were more numerous, and consisted of 5

1 In 1892 the Unionists had led the Liberals and Labour by 1·7%; in December 1910 the Liberals and Labour led the Unionists by 4·5%. This represented a swing to the Liberals and Labour of 3·1%. However, there had been only 41 unopposed Unionists in 1892, while there were 72 unopposed in December 1910. The real swing was therefore about 2·7 or 2·8%

2 Areas voting Unionist in both elections were: West Midlands, West Lancashire, London and the South-east (except the East End of London), and most English agricultural seats. Areas remaining Liberal were: West Yorkshire, most mining seats, Wales, East Anglia, East Central Scotland and Scottish Highlands

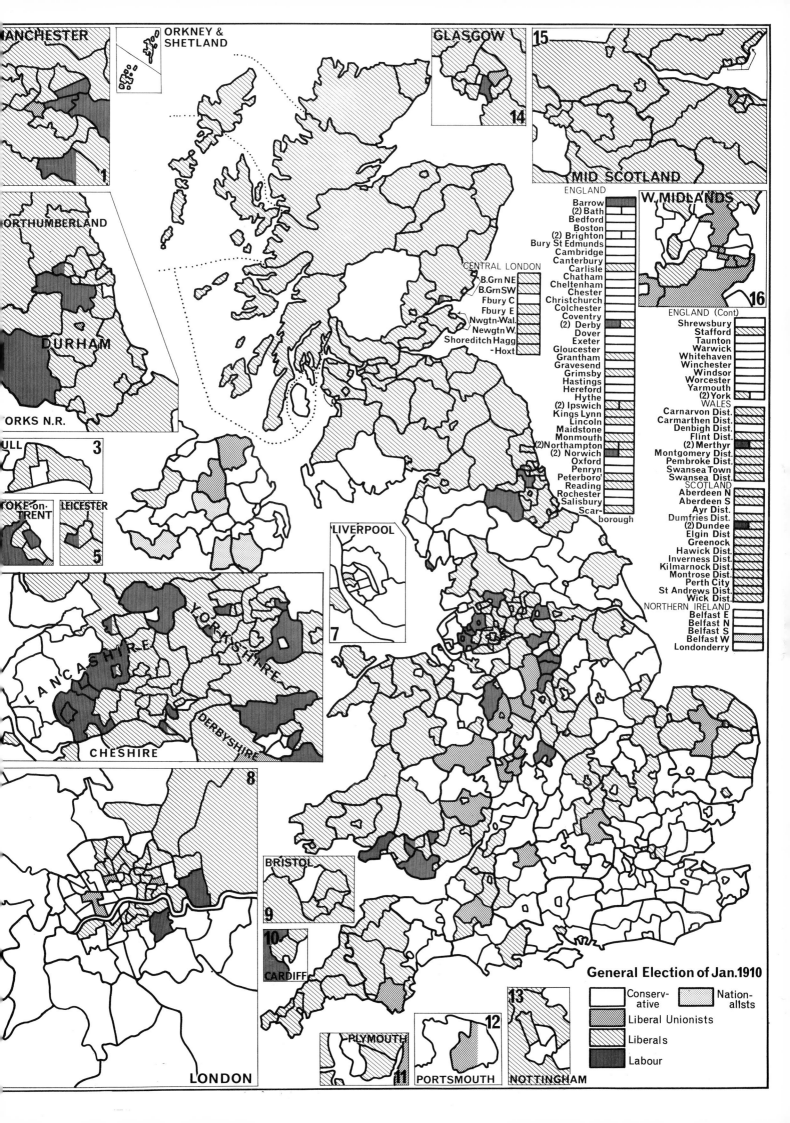

General Election of Jan.1910

Legend:
- Conservative
- Liberal Unionists
- Liberals
- Labour
- Nationalists

Inset maps
1. MANCHESTER
— ORKNEY & SHETLAND
— NORTHUMBERLAND
— DURHAM
— YORKS N.R.
3. HULL
— STOKE-on-TRENT
5. LEICESTER
7. LIVERPOOL
8. LANCASHIRE — YORKSHIRE — CHESHIRE — DERBYSHIRE
9. BRISTOL
10. CARDIFF
11. PLYMOUTH
12. PORTSMOUTH
13. NOTTINGHAM
14. GLASGOW
15. MID SCOTLAND
16. W.MIDLANDS
— LONDON

CENTRAL LONDON
- B.Grn NE
- B.Grn SW
- Fbury C
- Fbury E
- Nwgtn-Wal.
- Newgtn W.
- Shoreditch Hagg
- Hoxt

ENGLAND
- Barrow
- (2) Bath
- Bedford
- Boston
- (2) Brighton
- Bury St Edmunds
- Cambridge
- Canterbury
- Carlisle
- Chatham
- Cheltenham
- Chester
- Christchurch
- Colchester
- Coventry
- (2) Derby
- Dover
- Exeter
- Gloucester
- Grantham
- Gravesend
- Grimsby
- Hastings
- Hereford
- Hythe
- (2) Ipswich
- Kings Lynn
- Lincoln
- Maidstone
- Monmouth
- (2) Northampton
- (2) Norwich
- Oxford
- Penryn
- Peterboro'
- Reading
- Rochester
- Salisbury
- Scar-borough

ENGLAND (Cont)
- Shrewsbury
- Stafford
- Taunton
- Warwick
- Whitehaven
- Winchester
- Windsor
- Worcester
- Yarmouth
- (2) York

WALES
- Carnarvon Dist.
- Carmarthen Dist.
- Denbigh Dist.
- Flint Dist.
- (2) Merthyr
- Montgomery Dist.
- Pembroke Dist.
- Swansea Town
- Swansea Dist.

SCOTLAND
- Aberdeen N
- Aberdeen S
- Ayr Dist.
- Dumfries Dist.
- (2) Dundee
- Elgin Dist
- Greenock
- Hawick Dist.
- Inverness Dist.
- Kilmarnock Dist.
- Montrose Dist.
- Perth City
- St Andrews Dist.
- Wick Dist.

NORTHERN IRELAND
- Belfast E
- Belfast N
- Belfast S
- Belfast W
- Londonderry

main groups: 13 seats in the East and South-east of London; 14 in East Lancashire; 12 in the smaller English boroughs; 9 in South-west Scotland; and 7 agricultural seats in England. There were also some other scattered Liberal gains.

The Liberal gains in Lancashire came in 2 places: in Manchester and district,[1] and in the area between Ince and Blackburn. Many seats in the Manchester district probably went Liberal because of the Unionist policy of tariff reform; also, the Liberal campaign for social reform in the period just before 1910 probably kept some of those seats from going back to the Unionists. In the West Lancashire mining district, the replacement of Liberal candidates by Labour men almost certainly cost the Unionists the seats. Social reform helped these Labour candidates, as it helped the Liberals and Labour in London.

A major factor influencing the changes in both the smaller boroughs and in the agricultural seats appears to have been the degree of Nonconformity of the constituencies. In these seats the percentage of Nonconformists was the dividing line between Liberal and Unionist gains; in December 1910 as compared with 1892 it was 7·5%. That is, if seats changed at all between the two elections, where there were more Nonconformists than 7·5% they were likely to go Liberal. Where there were fewer Nonconformists than 7·5%, they were likely to go Unionist.[2] The following table illustrates the division:

	Nonconformist Under 7·5%	Over 7·5%
Agricultural and small borough seats going Unionist 1892 – December 1910 [3]	12	10
Agricultural and small borough seats going Liberal 1892 – December 1910 [3]	2	16

The probable reason for the Liberal advantage in Nonconformist seats over 1892 is that between 1902 and 1906, the Nonconformists had agitated for repeal of Balfour's Education Act, and many Nonconformists who had previously supported the Unionists

changed sides. Apparently many of them remained with the Liberals, at least in the 1910 elections.

Some seats went against the general trend. For example, East Dorset changed to the Liberals, although it had under 7·5% Nonconformists. In this seat as well as in several others, local factors were probably decisive. In East Dorset the Liberal candidate in December 1910 was F. E. Guest, a member of a prominent local family which had left the Conservative Party for the Liberals in 1904, over Free Trade. Despite such local factors, however, the general tendency remains clear, that there was a sharper division between the parties on religion in 1910 than there had been in 1892.

The mobilisation of the Nonconformists may have saved some seats for the Liberals, especially in the agricultural districts. Their gains in the boroughs were probably tied up with social reform as well as with religion; but in the country, religion may have been the dominant factor. The Liberals won very few agricultural seats in December 1910 compared with 1892. Perhaps this is because several social reforms proposed by the Liberals in 1910 had less appeal to the rural than to the urban poor. For example, unemployment insurance probably had a greater appeal in urban areas. After 1910 the Liberals organised a 'Land campaign' to rectify this, with noticeable results. While the Liberal vote declined seriously in most seats, it held more steadily in agricultural seats:

Swing against the Liberals in by-elections 1911-13[4]

year	% non-agricultural seats	% agricultural seats
1911	−1·6	−0·9
1912	−5·2	−2·8
1913	−5·0	−2·0

Although by-election figures are not always good indications of changes in party strength, they are the only ones available for the period 1910-14. They show that the Liberals had made up some of their deficit of 1910 in the rural areas. This is borne out by the results of elections of 1922 and 1923, when the Liberals retained a large number of agricultural seats in Great Britain.[5]

1 The Cheshire division of Hyde is included in the Manchester district figures
2 The Nonconformist vote has been calculated for 1922. See map, Distribution of Nonconformists in England in 1922, p. 127. Although there may have been slight changes in the distribution of Nonconformists between 1910 and 1922, they cannot have been great, especially in the small boroughs and agricultural seats which are considered here. Major changes, if they occurred at all, probably took place in the larger boroughs. A second possible objection to the use of the 1922 figures is that the boundaries were different in 1922 from those of 1910. To eliminate this as much as possible, seats with different boundaries have been ignored, unless the changes were very small

3 In this table 'agricultural seats' included seats which in 1921 had over 20% engaged in agriculture; 'small boroughs' includes seats in England and Wales which were not in the London area, Lancashire, Yorkshire, or the West Midlands urban complex
4 Only seats contested by Unionists and Liberals in December 1910 and the by-elections are considered. In 1914 there were only four comparable by-elections, as Labour intervened in most. In the table, 'agricultural seats' are those with over 20% in the adult male population engaged in agriculture. See map, Farm Voters in 1921, p. 121
5 See maps, General Elections of 1922 and 1923, pp. 41 and 45

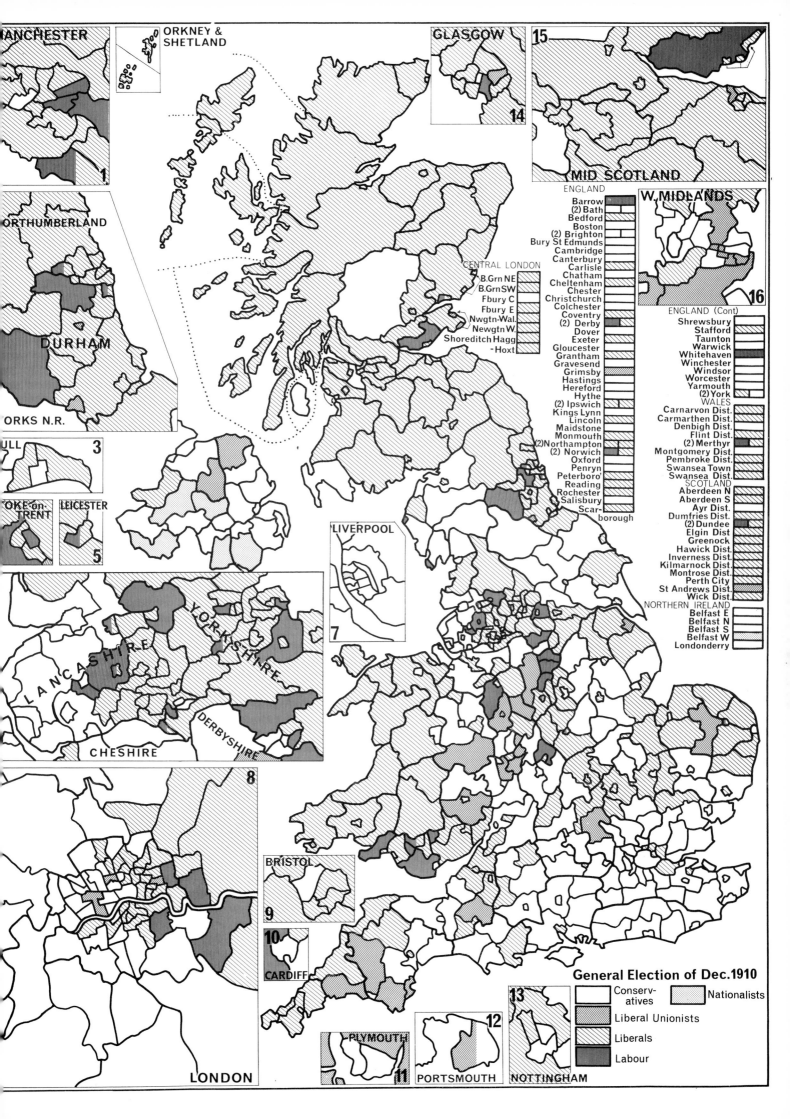

Party Gains January – December 1910

The overall results of the December election showed few changes from January 1910. In terms of votes, there was an apparent swing of 0·6% to the Liberals; while the net changes in seats were one Unionist and 3 Liberal losses, and 2 gains each for the Irish Nationalists and Labour. Neither figure indicates the real change in seats or votes. The apparent swing of 0·6% to the Liberals was caused by the increase of unopposed Unionists from 19 to 72.[1] The swing figure does not count the many Unionist votes in safe seats which were contested in January, but not in December. If all the seats had been contested the swing could even have been towards the Unionists.

The small net changes in seats masked considerable actual changes. To assess the significance of these changes, one must first examine the areas which changed. If several seats in a given area changed hands, it was probably caused by a regional trend; but if only widely scattered seats changed, then local factors such as differential turnout or the personalities of the candidates may have caused the changes. In only two areas did many seats change sides between January and December 1910. They were the North-west and the extreme South-west. In each area, the Unionists made substantial gains in votes as well as in seats.[2] Only one large group of seats showed any significant Liberal gains: the agricultural seats of the South Midlands. In that area majorities tended to be small, so that slight swings brought the Liberals several seats. Elsewhere, Liberal gains were very scattered. The Unionist gains in December 1910 therefore indicate that at least 2 parts of the country had moved against the Liberals; but the Liberal gains do not necessarily indicate that any area had moved away from the Unionists. The Liberal gains may merely indicate that local factors in scattered seats helped them more than they helped the Unionists.

Two factors may have led to Unionist gains in the North-west. First, between January and December 1910 the Irish Nationalists held the balance of power for the first time since 1895, and the old feelings about Home Rule may have driven Unionists in the North-west closer together than they had been in January. Second, in November 1910 Balfour announced that if returned to power, he would not introduce tariffs without a referendum. Some historians have held that this satisfied many Unionists in the North-west who had previously been worried about Free Trade.[3] The same factors probably influenced the South-west.

Four Liberal and Labour gains resulted from pacts between the parties. In Cumberland a Liberal withdrew from Whitehaven, and a Labour candidate from Cockermouth. In each case the Unionists lost the seat. A Labour withdrawal also accounted for the Liberal victory in Wakefield, and probably allowed the Liberals to keep their seat in Hyde. A Liberal withdrawal allowed Labour to gain Bow and Bromley. Thus the Liberals and Labour gained 4 seats and kept one in December 1910, primarily because of deals between themselves, not because of shifts in public opinion. Labour gained West Fife from the Liberals, presumably because Unionist voters supported Labour to defeat the Liberal.[4] Perhaps Unionists in West Fife feared little from the Labour candidate, W. Adamson. Adamson, leader of the Parliamentary Labour Party from 1917 to 1921 was, to say the least, exceedingly un-revolutionary.[5] Though the trends of the December 1910 election indicated that some parts of the country were moving away from the Liberals, those areas were limited. Even if the Unionists won them solidly, the Liberals would have had a majority, though it would have been reduced. An even more important factor in reducing the Liberal majority was the redistribution of seats, which is examined in the map on p. 71.

---

1 In January one Liberal was unopposed. In December 35 were unopposed
2 On the map Exeter is shown as a Liberal gain. On the first count the Liberals won it, but this was later reversed and the Unionists kept it
3 Ensor, *England 1870-1917*, 426; Halévy, *Rule of Democracy*, 341

4 The change is not shown on the map as it was not a Government or an Opposition loss. The January 1910 figures had been: Liberal 6,159, Labour 4,736, Conservative 1,994. Those of December were: Labour 6,128, Liberal 5,425
5 See Gallacher, *Revolt on the Clyde*, 280-7. Gallacher, a Communist, defeated Adamson in 1935

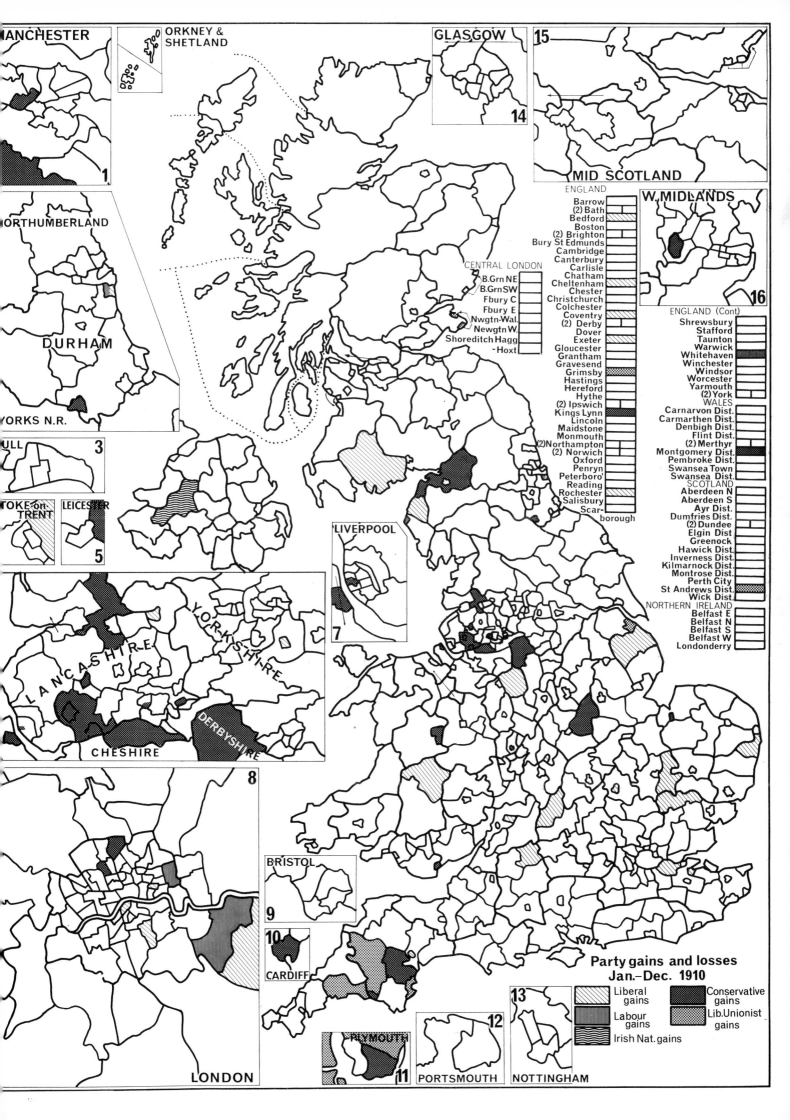

Party gains and losses Jan.–Dec. 1910

General Election of 1918

Overall results

party	total votes	% of total
Coalition	5,180,227	48·0
Non-Coalition Liberal	1,320,345	12·2
Labour, I.L.P., Socialist	2,398,773	22·2
Sinn Fein	496,961	4·6
Nationalist	233,690	2·2
Others	1,158,661	10·8
Total	**10,788,657**	**100·0**

Source: *Constitutional Year Book, 1923*, 252-3

Seats won by area

	Co. Cons.	Co. Lib.	Co. Other	Asquith Cons.	Other Lib.	Nat. Lib.	Nat. Pty.	D.S.S.	Lab.	Nat.	S.F.	Other	Total
England	293	87	13	21	13	7	2	1	44	1	—	3	485
Wales	1	18	1	3	—	2	—	—	9	—	—	1	35
Scotland	28	26	1	2	5	2	—	—	7	—	—	—	71
N. Ireland	3	—	—	19	—	—	—	—	—	4	3	—	29
S. Ireland	—	—	—	1	—	—	—	—	—	2	69	—	72
Universities	9	3	—	2	—	—	—	—	—	—	1	—	15
Total	**334**	**134**	**15**	**48**	**18**	**11**	**2**	**1**	**60**	**7**	**73**	**4**	**707**

Source: Kinnear, *General Election of 1922*
Nat. Pty. – National Party, a right-wing Conservative group
D.S.S. – Discharged Soldiers and Sailors; also known as the 'Silver Badge League'
S.F. – Sinn Fein
Co-op and Socialist M.P.s are counted as Labour M.P.s

Unopposed returns by area

area	Co. Cons.	Co. Lib.	Co. other	Sinn Fein	Nat.	other Lib.	Lab.	others	total
England	40	13	2	—	1	—	6	1	63
Wales	—	4	—	—	—	2	5	—	11
Scotland	1	7	—	—	—	—	—	—	8
N. Ireland	—	—	—	—	—	—	—	—	
S. Ireland	—	—	—	25	—	—	—	—	25
Universities	—	—	—	—	—	—	—	—	
Total	**41**	**24**	**2**	**25**	**1**	**2**	**11**	**1**	**107**

Comments

The 1918 election, which was the first fought on the basis of universal adult male suffrage, resulted in an overwhelming victory for the Lloyd George Coalition. Since the 73 Sinn Fein M.P.s did not take their seats, and since most of the un-couponned[1] Conservatives supported the Coalition, the effective Coalition majority was about 400. No other government since 1832 has had a majority even approaching this, except the National Government in 1931.[2] The figures for the total vote are misleading, as they indicate that the Coalition won only 48%. Since 67 Coalitionists were unopposed, the Coalition probably would have received over 50% of the total if all seats had been contested. In addition, many Liberal candidates who did not receive coupons nevertheless considered themselves Coalitionists.

The major partner in the Coalition, the Conservative Party, won 382 seats, or 108 more than they had won in December 1910. As the map on p. 71 indicates, most Conservative gains can be attributed either to the Redistribution of 1918, or to the continuation of pre-war trends. Only a quarter of all the Conservative gains can convincingly be attributed solely to the War or to the use of the coupon. Most such gains were agricultural seats the Liberals recovered in 1922 or 1923. The other areas with substantial Conservative gains in comparison with December 1910 were East Lancashire, Mid-Scotland, and East London. All 3 districts had shown marked trends to the Conservatives in by-elections between 1911 and 1914. To a considerable degree, then, the electoral map of Britain in 1918 indicated that the War had frozen the effective distribution of electoral strength at the 1914 position. This can be attributed to two things. First, there was a suspension of political activities during the war, at least by most Liberal and Conservative groups. Consequently, those groups were often ready in 1918 to resume the relative positions they had held in 1914. Second, and perhaps more important, the main reason for the Liberal decline in Central Scotland, East Lancashire and East London had been competition from Labour. In 1918, this competition still existed. A map showing the Conservative percentage vote in 1918 has many similarities to one showing their percentage in December 1910. However, maps of the Liberal percentages in the 2 elections do not show as many similarities, mainly because of increased competition from Labour in 1918. If the Liberals and Labour had been able to agree in the 3 areas, the Conservatives would not have scored the great victory they did.

Labour won few seats on its own in 1918. Eleven of their victors were unopposed, and several others were opposed only by left-wing 'Socialist' candidates. Even Labour strength in the 3 mining areas of South Wales, West Lancashire and West Yorkshire was only partial. In South Wales, Labour candidates defeated only one Coalition Liberal. Elsewhere, they were either unopposed, or their opponents were split. Labour victories in the West Lancashire mining district were also close in the few seats where Labour men had couponned opponents. Only in Yorkshire did Labour candidates trounce several couponned opponents in mining seats.

Labour remained weak in Greater London, where it elected only 4 M.P.s. Three had Coalition support, while the fourth, Jack Jones in West Ham – Silvertown, was well-known as a right-winger. He probably gained many votes from moderate Liberals who preferred him to his I.L.P. and Conservative rivals.[3] Labour also won 3 agricultural or partly agricultural seats. In Barnard Castle and Clitheroe, the anti-Labour vote was split; and in any case both seats were mixed mining and agricultural. Clitheroe had been

1 The 'coupon' generally took the form of a telegram from Lloyd George and Bonar Law. A typical coupon read: 'Dear . . . , We have much pleasure in recognising you as Coalition Candidate for . . . . We have every hope that the Electors will return you as their Representative in Parliament to support the Government in the great task which lies before it. Yours truly, D. Lloyd George. A. Bonar Law.' Many examples of this telegram were quoted in local newspapers in 1918, with the names of the appropriate candidate and constituency in place of the two blanks
2 Excluding wartime governments
3 When the Labour Party had decided to leave the wartime Coalition, Jones had said 'he was not going to change Lloyd George for Lord Lansdowne. He was not going to turn out the "Right Hon. 9d for 4d" for the "Right Hon. 4d for 9d" ' *(Report of the Annual Conference of the Labour Party, 1918*, part 2,36*)*

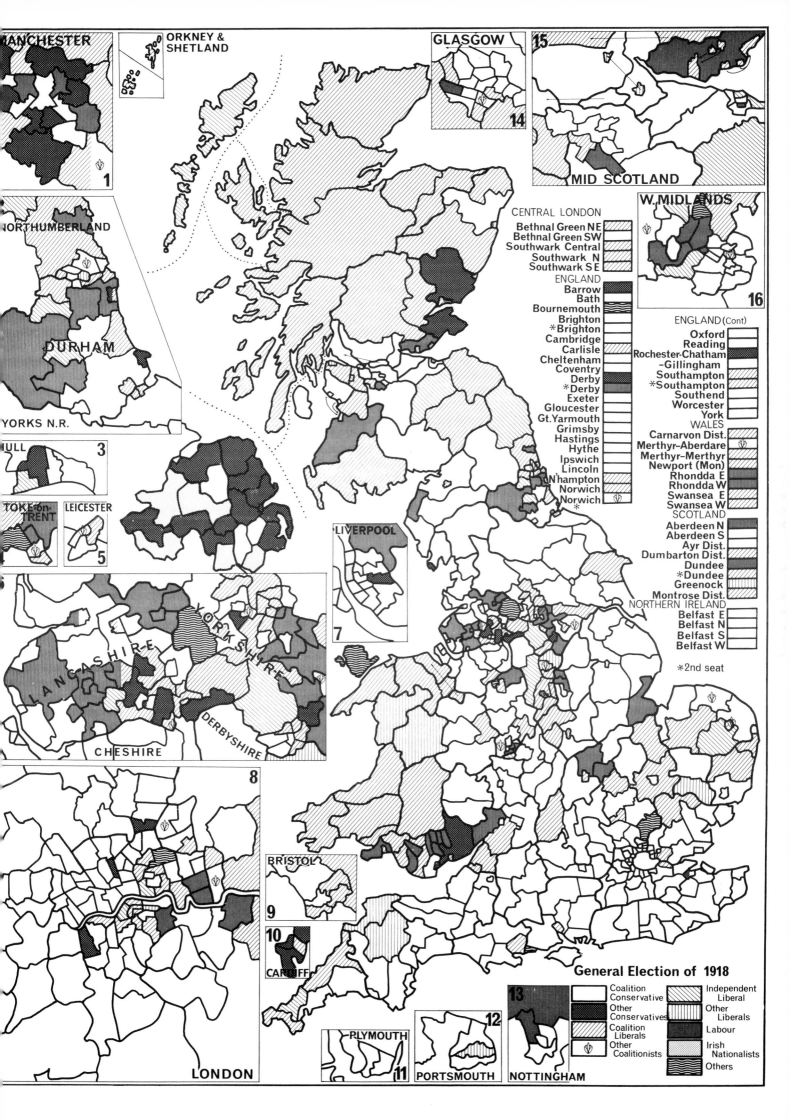

General Election of 1918

Labour since 1906, and Barnard Castle since 1903. Of the 3, only Holland-with-Boston was primarily agricultural. There, the successful Labour candidate in 1918 had been the Conservative candidate in December 1910. Apparently he had a strong local following, for on his death the seat went Conservative and has never returned to Labour since.

The overall performance of Labour in 1918 was weak: many Labour seats were held by grace of the Coalition, and many others were very near things, even in mining districts. Consequently, one could not have predicted, on the basis of the 1918 results, that in a little more than 5 years Labour would form the government.

The Liberals in 1918 were split between supporters of Lloyd George and supporters of Asquith. The figure of 29 given for non-Coalition Liberals in the *Constitutional Year Book*[1] includes at least 11 who were elected without coupons but who had not campaigned during the election as followers of Asquith.[2] The overwhelming majority of other Liberal M.P.s had run as Coalitionists and supporters of Lloyd George. Coalition Liberals were strong in industrial seats in West Yorkshire, East Lancashire, North Staffordshire and the North-east; in the East End of London; in mining seats in Derbyshire, South Wales and West Yorkshire; and in agricultural seats in Wales, Northern Scotland, the South-west and East Anglia. The areas of Coalition Liberal strength in 1918 largely corresponded to the areas of Liberal strength between 1885 and 1910.[3] However, some groups of seats won by Coalition Liberals fluctuated frequently between 1922 and 1924. The Coalition Liberal base in 1918 was therefore weaker than it appeared, as the Coalition Liberals could count on retaining only 50 or 60 of their seats in subsequent elections. Seats such as Bridgeton, Gorbals or Aberdare were won only, apparently, by chance, and they could not be regarded as Coalition Liberal strongholds. The eclipse of the Coalition Liberals in 1922 was therefore foreshadowed in 1918.

1 1923 edition, 267
2 These M.P.s are shown in the map as 'Other' Liberals

3 See map, Liberal Seats 1885 – December 1910, p. 83

General Election of 1922

Overall results

party	total votes	% of total
Conservative	5,281,555	36·7
Independent Conservative	222,410	1·5
Other Conservative	38,109	0·3
Total Conservative	**5,542,074**	**38·5**
Constitutionalist	48,748	0·3
Lloyd George Liberal	1,320,935	9·2
Asquith Liberal	2,098,732	14·6
Prefixless Liberal	763,315	5·3
Total Liberal	**4,182,982**	**29·1**
Labour, Co-op. and Socialist	4,237,769	29·4
Irish Nationalist and Sinn Fein	102,667	0·7
Communist (inc. 'Independent Labour')	38,134	0·3
Others	241,258	1·7
Total	**14,393,632**	**100·0**

Source: Kinnear, *General Election of 1922* (1965)

Seats won by area

Area	Cons.	Ind. Cons.	Other Cons.	L.G. Lib.	Asq. Lib.	Oth. Lib.	Constit.	Lab.	Nat. S.F.	Oth.	Tot.
England	293	10	3	30	29	17	4	95	1	3	485
Wales	6	—	—	6	—	4	—	18	—	1	35
Scotland	10	3	—	8	11	8	—	29	—	2	71
N. Ireland	10	—	—	—	—	—	—	—	2	—	12
Universities	8	—	—	3	—	—	—	—	—	1	12
Total	**327**	**13**	**3**	**47**	**40**	**29**	**4**	**142**	**3**	**7**	**615**

'Other Cons.' included one 'Unionist and agriculturist' and 2 'Unionist and Anti-Waste' candidates

Unopposed returns by area

area	Cons.	L.G. Lib.	other Lib.	Lab.	other	total
England	30	1	3	2	1	37
Wales	1	1	1	1	—	4
Scotland	—	—	2	1	—	3
N. Ireland	9	—	—	—	—	9
Universities	3	1	—	—	—	4
Total	**43**	**3**	**6**	**4**	**1**	**57**

Comments

The election of 1922 was the most confused between 1885 and 1966. Hundreds of candidates stood as representatives of one of a dozen parties or groups, as representatives of 2, 3 or more, or even as representatives of no party at all. Consequently, the figures showing the total votes cast for each party are seriously misleading. The only thing which is certain is that the Conservatives won a majority of seats, although they came nowhere near winning a majority of the votes cast. A reasonable estimate is that between 35% and 40% of the electorate supported the Conservatives. It is not possible to be more precise, because 43 Conservatives were unopposed, while many Lloyd George Liberals won primarily because of Conservative support. On the other hand, the Conservative candidates had much Liberal, and even some Labour, support.[1]

It is also impossible to state a precise figure for the Conservative majority, because many candidates ran as 'Independent Conservatives', 'Anti-Wasters', or 'Constitutionalists'. If the M.P.s elected under such labels are excluded, the Conservative majority was 39. However, some of the 39 gave only half-hearted support to the Government, while some 'Independent' Conservatives gave it very strong support. In addition, the Conservative Government could

1 In the 7 two-membered seats contested in 1922, by both Conservatives and Labour, 7,362 persons voted for one Labour and one Conservative; while 99,462 voted only for Labour candidates, and 104,088 voted only for Conservatives. These figures do not include Derby, for which a breakdown of voting was not published. They indicate that 3·5% of the Conservative and Labour voters split their votes between the two parties. There was even more splitting of votes between the Liberals and Labour, and between the Liberals and Conservatives

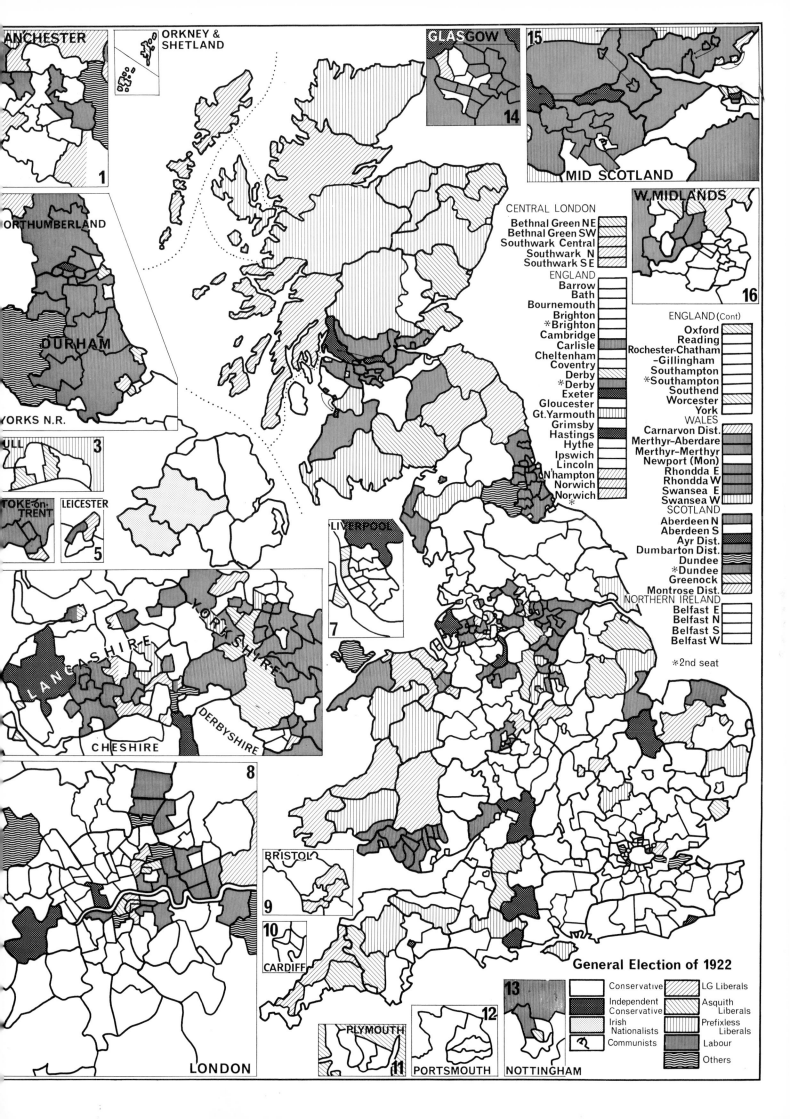

General Election of 1922

rely on the support of at least a third of the Lloyd George Liberal M.P.s on most questions. Consequently, the Government majority, though imprecise, was adequate to maintain it in office for a full 4- or 5-year term. Although the Government proved ineffective in Parliament, it was defeated only on a few occasions, none of them serious enough to bring it down. The Government could rely on a usual minimum majority of about 20, and on a maximum of about 150 if most Lloyd George Liberals supported it.

As in most interwar elections the chief areas of Conservative strength were London and the South-east, Birmingham, West Lancashire and the agricultural seats in Northern Yorkshire, and in the West and South Midlands. The Conservatives won 48 seats where over 30% of the population was employed in agriculture and 158 where over 20% was middle-class.[1] As there were 276 seats in these two categories, the Conservatives won 73% of them. The Conservatives won 122 of the remaining 315 territorial seats in Great Britain, or only 38%. Thirteen Unionist victories in agricultural seats were gains from Liberals, mostly from Lloyd George Liberals. Most of these gains can be attributed to an agricultural rebellion against sitting Government M.P.s, because the Conservatives lost 15 agricultural seats to the Liberals, mostly supporters of Asquith. Conservative candidates opposing sitting Lloyd George Liberals were able to criticise the Coalition agricultural policy more readily than sitting Conservatives.

The Asquith Liberals had no major area of strength in 1922, although they did win 4 neighbouring seats in North-eastern Scotland. Elsewhere they had only scattered wins. Sometimes maps of party victories disguise substantial strength of a losing party in the country, but this was not so with the Asquith Liberals in 1922. There was no major area where the Asquith Liberals even came close to winning, except in the agricultural seats of the South Midlands, Lincolnshire and the South-west. Few Asquith Liberal candidates won as much as 40% of the vote, and most of their best polls were in seats with Lloyd George Liberals as their only rivals. The Liberals without prefix did better, on the whole, than the straightforward supporters of Asquith or Lloyd George: a quarter of the prefixless Liberals were successful compared with only a sixth of the others. The successful prefixless Liberals were elected from various parts of the country but they were most numerous in rural Scotland.[2]

The Lloyd George Liberals, who slightly outnumbered the Asquith Liberals, retained numerous seats in East Lancashire, rural Wales and North-western Scotland. However, they lost mining seats they had won in 1918, as well as most of their 1918 wins in West Yorkshire, East Anglia and London. Many seats they did retain were held with Conservative support, although their seats in rural Wales and Scotland represented continuing Liberal strength.

The overall position of the Liberals after the 1922 election was one of considerable weakness. Although 116 Liberals of all factions were elected, they were seriously divided over leadership and over the attitude they should adopt towards co-operation with the Conservatives. In effect this meant that for the duration of the 1922 Parliament the Liberals did not possess the influence which a united party would have had. By maintaining the factional divisions which had existed prior to the election, the Liberals lost what chance they had to appear as an alternative government in subsequent elections.

A clear result of the 1922 election was the rapid growth of the Labour Party from the position of an ineffective minor group in Parliament to that of a vigorous and determined Opposition. Although they won 142 seats, that is, only 26 more than the Liberals, the Labour Party was far more united and presented a far more coherent challenge to the Government than the disunited Liberal factions could. In addition, Labour won 89 seats with more than 50% of the vote cast (including 4 unopposed seats), while the Liberals generally won on minority votes. Labour wins were also concentrated in a few well-defined areas, while Liberal wins were scattered throughout the country. Although this provided a solid base for Labour, it had a drawback. This was that the Labour Party was less able to expand into new areas than were the Liberals.

Mining districts provided 39 of the 82 Labour gains, while Glasgow, Greater London, Newcastle, Gateshead and Sheffield provided 28 more. Probably the Labour sweep in Glasgow was the most spectacular result of the election. There, Labour won 10 of the 12 seats it contested, mostly with very large swings.[3] The working-class seats in Eastern Sheffield also had uniformly large swings to Labour and away from the Lloyd George Liberals. Thenceforth, Glasgow remained solidly Labour even in 1931; while Sheffield gave Labour candidates large majorities in most elections except that of 1931.

Labour did not make progress in all parts of the country in 1922: in 77 seats it actually lost ground in comparison with 1918, and in 63 more, Labour did not contest seats it had fought in 1918. By no means all the Labour withdrawals took place in seats where Labour candidates had done badly in 1918. In 12, the Labour vote had been over 30%, and in 2 of them it had been 38%.[4] Most seats where Labour lost heavily in comparison with 1918 were agricultural seats in the South Midlands or seats in the textile districts of East Lancashire and West Yorkshire. Generally, where there was a substantial Labour loss or where Labour withdrew in 1922, there was a significant increase in the Liberal vote. Seven Liberal wins in 1922 can probably be attributed to Labour withdrawals.[5]

Labour made considerable progress in 1922, but even though it more than doubled its representation, with only 142 seats it was not yet in a position to make a serious challenge for power; and outside the Labour strongholds, there were few seats which seemed ripe for a Labour conquest.

---

1 For a total of 200, since 6 of the seats were in both groups, See map, The Agricultural Vote in 1921, p. 121; and map, The Middle-class vote in 1921, p. 123. For the purpose of the following calculations, Independent Conservatives have been included with Conservatives, and constituencies in Northern Ireland or Universities have been excluded
2 See map, Prefixless Liberals in 1922, p. 95

3 See map, parts D, E, F and G, Glasgow in 1921-2, p. 131
4 Southport and St. Ives
5 Birkenhead East, Bootle, Hartlepools, Middlesbrough West, Taunton, Edinburgh West and Greenock. In Greenock the Liberal winner had 36·7% to 36·0% for a Communist

General Election of 1923

Overall results

party	total votes	% of total
Conservative	5,538,824	38·1
Liberal	4,311,147	29·6
Labour	4,438,508	30·5
Others	260,042	1·8
Total	**14,548,521**	**100·0**

Source: *Constitutional Year Book, 1925*, 274

Seats won by area

area	Cons.	Lib.	Lab.	Nat.	other	total
England	221	123	138	1	2	485
Wales	4	12	19	—	—	35
Scotland	14	22	34	—	1	71
N. Ireland	10	—	—	2	—	12
Universities	9	2	—	—	1	12
Total	**258**	**159**	**191**	**3**	**4**	**615**

Unopposed returns by area

area	Cons.	Lib.	Lab.	Nat.	total
England	24	3	1	1	29
Wales	—	3	2	—	5
Scotland	—	4	—	—	4
N. Ireland	8	—	—	—	8
Universities	3	1	—	—	4
Total	**35**	**11**	**3**	**1**	**50**

Comments

In 1923, the parties obtained representation in rough proportion to their votes. However, if the Liberals and Labour had been as united as in pre-war years, the Conservative defeat would have assumed proportions similar to those of 1906. In every part of the country the Conservatives had serious losses in seats as well as in votes. Some of the safest Conservative seats voted Liberal or Labour, including many which had been consistently Conservative since at least 1885.[1] The distribution of Conservative seats showed many similarities to 1906 except that in 1923 the Conservatives won more seats in Cheshire, Suffolk and Derbyshire than they had won in 1906. However, most of the Conservative gains in comparison with 1906 were in seats where the opposition was divided. In the few seats where it was not, the Conservatives won with small majorities. Only in a few places did Conservatives win majority support. Among such places were Birmingham, Surrey and the agricultural seats around York[2] and Worcester.

In 1923 the Conservatives benefited more than in any other election from the redistribution of 1918. The Conservative strong-holds of Birmingham and the London suburbs had gained many seats in comparison with the pre-war period. Most of these gains came at the expense of small agricultural seats which went Liberal in 1923, and if the redistribution had not taken place it is fair to assume that about 25 more Liberals would have been elected. The redistribution had less effect on the Labour Party, because some Labour areas in 1923 had lost seats, while other areas had gained them, in comparison with the old distribution. The Conservatives could consider themselves fortunate to win as many as 258 seats, when by a strict application of proportional representation they would have won only about 230.

In 1923 the Liberals won 43 of the 86 seats in which agriculturists formed more than 30% of the population, while the Conservatives won only 38. In most agricultural seats they contested, and which they did not win, the Liberals came very close, usually within a few hundred votes of the Conservatives. For instance, in Melton they received only 44 votes less than the Conservatives, and in Knutsford only 80 votes less. This was the only election between 1918 and 1966 in which the Conservatives did not win a majority of the agricultural seats. Most Liberal gains in comparison with 1922 were in the South Midlands and South-west. Between 1918 and 1924, as between 1885 and 1910, these areas contained more effectively marginal seats than any other part of the country. That is, they had more seats which changed hands frequently. Some changed hands in every election between 1918 and 1929.[3] A shift in their favour of a few hundred votes in each agricultural seat would have given the Liberals a very large proportion of the agri-cultural seats. This would have meant that the Liberals would have had roughly the same number of M.P.s as Labour.

Probably the main reason for the Liberal victory in the agri-cultural seats was that the Conservative Government had failed to do anything about farm prices. The prices of two key farm products, wheat and barley, were above their pre-war level in 1923. However, this represented a decline of 59% from the very high prices of 1920.[4] It was no consolation for farmers to realise that they were better off than 13 years before, because debts they had incurred in 1920 had to be paid off as if the high prices of 1920 were still in effect. This was especially irritating, as the farmers had been promised in the Agriculture Act of 1920 that prices would be maintained at the higher level.[5]

1 For example, Basingstoke, Blackpool, Chelmsford, Chichester, Finchley, Liver-pool – Wavertree, Liverpool – West Derby, Lonsdale and Shrewsbury had all voted Conservative in general elections from 1885 to 1922, but voted Liberal in 1923
2 This includes three agricultural seats in North Yorkshire, three in East Yorkshire and two in West Yorkshire
3 For instance, the Isle of Ely and St. Ives both elected Liberals in 1918, Conservatives in 1922, Liberals in 1923, Conservatives in 1924 and Liberals in 1929. In 1923 the Conservatives gained 8 agricultural seats from the Liberals, but in 6 of them there had been no Conservative candidate in 1922, while in the seventh the 1922 Liberal candidate did not run in 1923
4 The following index shows the change in the price of wheat and barley between 1914 and 1924. It is based on prices listed in *Agricultural Statistics for England and Wales*, 1921, iii, 110; and 1924, iii, 125. It is based on the calculation that one quarter

wheat = 4·3 cwt, and that one quarter barley = 3·55 cwt. This calculation is necessary because the prices were quoted per quarter up to 1921, and per cwt thereafter.

Year	Wheat	Barley
1910	34	21
1918	77	53
1919	77	112
1920	100	100
1921	52	54
1922	45	45
1923	41	42
1924	57	63

5 See 10 & 11 Geo.V, Ch.76; and Kinnear, *Fall of Lloyd George*

Within the Liberal Party there was a shift towards Asquith as a result of the 1923 election. Viscount Gladstone estimated that the Lloyd George Liberals lost on balance 7 seats, while the Asquith faction gained 50. The Lloyd George Liberal losses were mainly to Labour, in seats where Conservatives had supported the Lloyd George Liberal candidate in 1922. If there had been no such co-operation in 1922, some of these seats might have gone Labour then. The figures in Gladstone's estimate were:

faction	gains	losses	net change[1]
Asquith	74	24	+50
Lloyd George	18	25	−7

Liberal gains were significant in 2 areas, other than agricultural ones. These were the West Yorkshire textile seats and a number of seats in London with a mixed social composition. Liberals won few seats in London which were predominantly slums, but they won 11 which were on the fringes of Labour-held slum districts. In West Yorkshire the Liberals and Labour eliminated the Conservatives from every seat in which the woollen industry was significant; in East Lancashire they all but eliminated the Conservatives in cotton seats. The 13 seats in Manchester and Salford which had elected 9 Conservatives in 1922, elected only one in 1923. A major factor in the Conservative defeat in East Lancashire and West Yorkshire was probably the Conservative endorsement of tariffs.

Labour made relatively few gains in 1923 except in seats where Conservatives had co-operated with Lloyd George Liberals in 1922. Labour gained 18 such seats from the Lloyd George Liberals.[2] Labour also made substantial gains in East London. Labour advances in London were continuous in all elections of the 1920s with the exception of 1924. In each election, Labour expanded slightly, usually displacing Liberals. The advance was slower than in many other parts of the country, but it was more secure. In 1931, when Labour lost most of its seats in the country, only mining seats and slums in London and Glasgow held firm. In 1923, Labour made few advances in other parts of the country, in seats or in votes. Their total vote was only half a million more than in 1922, and was not to be compared with their gain of a million in 1924, or their gain of 2½ million in 1922. Labour remained frustrated by the continuing Liberal hold on such industrial areas as West Yorkshire, East Lancashire, Tyneside and Tees-side.

C. P. Cook has examined the 1922–23 elections using the demographic figures provided on pages 116–129 of this book. His figures show that in seats which had straight Conservative-Liberal fights in both 1922 and 1923, the swing to the Liberals was 1·2% in agricultural and 9·1% in middle-class seats (as defined on pages 119 and 122). He also shows that in seats contested by all three parties in 1922 and 1923, the changes in vote were as follows:

	Boroughs	Counties	All seats
Conservative	−5·5%	−3·6%	−4·9%
Liberal	+3·1	+6·8	+4·1
Labour	+2·4	−3·2	+0·8

Cook's analysis shows that Labour had peaked by 1922 in most rural constituencies, but that in borough seats, especially those with heavy industry, Labour fortunes were still rising. The Liberals recaptured very little of the industrial vote they had lost to Labour in 1922; on the other hand, the Liberals did very well in non-industrial seats, a phenomenon which foreshadowed the Liberal revivals of the 1960s and 1970s.[3]

Cook points out, in addition, that many of the 1923 Liberal wins were due to the lack of a Labour candidate in seats which Labour could not win itself, but where Labour interventions would probably have taken just enough Liberal votes away to assure a Tory victory. He notes that the large number of Labour interventions in 1924 were what really sealed the fate of the Liberal Party in that election.[4]

The Liberal revival of 1923 can be compared with those of 1970–74 in that many voters went Liberal in the short run in different types of constituency, then drifted back to their original allegiances. In 1970, half of a sample of Liberal voters said they would vote for another party in the following election, and only 36% said they had voted Liberal in 1966.[5] Between the two 1974 elections, 2 million voters floated to the Liberals, and 2.5 million floated away.[6] This showed the shallowness of Liberal adherence, but at the same time showed the very large potential following for the party if, for once, the short-term factors mostly favoured it.

---

1 *Viscount Gladstone Papers,* Add. MSS 46480 ff. 63-4

2 Berwick-and-Haddington, Bolton (one seat), Bristol East, Bristol North, Kirkcaldy District, Leeds West, Leicester East, Lichfield, Mansfield, Northampton, Norwich (2 seats), Partick, Shipley, Shoreditch, Southwark North, Southwark South-east, Wellingborough

3 See pages 87 and 142 of this book.

4 Cook, *The Age of Alignment,* 161–170.

5 Gallup figures cited in Rose, *Electoral Behaviour,* 497.

6 J. Alt, *et. al.,* 'Angels in Plastic', as cited by Butler & Kavanagh, *British General Election of 1979,* 87.

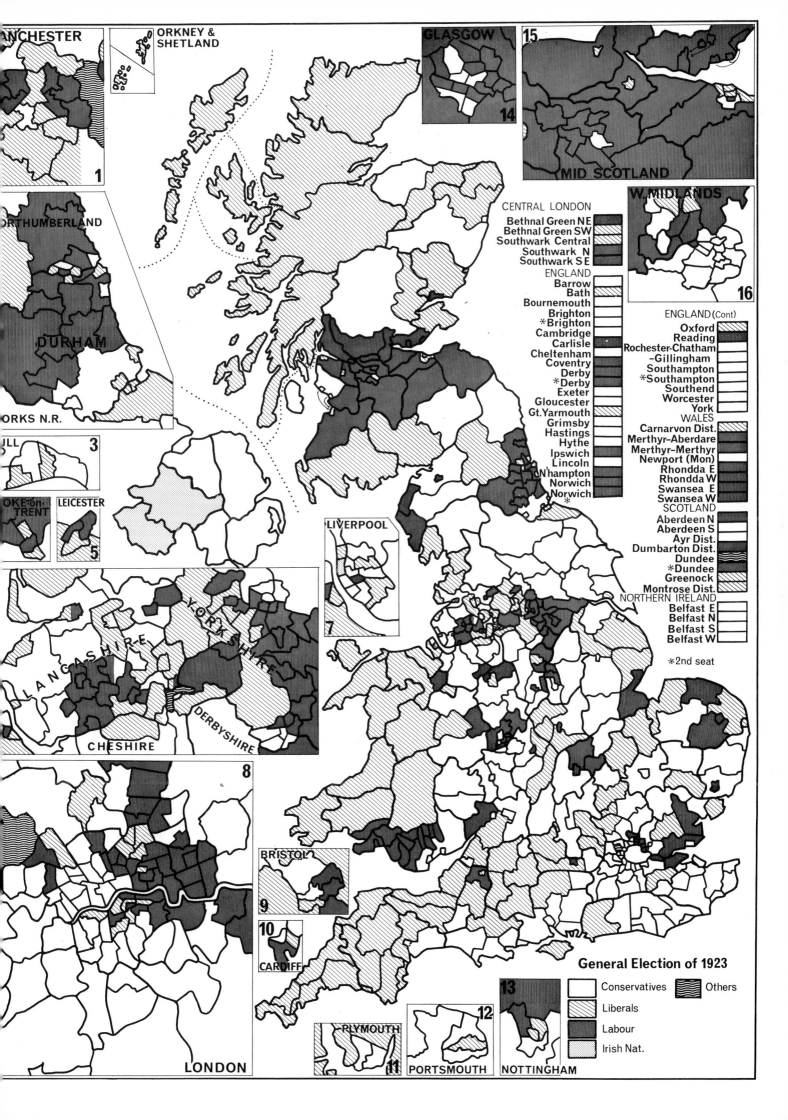

MANCHESTER

ORKNEY & SHETLAND

1

NORTHUMBERLAND

DURHAM

YORKS N.R.

HULL

3

STOKE-on-TRENT

LEICESTER

5

LANCASHIRE

YORKSHIRE

DERBYSHIRE

CHESHIRE

LIVERPOOL

7

GLASGOW

15

14

MID SCOTLAND

W. MIDLANDS

16

CENTRAL LONDON
Bethnal Green NE
Bethnal Green SW
Southwark Central
Southwark N
Southwark S E
ENGLAND
Barrow
Bath
Bournemouth
Brighton
*Brighton
Cambridge
Carlisle
Cheltenham
Coventry
Derby
*Derby
Exeter
Gloucester
Gt. Yarmouth
Grimsby
Hastings
Hythe
Ipswich
Lincoln
N'hampton
Norwich
Norwich
*

ENGLAND (Cont)
Oxford
Reading
Rochester-Chatham
-Gillingham
Southampton
*Southampton
Southend
Worcester
York
WALES
Carnarvon Dist.
Merthyr-Aberdare
Merthyr-Merthyr
Newport (Mon)
Rhondda E
Rhondda W
Swansea E
Swansea W
SCOTLAND
Aberdeen N
Aberdeen S
Ayr Dist.
Dumbarton Dist.
Dundee
*Dundee
Greenock
Montrose Dist.
NORTHERN IRELAND
Belfast E
Belfast N
Belfast S
Belfast W

*2nd seat

8

BRISTOL

9

10

CARDIFF

13

PLYMOUTH

11

12

PORTSMOUTH

NOTTINGHAM

LONDON

General Election of 1923

Conservatives ▢   Others ▨

Liberals ▨

Labour ■

Irish Nat. ▩

General Election of 1924

Overall results

party	total votes	% of total
Conservative	7,854,523	47·2
Constitutionalist	185,075	1·1
Liberal	2,928,747	17·6
Labour	5,489,077	33·0
Communist	55,436	0·3
Irish Nationalist	46,457	0·3
Others	81,054	0·5
Total	**16,640,369**	**100·0**

Source: for all elections 1924-64, *Campaign Guide 1966*, 352

Seats won by area

area	Cons.	Constit.	Lib.	Lab.	Nat.	other	total
England	347	7	19	109	1	2	485
Wales	9	—	10	16	—	—	35
Scotland	36	—	8	26	—	1	71
N. Ireland	12	—	—	—	—	—	12
Universities	8	—	3	—	—	1	12
Total	**412**	**7**	**40**	**151**	**1**	**4**	**615**

Unopposed returns by area

area	Cons.	Constit.	Lib.	Lab.	Nat.	total
England	13	—	2	2	1	18
Wales	—	—	1	7	—	8
Scotland	—	—	3	—	—	3
N. Ireland	2	—	—	—	—	2
Universities	1	—	—	—	—	1
Total	**16**	**—**	**6**	**9**	**1**	**32**

Comments

The chief feature of the 1924 election was the virtual elimination of the Liberals. On balance, the Liberals lost 119 seats, including all their agricultural seats in England and most of their industrial seats throughout the country. As they had brought the Labour Government to office by their Parliamentary support, and as they had brought that Government down, the Liberals simultaneously lost the goodwill of both other parties. Before 1924 there was always a strong possibility that the Liberals would opt for an alliance of some kind with the Conservatives or with Labour. The events of 1924 showed that they could not decide for either.

In 1922 and 1923 many Liberal victories had been in seats where there had been no Labour candidate and where Labour had actually given support to the Liberals in return for concessions elsewhere. In some other seats in 1923 Liberals had had the support of Conservatives. In 1924 both Labour and the Conservatives realised the Liberals were undependable allies and withdrew support. By their activities in 1924 the Liberals virtually wrote themselves off as a major party. Some Liberals sensed this and did not even run in 1924 as Liberals but as 'Constitutionalists'. The most famous of these was the ex-Liberal Winston Churchill. Churchill quickly moved into the ranks of the Conservative Party, which he had previously left in 1904.

The Conservatives won nearly everywhere, with the largest majority won by a single party from 1832 to that time. The map shows the extent of their victory, most of which was at the expense of the Liberals. The Conservatives were almost completely unable to penetrate the mining seats, rural Wales, East London, Glasgow or most of the Black Country. All but rural Wales were Labour strongholds and remained so in every election from 1922 to 1966, with the exception of 1931.

Few constituencies voted Labour in 1924, unless they consisted of an overwhelmingly working-class electorate. Nevertheless Labour did win one agricultural seat, North Norfolk, where their candidate had won in 1922 and 1923. This candidate had sat for the same constituency as a Liberal before 1918. Labour gained several seats in the textile district of West Yorkshire and on Tyneside, but most industrial seats won by the Liberals in 1923 went Conservative. The main effect of the 1924 election was to destroy the Liberal allegiance many industrial seats had previously had. Although it did not win many seats directly from the Liberals in 1924, at least Labour eliminated a serious threat to its own expansion. Consequently the destruction of the Liberals in 1924 paved the way for the great Labour expansion in non-mining industrial districts in 1929.

T. J. Nossiter has performed a multiple regression analysis of the data in this book on the Nonconformist percentage and on Conservative seats in 1924. He shows that there was a strong correlation between the two, and that this was independent of the middle-class percentage. Nossiter has also done similar, though smaller-scale computations for the 1910 elections, and has arrived at similar conculsions. These conclusions go contrary to the accepted view that Nonconformity was related positively to the Liberal percentage, rather than to the Conservative percentage.[1]

Perhaps the greatest problem of using ecological data in analysing elections is that one can see what happened, but not why it happened. In case of the Nonconformist vote, it is quite possible that factors other than Nonconformity were involved, at least in a few elections. There were only 21 constituencies where even 15% of the population was Nonconformist, and they fell into just three categories: a handful of rural seats on the fringes of England, another handful on the Yorkshire-Lancashire border, and some scattered seats elsewhere. When one has only these few seats to go on, one cannot make definitive conclusions about the performance of the Nonconformist vote as a whole in the rest of England. The very simplified calculations done on page 129 of this book take the question about as far as one can with any degree of accuracy; but Nossiter's analysis, which is both stimulating and challenging, should provoke further research ot a detailed nature into the relationship of Nonconformists and the political parties.

1 Nossiter, T. J., 'Recent Work On British Elections, 1832–1935', *Political Studies*, Dec. 1970, 525–528.

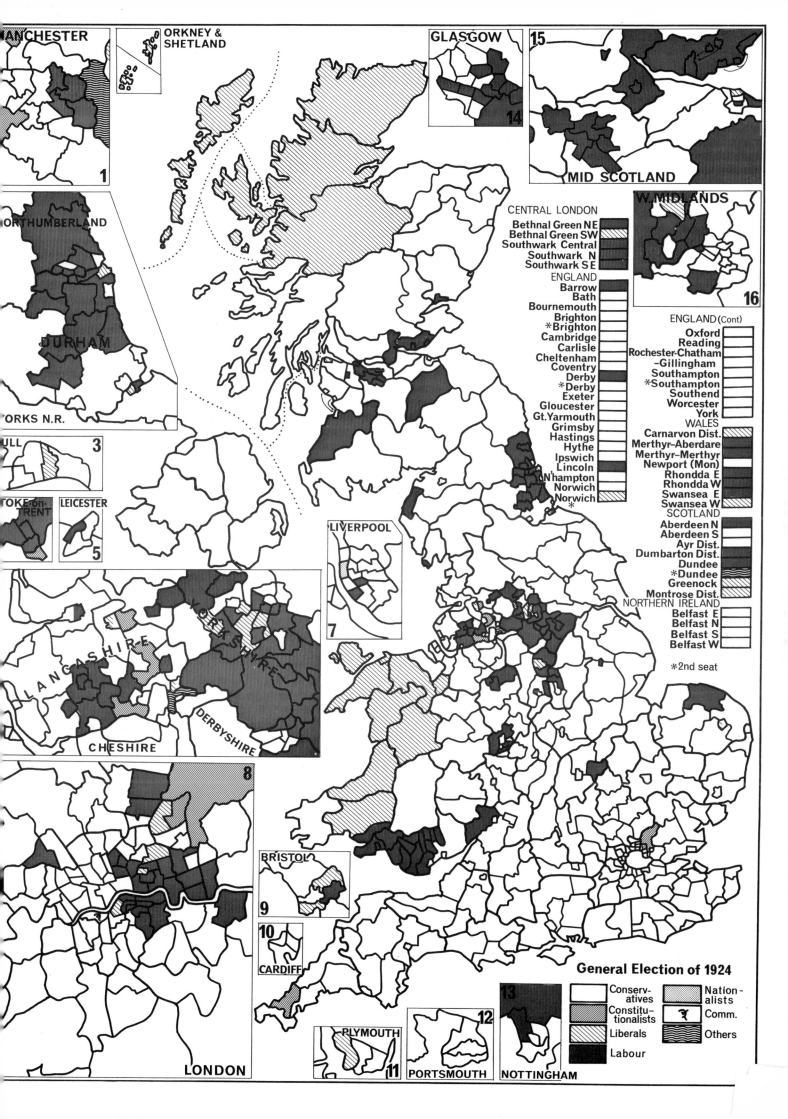

MANCHESTER
1

ORKNEY & SHETLAND

NORTHUMBERLAND

DURHAM

YORKS N.R.

HULL
3

STOKE-on-TRENT

LEICESTER
5

LANCASHIRE

YORKSHIRE

DERBYSHIRE

CHESHIRE

8

LIVERPOOL
7

BRISTOL
9

10

CARDIFF

LONDON

PLYMOUTH
11

12

PORTSMOUTH

13

NOTTINGHAM

GLASGOW
14

15

MID SCOTLAND

W. MIDLANDS
16

CENTRAL LONDON
Bethnal Green NE
Bethnal Green SW
Southwark Central
Southwark N
Southwark SE

ENGLAND
Barrow
Bath
Bournemouth
Brighton
*Brighton
Cambridge
Carlisle
Cheltenham
Coventry
Derby
*Derby
Exeter
Gloucester
Gt.Yarmouth
Grimsby
Hastings
Hythe
Ipswich
Lincoln
N'hampton
Norwich
Norwich
*

ENGLAND (Cont)
Oxford
Reading
Rochester-Chatham
-Gillingham
Southampton
*Southampton
Southend
Worcester
York

WALES
Carnarvon Dist.
Merthyr-Aberdare
Merthyr-Merthyr
Newport (Mon)
Rhondda E
Rhondda W
Swansea E
Swansea W

SCOTLAND
Aberdeen N
Aberdeen S
Ayr Dist.
Dumbarton Dist.
Dundee
*Dundee
Greenock
Montrose Dist.

NORTHERN IRELAND
Belfast E
Belfast N
Belfast S
Belfast W

*2nd seat

General Election of 1924

Conservatives
Constitutionalists
Liberals
Labour
Nationalists
Comm.
Others

General Election of 1929

Overall results

party	total votes	% of total
Conservative	8,656,473	38·2
Liberal	5,308,510	23·4
Labour	8,389,512	37·1
Others	293,880	1·3
Total	**22,648,375**	**100·0**

Seats won by area

area	Cons.	Lib.	Lab.	Nat.	other	total
England	221	35	226	1	2	485
Wales	1	9	25	—	—	35
Scotland	20	13	37	—	1	71
N. Ireland	10	—	—	2	—	12
Universities	8	2	—	—	2	12
Total	**260**	**59**	**288**	**3**	**5**	**615**

Note: Sir William Jowett, elected as a Liberal in Preston, became Attorney-General in the Labour Government after the election. He is counted as a Liberal in the above table. Neil Maclean, in Govan, did not receive the official support of the Labour Party in the election; however, as he was not opposed by an official Labour candidate, he is counted as Labour in the table. Sir Robert Newman, who had sat as Conservative M.P. for Exeter from 1918 to 1929, was not readopted by his constituency party. He ran as an Independent against the official Conservative, and won. In the table, he is counted under 'Others'

Unopposed returns

Irish Nationalist	3	(Liverpool – Scotland and 2 seats in Fermanagh and Tyrone)
Conservative	4	(Belfast University, Daventry, Londonderry County and Paddington South)

Comments

In 1929 most industrial seats won by the Liberals in 1923 completed their transfer to Labour. Only in East Lancashire was Labour unable to win the majority of such seats. In East Lancashire the Liberals remained stronger than in many other parts of the country. The relative political stability in East Lancashire is also shown by the fact that the Conservatives won several predominantly working-class seats there as late as 1959.

In other parts of the country Labour made striking advances, in terms of seats won if not in terms of increased votes. Altogether, Labour won two-thirds of the borough seats in England, and 10 of the 11 borough seats in Wales. In Birmingham they won half the 12 seats. This was the first time since 1886 that the Conservatives had lost more than one seat there. Outside the mining and other industrial areas Labour was hardly ever strong enough to win. Only 5 agricultural seats voted Labour of which 2 (Carmarthen and Brecon-and-Radnor) were also mining seats. Two more (Norfolk South-west and Norfolk North) were areas of rural radicalism which dated to the pre-war period. In most agricultural seats Labour did badly; but usually they got just enough votes to deny

victory to the Liberals. For example, in the 4 agricultural seats in Wiltshire, the increased Labour vote, in comparison with 1923, appeared to come almost exclusively from the Liberals. The result was that while the Liberals had won all 4 agricultural seats there in 1923, they won none in 1929. The figures in the agricultural seats in Wiltshire were:

	Lab.	Lib.	Cons.
% 1923	4·9	49·2	45·9
% 1929	14·9	40·1	45·0
Change	+10·0	−9·1	−0·9
Seats, 1923	—	4	—
Seats, 1929	—	—	4

Similar developments took place in many agricultural districts. Labour, though not strong enough to win, was strong enough to cause a Liberal defeat. In 1924 Labour had done the same thing in the industrial seats held by the Liberals, but the difference was that Labour at least had a chance to win in the industrial seats. In the agricultural seats, on the other hand, it had little or no chance. Even in the Labour landslide of 1945 only a handful of agricultural seats voted Labour.

The Conservatives won much the same areas as in 1923, although they increased their support in agricultural seats to the highest point they had yet reached in the inter-war period, except for 1924; while they lost some socially mixed seats in London to Labour. In 1929 the Conservatives depended more than in any other inter-war election on middle-class and agricultural seats. Of the 242 they won in Great Britain,[1] 177 had more than 30% agriculturists or more than 20% middle-class voters, or both. This represented 73% of the seats they won in Great Britain. In 1923 they had won 239 seats in Great Britain, of which only 150, or 63%, had more than 30% agriculturists or more than 20% middle-class voters. The Conservatives in 1929 were evidently being pressed back more on their middle-class and agricultural strongholds than they had been in 1923, with the advantage to them that they did not have so much to fear from Liberal opponents in such seats as in 1923.

The Liberals could maintain that there was still much strength left in their party, because they won over 5 million votes and because they won several seats for the first time since at least 1918.[2] They could also point out that whereas in previous elections they had often relied on much Labour or Conservative support, in 1929 they won most of their seats in three-cornered contests. Despite these things, their 59 wins were an improvement only in comparison with the disastrous year of 1924, when they had been demoralised, divided and almost without a programme. In 1929 the Liberals had patched up at least a temporary unity, and they had put great efforts into developing a coherent programme. Consequently their net gain of only 19 seats was disappointing.

---

1 Excluding Northern Ireland and University seats

2 Ashford, Eddisbury and Holland-with-Boston

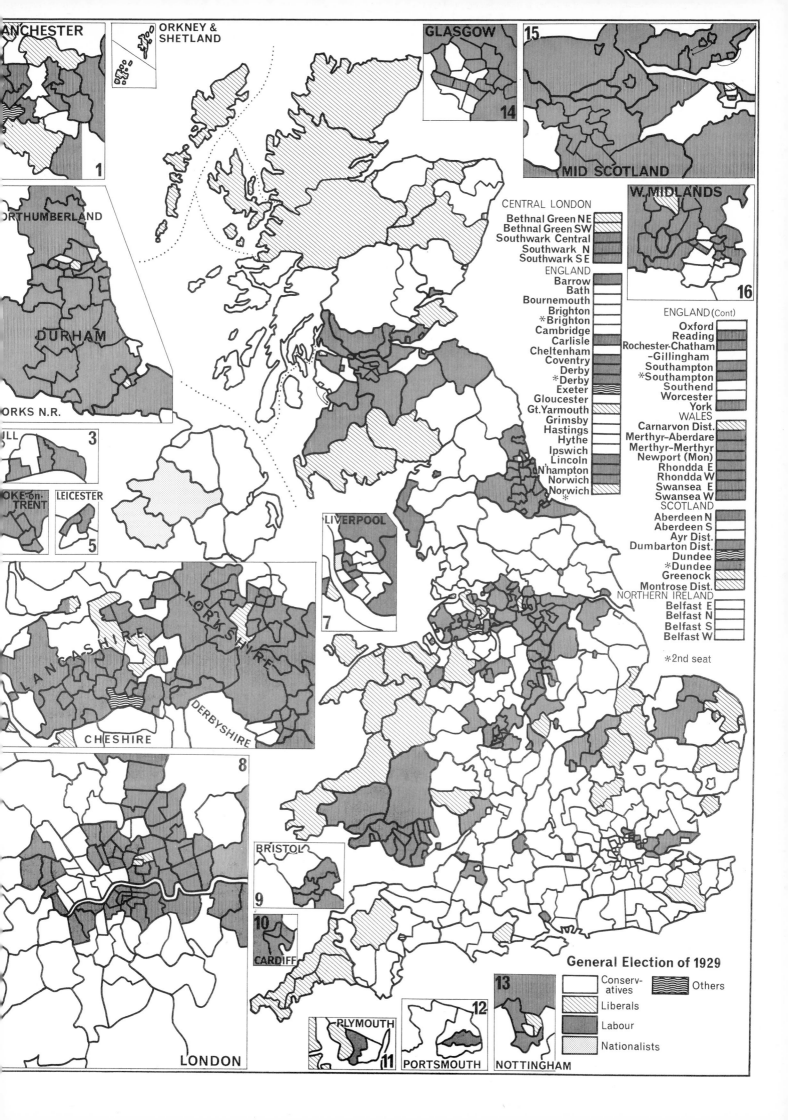

General Election of 1929

General Election of 1931

Overall results

party	total votes	% of total
National Government:		
Conservative	11,905,925	55·0
National	72,820	0·3
National Liberal	809,302	3·7
Liberal	1,403,102	6·5
National Labour	341,370	1·6
Total Govt. vote	**14,532,519**	**67·1**
Opposition:		
Labour	6,649,630	30·7
Independent Liberal (L.G.)	106,106	0·5
New Party (Mosley)	36,377	0·2
Communist	74,824	0·3
Irish Nationalist	123,053	0·6
Others	133,864	0·6
Total Opp. vote	**7,123,854**	**32·9**
Total vote cast	**21,656,373**	**100·0**

Seats won by area

area	Cons.	Nat Lib.	Nat.	Nat. Lab.	Lib.	L.G. Lib.	Lab.	Irish Nat.	other	total
England	399	23	3	10	20	—	29	—	1	485
Wales	6	4	—	1	4	4	16	—	—	35
Scotland	48	8	—	1	7	—	7	—	—	71
N. Ireland	10	.	—	—	—	—	—	2	—	12
Universities	8	—	—	—	2	—	—	—	2	12
Total	**471**	**35**	**3**	**12**	**33**	**4**	**52**	**2**	**3**	**615**

Note: J. A. Lovat-Fraser in Lichfield is listed as a 'National' M.P. in *The Constitutional Year Book, 1936. The Times Guide to the House of Commons, 1931* lists him as a National Labour M.P. He is listed in the above table as a 'National' M.P.

Unopposed returns by area

area	Cons.	Nat. Lib.	Lib.	Lab.	total
England	31	3	1	2	37
Wales	—	2	—	4	6
Scotland	3	2	3	—	8
N. Ireland	8	—	—	—	8
Universities	7	—	1	—	8
Total	**49**	**7**	**5**	**6**	**67**

Comments

Although the election of 1931 was an overwhelming defeat for Labour, the party won a greater percentage of the total vote than in any previous election except those of 1924 and 1929. In 1923 it had won 0·2% less than in 1931 but it had formed the Government. If the increased number of Labour candidates is taken into account, the average percentage obtained by all Labour candidates was still greater than in 1918 and 1922. The reason why Labour lost over four-fifths of its seats in 1931 is that for the first time its opponents were united. 1931 may be considered the Liberal revenge for their defeat in 1924. Although Labour lost some votes to the 'National Government' candidates, what really hurt was the solid Liberal support for those candidates. Apparently few Liberal voters in 1931 heeded Lloyd George's advice to vote Labour where there was no Liberal candidate. Consequently, Labour was forced back on the seats where it could count on a clear majority of the voters. It lost even some of these, notably in the mining seats in Durham, Central Scotland and Derbyshire.[1]

Most seats with a high index of unemployment showed only slight Labour losses in 1931, and some showed Labour gains, in votes. Labour did not win many seats where unemployment was high, mainly because they had never been strong in some of them and because their opponents were united. However, Labour candidates did maintain their total votes in most borough seats in Durham and Northumberland. Unemployment as measured in the Census of 1931 was between 25% and 35% in all boroughs in the 2 counties.[2] Two railway centres, Swindon and Carlisle, had increased Labour votes in 1931, while 2 more, Crewe and York, had only slight declines. A fifth, Derby, was contested by J. H. Thomas, the railwaymen's leader. There the Labour vote declined seriously in comparison with 1929, although unemployment was slightly higher than in the other 4 railway centres. Probably Thomas had a large personal following in Derby; this can be seen by the fact that in elections from 1918 to 1929 he had led his nearest rival in the two-membered seat by from 1,147 to 10,225 votes.

The personal influence of Ramsay MacDonald in Durham may have been important in changing the allegiance of mining seats there. However, it is more likely that the Liberals were the decisive factor. In 1929 the Liberals had been fairly strong in Durham and Northumberland, perhaps because of the large numbers of Nonconformists (Presbyterians in Northumberland, and mainly Primitive Methodists in Durham). In any event, several National Liberals and Liberals defeated Labour candidates in mining seats in Durham. In Northumberland the Liberals backed Conservative winners. Another factor causing some mining constituencies to desert Labour was the proportion of middle-class voters: Labour won three-quarters of the mining seats where under 10% of the population was middle-class, but only one-fifth of the mining seats where over 10% was middle-class.[3]

The Labour Party retained many seats in 5 areas: slums in East London and Glasgow; and mining districts in South Wales, West Lancashire and West Yorkshire. Many seats they held in 1931 had been won for the first time in 1922 or 1923. Most of their seats in Glasgow and East London were in this category. However, these seats could be regarded as the absolute rock-bottom Labour

---

In this book, the term 'National Liberal' refers to Liberal and semi-Liberal associates of the Conservative Party from 1931 to the present. It does not include orthodox Liberals, who supported Free Trade after 1932. The 'National Liberals' did not officially adopt their title until 1948. Prior to 1948, they were generally known as 'Liberal Nationals'. After 1948, the National Liberals were virtually indistinguishable from the Conservatives. Some candidates still ran as National Liberals, or as Conservative-and-National Liberals or under some similar device. M.P.s elected under any of these banners have been considered as National Liberals

1 See map, p. 117, for a discussion of the mining seats in 1921
2 The Census of 1931 was the first Census which gave figures of unemployment. The 10 areas with the highest unemployment in England and Wales were: Rhondda U.D. (25·9%), Newcastle-on-Tyne (26·9%), Gateshead (27·2%), Middlesbrough (27·7%), Tynemouth (28·3%), West Hartlepool (34·7%), Merthyr Tydfil (35·8%), South Shields (35·9%) and Sunderland (36·6%). (*Census of 1931*, General Report, 162)
3 See map, p. 117, for a table illustrating this

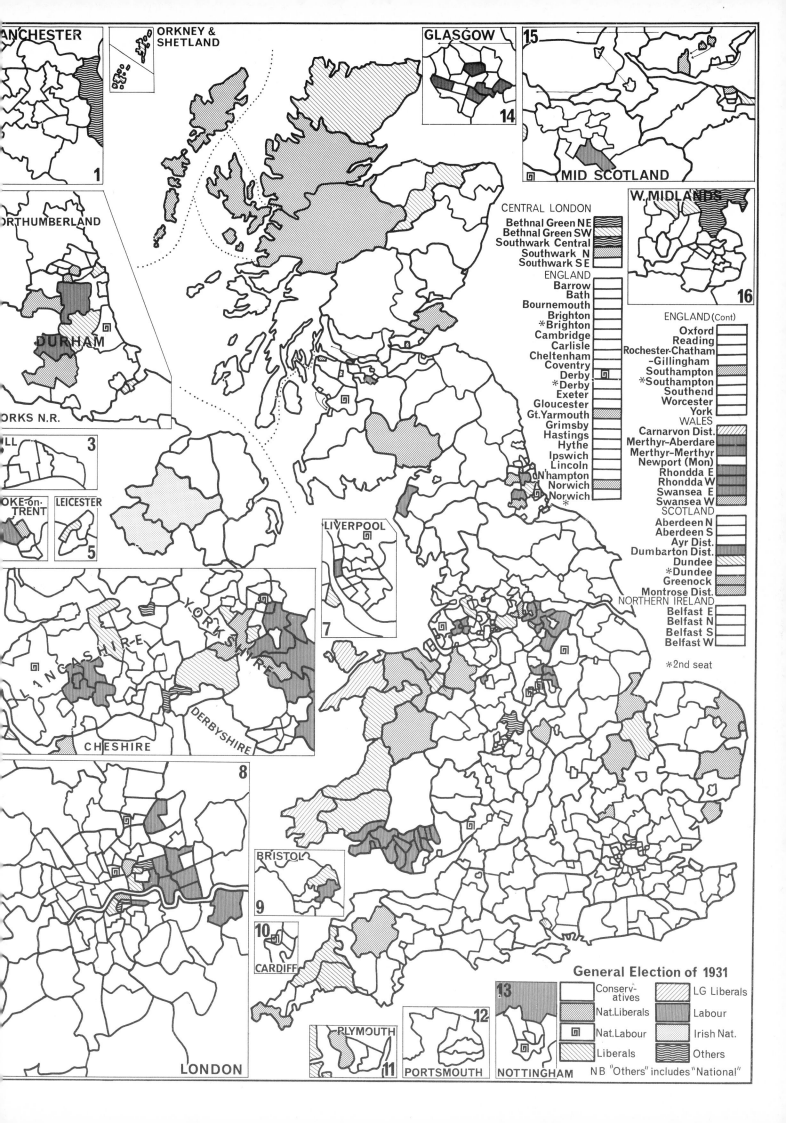

MANCHESTER

ORKNEY & SHETLAND

1

GLASGOW

14

15

MID SCOTLAND

RTHUMBERLAND

DURHAM

ORKS N.R.

3

LL

OKE-on-TRENT

LEICESTER

5

W. MIDLANDS

16

CENTRAL LONDON
Bethnal Green NE
Bethnal Green SW
Southwark Central
Southwark N
Southwark SE
ENGLAND
Barrow
Bath
Bournemouth
Brighton
*Brighton
Cambridge
Carlisle
Cheltenham
Coventry
Derby
*Derby
Exeter
Gloucester
Gt.Yarmouth
Grimsby
Hastings
Hythe
Ipswich
Lincoln
N'hampton
Norwich
Norwich
*

ENGLAND (Cont)
Oxford
Reading
Rochester–Chatham
–Gillingham
Southampton
*Southampton
Southend
Worcester
York
WALES
Carnarvon Dist.
Merthyr–Aberdare
Merthyr–Merthyr
Newport (Mon)
Rhondda E
Rhondda W
Swansea E
Swansea W
SCOTLAND
Aberdeen N
Aberdeen S
Ayr Dist.
Dumbarton Dist.
Dundee
*Dundee
Greenock
Montrose Dist.
NORTHERN IRELAND
Belfast E
Belfast N
Belfast S
Belfast W

*2nd seat

LIVERPOOL

7

YORKSHIRE

LANCASHIRE

DERBYSHIRE

CHESHIRE

8

BRISTOL

9

10

CARDIFF

General Election of 1931

13

12

PLYMOUTH

11

PORTSMOUTH

NOTTINGHAM

LONDON

	Conserv-atives		LG Liberals
	Nat.Liberals		Labour
	Nat.Labour		Irish Nat.
	Liberals		Others

NB "Others" includes "National"

strongholds, because Labour support in them had been growing in most elections since 1918. The 52 seats they won in all parts of the country therefore represented a much surer base for future expansion than the 60 they had won in 1918.[1]

Although Liberal votes helped the Conservatives win the largest majority in modern times, they did little to revive the Liberal Party The miscellaneous collection of 72 Liberals, National Liberals and Lloyd George Liberals were united on few things and were unable to influence the course of events in significant manner. Henceforth, more than before the election, the Liberals could be discounted as a major, or even as a minor force. Not until the Liberal revival of the late 1950s did the party again count.

The Conservatives won nearly everything in 1931, and had sufficient M.P.s from England alone to govern with an overwhelming majority. Only in Wales did they fail to win a majority, because of continuing Labour strength in the mining districts of South Wales. The Conservatives also did not penetrate the slums of

1 See map, Election of 1918, p. 39, for a discussion of Labour weakness then

East London. National Government victories there were primarily Liberal, or National Liberal victories, not Conservative ones.

The Communists ran 26 candidates, 5 of whom managed to save their deposits. If the Communists had put up no candidates, probably nearly all their supporters would have voted Labour. If this assumption is correct the Communists caused Labour losses in 5 seats:

seat	Lab.	Comm.	Lab. and Comm.	National
Attercliffe	15,020	2,790	17,810	15,185
Bothwell	14,423	2,163	16,586	16,571
Springburn	16,058	1,997	18,053	16,092
West Fife	11,063	6,829	17,892	12,977
Whitechapel	9,864	2,658	12,522	11,103

The 5 seats would have made little difference to Labour strength, even if Labour had won them. However, it helped maintain bitterness between the 2 parties. The only seat listed in which the Communist made a good showing was West Fife. In 1935 the Communist candidate, W. Gallacher, won.

General Election of 1935

Overall results

party	total votes	% of total
National Government:		
Conservative	10,496,300	47·7
National	86,716	0·4
National Liberal	887,331	4·0
National Labour	339,811	1·6
Total Govt. vote	**11,810,158**	**53·7**
Opposition:		
Liberal and L.G. Liberal	1,422,116	6·5
Labour	8,325,491	37·8
Communist	27,117	0·1
Others	412,172	1·9
Total Opp. vote	**10,186,896**	**46·3**
Total vote cast	**21,997,054**	**100·0**

Seats won by area

Area	Cons.	Lib. Nat.	Nat.	Nat. Lab.	Lib.	L.G. Lib.	Labour	I.L.P.	Comm-unist	Irish Nat.	Ind.	Total
England	329	22	1	6	11	—	116	—	—	—	—	485
Wales	6	3	1	1	2	4	18	—	—	—	—	35
Scotland	35	7	—	1	3	—	20	4	1	—	—	71
N. Ireland	10	—	—	—	—	—	—	—	—	2	—	12
Universities	7	1	1	—	1	—	—	—	—	—	2	12
Total	**387**	**33**	**3**	**8**	**17**	**4**	**154**	**4**	**1**	**2**	**2**	**615**

Unopposed returns by area

area	Cons.	Nat. Lib.	Lab.	others	total
England	14	2	3	—	19
Wales	—	1	10	—	11
Scotland	1	—	—	—	1
N. Ireland	6	—	—	—	6
Universities	2	—	—	1	3
Total	**23**	**3**	**13**	**1**	**40**

Comments

The results of the election of 1935 were more closely related to class divisions than those of any previous election. This was primarily due to the disintegration of the Liberals. In the 1920s the Liberals had had a wide appeal to all classes and they had often helped Labour or Conservative candidates win seats they probably would not otherwise have won, because of their class structure. By 1935 the Liberals still appealed across class lines, but their appeal had shrunk considerably in comparison with the 1920s. By 1935 Liberal strength in the country had eroded to such a degree that the Liberals probably had little effective influence even in determining which other party should win.

The election of 1935 inaugurated the third period in modern British politics, the period of Labour–Conservative predominance. The first 2 periods had been 1885 to 1910, with Liberal–Conservative predominance, and 1918 to 1931, a confused transition period when all 3 parties were strong. From 1935 to 1970 there were far fewer anomalies of the sort which had marked the elections of the 1920s, and most seats were won or lost on a fairly predictable basis, related to their social composition. After 1935 the Conservative and Labour parties held well-defined groups of seats with relatively homogeneous social composition, and they divided the seats with a more mixed social composition. Few seats diverged from this pattern, although in 1945 some did so. However, the exceptional seats even in 1945 were few in comparison with those in elections of the 1920s.

In 1935 the Liberals won only half the number of seats they had won in their previous disaster year of 1924. Their 21 seats reduced

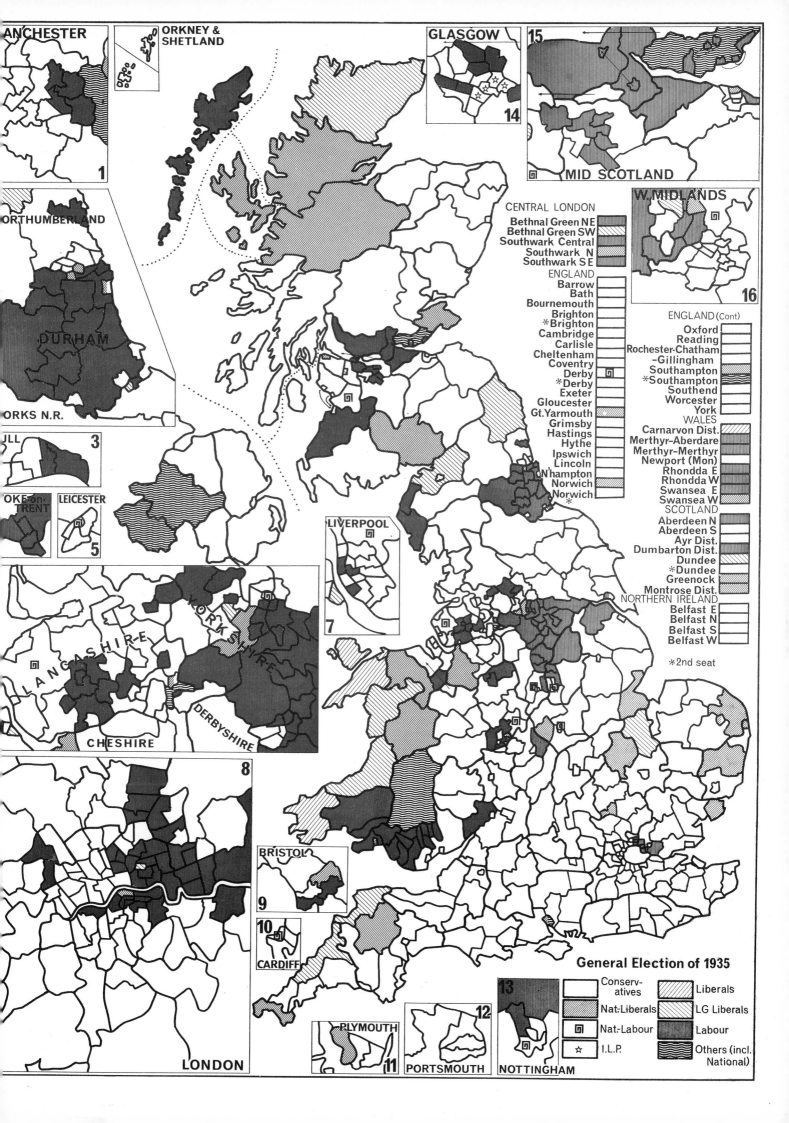

MANCHESTER 1

ORKNEY & SHETLAND

ORTHUMBERLAND

DURHAM

ORKS N.R.

ULL 3

OKE-on-TRENT **LEICESTER** 5

LIVERPOOL 7

LANCASHIRE-E

YORKSHIRE-E

CHESHIRE

DERBYSHIRE

GLASGOW 14

MID SCOTLAND 15

W.MIDLANDS 16

CENTRAL LONDON
Bethnal Green NE
Bethnal Green SW
Southwark Central
Southwark N
Southwark S E
ENGLAND
Barrow
Bath
Bournemouth
Brighton
*Brighton
Cambridge
Carlisle
Cheltenham
Coventry
Derby
*Derby
Exeter
Gloucester
Gt.Yarmouth
Grimsby
Hastings
Hythe
Ipswich
Lincoln
N'hampton
Norwich
Norwich
*

ENGLAND (Cont)
Oxford
Reading
Rochester-Chatham
-Gillingham
Southampton
*Southampton
Southend
Worcester
York
WALES
Carnarvon Dist.
Merthyr-Aberdare
Merthyr-Merthyr
Newport (Mon)
Rhondda E
Rhondda W
Swansea E
Swansea W
SCOTLAND
Aberdeen N
Aberdeen S
Ayr Dist.
Dumbarton Dist.
Dundee
*Dundee
Greenock
Montrose Dist.
NORTHERN IRELAND
Belfast E
Belfast N
Belfast S
Belfast W

*2nd seat

LONDON 8

BRISTOL 9

CARDIFF 10

PLYMOUTH 11

PORTSMOUTH 12

NOTTINGHAM 13

General Election of 1935

Conserv-
atives

Nat-Liberals

Nat-Labour

I.L.P.

Liberals

LG Liberals

Labour

Others (incl.
National)

them to almost complete Parliamentary impotence, an impotence which reflected their position in the country. Only a few areas elected any Liberals, most being agricultural districts where Labour had small appeal and where the Liberals could realistically challenge the charge of splitting the anti-Labour (or anti-Conservative) vote. They gained two agricultural seats in 1935, one of which (North Cumberland) had last elected a Liberal in January 1910. Their other gain, Berwick-on-Tweed, was probably due at least in part to the large number of Nonconformists there.[1] The Liberals won only 6 urban seats, 3 of them in straight fights. In a fourth, Middlesbrough West, there was no Conservative candidate, so that the Liberals won only 2 urban seats in contests involving Conservatives and Labour. These seats were Wolverhampton East and Birkenhead East.

The National Liberal group had little influence, as a group, though some National Liberal M.P.s such as Sir John Simon and Sir Walter Runciman had considerable influence as individuals. The Liberals and Lloyd George Liberals, however, were mere voices, with little influence either in the country or in Parliament.

The Labour Party won 154 seats, 12 more than it had won in 1922. Nearly half the seats Labour won in the 2 elections were different. Consequently, a comparison of the results of the elections gives some information about long-term trends of the 1920s and early 1930s. This comparison shows that in relation to 1922, Labour lost ground in Central Scotland and on Tyneside, and that it gained ground in East London, Liverpool and West Yorkshire.[2] Labour also lost several agricultural and partly-agricultural seats it had won in 1922 with Liberal support, but it gained one agricultural seat, the Western Isles.[3] Labour also won some partly-mining seats which had eluded it in 1922, and another seat, Bassetlaw, where mining had become increasingly important in the 1920s and 1930s.[4] Labour also did well in the Penryn-and-Falmouth division

of Cornwall, where A. L. Rowse came within 3,031 votes of winning. His high poll was due in part to the very high percentage of tin-miners unemployed in a constituency where a sixth of the population was engaged in tin-mining.[5]

One mining area where there was apparently a Labour recession in 1935 in comparison with 1922 was Central Scotland. Labour failed to win 2 mining seats, and one partly-mining seat which it had won in 1922. Their loss in North Lanark was due to a split between the I.L.P. and the Labour Party, which allowed the Conservative candidate to win on a minority vote. Rutherglen failed to go Labour as it had done in 1922, probably because of an influx of middle-class voters into the Western part of the constituency. This probably explains why Rutherglen voted Conservative in several elections after 1935.[6] In Peebles-and-South Midlothian, the opposition to Labour had been divided in 1922, and Labour failed to win in 1935 because there was a united front against it. Thus the apparent Labour recession in the mining district of Central Scotland was not really a recession at all. By 1935, therefore, the Labour Party had an even stronger hold on the mining vote than it had had in the early 1920s, and this hold continued to be evident in all subsequent elections.

Despite the high unemployment in the area[7] Labour failed to win many Tyneside seats it had swept in 1922. Their one win was Jarrow, where the Conservative lost by only 2,350 votes. In most Tyneside seats the Conservatives and their allies won fairly comfortably, and Labour did not greatly improve on their 1931 votes.

Apart from a few exceptional areas such as Tyneside, a comparison of the 1922 and 1935 results indicates that Labour had made substantial progress. Their performance in 1935 gave much more indication of hopeful Labour prospects than their performance in 1922 had given.

---

1 Berwick-on-Tweed had 28·5% Nonconformists, mostly Presbyterians. This was the highest proportion of Nonconformists in any constituency in England. See map, Distribution of Nonconformists in England in 1922, p. 127

2 In this comparison, Communist and I.L.P. M.P.s are counted with Labour

3 The radical tradition there dated to at least 1885. See map, General Election of 1885, p. 15

4 According to Sir E. Hume-Williams, *The World, the House and the Bar*, 238

5 The *Census of 1931*, General Report, 158, stated that 61·1% of all tin, lead and copper miners had been unemployed in 1931

6 Rutherglen voted Conservative in 1951, 1955 and 1959

7 See map, General Election of 1931, p. 51, for a discussion of Tyneside then

General Election of 1945

Overall results

party	total votes	% of total
Conservative	9,087,238	36·1
National Liberal	759,884	2·9
National	175,701	0·7
Conservatives and allies	**10,022,823**	**39·7**
Liberal	2,227,400	8·9
Labour	11,967,985	48·2
Communist	102,780	0·4
Others	782,563	2·8
Total	**25,103,551**	**100·0**

Seats won by area

Area	Cons.	Lib. Nat.	Nat.	Lab.	Common- wealth	I.L.P.	Lib.	Com- munist	Irish Nat.	Other	Total
England	158	7	1	332	1	—	5	1	—	5	510
Wales	3	1	—	25	—	—	6	—	—	—	35
Scotland	24	5	—	36	—	4	—	1	—	1	71
N. Ireland	8	—	—	1	—	—	—	—	2	1	12
Universities	3	—	1	—	—	—	1	—	—	7	12
Total	**196**	**13**	**2**	**394**	**1**	**4**	**12**	**2**	**2**	**14**	**640**

In the above table, D. N. Pritt (Hammersmith North) is counted with Labour; D. L. Lipson (Cheltenham) with 'Others'; and G. Buchanan (Gorbals) with the I.L.P. Listings are as found in *Dod's Parliamentary Companion, 1947*. Except in the cases mentioned, the listings are the same as in *The Times Guide to the House of Commons, 1945*.

Unopposed returns

Labour: Rhondda West, Liverpool–Scotland
Conservative: Armagh
Total: 3 seats

Comments

The election of 1945 was the third 'khaki' election of the century. Unlike the others, it was a serious defeat for the Government of the day. The Conservative defeat in 1945 assumed the proportions of their defeat in 1906, and their loss of over 200 seats seemed to some contemporary observers the 'Waterloo of the Conservative Party'.[1] However, as with the election of 1906, it was not a Waterloo at all; it was not even a retreat from Moscow. It was merely a temporary setback which the Conservatives made good at the next election. Within 6½ years of the 1945 election, the Conservatives once more formed a Government. That Government stayed in office longer than any other since the passage of the Reform Bill of 1832.

There was certainly good ground just after the election of 1945 for believing that the Conservatives were due for a long period in opposition. Not only were they demoralised and apparently with little popular appeal, they had also lost many Conservative strong-holds which had withstood even the Liberal sweep of 1906. For instance, Birmingham and Liverpool had rejected the Liberals in 1906, but in 1945 both cities elected a strong majority of Labour M.P.s. These victories had been foreshadowed by Labour strength in Liverpool and Birmingham in 1929, but some other 1945 Labour victories had not been foreshadowed then. The chief difference between the election of 1929 and 1945 was that in 1929 Labour had just missed getting a majority, while in 1945 it won a comfortable one. The main increase in Labour representation in comparison with 1929 came in the South-east, especially in the suburbs of London. If Labour had won fewer seats in this area, it would have had a much smaller majority in 1945. The seats Labour won in this area in 1945, but not in 1929, were predominantly middle-class in character; they included, for instance, Mitcham and Wimbledon. Labour also won some agricultural seats in the South-east, such as Cambridgeshire and Sudbury, which had fairly small industrial working-class populations. In most of these seats, there was a very high swing to Labour, averaging 17·5% to 22%, in comparison with the national average of 12%. Most places in the country as a whole which had such large swings were either middle-class residential areas, or long-time Conservative strongholds, or both. On the other hand, nearly all places with relatively low swings to Labour had had a high Labour vote in 1935, or else they had had high Liberal votes in 1945. Twelve of the 14 areas which had Liberal votes exceeding 20% in 1945 also had below-average swings to Labour, while the remaining two had only average swings to Labour.[2] Possibly the Liberal Party acted in 1945 as a sort of safety-valve, which attracted Conservative protest voters who did not wish to go all the way toward Labour.

The places with high and low swings to Labour in 1945 were:

Swing to Labour under 6%[3]

area	av. swing	seats
Glasgow	2·5	15
North Wales	4·5	12
Scottish Highlands	5·0	8
Liverpool	6·5	11
Total number of seats		**46**

Swing to Labour over 17%

area	av. swing	seats
North-west Kent	22·0	7
West Midlands	20·0*	32*
London, residential	18·5	12
Fulham, Hammersmith, Islington and St. Pancras	18·5	11
Middlesex	18·5	24
Portsmouth, Plymouth and Southampton	18·0	8
North Surrey	17·5	11
Total number of seats		**105**

* includes Birmingham

This table may be compared with the table given with the following map and with the map on p. 79, which shows the swing in each constituency between 1959 and 1964. It may be seen that only

---

1 R. B. McCallum and A. Readman, *The British General Election of 1945*, 243. This book inaugurated the series of post-war election studies sponsored by Nuffield College, Oxford

2 The areas are those defined in McCallum and Readman, *op.cit.*, 293-5. The Liberal vote is the average % cast for each Liberal candidate in the area

3 Based on R. B. McCallum and A. Readman, *The British General Election of 1945*, 293-5

2 groups of seats had a high swing in all 3 elections, the suburbs of London and the seaports of Portsmouth, Plymouth and Southampton. Birmingham had a high swing to Labour in 1945, a moderate swing to the Conservatives in 1950, and a low swing to Labour in 1964; on the other hand, Liverpool and Glasgow acted in contrary directions and cancelled the effect of the Birmingham swing. The suburbs of London were less stable than other parts of the country in each of these elections. This instability was reflected in the large number of seats there which changed hands.[1] In effect, the high swing to Labour in the London suburbs in 1945 produced the large Labour majority in that election; the high swing to the Conservatives in 1950 deprived Labour of their working majority; and the high swing to Labour in 1964 gave Labour a majority once more.

Shortly before the 1945 election, the 20 most populous seats were divided to form 25 additional smaller seats for a total of 45 seats. The Labour Party won 16 of the new seats in 1945, while the Conservatives won only 9. At first glance, this indicates that the redistribution favoured Labour, but this was not the case. Most of the new seats were in the suburbs of London, and the Conservatives quickly gained them. By 1959 the Conservatives held 20 of the seats set up in 1945. If one compares the Conservative improvement in these seats[2] with their improvement in the rest of the country,[3] it is apparent that the new seats had a far above average inclination to the Conservatives. In 1945 Labour won most of the new seats, when it did not need them. Thereafter, the Conservatives won the seats, when they made a difference. Consequently, one must conclude that the Redistribution of 1945, small though it was, favoured the Conservatives.

1 See map, Labour Seats, 1955-1966, p. 115
2 Eleven gains compared with 9 held in 1945, or an improvement of 121% between 1945 and 1959

3 161 gains compared with 205 held in 1945, or an improvement of 56% between 1945 and 1959

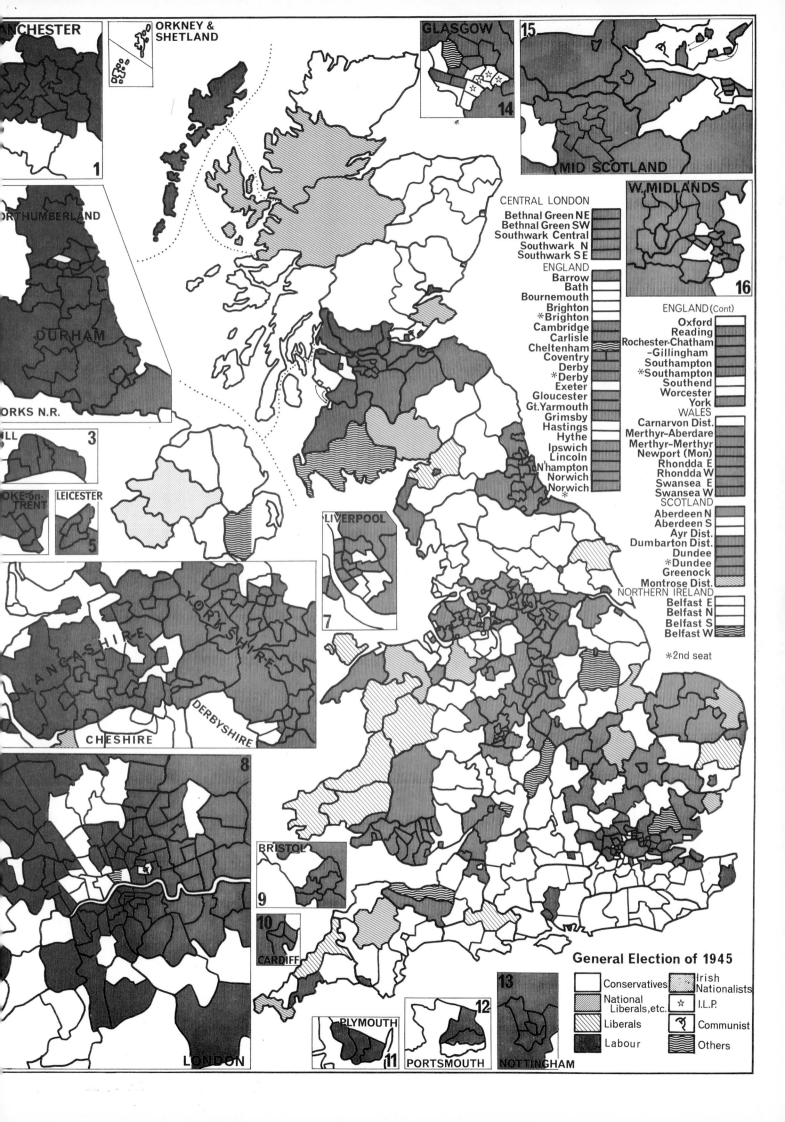

General Election of 1945

CENTRAL LONDON
Bethnal Green NE
Bethnal Green SW
Southwark Central
Southwark N
Southwark SE

ENGLAND
Barrow
Bath
Bournemouth
Brighton
*Brighton
Cambridge
Carlisle
Cheltenham
Coventry
Derby
*Derby
Exeter
Gloucester
Gt. Yarmouth
Grimsby
Hastings
Hythe
Ipswich
Lincoln
N'hampton
Norwich
Norwich *

ENGLAND (Cont)
Oxford
Reading
Rochester-Chatham
—Gillingham
Southampton
*Southampton
Southend
Worcester
York

WALES
Carnarvon Dist.
Merthyr-Aberdare
Merthyr—Merthyr
Newport (Mon)
Rhondda E
Rhondda W
Swansea E
Swansea W

SCOTLAND
Aberdeen N
Aberdeen S
Ayr Dist.
Dumbarton Dist.
Dundee
*Dundee
Greenock
Montrose Dist.

NORTHERN IRELAND
Belfast E
Belfast N
Belfast S
Belfast W

*2nd seat

1 — MANCHESTER
ORKNEY & SHETLAND
NORTHUMBERLAND
DURHAM
YORKS N.R.
3
HULL
STOKE-on-TRENT
LEICESTER — 5
LANCASHIRE
YORKSHIRE
CHESHIRE
DERBYSHIRE
LIVERPOOL — 7
8
BRISTOL — 9
10
CARDIFF
13
PLYMOUTH — 11
PORTSMOUTH — 12
NOTTINGHAM
LONDON
GLASGOW
14
15
MID SCOTLAND
W. MIDLANDS
16

Conservatives
National Liberals, etc.
Liberals
Labour
Irish Nationalists
I.L.P.
Communist
Others

General Election of 1950

Overall results

party	total votes	% of total
Conservative	11,505,164	40·0
National Liberal	985,343	3·4
Conservatives and allies	**12,490,507**	**43·4**
Labour	13,267,466	46·1
Liberal	2,621,489	9·1
Communist	91,812	0·3
Others	301,043	1·1
Total	**28,772,317**	**100·0**

Seats won by area

area	Cons.	Nat. Lib.	Lib.	Lab.	Irish Nat.	total
England	243	10	2	251	—	506
Wales	3	1	5	27	—	36
Scotland	26	6	2	37	—	71
N. Ireland	10	—	—	—	2	12
Total	**282**	**17**	**9**	**315**	**2**	**625**

Unopposed returns

Conservatives: Antrim, Armagh
Total: 2

Comments

In 1950, as in 1945, there were substantial regional variations in the swing to or from the Conservatives. The national average for the swing to the Conservatives in 1950 was 2·9%,[1] but 8 groups of seats consisting of 92 seats in all had average swings to the Conservatives exceeding 7% while 4 groups of seats consisting of 48 seats had average swings to Labour. The groups of seats were:

Swing to Conservatives over 7%[2]

area	av. swing	seats
North Lancashire	8·8	10
Kent, Sussex Boroughs	8·8	13
Hull	8·6	4
Essex Boroughs	8·2	14
Essex County Divs.	8·1	10
Hampshire Ports	7·6	6
Leeds	7·6	7
Middlesex Boroughs	7·1	28
Total number of seats		**92**

Swing to Labour over 0·0%

area	av. swing	seats
Mining Wales	2·3	17
Durham County Divs.	0·9	10
Rural Wales	0·6	13
Fife, Stirling and Linlithgow	0·0	8
Total number of seats		**48**

Nearly all the areas with a high swing to the Conservatives were predominantly middle-class. This suggests that the middle-class voters as a whole were more likely to change allegiance in 1950 than were other groups. This was apparently a feature of the 1964 election, when there was also considerable regional variation in swing; and it may have been a feature of other elections. As in 1964 the high swing in middle-class seats caused many changes in representation, as can be seen by comparing this map with the preceding one. Such a comparison indicates that the Labour recession in the suburbs of London was by far the most striking thing about the election of 1950.

Major variations in swing in 1950 had also been notable in 1945, and were to be notable again in 1964. Such variations tend to undermine the concept of a national swing, but they do not undermine it completely. In all three elections high swings in some areas tended to cancel low swings in others. Consequently, although the theoretical concept of a national swing is suspect, in practice it is still useful. However, it is easy to conceive of an election in which high and low swings do not cancel each other. For instance, in the election of 1950 they did not cancel each other completely, as there were almost twice as many seats with a very high swing as there were with a very low swing.

The Liberal vote in 1950 was distributed fairly evenly throughout Britain. However, Liberal candidates won more than 20% of the votes in 3 districts. These were the South-west, North-eastern Scotland and North Wales. All 3 had been traditional Liberal strongholds. In addition, Liberal candidates won over 20% in many scattered agricultural seats. The only urban seats where Liberals won more than 20% were Bolton West, Luton and Bethnal Green. Otherwise, the Liberals in 1950 were reduced to dependence almost entirely on agricultural seats, probably because of the inherent weakness of Labour in such seats. In the agricultural seats won by Labour in 1945, the Liberals did very badly in 1950. Three groups of agricultural or partly agricultural seats had had a Liberal tradition as recently as the 1920s, but voted Labour in 1945. These were seats in Norfolk, Gloucestershire and Southern Scotland. The Liberals did badly in 1950 in all of them. There was little sign, in 1950, of Liberal strength in middle-class seats, which marked the election of 1964.[3] This leads one to conclude that the Liberal 'revival' in 1964 was a conversion rather than a revival in middle-class seats.

---

1 Nicholas, *The British General Election of 1950,* 306, states that the swing was 3·3%. This refers, not to the total change, but to the change in seats contested by both Conservatives and Labour in 1945 and 1950. As a redistribution of seats intervened, this figure is only approximate. The net change in the total vote was a Labour loss

of 2·1% and a Conservative gain of 3·7%, making a swing in the whole country of 2·9%
2 *Ibid.,* 306-15
3 See map, The Liberal Vote in 1964, p. 87

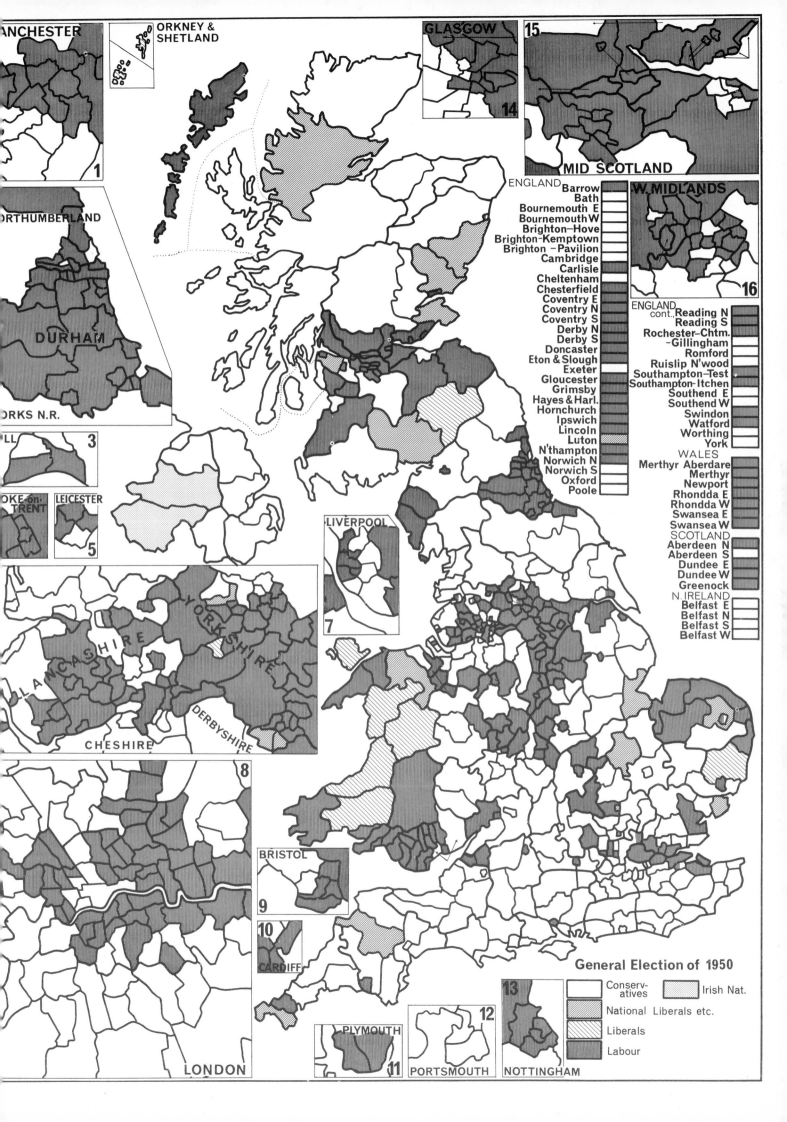

General Election of 1950

Inset maps:
1. MANCHESTER
2. ORKNEY & SHETLAND
3. NORTHUMBERLAND / DURHAM / YORKS N.R. / HULL
5. STOKE-on-TRENT / LEICESTER
7. LIVERPOOL
8. LONDON
9. BRISTOL
10. CARDIFF
11. PLYMOUTH
12. PORTSMOUTH
13. NOTTINGHAM
14. GLASGOW
15. MID SCOTLAND
16. W. MIDLANDS

ENGLAND
Barrow
Bath
Bournemouth E
Bournemouth W
Brighton–Hove
Brighton–Kemptown
Brighton–Pavilion
Cambridge
Carlisle
Cheltenham
Chesterfield
Coventry E
Coventry N
Coventry S
Derby N
Derby S
Doncaster
Eton & Slough
Exeter
Gloucester
Grimsby
Hayes & Harl.
Hornchurch
Ipswich
Lincoln
Luton
N'thampton
Norwich N
Norwich S
Oxford
Poole

ENGLAND cont.
Reading N
Reading S
Rochester–Chtm.
–Gillingham
Romford
Ruislip N'wood
Southampton–Test
Southampton–Itchen
Southend E
Southend W
Swindon
Watford
Worthing
York

WALES
Merthyr Aberdare
Merthyr
Newport
Rhondda E
Rhondda W
Swansea E
Swansea W

SCOTLAND
Aberdeen N
Aberdeen S
Dundee E
Dundee W
Greenock

N. IRELAND
Belfast E
Belfast N
Belfast S
Belfast W

Legend:
Conservatives
National Liberals etc.
Liberals
Labour
Irish Nat.

General Election of 1951

Overall results

party	total votes	% of total
Conservative	12,734,120	44·5
National Liberal	984,079	3·5
Conservatives and allies	**13,718,199**	**48.0**
Liberal	743,512	2·6
Labour	13,935,917	48·7
Communist	21,640	0·1
Others	177,326	0·6
Total	**28,596,594**	**100·0**

Seats won by area

area	Cons.	Nat. Lib.	Lib.	Lab.	Irish Nat.	other	total
England	259	12	2	233	—	—	506
Wales	5	1	3	27	—	—	36
Scotland	29	6	1	35	—	—	71
N. Ireland	9	—	—	—	2	1	12
Total	**302**	**19**	**6**	**295**	**2**	**1**	**625**

Unopposed returns

Conservatives: Antrim North, Antrim South, Armagh and Londonderry, **Total 4**

Comments

In 1951 the Conservatives had 217,718 votes fewer than Labour, but they won 26 more seats. This bias existed in nearly every election between 1918 and 1966, but was most noticeable in elections held shortly after redistributions. The main reason for this bias in the electoral system is that Labour won very large majorities in mining and slum seats in most elections, while the Conservatives won many suburban seats with small but comfortable majorities. In 1951, for example, 20 seats had majorities exceeding 25,000 votes. Seventeen voted Labour, and only 3 voted Conservative. In these very safe seats, therefore, Labour wasted many more votes than did the Conservatives. On the other hand, the Conservatives won numerous seats in the suburbs of London with majorities ranging from 2,000 to 5,000. Such seats were safe in most elections.[1]

Since the suburbs of London were the fastest growing part of the country throughout the period since 1885, redistributions added more seats there than elsewhere. Consequently, the Conservatives benefited more than other parties from redistributions. When redistributions were delayed, the bias in favour of the Conservatives became less noticeable. Although the Conservatives still won roughly the same percentages in the growing suburbs, their absolute majorities were greater, and these majorities tended to balance large Labour majorities in places with a more static population. If the redistributions had been intended to produce equality of votes, they did not achieve it. All they achieved was a rough equality in the size of constituency, but this equality in the size of the electorate in the constituencies was less significant than equality in the size of majorities.

The election of 1951 was the first in a series of 3 elections in which the swing to the Conservatives was uniform. To some extent, the uniformity in 1951 was explained by the closeness of the previous election, held only a year and a half before. It may be assumed that regional factors, such as differences in prosperity, had already affected the swing in 1950, so that a fairly uniform swing in 1951 was only to be expected. The election of 1951 may be compared with the election of 1966. Like the election of 1966, 1951 followed shortly after another election in which there had been considerable regional variations in swing. Both 1966 and 1951 had far smaller variations in swing, although in both there was 'compensation' in a few places for low or high swings in the previous election. In 1951, for instance, the swing to Labour in London suburbs was slightly less than the national average, while in 1950 it had far exceeded the national average. In 1966 a few areas also exhibited such compensation.[2]

Another explanation for the uniformity of swing in 1951 is that there were few new issues in 1951 which could have affected different parts of the country in different ways. This may also explain the uniformity in 1955 and 1959, when there were few major issues which had not been present in 1951.

1 The Conservatives and Labour divided seats with majorities under 1,000 fairly evenly in 1951. Labour won 20, the Conservatives 22, the Liberals one and Irish Labour one

2 See map, Swing to Labour, 1964-1966, p. 81

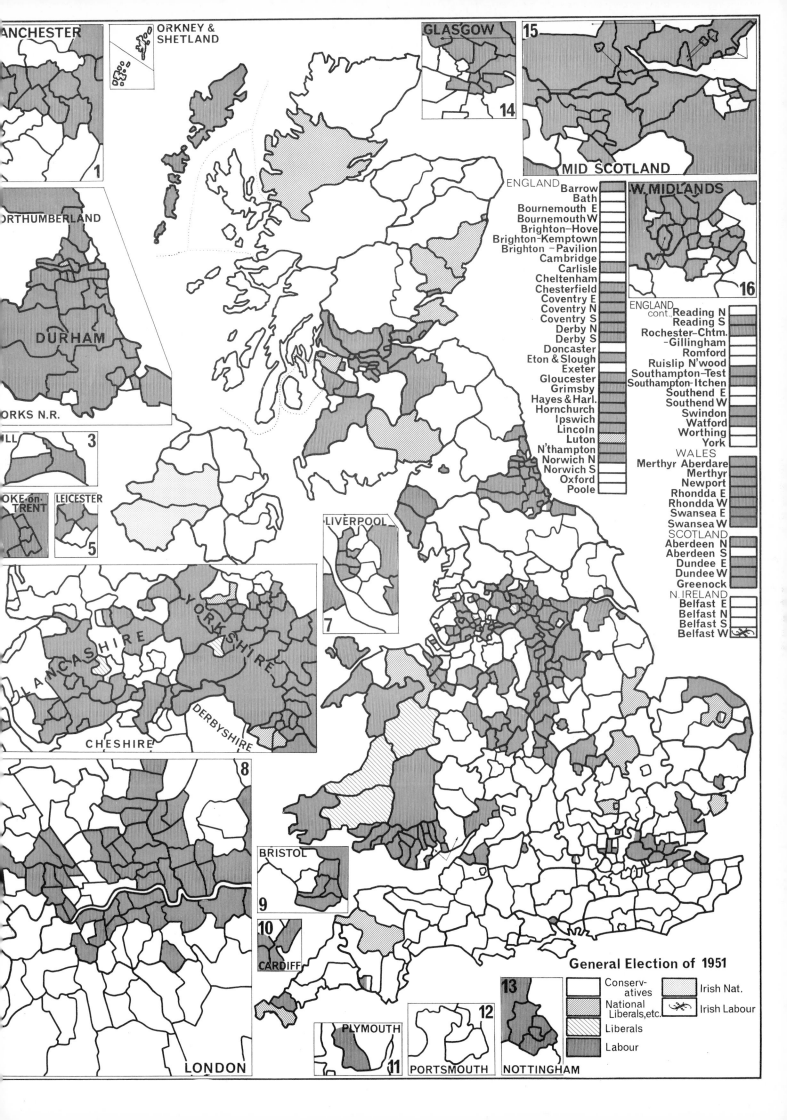

MANCHESTER

ORKNEY & SHETLAND

1

NORTHUMBERLAND

DURHAM

YORKS N.R.

HULL

3

STOKE-on-TRENT

LEICESTER

5

LIVERPOOL

7

GLASGOW

14

15

MID SCOTLAND

W. MIDLANDS

16

LANCASHIRE

YORKSHIRE

DERBYSHIRE

CHESHIRE

8

BRISTOL

9

10

CARDIFF

13

LONDON

PLYMOUTH

11

PORTSMOUTH

12

NOTTINGHAM

ENGLAND
Barrow
Bath
Bournemouth E
Bournemouth W
Brighton–Hove
Brighton–Kemptown
Brighton–Pavilion
Cambridge
Carlisle
Cheltenham
Chesterfield
Coventry E
Coventry N
Coventry S
Derby N
Derby S
Doncaster
Eton & Slough
Exeter
Gloucester
Grimsby
Hayes & Harl.
Hornchurch
Ipswich
Lincoln
Luton
N'thampton
Norwich N
Norwich S
Oxford
Poole

ENGLAND
cont.
Reading N
Reading S
Rochester–Chtm.
–Gillingham
Romford
Ruislip N'wood
Southampton–Test
Southampton–Itchen
Southend E
Southend W
Swindon
Watford
Worthing
York
WALES
Merthyr Aberdare
Merthyr
Newport
Rhondda E
Rhondda W
Swansea E
Swansea W
SCOTLAND
Aberdeen N
Aberdeen S
Dundee E
Dundee W
Greenock
N. IRELAND
Belfast E
Belfast N
Belfast S
Belfast W

General Election of 1951

Conservatives

National Liberals, etc.

Liberals

Labour

Irish Nat.

Irish Labour

General Election of 1955

Overall results

party	total votes	% of total
Conservative	12,416,293	46·4
National Liberal	869,226	3·2
Conservatives and allies	**13,285,519**	**49.6**
Labour	12,405,254	46·4
Liberal	722,402	2·7
Communist	33,144	0·1
Others	313,410	1·2
Total	**26,759,729**	**100·0**

Seats won by area

area	Cons.	Nat. Lib.	Lib.	Lab.	Irish Nat.	total
England	278	14	2	216	—	511
Wales	5	1	3	27	—	36
Scotland	30	6	1	34	—	71
N. Ireland	10	—	—	—	2	12
Total	**323**	**21**	**6**	**277**	**2**	**630**

Unopposed returns

None

Comments

In 1954 there was a redistribution of seats. Since only 6 years had elapsed since the previous major redistribution, the changes in 1954 had much less effect on party strength than other redistributions had had. The redistribution of 1954 probably favoured the Conservatives to the extent of 2-10 seats,[1] but this was not a major cause for Labour complaint. A more valid reason for complaint was the continuing existence of a bias in the electoral system which the 1954 redistribution exaggerated slightly. This bias was not the result of a faulty job by the Boundary Commissioners: it lay in the method of distributing seats according to the size of the population in each seat.

The swing to the Conservatives in 1955 was nearly uniform, although a few places such as Hull had a slight swing to Labour, while some other places such as Middlesbrough and Coventry had above average swings to the Conservatives. Another area with relatively low swings to the Conservatives was Norfolk, where Labour improved its position in 6 of the 10 seats. A major factor causing this improvement was the slow increase in agricultural wages. These wages rose between 1951 and 1955 no faster than the cost of living, while industrial wages rose faster than the cost of living. Consequently, agricultural workers were slightly worse off in relation to other workers in 1955 than they had been in 1951. This probably explains the 3 Labour gains in Norfolk.[2]

This election was the first since 1929 in which the Liberals improved their percentage of the vote in comparison with the preceding election. The Liberal share of the vote rose from 2·6% to 2·7%. As in 1950 the Liberal vote was concentrated in agricultural seats. Sixteen of the 18 seats in which the Liberals won over 20% were primarily agricultural, while the remaining 2, Bolton West and Huddersfield West, had no Conservative candidates. Two suburban constituencies which the Liberals won in 1966, Cheadle and Orpington, had only average Liberal votes, 15·6% and 12·4% respectively. The Liberal vote in 1950 as well as their vote in 1955 indicated no great strength in middle-class suburban seats, which characterised their vote in 1964.

1 D. E. Butler, *The British General Election of 1955*, 157, calculated that the net effect of the 1954 redistribution was a Conservative gain of 2-5 seats. *The Times Guide to the House of Commons, 1955*, 252, estimated the Conservative gains at 5-10 seats

2 See *The Campaign Guide, 1955*, 150, 176 and 192, for agricultural and industrial wages in 1951 and 1955, and for the change in the cost of living from 1951 to 1955

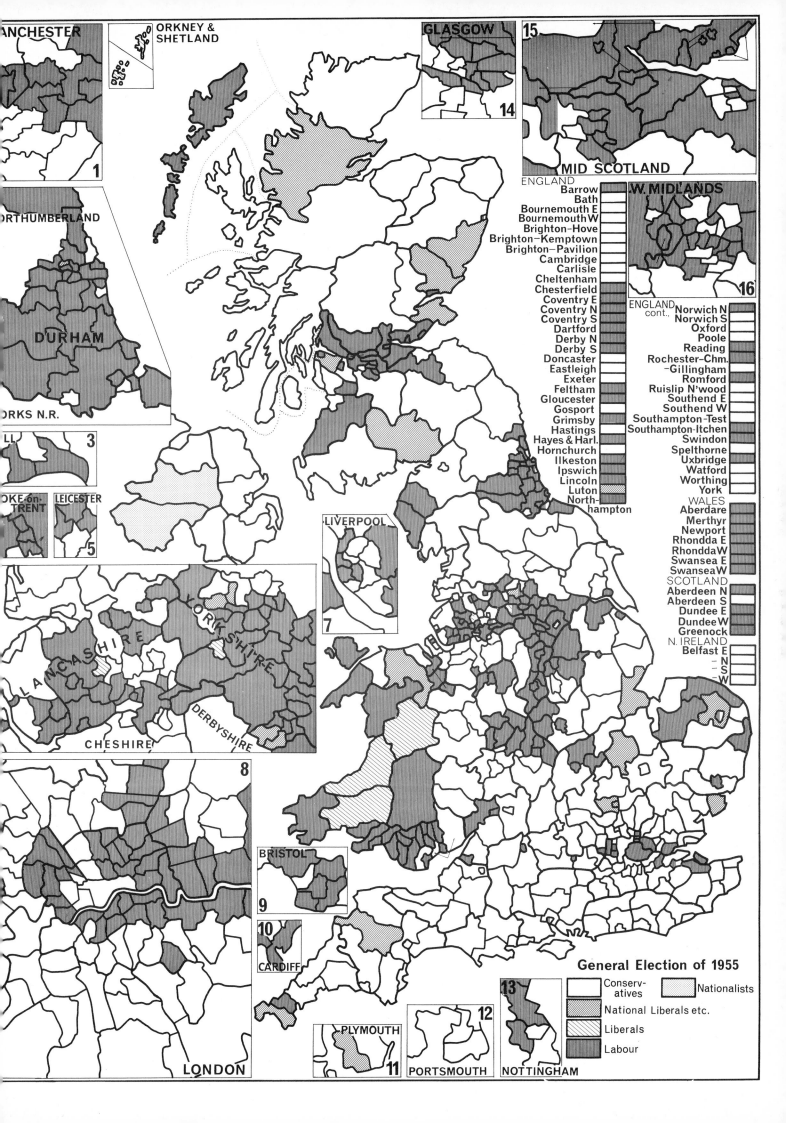

General Election of 1955

MANCHESTER **1**

ORKNEY & SHETLAND

GLASGOW **14**

15

MID SCOTLAND

NORTHUMBERLAND

DURHAM

YORKS N.R.

HULL **3**

STOKE-on-TRENT

LEICESTER **5**

LIVERPOOL **7**

LANCASHIRE

YORKSHIRE

CHESHIRE

DERBYSHIRE

8

BRISTOL **9**

CARDIFF **10**

13

PLYMOUTH **11**

PORTSMOUTH **12**

NOTTINGHAM

LONDON

Conservatives
National Liberals etc.
Liberals
Labour
Nationalists

General Election of 1959

Overall results

party	total votes	% of total
Conservative	13,068,175	46·8
National Liberal	682,760	2·6
Conservatives and allies	**13,750,935**	**49.4**
Liberal	1,640,761	5·9
Labour	12,216,166	43·8
Communist	30,897	0·1
Others	223,949	0·8
Total	**27,862,708**	**100·0**

Seats won by area

area	Cons.	Nat. Lib.	Lib.	Lab.	other	total
England	302	13	3	193	—	511
Wales	7	—	2	27	—	36
Scotland	25	6	1	38	1	71
N. Ireland	12	—	—	—	—	12
Total	**346**	**19**	**6**	**258**	**1**	**630**

Unopposed returns

None

Comments

Many regional variations in swing which characterised the 1964 election appeared, in a smaller degree in the election of 1959. In 1964 there was an above average swing to Labour in Lancashire and Central Scotland, and a below average swing to Labour in the Midlands and East Anglia. In 1959 Lancashire and Scotland favoured Labour slightly more than other parts of the country, while the Midlands and East Anglia favoured the Conservatives. In addition, the Liberal vote began to rise in 1959, especially in the suburban constituencies. The chief difference between the elections of 1959 and 1964 was that in 1959 the swing did not vary from one part of the country to another as much as it did in 1964.

The increase in the Liberal vote from 2·7% to 5·9% was probably the most striking feature of the 1959 election. In addition to winning more votes throughout the country, the Liberals won over 20% in 46 seats, compared with 18 in 1955. The Liberals tended, however, to do worst in their best seats. In 8 of the 13 seats where they had won over 30% in 1955, their vote dropped, although it dropped in only 2 other seats throughout the country.[1]

The Liberals won more than 20% of the vote in 14 urban seats. In 2 of these seats, Bolton West and Huddersfield West, they had won over 20% in 1955, with Conservative help. However, they had won over 20% in none of the remaining 12. Nearly all these seats were predominantly middle-class, which suggests that many middle-class voters had become dissatisfied with the Conservatives but were as yet unwilling to vote Labour. It is notable that in 1964 the Liberals won even more support in this type of constituency than they had done in 1959, while their support in many other parts of the country remained fairly stable.

1 D. E. Butler, *General Election of 1959*, 195

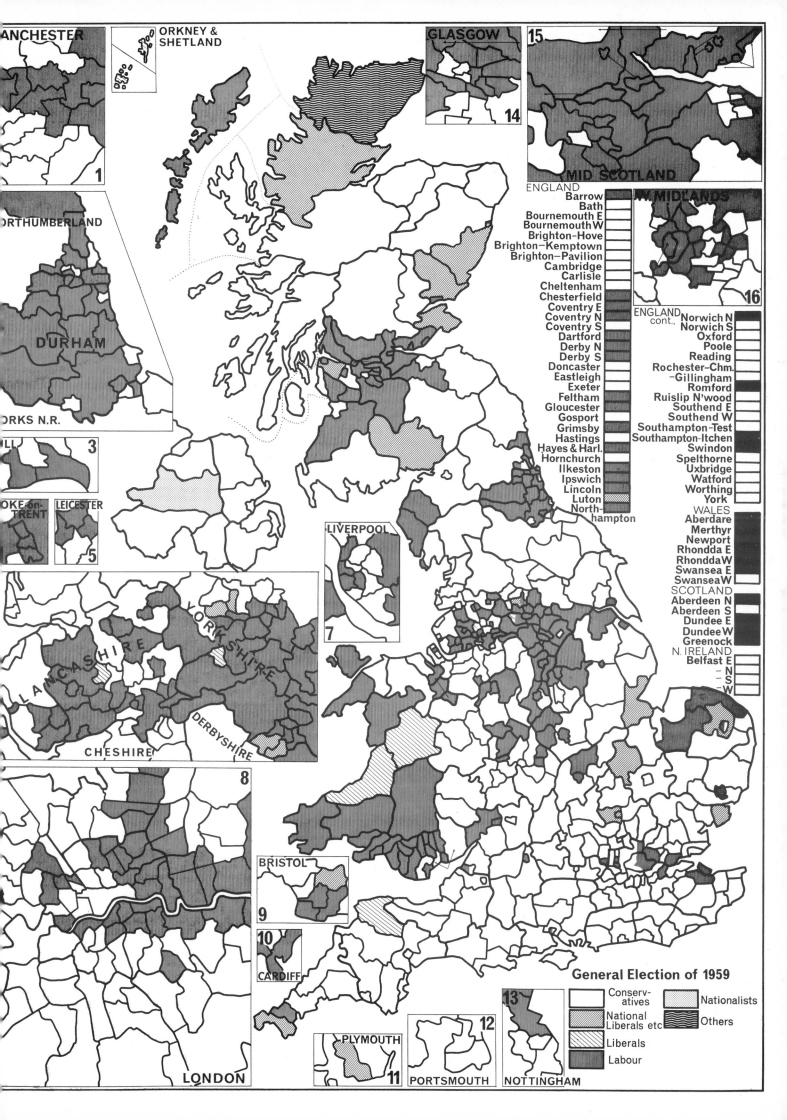

General Election of 1959

Legend:
- Conservatives
- National Liberals etc
- Liberals
- Labour
- Nationalists
- Others

Map insets:
1. MANCHESTER
   ORKNEY & SHETLAND
   NORTHUMBERLAND
   DURHAM
   YORKS N.R.
3. HULL
   STOKE-on-TRENT
5. LEICESTER
7. LIVERPOOL
8. LANCASHIRE / YORKSHIRE / CHESHIRE / DERBYSHIRE
9. BRISTOL
10. CARDIFF
11. PLYMOUTH
12. PORTSMOUTH
13. NOTTINGHAM
14. GLASGOW
15. MID SCOTLAND
16. W. MIDLANDS
    LONDON

ENGLAND
Barrow
Bath
Bournemouth E
Bournemouth W
Brighton-Hove
Brighton-Kemptown
Brighton-Pavilion
Cambridge
Carlisle
Cheltenham
Chesterfield
Coventry E
Coventry N
Coventry S
Dartford
Derby N
Derby S
Doncaster
Eastleigh
Exeter
Feltham
Gloucester
Gosport
Grimsby
Hastings
Hayes & Harl.
Hornchurch
Ilkeston
Ipswich
Lincoln
Luton
Northampton

ENGLAND cont.,
Norwich N
Norwich S
Oxford
Poole
Reading
Rochester-Chm.
-Gillingham
Romford
Ruislip N'wood
Southend E
Southend W
Southampton-Test
Southampton-Itchen
Swindon
Spelthorne
Uxbridge
Watford
Worthing
York

WALES
Aberdare
Merthyr
Newport
Rhondda E
Rhondda W
Swansea E
Swansea W

SCOTLAND
Aberdeen N
Aberdeen S
Dundee E
Dundee W
Greenock

N. IRELAND
Belfast E
– N
– S
– W

General Election of 1964

Overall results

party	total votes	% of total
Conservatives and allies	12,002,906	43·4
Labour	12,205,779	44·1
Liberal	3,101,103	11·2
Communist	44,576	0·2
Others	302,518	1·1
Total	**27,658,898**	**100·0**

Seats won by area

area	Cons.	Lib.	Lab.	total
England	261	3	247	511
Wales	6	2	28	36
Scotland	24	4	43	71
N. Ireland	12	—	—	12
Total	**303**	**9**	**318**	**630**

Unopposed returns

None

Comments

Many variations in the swing to Labour distinguished the election of 1964 from its immediate predecessors, and from the election of 1966. These variations, which are examined in the map on p.79, were probably due to two main factors, which differed in significance from one part of the country to another. The factors were the Liberal revival and the degree of economic prosperity. The map on p.87 shows that the Liberal vote in 1964 was not uniform, but that it was concentrated first in traditional Liberal areas, and second in middle-class suburban districts.[1] An opinion poll taken during the 1964 election indicated that the Liberals had roughly even support among all classes, but that they had rather more support among middle-class, than among working-class, voters.[2] If the middle-class vote had normally been divided evenly between the Conservatives and Labour, an increase in the Liberal proportion of that vote would have had little net effect on the relative standing of the two major parties. However, the middle-class vote was normally very strongly Conservative. Consequently, a large increase for the Liberals was almost bound to affect the Conservatives more than it affected Labour. The net change was an increase in the standing of Labour in comparison with the Conservatives. Since the middle-class vote was concentrated in suburban seats,[3] the Liberal revival affected the apparent swing to Labour more than in seats where the proportion of middle-class voters was low.

A second factor producing variations in the swing to Labour was the degree of economic prosperity. Some depressed places such as Glasgow and Liverpool had higher swings to Labour than more prosperous ones such as Birmingham and agricultural seats in East Anglia. A comparison of 2 opinion polls taken in 1955 and 1964 indicates that the main change between the 2 elections was an increase in the Liberal middle-class vote at the expense of the Conservatives. There was only a small net change in the working-class vote. The overall changes between 1955 and 1964 were:

	% net change, 1955-64 [4]			
	A and B	C1	C2	D and E
Conservative	−10	−9	−1	+1
Labour	−1	nil	−5	−6
Liberal	+10	+9	+6	+4

The polls gave figures only for the net changes throughout Britain, and not by region. However, the working-class vote probably stayed more solidly with Labour in depressed areas than in more prosperous ones. This would account for the fairly small net change in the working-class vote in the country as a whole.

The election of 1964 may usefully be compared with the election of 1950, which Labour also won with a very small majority. In 1950 Labour had won several seats in Birmingham and East Anglia which it did not win in 1964; and it won several seats in Glasgow, Liverpool and East Lancashire in 1964 which it had not won in 1950. In other parts of the country the distribution of seats in 1964 was remarkably similar to the distribution in 1950.

---

1 Although the Liberals had shown some strength in middle-class suburban seats in 1923, such seats had not traditionally been Liberal
2 The overall figures in this poll were:

	Social class			
	A and B	C1	C2	D and E
Conservative	75	61	34	31
Labour	9	25	54	59
Liberal	15	14	11	9

Source: Butler and King, *British General Election of 1964,* 296

3 See map, The Middle-class Vote in 1921, p. 123, for the distribution of middle-class voters then
4 Based on Butler and King, *British General Election of 1964,* 296, and on M. Abrams, 'Class Distinctions in Britain', *Future of the Welfare State,* Conservative Political Centre, 1958

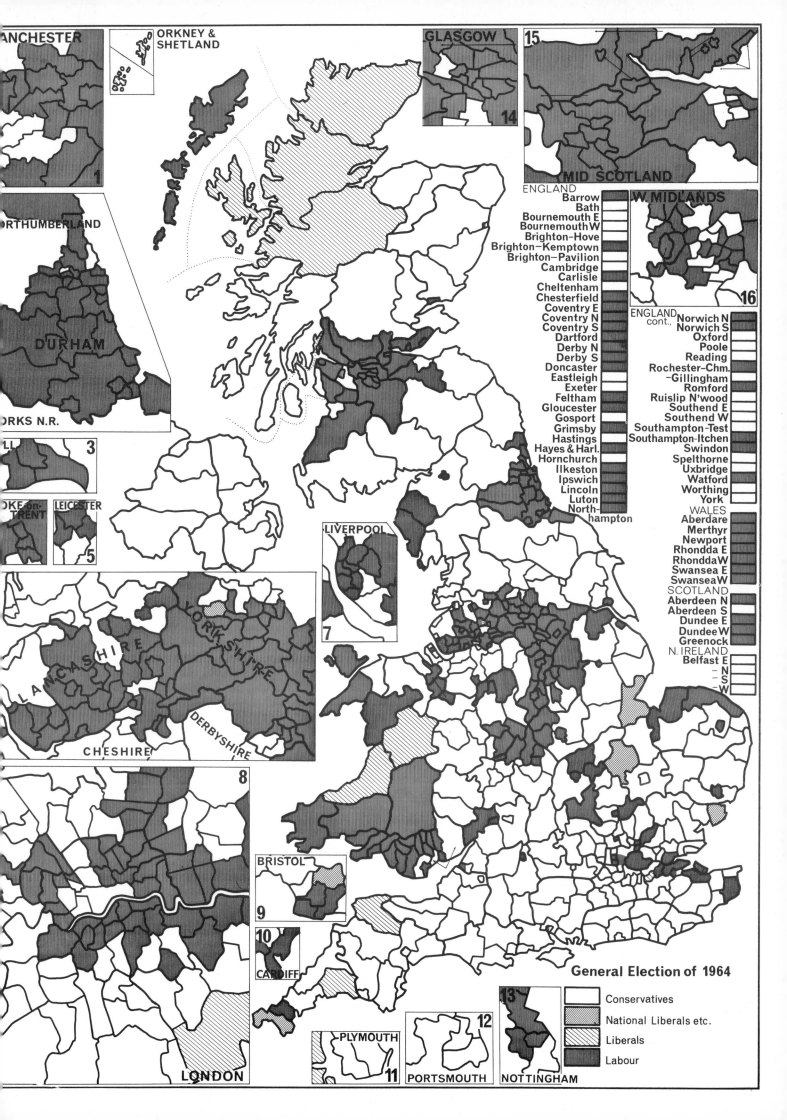

General Election of 1964

MANCHESTER
1

ORKNEY & SHETLAND

GLASGOW
14

15

MID SCOTLAND

NORTHUMBERLAND

DURHAM

YORKS N.R.

HULL
3

STOKE-on-TRENT

LEICESTER
5

W. MIDLANDS
16

LIVERPOOL
7

YORKSHIRE

LANCASHIRE

DERBYSHIRE

CHESHIRE

8

BRISTOL
9

CARDIFF
10

LONDON

PLYMOUTH
11

PORTSMOUTH
12

NOTTINGHAM
13

ENGLAND
Barrow
Bath
Bournemouth E
Bournemouth W
Brighton-Hove
Brighton-Kemptown
Brighton-Pavilion
Cambridge
Carlisle
Cheltenham
Chesterfield
Coventry E
Coventry N
Coventry S
Dartford
Derby N
Derby S
Doncaster
Eastleigh
Exeter
Feltham
Gloucester
Gosport
Grimsby
Hastings
Hayes & Harl.
Hornchurch
Ilkeston
Ipswich
Lincoln
Luton
North-hampton

ENGLAND cont.,
Norwich N
Norwich S
Oxford
Poole
Reading
Rochester-Chm.
-Gillingham
Romford
Ruislip N'wood
Southend E
Southend W
Southampton-Test
Southampton-Itchen
Swindon
Spelthorne
Uxbridge
Watford
Worthing
York

WALES
Aberdare
Merthyr
Newport
Rhondda E
Rhondda W
Swansea E
Swansea W

SCOTLAND
Aberdeen N
Aberdeen S
Dundee E
Dundee W
Greenock

N. IRELAND
Belfast E
- N
- S
- W

Conservatives
National Liberals etc.
Liberals
Labour

General Election of 1966

Overall results

party	total votes	% of total
Conservative	11,418,433	41·9
Liberal	2,327,533	8·5
Labour	13,064,951	47·9
Communist	62,112	0·2
Others	390,577	1·5
Total	**27,263,606**	**100·0**

Source: *The Times Guide to the House of Commons, 1966*, 232

Seats won by area

area	Cons.	Lib.	Lab.	others	total
England	219	6	285	1	511
Wales	3	1	32	—	36
Scotland	20	5	46	—	71
N. Ireland	11	—	—	1	12
Total	**253**	**12**	**363**	**2**	**630**

Unopposed returns   None

Comments

Note: the turnout in 1966, and the swing between 1964 and 1966 are examined in the maps on pp. 77 and 81

The most notable thing about the 1966 election was its uniformity of swing: half the constituencies had swings to Labour within 1% of the national average of 3·1%. Most other constituencies were also near this figure.[1] This uniformity of swing was a feature of most elections since 1945. In some, such as the elections of 1950 and 1964, the swing varied slightly from place to place, but not as much as it had done in elections of the 1920s. The chief reason for this relative uniformity of swing after 1945 was the decline of the Liberals as a major force. In the 1920s the Liberals had considerably different strength in different parts of the country. Not only that, but much of their appeal depended on the personality of individual Liberal candidates. For instance, left-wing Liberals with a strong personality such as J. M. Kenworthy or Frank Gray[2] had appealed successfully for working-class votes, while right-wing Liberals such as Sir Thomas Robinson and Col. England[3] had appealed successfully for middle-class votes. In addition, some Liberals such as the well-known cricketer C. B. Fry had had an appeal which cut across normal party and class lines.[4] The Liberals therefore varied considerably from place to place, not only in strength but in the groups from which they had drawn their support. Variation in Liberal activities in the country therefore had a far from uniform effect on voting patterns. The removal of the Liberals as an effective force in nearly all elections after 1945 consequently increased uniformity in those patterns. Some variation remained, mainly attributable to 2 factors, the personalities of the candidates and the variation in economic conditions from one part of the country to another. The personalities of the candidates probably affected few constituencies, and those in a negative way: unpopular candidates probably lost some votes,[5] but there is less evidence that popular candidates attracted many. A more important cause of heterogeneous voting patterns was variations in economic conditions: one would anticipate lower swings against the Government in prosperous areas than in depressed ones. For instance, in 1964 the prosperous West Midlands had had a low swing against the Conservative Government, while the depressed areas in Lancashire and around Glasgow had had high swings against it. In the country as a whole, such regional variations cancelled one another. At any rate, 2 opinion polls taken in 1955 and 1966 showed that the Conservative percentage of the working-class vote stayed almost constant, and that the major change was a heavy transfer of middle- and lower middle-class voters to the Liberals.[6] This probably accounted for the above average swings against the Conservatives and to the Liberals in middle-class suburban districts; while the small change among working-class voters reflects the cancellation of high swings in some places by low swings in others. Unfortunately, the polls did not publish results by region, so that this cannot be confirmed.

The map shows the continuing predominance of the Conservatives in middle-class areas and also in agricultural ones. Even though their proportion of the middle-class vote dropped heavily in comparison with 1955, almost three-quarters of the middle-class voters supported the Conservatives. Agricultural districts also supported the Conservatives strongly, except in Norfolk, Wales and the Scottish Highlands. In Norfolk and Wales the Labour Party won several agricultural seats, in several of which Labour candidates had received substantial Liberal support as early as 1922. The Liberals held a few seats in the Scottish Highlands which they had won in 1964, although they lost Caithness-and-Sutherland to Labour. They gained 2 working-class seats (Colne Valley and Roxburgh-and-Selkirk), both of which had a long Liberal tradition; and they also gained the suburban seat of Cheadle. The Liberal performance in 1966 can be viewed in two ways. In the country as a whole, their vote dropped; but in their strongholds it often went up, and the Liberals gained on balance 2 seats. Therefore the election could be viewed either as a very small step forward, or as another stage in the long Liberal decline.

Labour won fewer agricultural and middle-class seats in 1966 than it had won in 1945. The relative agricultural revival under the Conservatives probably accounted for the hesitancy of such seats to swing to Labour. The middle-class seats did not turn to Labour either, because the marked Liberal revival among middle-class voters split the anti-Conservative vote. In 1945, there had been no such revival, and Labour had been able to capture many protest votes in middle-class seats.[7]

1 See map, Swing to Labour, 1964-1966, p. 81
2 Liberal M.P.s for Central Hull and Oxford
3 Liberal M.P.s for Stretford and Heywood-and-Radcliffe
4 Liberal candidate for Brighton 1922
5 See maps on pp. 79 and 81 for a full discussion of this
6 The results of the 2 polls were:

1955

	Social classes			
	A and B	C1	C2	D and E
Conservative	85	70	35	30
Labour	10	25	60	65
Liberal	5	5	5	5

Source: M. Abrams, 'Class Distinctions in Britain,' *Future of the Welfare State,* Conservative Political Centre, 1958

1966	A and B	C1	C2	D and E
Conservative	72	59	33	26
Labour	16	30	59	65
Liberal	12	11	8	7

Source: Butler and King, *British General Election of 1966,* 264

Change, 1955-1966	A and B	C1	C2	D and E
Conservative	−13	−11	−2	−4
Labour	+4	+5	−1	nil
Liberal	+7	+6	+3	+2

7 See map, General Election of 1945, p. 57

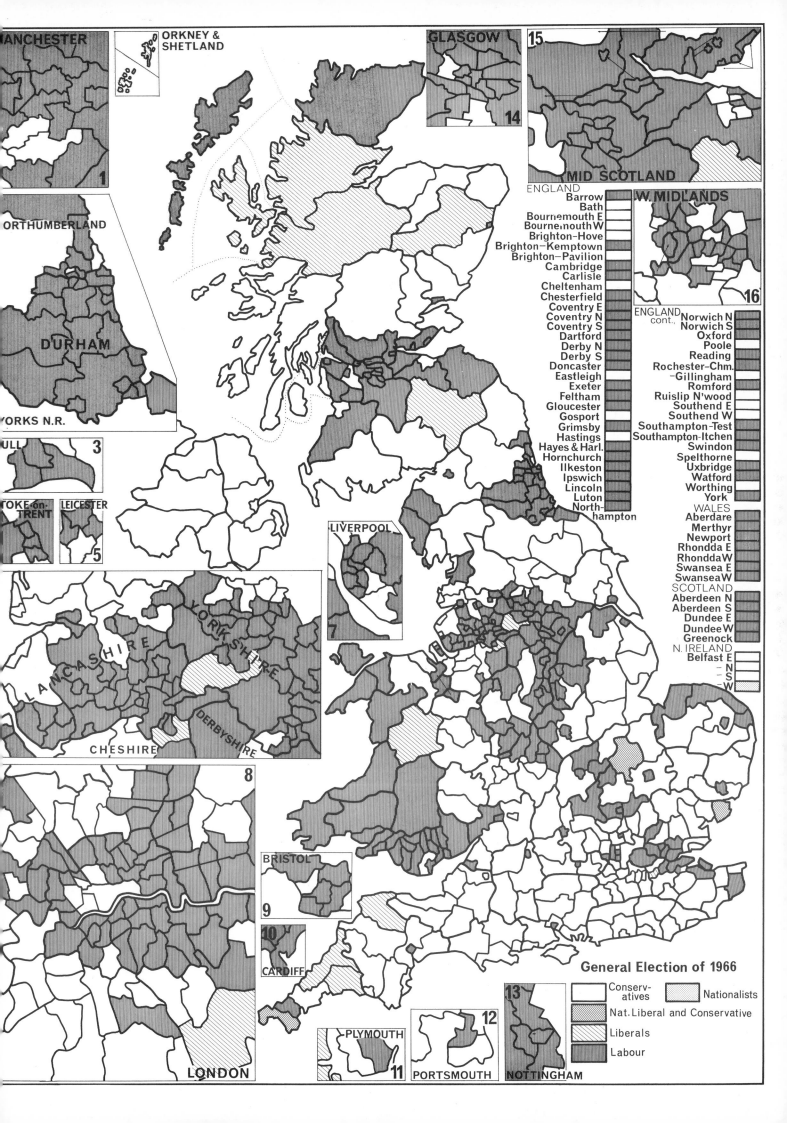

MANCHESTER

ORKNEY & SHETLAND

GLASGOW

15

NORTHUMBERLAND

DURHAM

MID SCOTLAND

W. MIDLANDS

16

YORKS N.R.

HULL

3

STOKE-on-TRENT

LEICESTER

5

LANCASHIRE

YORKSHIRE

DERBYSHIRE

CHESHIRE

LIVERPOOL

7

8

BRISTOL

9

10

CARDIFF

13

12

PLYMOUTH

11

PORTSMOUTH

NOTTINGHAM

LONDON

ENGLAND
Barrow
Bath
Bournemouth E
Bournemouth W
Brighton–Hove
Brighton–Kemptown
Brighton–Pavilion
Cambridge
Carlisle
Cheltenham
Chesterfield
Coventry E
Coventry N
Coventry S
Dartford
Derby N
Derby S
Doncaster
Eastleigh
Exeter
Feltham
Gloucester
Gosport
Grimsby
Hastings
Hayes & Harl.
Hornchurch
Ilkeston
Ipswich
Lincoln
Luton
North-
hampton

ENGLAND cont.,
Norwich N
Norwich S
Oxford
Poole
Reading
Rochester–Chm.
–Gillingham
Romford
Ruislip N'wood
Southend E
Southend W
Southampton-Test
Southampton-Itchen
Swindon
Spelthorne
Uxbridge
Watford
Worthing
York

WALES
Aberdare
Merthyr
Newport
Rhondda E
Rhondda W
Swansea E
Swansea W

SCOTLAND
Aberdeen N
Aberdeen S
Dundee E
Dundee W
Greenock

N. IRELAND
Belfast E
– N
– S
– W

General Election of 1966

Conservatives

Nationalists

Nat. Liberal and Conservative

Liberals

Labour

Effect of the Redistribution of 1918 on December 1910 Results

Between 1885 and 1918 there was no redistribution of seats, but there was a substantial redistribution of population. By 1915 the largest seat, Romford, had 36 times as many voters as the smallest, Kilkenny.[1] The biggest increases in population came in the suburbs of Birmingham, Glasgow, Liverpool and especially London. All the areas involved except the suburbs of Glasgow were strongly Unionist, and it is not surprising to find that when new seats were formed in these areas, practically all of them voted Unionist. On the other hand, the areas of greatest population decline from 1885 to 1915 were rural Scotland, Wales and Southern Ireland, none of which had elected many Unionist M.P.s in December 1910.

Despite the fact that the Unionists held 9 of the 13 largest seats[2] in December 1910, the electoral system caused the Unionists little hardship. If Southern Ireland is excluded from the calculations and only Great Britain and Northern Ireland are considered, the Unionists won 47·3% of the vote and 48·2% of the seats in December 1910. The distribution of seats in Great Britain and Northern Ireland therefore gave the Unionists a slight advantage over their opponents. The reason for this is that the Unionists won many small seats which counterbalanced their victories in the very large seats so that there was little net disadvantage to them.

A valid Unionist complaint was that Southern Ireland was grossly over-represented. With only 7% of the population it had 11·5% of the seats. In a redistribution strictly according to population, Southern Ireland would have lost exactly 30 seats; but according to the Home Rule Bill of 1912, Southern Ireland would have lost 48 seats, all of them Nationalists.[3] This Home Rule Bill would have become operative in any election held after 1914, but it was suspended for the duration of the War. If the Home Rule Bill had been applied, the effect on representation in the House of Commons would have been:

party	no Home Rule Bill	Home Rule Bill applied
Unionist	272	263
Liberal and Labour	314	313
Nationalist	84	32

The net effect of the Home Rule Bill would therefore have been to cut the majority of the Liberals and their allies over the Unionists from 126 to 80. This assumes that in all other respects, the distribution of votes remained unchanged from the election of December 1910.

By comparing the electoral map of December 1910 with the redistribution map of 1918 it is possible to estimate where party gains and losses would occur. If there were no changes in the results of the December 1910 election, the division of a Unionist seat into 2 seats would result in one Unionist gain. For example, the Unionist seat of Wandsworth was divided into 4 new seats. If the Unionist vote had been distributed evenly throughout the old constituency in December 1910, then the result of the re-distribution in Wandsworth would be 3 Unionist gains. Similarly, if a Unionist seat with a small majority were joined to a Liberal seat with a larger majority, the net result would be a Unionist loss. For example, Kings Lynn, with a Unionist majority of 97, was joined to the seat of Norfolk North-west, with a Liberal majority of 1,143. Assuming there was no change from the result of the December 1910 election in either seat, the result would be a Unionist loss of one seat.

In some places the estimate of the effect of redistribution is more complex. For instance, the Liberal seat of Romford was divided into 4 smaller seats: East Ham North and South, Romford and Ilford. East Ham North and South and Romford were slums similar to West Ham and Poplar, while Ilford was primarily a suburb similar to other suburbs in the southern and north-western parts of London. Probably, the Unionists would win in Ilford,[4] and the Liberals would win the other 3 seats.[5] Similarly South-east Durham was divided into 2 seats, the mining seat of Seaham and the partly agricultural seat of Sedgefield. As other agricultural seats in the area had voted Unionist in December 1910, while the mining seats had voted Liberal, the result of the division was probably that Sedgefield would go Unionist while Seaham would go Liberal.[6] The Appendix is based on calculations similar to those preceding.

The Home Rule Bill of 1912 was not applied in the redistribution of 1918. Instead, the worst anomalies of the existing distribution within Ireland were removed while the total number of Irish seats remained at 101.[7] The result was a net loss of 6 Nationalist seats, and a gain of 6 for the Unionists, as indicated in the Appendix. In England, Wales and Scotland the net effect of the redistribution was to add 27 more Unionist, 5 more Labour, and 3 more Liberal seats. One Unionist and one Nationalist seat were added in the University section. If the election of December 1910 had been fought on the revised boundaries, the result would have been:

party	no redistribution	redistribution applied
Unionist	272	306
Liberal and Labour	314	322
Nationalist	84	79

As the table shows, if the revised boundaries were applied, and there were no change from the December 1910 voting pattern, the Government majority would be cut from 126 to 95. However, there were significant changes in voting patterns between December

---

1 Romford had 60,878 voters and a population of 312,804; Kilkenny had 1,702 voters and a population of 13,112
2 The 9 Unionist seats were: Bootle, Cardiff, Croydon, Ealing, Enfield, Harrow, Lewisham, Wimbledon and Wandsworth. The 4 Liberal seats were Romford, Tottenham, Walthamstow and West Ham South. All had a population of at least 158,000
3 J. H. Campbell, *Guide to the Home Rule Bill, 1912*, 78-82. The total effect of this Bill on Irish representation would have been:

S. Ireland – 48 Nationalist losses
N. Ireland – 4 Nationalist, one Liberal and 9 Unionist losses
4 Ilford elected a Conservative in every election from 1918 to 1966, except 1945
5 Liberals won all 3 seats in 1918
6 In 1918 Sedgefield voted Conservative while Seaham voted Liberal
7 The Unionists and Nationalists gained one University seat each in Ireland. These are tabulated under extra University seats

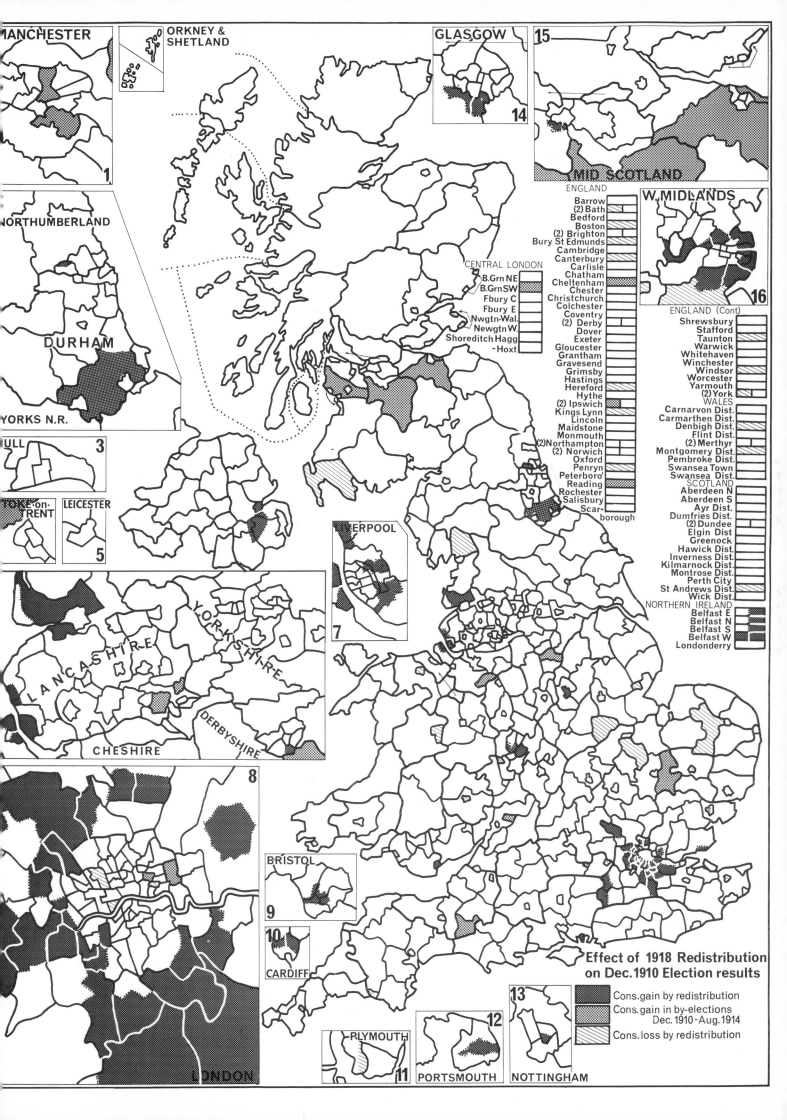

MANCHESTER

1

ORKNEY & SHETLAND

GLASGOW

14

15

MID SCOTLAND

NORTHUMBERLAND

DURHAM

YORKS N.R.

HULL

3

W. MIDLANDS

16

STOKE-on-TRENT

LEICESTER

5

LIVERPOOL

7

LANCASHIRE

YORKSHIRE

CHESHIRE

DERBYSHIRE

8

BRISTOL

9

10

CARDIFF

13

12

PLYMOUTH

11

PORTSMOUTH

NOTTINGHAM

LONDON

**Effect of 1918 Redistribution
on Dec. 1910 Election results**

■ Cons. gain by redistribution

▨ Cons. gain in by-elections
Dec. 1910-Aug. 1914

▧ Cons. loss by redistribution

1910 and the outbreak of the First World War. In that period the Liberals lost 16 by-elections to the Unionists, 9 of them in the 3 areas of East Lancashire, East London and Mid-Scotland. In the absence of any statistical evidence to the contrary, one must assume that the Unionists would continue to hold the seats they had won in by-elections. This would have reduced the Government majority from 95 to 65.[1]

A further factor must be noted. In East Lancashire, East London and Mid-Scotland the by-elections indicated that a general election would result in a Unionist landslide in each area. In Mid-Scotland the swing against the Liberals was not only strong. It was intensified by Labour intervention in most by-elections after 1912. The result was that in the 10 by-elections in Mid-Scotland, the Liberals did very badly. In 3 of the 4 contested by Labour as well as by Liberals, the Unionists won. Two of these seats, Midlothian and Leith, had been Liberal without a break from 1885 to December 1910.[2] In the other 6 seats, which were not contested by Labour, the average swing from the Liberals was 4·8%.[3] If Labour continued to intervene on a large scale, and if the swing from the Liberals extended to other seats in the region, the Unionists stood to gain between 15 and 20 seats.

In East Lancashire the swings against the Liberals were almost the same as in Mid-Scotland, 4·9%.[4] Such a trend, if extended to other seats in East Lancashire, would cost the Liberals between 15 and 20 seats on the revised distribution. In East London the average swing was slightly higher, 5·5% to the Unionists.[5] Such a swing, if extended to other seats in East London, would give the Unionists 13 gains.

If all these regional and by-election trends remained as favourable to the Unionists as the by-elections indicated, the net result would be Unionist gains of between 49 and 69 seats.[6] This would give the Unionists between 355 and 375 seats. In the House of Commons after the redistribution of 1918, 354 seats were required for a clear majority over all other parties.

Although these calculations are all hypothetical, they are the most likely results of trends observable in the period between December 1910 and mid-1914. There is no guarantee that these trends would have continued in the general election due in 1914 or 1915, but it is possible to compare the results of the 1918 election with those predicted on the basis of pre-war trends. To do this, we must eliminate seats where Unionist gains were predicted but where the Unionists backed Liberals in 1918. For example, pre-war trends indicated a Unionist victory in Glasgow–Cathcart; but in the 1918 election the Unionists backed the Coalition Liberal, so that it is not possible to say whether the Unionists would have won if they had put up a candidate. By eliminating the few seats in such categories, it is possible to arrive at the following prediction, assuming there had been no change whatever in the electoral structure of Britain between 1914 and 1918:

Unionist gains	15–20	in Mid-Scotland
	15–20	in East Lancashire
	13	in East London
	47	by redistribution
	6	in scattered by-election wins, 1911-14
	———	
	96–106	
Unionist losses	14	by redistribution

Net Unionist gains 82–92

1 The Unionists lost one by-election to the Nationalists, so that their net gain was 15, which made a difference of 30 on a division
2 The seat remaining Liberal was North-East Lanark. There, the Liberal majority was cut from 2,706 to 1,200
3 Swings against the Liberals in Mid-Scottish by-elections were: −2·3% in Tradeston; −3·4% Govan; −2·1% N. Ayrshire; −8·0% Edinburgh East; −4·4% St. Rollox; −8·4% Linlithgow

The result of the 1918 election indicates that all 6 by-election victories remained Unionist;[7] that 44 of the 47 predicted Unionist gains by redistribution went Unionist; that 12 of the 14 predicted Unionist losses by redistribution went Liberal or Labour while 2 went Unionist; and that Unionists gained 50 in the 3 areas of East London, Mid-Scotland and East Lancashire,[8] for a total net gain of 84. This compares very closely with the prediction. In the election of 1918 the Unionists won 108 more seats than they had in December 1910. According to the previous calculations 84 of these gains can be attributed to pre-war factors, leaving only 24 attributable to other factors. Since so few may be attributed to other factors, it seems improbable that the election of 1918 was won by the Unionists primarily because of the War,[9] or the use of the 'coupon'.[10]

Probable net effect of the 1918 redistribution

county	Unionist	Lab.	Lib.
Berkshire	−1	—	—
Cambridgeshire	—	—	−1
Cheshire	2	—	−1
Cornwall	−1	—	−1
Cumberland	—	−1	—
Devon	−1	—	−1
Derbyshire	—	—	1
Durham	1	1	1
Essex	1	1	5
Gloucestershire	1	—	—
Hampshire–Wight	1	—	—
Herefordshire	−1	—	—
Hertfordshire	1	—	—
Huntingdonshire	−1	—	—
Kent	1	—	—
Lancashire	4	—	4
Leicestershire	—	—	1*
Lincolnshire	−2	—	−1
London	6	—	−3
Middlesex	9	—	1
Monmouthshire	—	2	—
Norfolk	−2	—	—
Northamptonshire	—	—	−2
Northumberland	1	1*	—
Nottinghamshire	1	—	1
Oxfordshire	—	—	−1
Shropshire	—	—	−1
Somerset	−2	—	−1
Staffordshire	2	1	−2
Suffolk	−1	—	−1
Surrey	4	—	—
Warwickshire	5	—	—
Westmorland	−1	—	—
Wiltshire	−1	—	1
Worcestershire	−2	—	—
Yorkshire	—	—	5
Wales (excl. Mon.)	—	—	−3
Scotland	—	—	1
N. Ireland	6	—	—	−1 Nationalist
S. Ireland	—	—	—	−5 Nationalist
Universities	4	—	1	1 Nationalist
Total	**34**	**5**	**3**	**−5**

Total number of seats added: 37

* Might be Liberal or Labour gain of one

4 Swings against the Liberals in East Lancashire had been: −1·4% Middleton; −11·0% Manchester South; −8·1% Manchester North-west; −1·0% Bolton; −3·2% Altrincham
5 Swings against the Liberals in East London had been: +0·4% West Ham North; −5·3% Bethnal Green South-west; −8·5% Hackney South; −6·7% Whitechapel; −2·0% Bethnal Green South-west (second by-election). In Bow and Bromley there had been a swing against Labour of 10·7% in a straight fight with a Unionist. this swing is not counted in the London average
6 15-20 in Mid-Scotland; 15-20 East Lancashire; 13 East London; 6 other by-election gains
7 The Unionists lost 3 seats they had won in by-elections, 2 because they supported a Coalition Liberal in 1918, and the third because there was a Unionist split in 1918. These 3 by-elections are not listed above
8 20 in Mid-Scotland, 18 in East Lancashire, 12 in East London
9 As suggested by T. Wilson, *Downfall of the Liberal Party*, 15-8
10 As suggested by J. M. Robertson, *Mr. Lloyd George and Liberalism*, 91-2; and H. H. Asquith, *Memories and Reflections*, II, 238-9

Turnout in the Elections of 1918, 1922, 1966 and 1979

The elections considered in these 4 maps are the first 2 where universal male suffrage applied, and 2 recent ones.[1] As 61 years separate the first from the last, one would expect many changes in the regional variation in turnout. There were some changes, but the basic pattern was similar in all 4 elections. The areas of high turnout included Northwest Yorkshire, Northeast Lancashire, the Southwest, and the Northampton District. Areas of low turnout in all 4 elections included the Southeast, Central London, Liverpool, Birmingham, and rural Scotland. Only in the case of rural Scotland is it likely that geographical factors such as weather and distance caused low turnout.[2]

There may have been a connection between working-class areas and low turnout in these elections, but it was not universal. In London, the connection was clearer than elsewhere: in 1918, turnout was lowest in Bethnal Green and neighbouring slum seats; next-lowest in slightly more prosperous nearby seats; and highest in the outer suburbs. This pattern in London was also noticeable in the other 3 elections. The 1966 and 1979 similarities may have been due to the fact that by that time, the seats in London with a low turnout were nearly all safely Conservative or Labour. But the degree of safeness was not decisive in London in 1918 or 1922, since most slum seats there changed hands several times in the 1920s, and still had low turnout. A more likely explanation for higher turnout in the suburbs is that working-class voters in the core were more apathetic than middle-class suburban voters. This was borne out by numerous opinion polls.[3] The opinion polls may merely have reflected the fact that by the 1960s, predominantly working-class seats were safely Labour, while seats with mixed populations were more marginal. Thus what seemed to be working-class apathy may have shown that workers lived in safe Labour seats, not that the working-class as a whole was more apathetic than other groups. The low turnout in all these elections in the few core-area seats with a high middle class component tends to confirm this: where the seats were overwhelmingly safe for the Conservatives, turnout was often low despite the high middle-class percentage. An examination of voter apathy in safe and unsafe seats must be made before drawing firm conclusions about working-class apathy in elections, even where those conclusions seem to be backed up by evidence from opinion polls.

In 1918 and 1922 the working class was apparently more apathetic in some places than in others. In the 2 elections there was above average turnout in most mining seats and in Glasgow than in the country as a whole; yet the mining areas and Glasgow were strongly working class.[4] The high turnout in the 2 groups of seats may have been the reason why Labour displaced the other parties there sooner than in most other places. There is no reason to assume that the working-class vote behaved in a uniform manner throughout the country, in respect to turnout at any rate. This was more noticeable in 1918 and 1922 than in 1966 or 1979; but even in 1979, the question of the uniformity of working-class turnout remains open.

In all 4 elections, the textile areas of West Yorkshire and eastern Lancashire had above average turnout. This was partly because the areas had many marginal seats in all the elections; but partly it was because the areas were apparently more politically conscious than most others. A comparison of the turnout maps with those showing the growth of the local Labour Party organisations shows that the textile districts contained many of the earliest divisional Labour Parties. It may also be significant that the textile areas had a high proportion of Nonconformists and a long Liberal tradition prior to 1918.

Another possible influence in the 4 elections was the Liberal vote. Where there was a Liberal tradition, turnout was usually higher than where there was not. The southwest, the Yorkshire-Lancashire textile districts, and Wales all had Liberal traditions and high turnout in most if not all of the elections considered here. On the other hand, western Lancashire, the southeast, Birmingham, and the area between Lincoln and Scarborough all had a Conservative tradition before 1918, and low turnout. It is not possible to calculate the precise effect of the presence or absence of Liberal candidates on turnout,[5] but the overall impression is that places with a Liberal tradition and a Liberal candidate usually had a high turnout as well, regardless of the social or economic makeup of the constituency.

Some changes may be seen between the turnout in 1918-22 and in 1966-79. In the earlier years, turnout was high in the mining seats and Glasgow, probably because of intense Labour Party activity there. By 1966, these places contained many of the safest Labour seats in the country, so that Labour voters probably did not feel the need to vote as keenly as in more closely fought seats. In some seats in the Black Country, a similar situation caused a relatively high turnout in 1918 and 1922, and a fairly low turnout in both 1966 and 1979.

It should not be assumed that turnout in every election between 1918 and 1979 showed the same variations as those indicated in these maps. A wide variety of factors affect turnout, and these change with each election. Nevertheless, the basic similarity of the patterns of turnout in each of the four elections considered is very striking.

---

1 The statistics on which the maps are based can be found in Kinnear, *General Election of 1922*, and *The Times Guide to the House of Commons* for 1966 and 1979. The statistics for 1918 and 1922 for 2-membered seats take 'plumpers' (people who voted for only one candidate) into account. There were 88,103 plumpers in 1918, and 122,721 in 1922, compared with 288,382 people voting for 2 candidates in 1918, and 498,751 in 1922. Kinnear, *General Election of 1922*, Appendix XXX
2 In 1918 and 1922 the elections were held in December and November respectively, and cold weather affected many of the widely-scattered seats in rural Scotland more than it did in more southerly seats. Even there, political influences may have been decisive, since many seats in Scotland had either no Liberal or no Conservative candidates in 1918-22; and strong third and fourth parties in 1979

3 See, for example, Butler and King, *British General Election of 1964,* 294
4 It has been calculated that in 1966, in the 31 seats where Liberals intervened, turnout rose by 0·7%, while in the 84 seats where they withdrew, turnout fell by 2·6%. However, three-quarters of the Liberal withdrawals were in Labour seats, and turnout fell in Labour seats generally in 1966, whether or not the Liberals withdrew. In 1970, the differential between seats with Liberal interventions and withdrawals was 3·2%; in February 1974, Liberals withdrew in only 11 seats, so it would be misleading to calculate an average differential. In October 1974, there were no Liberal withdrawals, but turnout dropped by only 4·5% in seats with Liberal interventions compared with a drop of 6·3% in all seats. Butler, *et. al., The British General Election of 1966,* 273-275; *BGE of 1970,* 388; *BGE of October 1974,* 334

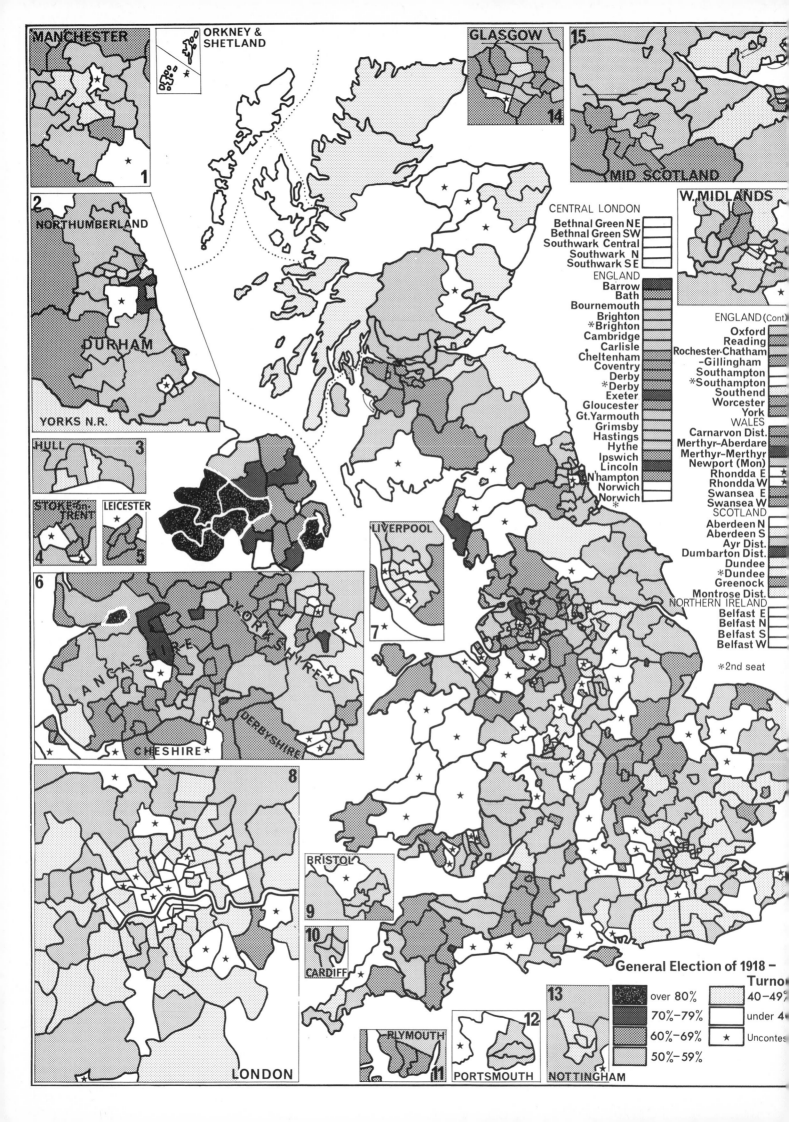

MANCHESTER

ORKNEY & SHETLAND

1

GLASGOW

15

14

MID SCOTLAND

2

NORTHUMBERLAND

DURHAM

YORKS N.R.

W. MIDLANDS

HULL **3**

STOKE-on-TRENT **4**

LEICESTER **5**

6

LANCASHIRE

YORKSHIRE

CHESHIRE

DERBYSHIRE

LIVERPOOL

7

CENTRAL LONDON
Bethnal Green NE
Bethnal Green SW
Southwark Central
Southwark N
Southwark S E

ENGLAND
Barrow
Bath
Bournemouth
Brighton
*Brighton
Cambridge
Carlisle
Cheltenham
Coventry
Derby
*Derby
Exeter
Gloucester
Gt.Yarmouth
Grimsby
Hastings
Hythe
Ipswich
Lincoln
N'hampton
Norwich
Norwich

ENGLAND (Cont)
Oxford
Reading
Rochester-Chatham
-Gillingham
Southampton
*Southampton
Southend
Worcester
York
WALES
Carnarvon Dist.
Merthyr-Aberdare
Merthyr-Merthyr
Newport (Mon)
Rhondda E   ★
Rhondda W   ★
Swansea E
Swansea W
*
SCOTLAND
Aberdeen N
Aberdeen S
Ayr Dist.
Dumbarton Dist.
Dundee
*Dundee
Greenock
Montrose Dist.
NORTHERN IRELAND
Belfast E
Belfast N
Belfast S
Belfast W

*2nd seat

8

9 BRISTOL

10 CARDIFF

12 PORTSMOUTH

11 PLYMOUTH

13 NOTTINGHAM

LONDON

General Election of 1918 –
Turno

over 80%   40–49%
70%–79%   under 4
60%–69%   ★ Uncontes
50%–59%

General
Election of 1922 –Turnout

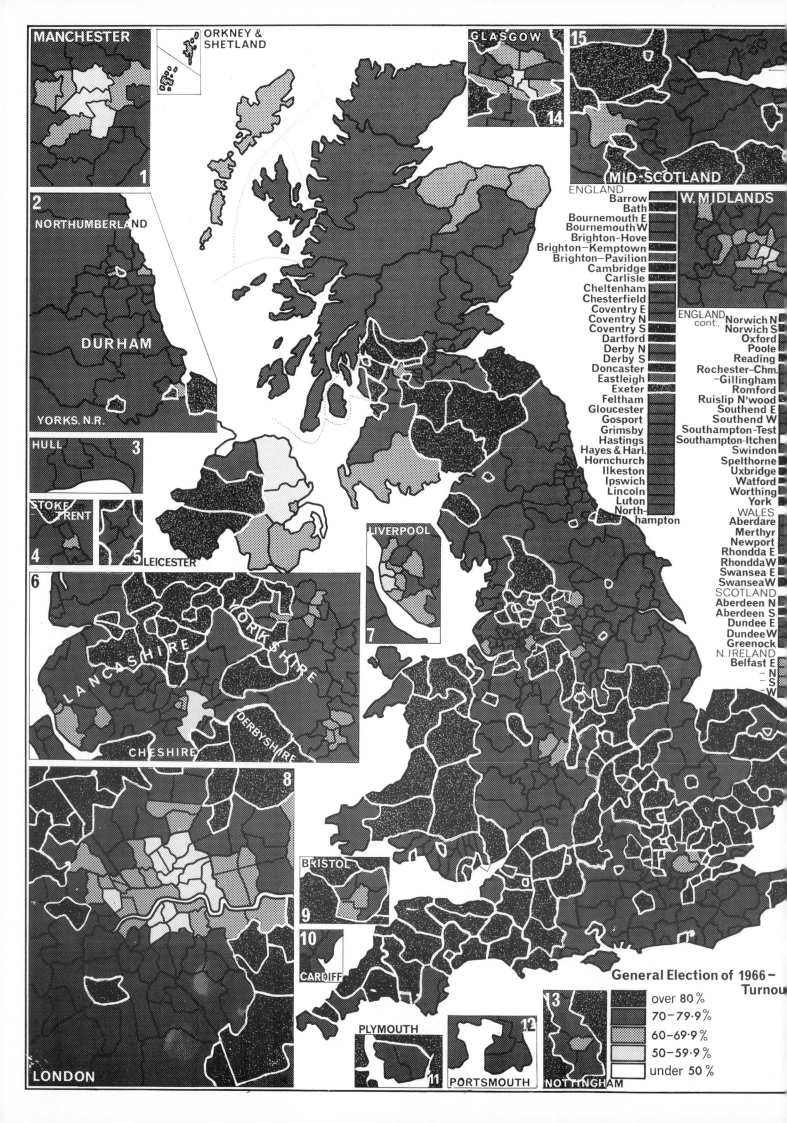

MANCHESTER **1**

ORKNEY & SHETLAND

2
NORTHUMBERLAND

DURHAM

YORKS. N.R.

HULL **3**

STOKE TRENT

4

5 LEICESTER

6

LANCASHIRE

YORKSHIRE

CHESHIRE

DERBYSHIRE

8

LIVERPOOL

7

GLASGOW

14

15

MID·SCOTLAND

W. MIDLANDS

8

BRISTOL **9**

10
CARDIFF

13

PLYMOUTH

12

11 PORTSMOUTH

NOTTINGHAM

LONDON

General Election of 1966 –
Turnou

over 80 %
70–79·9 %
60–69·9 %
50–59·9 %
under 50 %

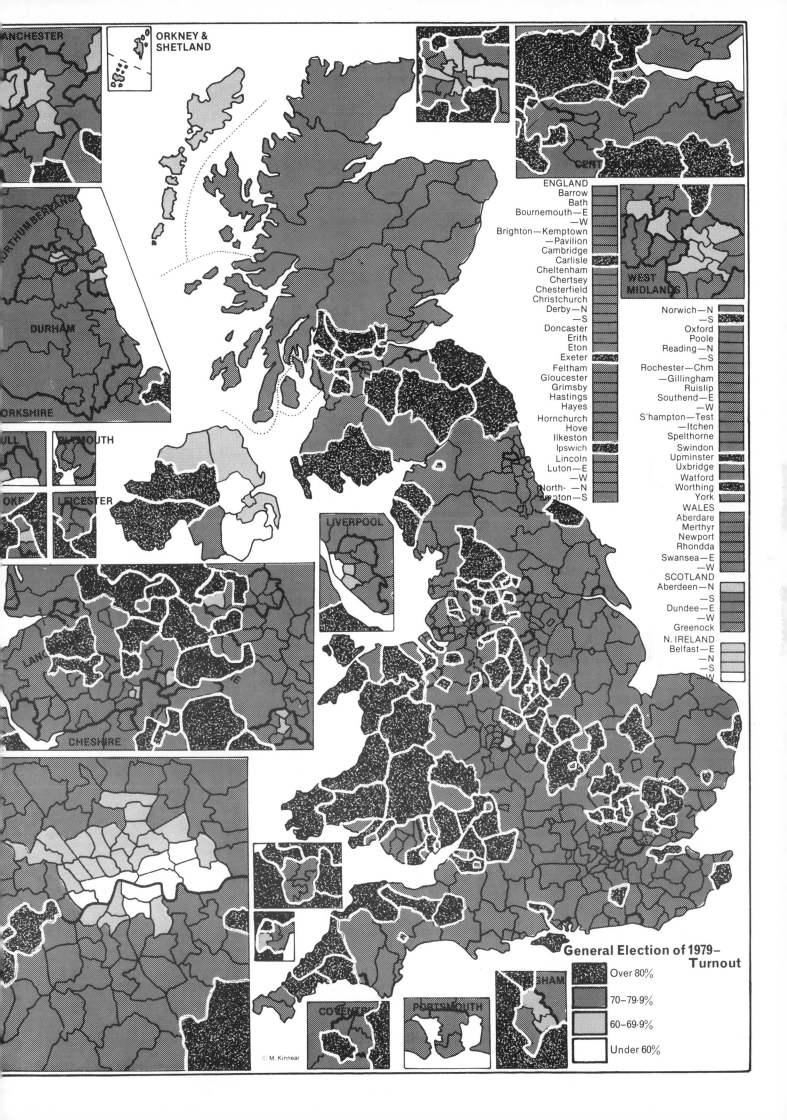

Swing to Labour 1959-64[1]

The figure showing the average swing to Labour throughout Britain was less meaningful for 1964 than similar figures had been for the elections of 1955 and 1959. In 1955 half the constituencies had had swings within 1% of the national average; in 1959 half had had swings within 1·25%; but in 1964 half had swings within 1·75%.[2] Although this showed an increasing tendency for constituencies to diverge from the national average, there was no return to the extremely wide variations of the pre-1931 period. In 1964 some fairly clear regional trends can be discerned. A Gallup Poll published in the *Sunday Telegraph* for 11 October 1964 shows that the decisive factors affecting swing were associated either with economic problems or with the personalities of the party leaders. According to the persons interviewed, the significant changes between 1959 and 1964 were that Labour had made much progress in economic policies as well as in the field of party leadership. Although opinions of the party leaders may have differed throughout the country, it is more likely that variations in economic prosperity caused the variations in swing. For instance, there was an above average swing to Labour in the depressed areas of South-east and South-west Lancashire, the Scottish Highlands and Central Scotland. On the other hand, relative prosperity in the West Midlands and in agricultural seats probably contributed to the low swing to Labour. An additional factor of prejudice against immigrants may have aided the Conservatives in the West Midlands, but this was not the only explanation for the low swing to Labour there.[3]

The relatively low swing to Labour in most agricultural seats did not result from some permanently stable voting habits in such seats: before 1931 the same seats had changed hands more frequently than almost any other group of seats in the country. The relative stability in 1964 can be attributed to two factors, economic prosperity and the Liberal revival. Between 1959 and 1964 the increase in living standards of farmers and farm labourers was only marginally greater than the increase in such standards in the country as a whole.[4] However, this marked a change from the pre-1939 period, when agriculture had been in a long decline; and this may account for the apparent reluctance of the agricultural seats to swing towards Labour. Another influence was that the Liberals provided a real alternative to Labour in most of the seats involved. Some voters who might otherwise have switched directly from the Conservatives to Labour voted Liberal instead. The swing varied from one agricultural district to another, although it was below the national average in all of them. Part of this variation may have been due to regional differences in agricultural production, while part may have been due to differences in Liberal strength in the seats involved.[5] Since two factors could vary, perhaps in different ways in different places, it would be misleading to attempt to isolate either of them and maintain that it alone was decisive. For instance, the seats in the South-west and in East Anglia both showed low swings to Labour, although the Liberal vote was fairly high in the South-west and low in East Anglia. If these were the only 2 agricultural districts, one might be justified in assuming that Liberal strength made little difference to the swing. However, if one compares the South-west to the partly agricultural seats near Oxford, most of which had a low Liberal vote and an average swing to Labour, one might assume that the differences in Liberal strength were very significant in determining the swing. As it is, one must conclude that at least two variable factors were influential, and that the statistics do not allow one to state definitely which was decisive in any particular case. Until election figures are made available by polling division, such imprecision will remain.

The swing to Labour was above average in almost all large cities outside the West Midlands. Generally, there were higher swings on the declining fringes of the cities than in the centre or in the more prosperous suburbs. This is perhaps clearest in the case of London: there, the safe Labour seats in the East End showed very low swings to Labour, probably because their safeness encouraged apathy. The high swings in the outskirts were likely caused by an influx of Labour voters. Similar phenomena can be observed in most other large cities, although in Glasgow some fairly prosperous seats in the West–Central part of the city showed low swings to Labour, while slum districts in the East showed high swings. A small group of prosperous seats in the West End of London also had high swings to Labour, but in most of them local factors were probably decisive.[6]

---

1 'Swing' is defined for the purpose of the maps on pp. 79 and 81 as the mean of the Conservative % loss and the Labour % gain, both figures being percentages of the total vote cast. The two maps are based on statistics in *The Times Guide to the House of Commons, 1964*, 247-67. The swing in seats won by Liberals is calculated on the same basis as the swing in seats won by the Conservatives or Labour. The national average figures of swing in Great Britain were 2·9% in 1964 and 3·1% in 1966
2 R. Rose, 'The Voting Surveyed', in *The Times Guide to the House of Commons, 1964*, 240
3 Race relations, especially in the West Midlands, are examined in P. Foot, *Immigration and Race in British Politics* (Penguin Special, 1964), and in N. Deakin (ed.), *Colour and the British Electorate, 1964* (Pall Mall, 1965)

4 The average weekly earnings of agricultural labourers rose by 15% between 1959 and 1964, while the average weekly earnings of all workers, including agricultural workers, rose by only 14·7% in the same period (*Campaign Guide, 1964*, 125, 162, 177)
5 See map, The Liberal Vote in 1964, p. 87
6 In the Cities of London and Westminster the Speaker ran as an Independent, whereas he had run in 1959 as a Conservative; in St. Marylebone and Hampstead, two Conservative Ministers, Mr Quintin Hogg and Mr Henry Brooke, apparently had substantial adverse personal votes

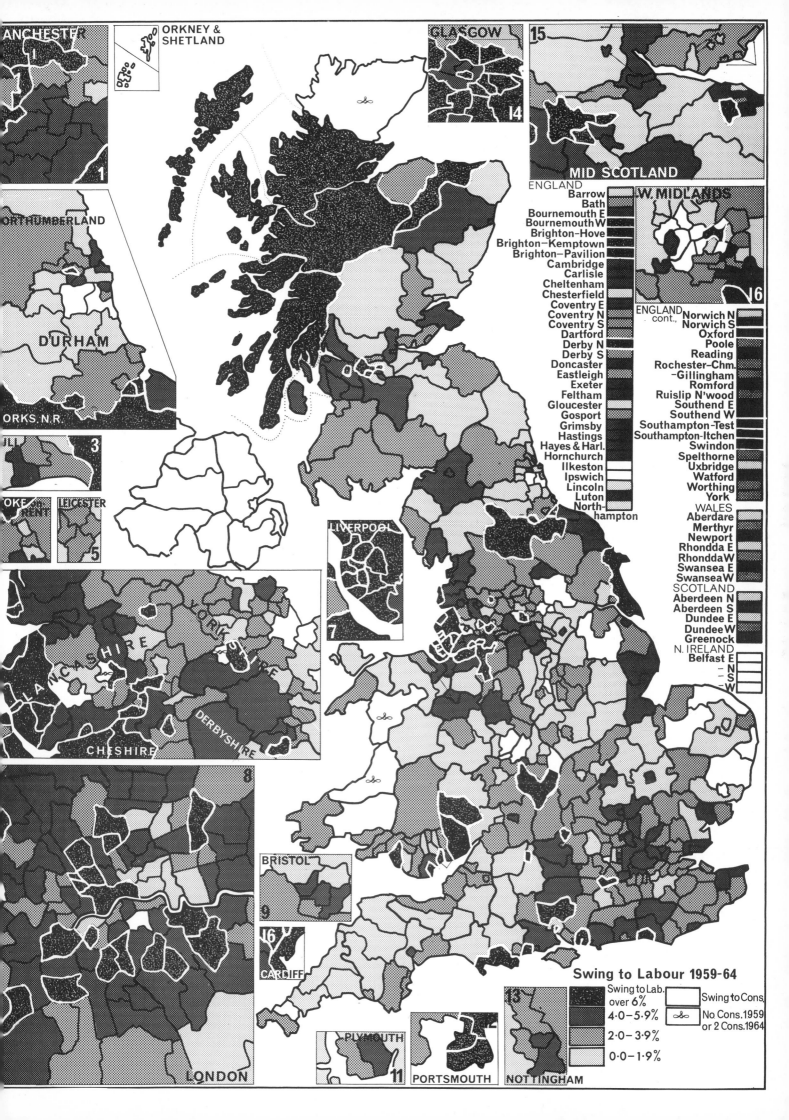

Swing to Labour 1964-66

In 1966 half the constituencies had swings within 1% of the national average of 3·1%. This compares closely with the election of 1955, when half the constituencies also had swings within 1% of the average, but it was a change from 1964, when half were within 1·75%.[1] Probably the swing to Labour was more nearly uniform in 1966 than in 1964 because no major changes had taken place between 1964 and 1966 in the patterns of regional economic prosperity. Consequently, national issues had roughly similar effects in most parts of the country.

Because the swing to Labour in 1966 was more uniform than it had been in 1964, exceptional areas stood out with greater clarity. Such areas included Birmingham, which had a low swing to Labour in 1964, and a high swing in 1966; East Anglia and the South-west, which had below average swings to Labour in both elections. The above average swing to Labour in 1966 in Birmingham, Leicestershire and some seats in London may be regarded as 'compensation' for the relatively low swings there in 1964. However, such 'compensation' did not form a noticeable pattern throughout the country. Groups of seats showing above average swings to Labour in both elections included the Southern outskirts of London, South-east and North-west Lancashire, and several seats around Hull. Even within those places there was often no relative 'compensation'. For example, the 2 seats with the highest swings in Manchester and Salford in 1964 were Blackley and Salford East. In 1966 both seats again had the highest swings to Labour in their cities. In Hull one seat had the highest swing in both elections. This was Hull West.

As in 1964 some Conservative candidates seemed to have strong adverse personal votes, because the swing against them in both 1964 and 1966 was noticeably higher than the swing in surrounding seats. Such Conservative candidates included Mr Brooke (Hampstead), Mr Berkeley (Lancaster) and Mr Thorneycroft (Monmouth). In St. Marylebone the high swing against Mr Hogg in 1964 was offset by a relatively low swing against him in 1966. Labour candidates apparently having adverse personal votes included Mr Brown (Belper), Mr Cousins (Nuneaton) and Mr Greenwood (Rossen-

dale). On the other hand, Mr Silverman's advocacy of the abolition of capital punishment seemed to do him little harm in Nelson and Colne.

There was no clear relationship between turnout and the swing to Labour. Figures for the swing to Labour in all seats with increased or decreased turnout indicate that the mean swing to Labour was usually higher where turnout increased, and lower where it decreased. Labour may well have suffered more than the Conservatives from increased turnout, but the statistics contain so many exceptions that one cannot state definitely that this was the case.[2]

There was also no clear evidence that the Liberal vote came primarily from one party or the other. In the 84 seats where Liberals ran in 1964, but not in 1966, there was a below-average swing to Labour. This apparently shows that when Liberal voters were faced with a choice, they favoured the Conservatives. On the other hand, in the 25 seats with an increase in the Liberal vote, there was a below average swing to Labour. This apparently shows that the Liberal votes came more from Labour than from the Conservatives. These two phenomena can be reconciled if one assumes that Liberal voters in different parts of the country behaved in slightly different ways. There is, indeed, no reason to suppose that they behaved in a more uniform manner than Conservative or Labour voters. In connection with this, it should be noted that three-quarters of the seats where the Liberals withdrew were won by Labour in 1966. Many were safe Labour seats where the Liberal vote had been small in 1964. On the other hand, Labour won only 5 of the 25 seats where the Liberal vote rose, and 3 of the 5 were in Wales. Most of the remaining 20 were either won by Liberals or had had a strong Liberal vote in 1964. The below-average swing to Labour in the seats examined therefore reflects Liberal behaviour in only 2 general groups of seats, that is, in Labour strongholds, and in seats where the Liberals had done well in 1964. This is insufficient evidence to allow one to draw firm conclusions about the behaviour of Liberal voters in the country as a whole.

---

1 R. Rose, 'The Voting Surveyed', *Times Guide to the House of Commons, 1966*, 234
2 According to Butler and King, *The British General Election of 1966*, 273, in 163 seats with increased turnout, the mean swing to Labour was 3·7%; in 324 where turnout decreased by up to 2·9%, the mean swing was 3·5%; and in the 130 where turnout decreased by more than 3·0%, the mean swing was 3·1%. However, there was wide variation within the three groups, as is demonstrated clearly by the complete table in *ibid.*, 273

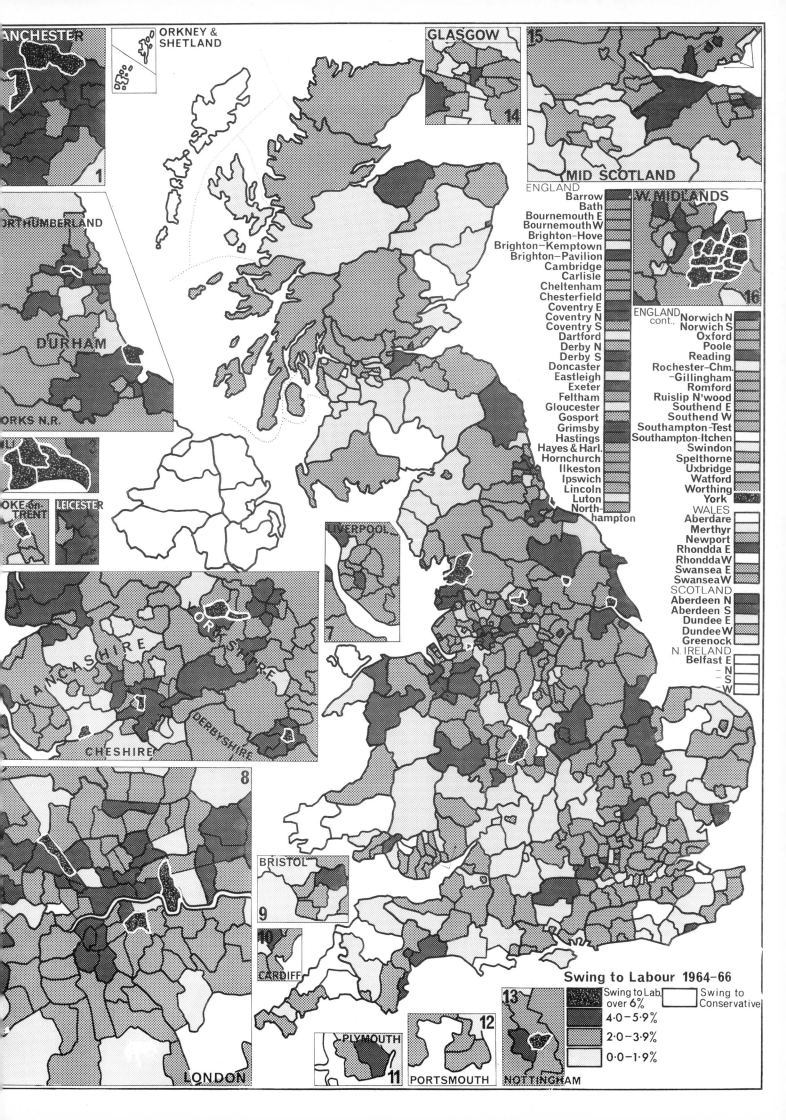

Liberal Seats 1885 — December 1910

Between 1885 and December 1910 the Liberals were very weak in most of the large cities, and strong in mining districts and in the rural areas of Scotland and Wales. Nearly all the Liberal victories in the large cities were in slum areas; only occasionally did the Liberals do well in middle-class urban districts. Of the 11 largest cities in Great Britain the Liberals won only Edinburgh in all elections in this period; and in the remaining 10 they normally won a majority of the seats in only 2.[1] The Liberals were weakest of all in the 4 largest cities, London, Liverpool, Birmingham and Glasgow. As the Liberals were slightly to the left of the Unionists in this period, their weakness in large urban centres is at first surprising. Probably the Liberals did badly because a large number of out-voters[2] were registered in constituencies in large cities; in addition, many working-class men did not have the vote. If the principle of 'one man, one vote' had been established, Unionist predominance in many large cities probably would have been challenged severely.

The Liberals were weak in the suburbs of large cities and in heavily middle-class seats.[3] The areas where the middle class was strongest, that is the suburbs of Manchester and London, the South-east, some seats around Colchester and some more in the South-west, were less favourable to the Liberals than other nearby seats with fewer middle-class voters. Only in West Lancashire was the reverse apparently the case. Preston, Southport and Lancaster had more middle-class voters than most other seats in West Lancashire,[4] and they were also more favourable to the Liberals than neighbouring seats. This was also noticeable in the election of 1923, when the Liberal wins in West Lancashire virtually coincided with seats having over 20% of their population middle-class.[5]

Mining seats generally voted Liberal, but in some mining districts there was a distinct trend away from the Liberals towards Labour after 1906. The West Lancashire mining district had never voted Liberal between 1885 and 1906; but between 1906 and 1966 it voted Labour in every election. Trends to Labour were also noticeable in the mining areas of South Wales and West Yorkshire. In Durham and Northumberland, Labour was beginning to make headway by 1910, but the Liberals still predominated in the mining seats. In Derbyshire there was hardly any trend to Labour: the Derbyshire Miners' Federation had opposed affiliation with the Labour Party, and before the First World War the miners in Derbyshire were apparently committed strongly to the Liberals.[6] An official of the Derbyshire Miners' Federation sat as Liberal M.P. for Chesterfield until his retirement in 1929.

The numerous agricultural seats did not all vote in similar ways between 1885 and 1910. Those in Wales and Eastern Scotland were solidly Liberal in nearly every election, while those around Worcester, Exeter, York and Grantham were hardly ever Liberal. The agricultural belt in the South Midlands was sometimes Liberal and sometimes not. It was not an area on which the Liberals could depend in time of need, but one where they needed to show some strength if they were to win an election. The last time the Liberals won many seats in this district was in 1923, when they deprived the Conservatives of a majority. The Liberals also showed relatively more strength in East Anglia than they did in later years.

Although there was a connection between the percentage of Nonconformists and the areas of Liberal strength, it was not always straightforward. Between 1885 and 1910 the Liberals won all the English seats with over 15% Nonconformists in at least 7 of the 8 elections.[7] However, in the vast majority of English seats with under 15% Nonconformists, there was often little apparent connection between the degree of Nonconformity and the number of Liberal victories. For instance, in West Yorkshire the Liberals were as strong in the woollen as in the mining district, but the Nonconformists were much stronger in the woollen district. In Derbyshire, Durham and Northumberland the Liberals were as strong in seats with many Nonconformists as in those with relatively few. This does not indicate the lack of a connection between the Nonconformist vote and the Liberal vote; rather it indicates that the Liberals drew support from several different social groups. In the places mentioned the Liberals drew support from Nonconformists and miners, who were not necessarily the same people. The Nonconformist vote alone was hardly ever sufficient to bring about Liberal victories, and in most seats economic and other factors probably were decisive. However, the Nonconformists probably provided a useful base of Liberal support. Before 1918 the Nonconformists were only one group of many supporting the Liberals; after 1918 they were one of a very few groups, and their relative significance therefore grew. Because of this, the relation between Nonconformist and Liberalism became more apparent during the inter-war period.

In the rural areas supporting the Liberals, population was declining. A redistribution would take away many seats from them and increase the number of fast-growing Conservative suburbs. In addition, the Liberals depended on mining seats for much of their strength before 1910, and in most mining districts competition from Labour was increasing. Consequently, the Liberal proportion of seats in Parliament was bound to go down substantially.

---

1 Liberals won a majority of seats in all elections from 1885 to December 1910 in Edinburgh; in 7 of 8 in Leeds; in 6 in Bradford; in 4 in Nottingham and Bristol; in 3 in Manchester – Salford and Glasgow; in one in London and Birmingham; and in none in Sheffield and Liverpool
2 That is, persons possessing business, rather than residential qualifications for voting
3 See map, the Middle-Class Vote in 1921, p. 123

4 Blackpool had more than 30% middle-class voters in 1921, but before 1918 it had been part of Fylde, where there were under 20% middle-class voters
5 See map, General Election of 1923, p. 45
6 J. E. Williams, The Derbyshire Miners, 484-513, gives a full account of the political activities of the Federation before 1914
7 Based on the map on p. 127, which gives statistics for 1922 of the five largest Nonconformist groups

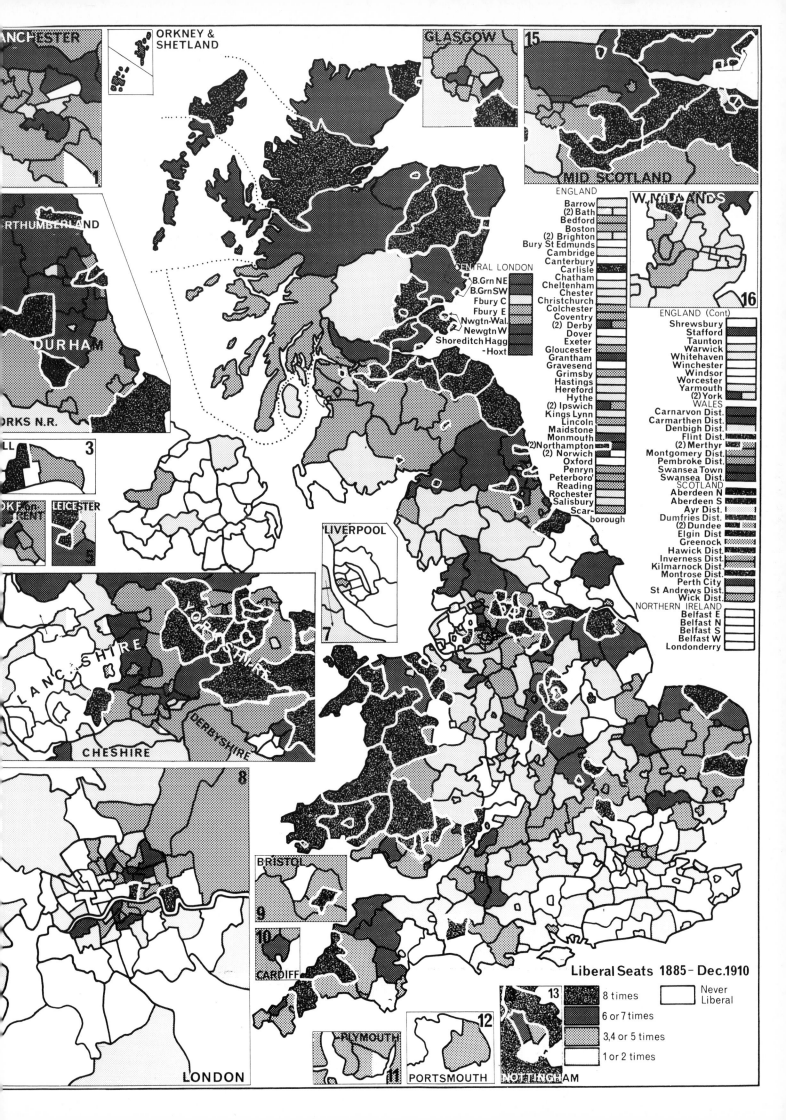

Liberal Seats 1885 – Dec.1910

Liberal Seats 1918-29

Although the 1920s are often considered a period of very rapid decline in Liberal fortunes, the party did well in the first 3 post-war elections. During the whole period 1918 to 1929 the Liberals won 281 seats at least once; this is only a few less than the 304 seats Labour won at least once in the same elections.[1] In normal times, if the Liberals won a seat at least once in a 10-year period, it generally indicated sufficient Liberal support for further victories in the same seat. The chief exceptions would be where the Liberal victory had been based on a freak split in the main opposition vote, or where it had been based on the personality of a Liberal candidate who was unable to contest the seat again because of death, illness or some other reason. Otherwise, the Liberals could have expected to win most of the 281 seats in a good year. They could also have expected to rely on nearly all the seats they won twice, and on at least half they won only once, in a moderate year. This would have given them about 210 seats. Yet the highest number of seats the Liberals won in any election in this period was only 163 in 1918.

The main problem for the Liberals was not winning seats once, but holding those they won. In the 1920s they won many seats which had eluded them in every election between 1885 and December 1910;[2] and they also held many mining and industrial seats which might have been expected to vote Labour at the first opportunity.[3] However, they rarely won those seats more than once. Several things may account for this ability to penetrate a wide variety of seats, and for the inability to retain them: individual candidates, the influence of protest votes, and the inconsistent Parliamentary policies of the Liberals all contributed.

Liberal candidates themselves were often important factors in providing the Liberal victories. For instance, Frank Gray cultivated Oxford assiduously from 1918 until his victory in 1922. Gray later said that he had visited every working-class house at least once and that he had preferred preparing meat teas for busy housewives to talking with them about the Ruhr.[4] His rewards were the only Liberal victories in Oxford between 1885 and 1979; but his victories meant that he had much less time to spend in his constituency, and if he had not been unseated for corruption Gray might well have had difficulty in retaining his seat. Other Liberals who were effective campaigners sometimes performed ineffectively in the Commons, and thereby lost some of the local goodwill which helped bring them victory in the first place.

A second reason for Liberal inability to retain seats was that they won many on a protest vote; if the Liberals were unable to remedy the situation causing the original protest, they were faced with a reaction. For instance, the Liberals won many agricultural seats in 1923, partly because of the continuing decline of farm prices from the very high levels of the immediate post-war period. In 1924 most of the agricultural seats went Conservative, perhaps because the farmers were disillusioned with the Liberals. It is interesting to note that a third of the English agricultural seats voting Liberal in 1929 had not gone Liberal in 1923, so that they had not had the chance to be disillusioned.

The failure of the Liberals to pursue a coherent policy in Parliament was also a great source of weakness. If they had acted consistently with the Conservatives or with Labour, the Liberals probably would have won fewer seats than they did, but they would have won them more often. As it was, many Liberals appeared in one election as partial supporters of Labour and in the next as partial supporters of the Conservatives. Such candidates could hardly expect to retain the trust of either party. However, some Liberals followed a consistent line, and were frequently successful. The Liberal M.P. for Central Hull, Cmdr J. M. Kenworthy, always sided with Labour and won every election he contested; in Bristol consistent co-operation between the local Liberals and Conservatives assured the Liberals of at least one seat in every election from 1918 to 1935, with the exception of 1929.

The map indicates that the Liberals retained substantial strength in nearly all the areas they had won before 1918. These areas represented about 30 fewer seats, however, because of the redistribution.[5] The only areas showing a major Liberal recession as compared with the pre-1918 period were mining seats and Central Scotland. In both groups of seats there had been a marked trend away from the Liberals before 1914, so that this cannot convincingly be attributed to the War. Otherwise, the Liberals remained relatively strong in all their old bailiwicks, the difference being that they seemed unable to win them more than once or twice.

In Scotland the division between East and West disappeared, and the Liberals were as strong in one side as in the other. The seat of Galloway, which had not voted Liberal between 1885 and 1918,[6] voted Liberal 3 times in the 1920s, indicating how much the electoral picture in Scotland had changed. The division in Scotland after 1918 was almost entirely that of urban against rural, with the Conservatives and Liberals alternating in the rural, and Labour remaining strong in the urban, districts.

In Wales the division between urban and rural areas was

---

1 The Conservatives won 445 seats in Great Britain at least once in the same elections. The overall figures (counting Independent Conservatives as Conservative wins, etc., and excluding Northern Ireland) were:

Times won	Conservatives	Liberals	Labour
5	154	22	49
4	105	19	63
3	76	34	48
2	54	69	53
1	56	137	91
nil	157	321	298

2 For instance, Finchley, Horncastle, Chelmsford, Tiverton, Liverpool – Wavertree, Bootle and Holderness
3 For instance, Lambeth North, Bethnal Green South-west, Spen Valley, Spennymoor, Barnsley, Greenock and Wolverhampton East
4 Gray, *Confession of a Candidate*, 38
5 See map, Redistribution of 1918, p. 71
6 Galloway had not existed as a seat before 1918, but its constituent parts, if grouped, had not given a Liberal majority between 1885 and 1910

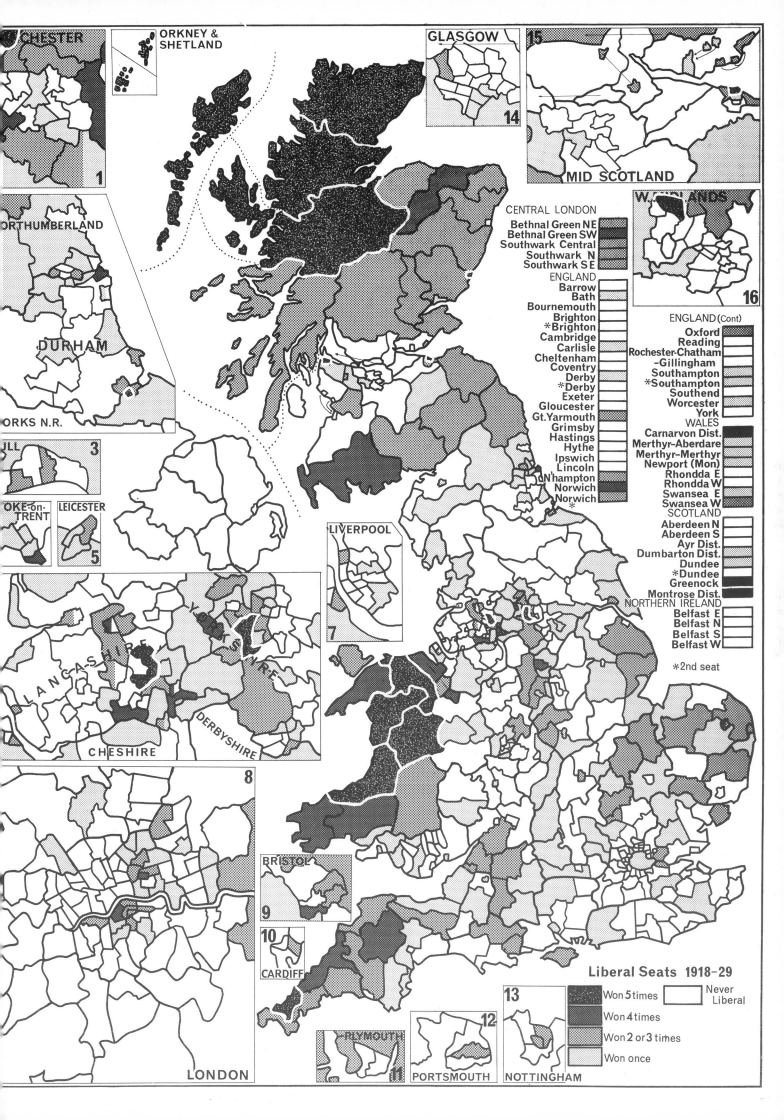

CHESTER

ORKNEY & SHETLAND

1

GLASGOW

14

15

MID SCOTLAND

NORTHUMBERLAND

DURHAM

YORKS N.R.

3

STOKE-on-TRENT

LEICESTER

5

W. MIDLANDS

16

LANCASHIRE

YORKSHIRE

LIVERPOOL

7

DERBYSHIRE

CHESHIRE

8

BRISTOL

9

CARDIFF

10

13

LONDON

PLYMOUTH

11

PORTSMOUTH

12

NOTTINGHAM

CENTRAL LONDON
Bethnal Green NE
Bethnal Green SW
Southwark Central
Southwark N
Southwark SE
ENGLAND
Barrow
Bath
Bournemouth
Brighton
*Brighton
Cambridge
Carlisle
Cheltenham
Coventry
Derby
*Derby
Exeter
Gloucester
Gt. Yarmouth
Grimsby
Hastings
Hythe
Ipswich
Lincoln
N'hampton
Norwich
Norwich
*

ENGLAND (Cont)
Oxford
Reading
Rochester-Chatham
-Gillingham
Southampton
*Southampton
Southend
Worcester
York
WALES
Carnarvon Dist.
Merthyr-Aberdare
Merthyr-Merthyr
Newport (Mon)
Rhondda E
Rhondda W
Swansea E
Swansea W
SCOTLAND
Aberdeen N
Aberdeen S
Ayr Dist.
Dumbarton Dist.
Dundee
*Dundee
Greenock
Montrose Dist.
NORTHERN IRELAND
Belfast E
Belfast N
Belfast S
Belfast W

*2nd seat

Liberal Seats 1918-29

Won 5 times   Never Liberal

Won 4 times

Won 2 or 3 times

Won once

also clear. In 1918 the Coalition Liberals and Labour shared the mining seats, but this stopped in 1922: between 1922 and 1966 hardly any mining seats in South Wales have ever voted anything but Labour. However, the rural seats remained Liberal throughout the 1920s, and Labour did not seriously penetrate the area until 1945.

Liberal areas in England remained substantially those of the pre-1918 period, with the exception already mentioned of the mining districts after 1922. The areas of Liberal weakness were still the West Midlands, the South-east and the agricultural district around York; but even in those places the Liberals often managed surpris-ing wins, such as those in Sevenoaks in 1923 and Ashford in 1929. The Liberals also retained many urban seats they had won before 1910, in Stoke, Hull, Bristol, Newcastle, Tees-side and other industrial areas. Liberal strength was most noticeable, however, in London. There, the Liberals won more seats than Labour in both 1918 and 1922, and managed to retain several in 1923 and in later elections, too. The Liberals continued to be relatively strong in the textile districts of West Yorkshire and East Lancashire in the early 1920s, but they lost most seats in these areas in 1924, and rarely came close thereafter.

The Liberal Vote in 1964

In 1964 the Liberals won more seats in 3-cornered fights than in any election between 1929 and that date. In terms of seats won, they remained weak, but they won their seats without depending on other parties. The distribution of Liberal strength in Scotland and Wales remained substantially what it had been in the inter-war years. In both places the Liberals did well in the rural areas, and very badly in the urban ones. However, in England there were many changes in the areas of Liberal strength and weakness. The strongest Liberal area remained the agricultural and semi-agri-cultural seats in the South-west, but the Liberals were very weak in most agricultural seats in the South Midlands and in East Anglia. On the other hand, in London and the South-east the Liberal areas were the reverse of what they had been 30 years before. In 1964 the Liberals showed substantial strength in middle-class suburban seats in Kent, Surrey and Sussex, while they did badly in inner London. In the inter-war years inner London had provided nearly all the Liberal wins in the South-east. Some observers[1] have dismissed Liberal strength in 1964 in the South-east and in suburban seats elsewhere by saying that the Liberals were even stronger in rural Wales and Scotland. However, the Liberal vote in Wales and Scotland was relatively stationary, while that in the South-east was increasing rapidly. Much more evidence is needed before the phrase 'Orpington Man' is discarded. Perhaps Liberal strength in the suburban districts was caused by a uniform swing of all classes to the Liberals in what seemed safe Conserva-tive seats. It is also possible that the swing to the Liberals was mainly among middle-class voters. The examination of election results proves neither viewpoint; such proof requires a detailed examination of the area by means of voter surveys. Such surveys do not, at present, exist for the area.

Some other constituencies where the Liberals did well in 1964, but where they had won infrequently, if at all, in the inter-war years, were Wirral, South Fylde, several suburban seats around Man-chester and some agricultural seats in Northern Yorkshire.[2] All but the latter group were suburban seats, and practically all were safely Conservative. As with the Liberal areas in the South-east it is uncertain whether the Liberals did well because there was little Labour strength or because there was a more marked swing among middle-class voters than others, to the Liberals. A partial indication that Liberal strength in middle-class districts was caused by a greater swing among middle-class voters is that the Liberals did badly in nearly every slum they contested in the large cities. This includes several areas where the Liberals had done well in the inter-war years: East London, Tees-side and Tyneside. In these places Liberal co-operation with the Conservatives after 1931 probably damaged Liberal chances of winning a large segment of the working-class vote.

1 See, for instance, Butler and King, *British General Election of 1964*, 351

2 For discussions of the effect of Liberal intervention, see R. Rose, 'The Voting Surveyed', in *The Times Guide to the House of Commons, 1964*, 241

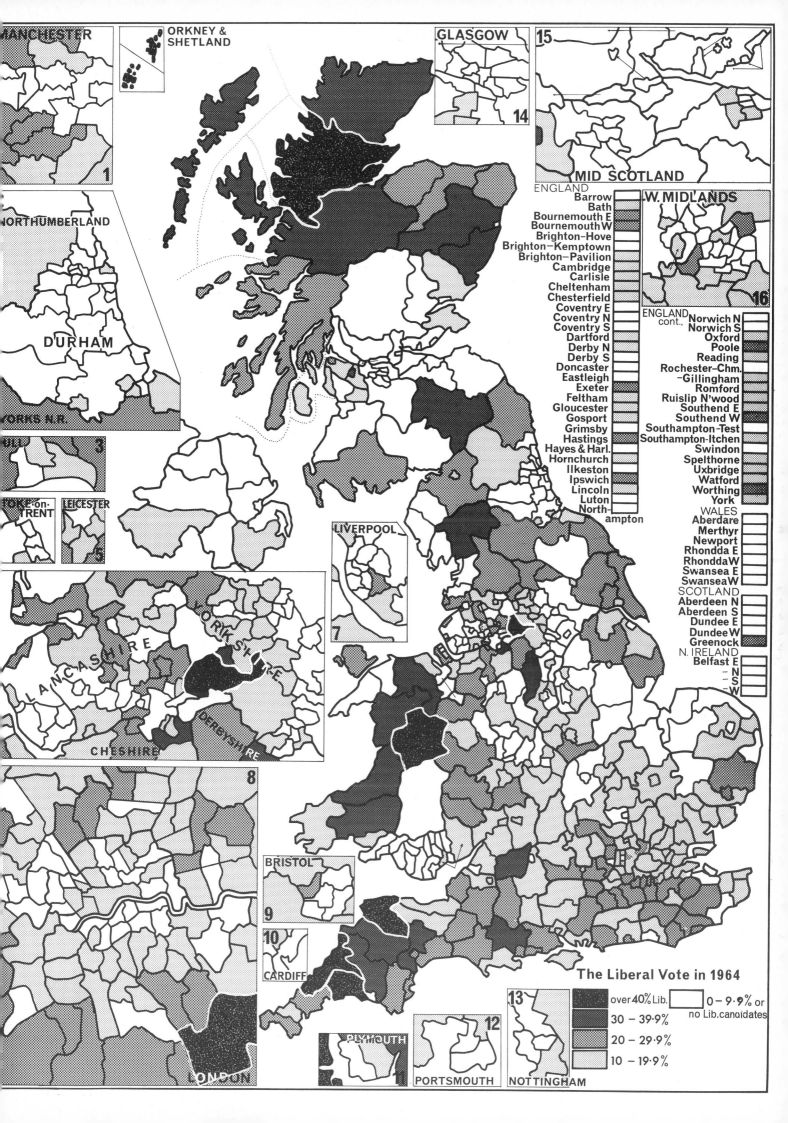

MANCHESTER

ORKNEY &
SHETLAND

1

NORTHUMBERLAND

DURHAM

YORKS N.R.

HULL

3

STOKE-on-TRENT

LEICESTER

5

LANCASHIRE

YORKSHIRE

DERBYSHIRE

CHESHIRE

8

LIVERPOOL

7

BRISTOL

9

10

CARDIFF

PLYMOUTH

11

PORTSMOUTH

12

NOTTINGHAM

13

LONDON

GLASGOW

14

15

MID SCOTLAND

W. MIDLANDS

16

The Liberal Vote in 1964

over 40% Lib.   0 - 9.9% or
                    no Lib. candidates
30 - 39.9%
20 - 29.9%
10 - 19.9%

Establishment of Lloyd George Liberal Constituency Parties 1920-22

The following table shows the date on which Lloyd George Liberal organisations were established in constituencies from 1920 to 1922. The letters 'L.A.' indicate that the local Liberal Association supported Lloyd George. The letters 'N.K.' indicate that although a Lloyd George Liberal Association is known to have existed, the date of its establishment is not known.

The table also lists social activities such as tea parties and garden fetes held by each local Lloyd George Liberal organisation from August 1922 to October 1923. Purely electoral activities such as election meetings are excluded from this list, although regular political education activities held outside elections are included. The number refers to the number of months in which social activities were reported in the *Lloyd George Liberal Magazine*.

The sign * before the name of a constituency indicates that in the constituency there was no Lloyd George Liberal candidate in either 1918 or in 1922, nor in by-elections between these elections.

constituency	year	activities
1 London Boroughs		
Battersea – North	1921	1
Bermondsey – West	1920	3
*Camberwell – Dulwich	1921	nil
North-west	1920	7
Peckham	L.A.	6
*Chelsea	1922	nil
*City of London (2 seats)	1921	nil
*Finsbury	1921	nil
*Fulham – East	1922	nil
Hackney – Central	L.A.	6
* North	1921	nil
South	L.A.	2
Hampstead	1921	2
*Holborn	1921	nil
*Islington – East	1921	nil
* South	1921	nil
* West	1921	nil
Kensington – South	1921	nil
Lambeth – Kennington	1920	6
*Lewisham – East	1922	nil
* West	1921	nil
Poplar – South	L.A.	nil
*St. Marylebone	1921	nil
Shoreditch	L.A.	1
Southwark – Central	L.A.	2
North	L.A.	nil
South-east	L.A.	6
*Wandsworth – Balham	1921	nil
Central	1920	nil
* Clapham	1921	nil
* Putney	1921	nil
* Streatham	1921	nil
*Westminster – Abbey	1921	nil
* St. Georges	1921	nil
2 English Boroughs		
Barnsley	1922	7
*Barrow	1922	nil
Bolton (2 seats)	1921	8
*Bradford – Central	1921	2
East	1921	2
* South	1921	2
* North	1921	2
Bristol – East	1920	4
North	1921	5
South	1922	3
* West	1922	nil
*Bromley	1921	nil
*Croydon – North	1921	nil
* South	1921	nil
East Ham – North	L.A.	3
*Exeter	1920	nil
*Gateshead	1921	1
Huddersfield	1920	nil
*Hull – Central	1921	1
* East	1921	nil
South-west	1921	5
Leeds – South-east	L.A.	5
West	L.A.	3
Leicester – East	1921	7
* South	1921	nil
West	1921	nil
*Leigh	L.A.	nil
Leyton – East	1920	8
* West	1921	nil
Manchester – Rusholme	N.K.	nil
Withington	N.K.	1
Middlesbrough – East	1921	3
West	1921	3
Newcastle-u-Lyme	1922	nil
Newcastle-on-Tyne – East	1921	8
* North	1922	4
West	1921	8
Northampton	L.A.	5
Norwich (2 seats)	L.A.	nil
Oldham (2 seats)	1921	2
Portsmouth – Central	1920	1
*Rotherham	1922	3
Salford – North	1922	nil
Sheffield – Attercliffe	L.A.	1
Brightside	L.A.	1
Hillsborough	L.A.	nil
Park	L.A.	1
Southampton (2 seats)	L.A.	2
Stockton	L.A.	1
Stoke – Burslem	1922	3
Hanley	L.A.	1
Stoke	L.A.	2
Sunderland (2 seats)	L.A.	3
*Wallasey	1922	nil
Wallsend	1922	1
Walthamstow – West	N.K.	8
3 English Counties		
Beds – Bedford	L.A.	nil
Cambridgeshire	L.A.	nil
*Cheshire – Northwich	1922	nil
Crewe	L.A.	2
Cornwall – Camborne	1922	nil
North	L.A.	nil
Derbyshire – Ilkeston	1922	1
* North-east	L.A.	nil
South	L.A.	4
Dorset – East	L.A.	nil
Durham – Bp. Auckland	1920	1
Blaydon	1921	4
* Chester	1922	2
Jarrow	1921	nil
*Spennymoor	1920	nil
*Essex – Maldon	1920	nil
Romford	L.A.	8
Saffron Walden	1921	nil
Gloucestershire – Thornbury	1920	nil
Herts – Hertford	L.A.	4
Isle of Ely	L.A.	nil
*Kent – Canterbury	1921	nil
Dartford	1921	nil
*Lancs – Farnworth	1921	nil
Heywood	L.A.	3
Middleton	L.A.	1
Stretford	L.A.	4
Westhoughton	1921	8
Leics – Bosworth	L.A.	3
Loughborough	L.A.	5
*Middlesex – Hendon	1921	nil
* Wood Green	1921	nil
*Norfolk – Kings Lynn	1922	nil
Northants – Kettering	L.A.	6
Wellingborough	1921	6
Northumberland – Berwick	1921	nil
Wansbeck	1922	3
Notts – Broxtowe	L.A.	9
Oxfordshire – Banbury	L.A.	5
Staffs – Kingswinford	1922	5
Lichfield	1922	1
Suffolk – Eye	1922	nil
Lowestoft	1921	nil
Sudbury	L.A.	1
W. Yorks – Elland	L.A.	1
Hemsworth	1921	4
Normanton	1920	2
Penistone	1921	1
Pontefract	1921	1
Pudsey	L.A.	nil
Shipley	L.A.	nil
Sowerby	1921	1
* Wentworth	1921	nil
4 Welsh Boroughs		
Cardiff – Central	L.A.	nil
East	L.A.	1
South	L.A.	nil
Carnarvon District	L.A.	1
Merthyr – Aberdare	L.A.	1
Merthyr	L.A.	1
Newport	L.A.	nil
Rhondda – East	L.A.	nil
* West	L.A.	nil
Swansea – East	L.A.	3
West	L.A.	4

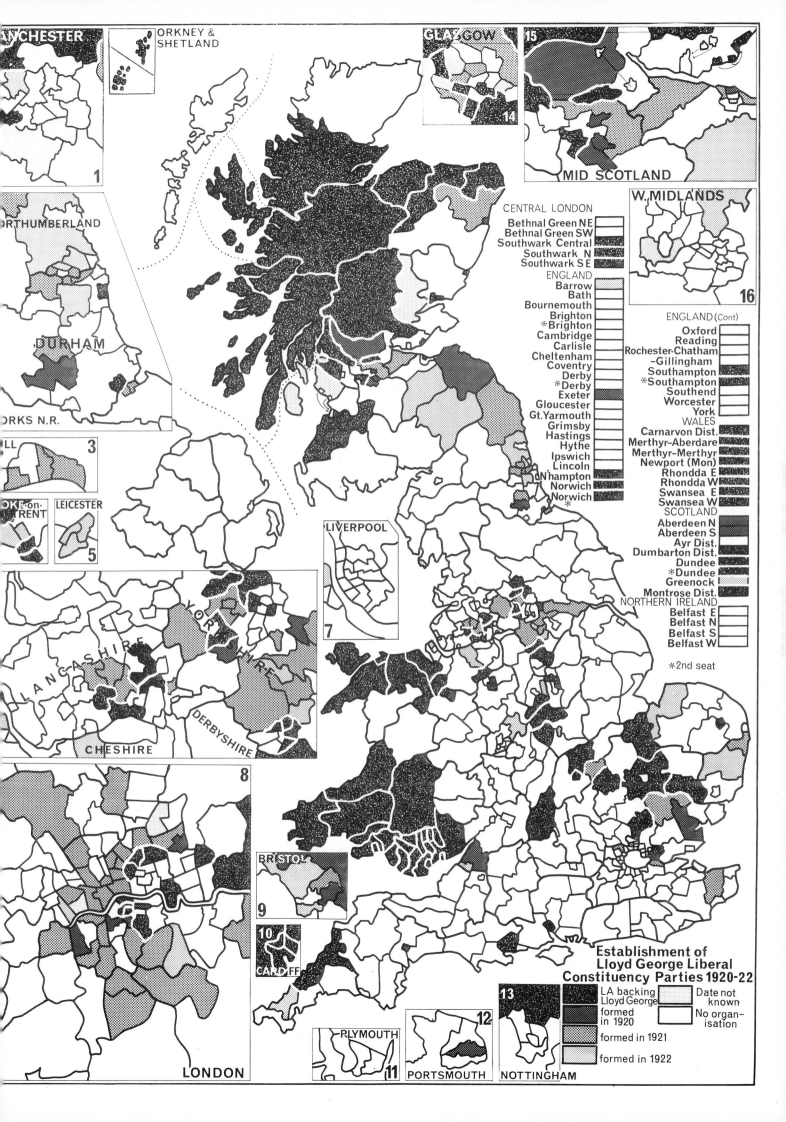

Establishment of Lloyd George Liberal Constituency Parties 1920-22

constituency	year	activities
5 Welsh Counties		
Anglesey	L.A.	nil
Brecon and Radnor	L.A.	nil
Cardigan	L.A.	nil
Carmarthen – Carm	L.A.	nil
Llanelly	L.A.	nil
Carnarvon	L.A.	nil
Denbigh – Denbigh	L.A.	nil
Wrexham	L.A.	1
Flint	L.A.	nil
Glamorgan – Aberavon	L.A.	3
Caerphilly	L.A.	2
Gower	L.A.	nil
* Llandaff	L.A.	2
Neath	L.A.	2
Ogmore	L.A.	nil
Pontypridd	L.A.	2
Monmouth – Abertillery	L.A.	nil
Bedwellty	L.A.	nil
Ebbw Vale	L.A.	nil
* Monmouth	L.A.	nil
* Pontypool	L.A.	nil
Pembroke	L.A.	nil
6 Scottish Burghs		
Aberdeen – North and South	1920	1

constituency	year	activities
Dumbarton District	L.A.	nil
Dundee (2 seats)	L.A.	nil
Edinburgh – Central	1922	1
East	1921	1
* West	1921	nil
Glasgow – Bridgeton	L.A.	nil
Cathcart	L.A.	nil
Govan	1922	nil
* Hillhead	1922	nil
* Kelvingrove	1921	1
Partick	L.A.	nil
* Pollok	1921	nil
* St. Rollox	1921	nil
Shettleston	1922	nil
* Tradeston	L.A.	nil
Greenock	1922	nil
Kirkcaldy District	L.A.	2
* Leith	1920	nil
Montrose District	L.A.	1
7 Scottish Counties		
* Aberdeenshire – Central	1921	nil
East	L.A.	nil
Argyll	L.A.	1
* Ayrshire – Bute and North	N.K.	nil
South	L.A.	nil

constituency	year	activities
Banff	L.A.	nil
Berwick and Haddington	1920	1
* Dumbartonshire	L.A.	nil
Inverness – Inverness	L.A.	nil
Ross and Cromarty	L.A.	nil
* Lanark – Coatbridge	1920	nil
* Hamilton	1920	nil
Motherwell	1920	1
* North	1921	nil
Rutherglen	L.A.	2
* Linlithgow	1921	nil
Moray and Nairn	L.A.	nil
Orkney and Shetland	L.A.	nil
* Peebles and South Midlothian	1922	nil
Perth – Kinross and West	L.A.	nil
Perth	N.K.	nil
Renfrew – West	L.A.	1
Roxburgh and Selkirk	1922	1
* Stirling – West	1920	nil
8 Universities		
** Oxford (2 seats)	1921	nil
* London	1921	nil
Wales	1921	nil
Scottish (3 seats)	1921	nil

Sources: *Lloyd George Liberal Magazine*, October 1920 – October 1923; *Minutes of the Scottish Liberal Association*, 1918-1923; *Nottingham Guardian*, 30 October 1922; *Berwick Mercury*, 21 January 1922

The breach between Asquith and Lloyd George was not official, so far as the Liberal organisation was concerned, until the meeting of the National Liberal Federation in May 1920. Before then, there had been open warfare between the 2 groups of Liberals, but the Lloyd George Liberals had preferred to retain as many ties as possible with official Liberal bodies. After their expulsion from the Party the Lloyd George Liberals tried to establish local organisations in seats they held, as well as in seats they hoped to contest in the forthcoming election. They did not, at first, try to set up many local organisations in places with sitting Conservative M.P.s. Presumably, they felt that Liberal voters in such seats might not respond to the call to support Conservatives against Asquith Liberals. Therefore, the growth and development of the Lloyd George Liberal organisation was hampered from the first. This caused much frustration among Lloyd George's organisers, one of whom wrote that his party was like a mule, with 'a capacity for hard work but a disappointing inability to reproduce its species'.[1] In a few cases the Lloyd George Liberals set up local organisations to co-operate with Conservative M.P.s. However, between October 1920 and December 1921 the *Lloyd George Liberal Magazine* reported only 7 cases of co-operation between Lloyd George Liberals and Conservatives at a local level.[2] Some Conservative M.P.s resented the fact that the Lloyd George Liberals did not give them more open support, and this may have helped turn some of them away from the Lloyd George Coalition.[3]

Generally, the Liberal M.P.s who supported Lloyd George were able to carry their local Liberal Associations with them. Only rarely did their local associations rebel.[4] Nearly all the Liberal Associations in Wales and the Scottish Highlands supported Lloyd George, as did several in the mining districts of Derbyshire. Most Liberal Associations which backed Lloyd George had a Lloyd George Liberal candidate in 1922. The 7 exceptions were Rhondda East, Ebbw Vale, Llandaff and Monmouth, in Wales; and Aberdeenshire Central, Dumbartonshire and Leigh. In Aberdeenshire Central the local Liberal Association withdrew its support from the Coalition in 1919 during a by-election, and a new organisation was not formed until 1921. In Dumbartonshire the Liberal organisation covered both the county and burgh seats jointly, one of which (the burghs) was held by a Lloyd George Liberal. In Leigh the local Liberal Association withdrew support from its Asquithian M.P., who ran elsewhere in 1922.[5] Where the local Liberal Associations did not openly support the Coalition, they were often unwilling to attack it openly either. For instance, in Wansbeck the Executive of the Liberal Association passed a resolution denouncing the Coalition. The Association then met and rescinded their Executive's resolution by a vote of 70 to 10, whereupon the Liberal agent resigned and emigrated to Canada.[6] The fact that the local Liberal Associations backed the Coalition in most places with an active Lloyd George Liberal M.P. or candidate suggests that many Liberals in the country did not want to see the party split extended, and that they wished to avoid damaging the chances of any kind of Liberal candidate.

After the split of May 1920 the Lloyd George Liberals began setting up constituency parties, at first in their own strongholds, and then in various other constituencies. There was no lack of money for organisational purposes, and the establishment of local parties proceeded rapidly.[7] Most of the local Associations were set up during 1921, though a few more were organised in 1922. The most extensive area of organisation was London, where few Liberal Associations supported Lloyd George. Most of the organisations in London, especially those in the suburbs, were apparently phantom affairs, as they held few meetings after their initial establishment. The collapse of these phantom organisations probably contributed to the growing feeling in 1922 that Lloyd George was losing popularity in the country.

1 *Lloyd George Papers*, F/16/2/2, S. Fildes to E. Evans, 23 March, 1922
2 In Stockton, Cambridgeshire, Bute and North Ayrshire, Kelvingrove, Bothwell and Rutherglen, Gateshead and Exeter
3 For instance, J. R. P. Newman, Conservative M.P. for Finchley, complained that he did not know of any Liberal, Coalition or otherwise, who had come forward to support him, and he saw no reason to stick with the Coalition. (*Finchley Press*, 3 November 1922)
4 One constituency organisation which did rebel was that of Clay Cross, which repudiated its M.P. in July 1920. However, the M.P. had maintained few connections with his constituency, and he did not bother to set up even a nominal Lloyd George

organisation (Williams, *Derbyshire Miners*, 816)
5 The M.P., P. Raffan, had obtained a coupon in 1918, but he had denounced it. In 1922 he ran as an Asquith Liberal in Ayr District against a Labour candidate. Despite this, he was supported by the Vice-President of the Labour Party (*Leigh Chronicle*, 29 November 1918, and *The Times*, 9 November, 1922)
6 *Newcastle Daily Chronicle*, 31 May 1920; and *Lloyd George Papers*, F/22/2/20 Report on Party Organisation, 16 November 1920
7 Some advisers of Lloyd George felt that money was used as a substitute for enthusiasm in many constituencies, and that 'one volunteer is worth ten pressed men' (*Lloyd George Papers*, F/16/2/2, Fildes to Evans, 23 March 1922)

Activities of Lloyd George Liberal Constituency Parties 1922-23

Monthly appearances in Lloyd George Lib. Magazine August 1922 – October 1923	Constituencies
9	1
8	6
7	3
6	7
5	7
4	8
3	14
2	18
1	37
nil	123
	224

In May and June 1922 the Lloyd George Coalition abandoned Free Trade to a limited extent, when it agreed to 'safeguarding of industries'. It might have been anticipated that this would lead to the collapse of many local Liberal organisations which backed Lloyd George, but this was rarely so. The local organisations continued their activities, except where they had been mere paper bodies, that is in London. Outside London, almost all held political activities such as election meetings, rallies, dinners, and so on. However, this might only have disguised a decay in the effective organisation of the local parties.

Because of this, purely electoral affairs conducted by the local parties have been ignored in assessing the activities of the Lloyd George Liberals after July 1922. Instead, social activities such as day trips to country houses, dances, picnics, and so on, have been considered. Nearly all such activities in any Lloyd George Liberal local organisation were reported in the constituency sections of the *Lloyd George Liberal Magazine,* the month after they happened. By seeing how many of these activities each local party held, it is possible to gauge the effectiveness of the organisation. The table on p. 89 lists the number of months in which each local organisation was reported to have held social or educational functions. Sometimes, one monthly appearance consisted of reports of several functions. For instance, the *Magazine* reported in June 1923 that the Association in Hackney Central had held a membership drive which resulted in the addition of 200 new members, several women's meetings, visits to hospitals, street collections for funds, and other activities. As these happened in the same month, they constitute one appearance in the *Magazine*.

In Scotland and Wales few Lloyd George Liberal associations had any social activities after July 1922. This did not reflect weakness in the organisations, but the distances involved, which prohibited such activities on a constituency basis. In England most of the local associations outside London had some social activities. The absence of many activities in London was probably a sign of weakness, whereas the number of social activities in the provincial cities and county divisions was a sign of relative strength. The most active local association was that in Bolton, which held at least 26 social functions from August 1922 to October 1923.[1] Several other constituencies were nearly as active as Bolton. Much of this activity was sponsored and subsidised by the Lloyd George Liberal headquarters in London, but it is unlikely that the headquarters would have bothered to subsidise, say, sewing circles, unless those circles showed some signs of life in any case. Consequently, the activities of the local associations can be taken as a sign of the real strength of the Lloyd George associations in the constituencies.

A sign that the Lloyd George organisations could have been more extensive if the organisers had wished, was that during the election of 1922 several candidates put themselves up as supporters of Lloyd George, usually against 'Diehard' Conservatives. In most cases the Lloyd George organisation put pressure on them to stand down.[2] In Jarrow they refused to supply a candidate to the local Lloyd George Liberals, who wished to run one.[3]

Some organisers of the Lloyd George local associations were perplexed at the desire of the headquarters to limit the number and activity of local parties.[4] In fact, the first local Lloyd George organisation, in Maldon, was set up without reference to the headquarters.[5] Probably the headquarters wished to limit Liberal splits in most constituencies, in order to capture the entire Liberal organisation later on. The establishment of numerous local parties competing with Liberal Associations would prevent this. In England, apart from London, only 21 new local parties were set up, unless there was a Lloyd George Liberal candidate in the constituency.

1 As they were all in 8 months, the table above lists 8 appearances in the *Lloyd George Liberal Magazine*. The activities included 5 outings, 5 sewing circle meetings, 4 socials, 3 balls and dances, 2 reports of ward meetings, one picnic, one dancing class, one formation of a football club, one formation of a Harmonic Concert Group, one concert, one tea party, and one Children's Party for 6,000 children
2 Some Conservative constituencies where this happened were Paddington North, Ealing and Canterbury

3 *Sunderland Daily Echo,* 4 November 1922; *Morning Post,* 6 and 7 November 1922; *South Eastern Gazette,* 7 November 1922
4 Sir William Sutherland wrote to Lloyd George in 1922 that he did not expect 'to have proper political influence unless we have our political force fully organised in every constituency. However, that has not been the view of our Chief Whips and it is their view naturally that prevails.' *(Lloyd George Papers,* F/35/1/39, Sutherland to Lloyd George, 18 March 1922)
5 *Lloyd George Liberal Magazine,* November 1921

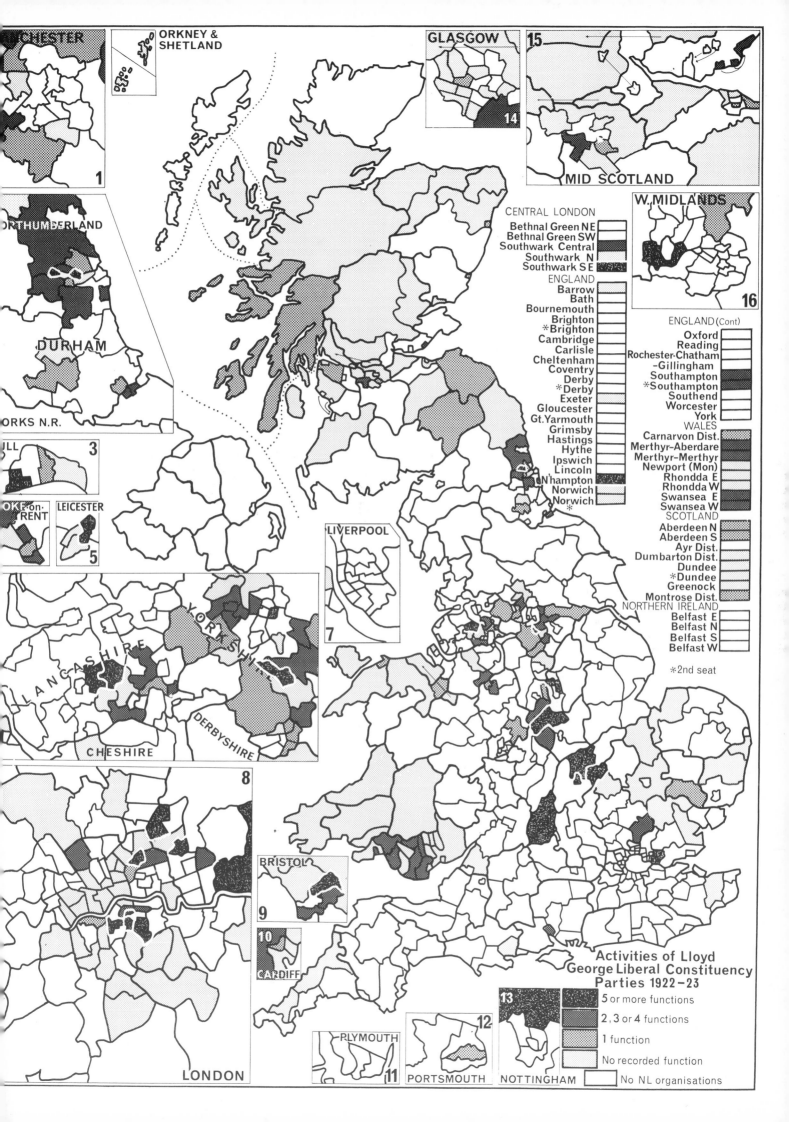

Activities of Lloyd George Liberal Constituency Parties 1922–23

Liberals without Prefix in 1922

Despite the split between Asquith and Lloyd George, at least 96 Liberal candidates ran 'without prefix' in the 1922 election. That is, they did not campaign as supporters of either leader against the other. Nearly all said they would follow whichever Liberal leader obtained the support of the majority of Liberal M.P.s after the election. The Liverpool Junior Reform Club proposed a platform for Liberals who wished to run as 'reunion' candidates, with the support of all Liberals. According to this platform such candidates should work for reunion, should support Liberal principles, especially Free Trade, and should waive the question of leadership until after the election. After the election, thought the Liverpool Junior Reform Club, a meeting of all Liberal M.P.s would choose the Liberal leader.[1] Liberal candidates and associations in all parts of the country supported these ideas. Many had previously been factional adherents of Asquith or of Lloyd George, but the fall of the Lloyd George Coalition removed that source of antagonism between many Liberals in the country, and they eagerly sought reunion. *The Constitutional Year Book, 1923,* listed the previous factional affiliations of all the Liberal candidates in 1922, and from that list it is apparent that many supporters of Asquith and of Lloyd George wished reunion:

'Constitutional Year Book' listing	all prefixless candidates	prefixless[2] M.P.s
'L' (Asquith)	45	13
'NL' (Lloyd George)	42	13
'IL'	5	3
'Independent'	3	—
'Independent NL'	1	—
	96	**29**

Lloyd George accepted the 'reunion' movement in the Liberal Party, probably because it represented the quickest way for him to regain influence after his expulsion from office. However, Asquith did not countenance it. In November 1922 his wife wrote to Bonar Law: 'Don't believe a word about Reunion. Never was a greater lie. We would rather be out for *ever'*.[3] After the election he rejected several offers from Lloyd George to reunite the Liberals in Parliament, on any basis except the complete submission of Lloyd George. However, more supporters of Lloyd George had been elected in 1922 than supporters of Asquith, so that Asquith had little to gain by allowing an open choice of Leaders.

As a result of the 1922 election neither leader had the support of a clear majority of Liberal M.P.s. 116 Liberal M.P.s included 47 open adherents of Lloyd George, 40 of Asquith and 29 'prefixless' M.P.s, who where in fact evenly divided between Asquith and Lloyd George. Perhaps if either Liberal leader had had an overwhelming majority among the Liberal M.P.s in 1922, the other leader would have given much more ground. As it was, Asquith was encouraged in his desire to humiliate Lloyd George, while Lloyd George was not cast down so far that he needed to grovel.[4] In the election of 1923 the Liberal split was supposedly healed. However, Viscount Gladstone, one of Asquith's closest advisers, continued to draw up lists showing which Liberal candidates supported Asquith and Lloyd George.[5] Although Gladstone's actions are understandable, they probably contributed to continuing ill-feeling in Liberal ranks.

---

1 *Bacup Times,* 4 November 1922
2 This table is based on Kinnear, *The Fall of Lloyd George,* Appendix 2
3 Blake, *Unknown Prime Minister,* 465
4 Asquith wrote in November 1922: 'I am all against forcing the pace (for Liberal reunion) and surrendering any of our ground. Meanwhile L.G. is evidently dallying with visions of reconciliation . . . [L.G.] declared that he was quite ready to serve with and under me, with whom he had never had a quarrel and whom he had never ceased to admire and respect.' *(Letters from Lord Oxford to a Friend,* II, 39-40)
5 One such list can be found in the *Viscount Gladstone Papers,* Add. MSS 46480-63-64, aide-memoire of Gladstone after the 1923 election

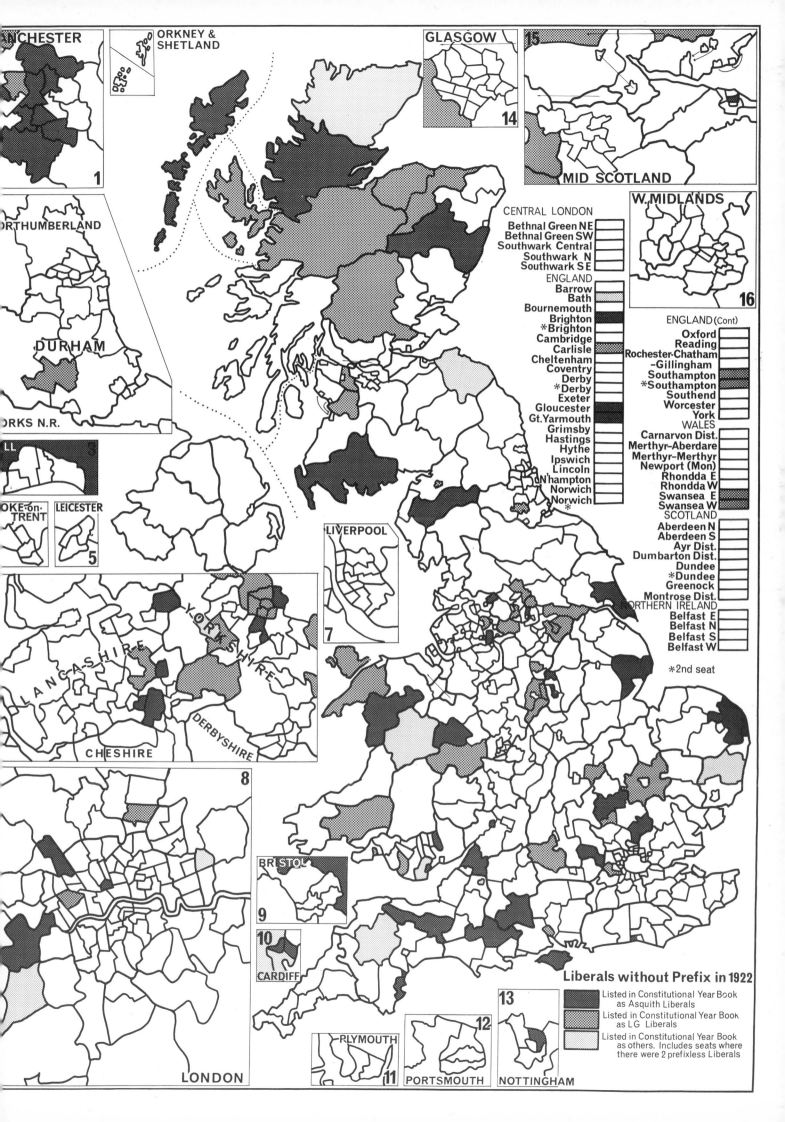

Conservatives and Lloyd George Liberals in 1922

In 1922 there was no national electoral co-operation between the Conservatives and Lloyd George Liberals. According to the Chairman of the Conservative Party, when local arrangements for co-operation were made, 'the Central Office will accept that arrangement'.[1] In 159 seats local Conservative and Lloyd George Liberal Associations made such arrangements. In a further 55 they fought each other. In the remaining 389 seats in England, Scotland and Wales they neither conflicted nor co-operated. The chief areas of co-operation were Scotland, Lancashire, Staffordshire and Wales, while the chief areas of conflict were East Anglia and the textile district of West Yorkshire. In these areas, however, there were numerous individual seats which went against regional trends. In some areas of co-operation there was a strong threat from Labour. Central Scotland, Staffordshire, Sheffield and Newcastle were examples. However, Labour was very weak indeed in rural Scotland, rural Wales, West Lancashire and rural Cheshire. In those places co-operation cannot be attributed to a major threat from Labour. Also, in Glamorgan, where Labour was very strong, there was co-operation in only 5 seats out of 12.

Although the national parties theoretically allowed constituency associations to decide whether or not they would co-operate, in a few seats the national parties clearly interfered. Several Lloyd George Liberals were persuaded to withdraw from contests against Conservatives,[2] and some Conservatives were persuaded to withdraw from contests against Lloyd George Liberals.[3] Perhaps because of such interventions by the central offices, there were relatively few open splits between the Conservatives and Lloyd George Liberals in 1922. Almost half the splits were in seats held neither by Lloyd George Liberals nor by Conservatives.[4] In 9 seats Lloyd George Liberals intervened against Conservatives, and in 24 seats Conservatives intervened against Lloyd George Liberals. Often the local splits were encouraged by persons living outside the constituencies involved. For instance, in the Forest of Dean the local Conservative Party supported Mrs Coombe Tennant, a Lloyd George Liberal. However, a group of publicans and brewers calling themselves the 'Fellowship of Freedom and Reform' nominated a candidate against her.[5] In East Dorset the Conservative Association endorsed Lloyd George's assistant, F. E. Guest, but other Conservatives nominated an Independent, R. Hall Caine.[6] It is uncertain whether Caine's greatest support came from Lord Beaverbrook or from Lord Croft, but it did not come from the executive of the local Conservative Association.[7]

Probably no one group or person organised most of the local splits between Conservatives and Lloyd George Liberals in 1922. The split in Lowestoft was encouraged by Lord Northcliffe's *Daily Mail* early in 1922,[8] while that in Sudbury was encouraged by Field-Marshal Sir William Robertson.[9] Both Northcliffe and Robertson were known opponents of Lloyd George. In the Forest of Dean the agents of disruption were the 'Fellowship of Freedom and Reform', and in Cambridgeshire the local Conservatives themselves probably wished to depose their M.P., Edwin Montagu.[10] It is improbable that Lord Beaverbrook engineered many of the local splits in 1922, as he later maintained. By late October 1922, when he wished to encourage the splits, most of the splits had already taken place. Probably Beaverbrook's activities were confined to a few favourable constituencies such as East Dorset.[11]

Some local conflicts were very complex. In 1922 many persons had votes in 2 constituencies; often neighbouring constituencies adopted different attitudes towards co-operation. For instance, the Conservatives in Leeds Central and North opposed Lloyd George Liberals, while Conservatives in Leeds South and West supported them. Some voters in the 4 constituencies were thus forced to vote one way in one place, and the contrary in another. In Doncaster and Don Valley the situation was still more confused. The Conservatives and Lloyd George Liberals fought each other in Doncaster; but in Don Valley they co-operated. Moreover, the organisation running the Lloyd George Liberal campaign in Don Valley was the Doncaster Conservative Association.[12]

---

1 Sir George Younger, *Bristol Adventurer*, 3 November 1922
2 See map on p. 97
3 For example, in Bedford the local Conservative Association nominated a candidate against the sitting Lloyd George Liberal. The Conservative Central Office persuaded the candidate to run elsewhere, but the local association insisted on opposing the Lloyd George Liberal and obtained another candidate. The Central Office eventually endorsed the second candidate (*The Chronicle*, 1 November 1922)
4 Seven were in Asquith Liberal, Labour or other seats, while 15 more were in seats where a Lloyd George Liberal ran as a prefixless Liberal. Some of the latter had been offered Conservative support if they would run as Lloyd George Liberals, but they had refused such conditions. W. Forrest in Pontefract was one of them. Forrest could not say whether he supported Lloyd George, Asquith, Bonar Law 'or any other leader' (*Pontefract Advertiser*, 1 November 1922)
5 *Gloucester Journal*, 30 September and 4 November 1922; *Western Independent*, 29 October 1922. According to H. A. L. Fisher, Dinnick, the candidate opposing Mrs Tennant 'is promising free beer and spending £10,000 in the constituency . . . Mrs C.T. says he is causing beer to flow everywhere and though he would undoubtedly be unseated for corruption if elected, he doesn't mind about this, as he hasn't a dog's chance of winning and he is only out to queer her pitch. It is sickening' (*H. A. L. Fisher Papers*, Fisher to Mrs Fisher, 10 November 1922)

6 Caine's brother contested Reading in 1922 as a Labour candidate
7 Croft, *My Life of Strife*, 165; *East Dorset Herald*, 23 November 1922; and *Dorset County Chronicle*, 26 October 1922
8 According to Sir G. Rentoul, the candidate in Lowestoft, *This is my Case*, 87
9 *Suffolk and Essex Free Press*, 2 November 1922
10 *Suffolk and Essex Free Press*, 2 November 1922
11 In his book, *The Decline . . . of Lloyd George*, 214 Beaverbrook stated that he had launched 56 candidates 'against Lloyd George's party men'. However, only 24 Conservatives intervened against Lloyd George Liberals, and many of them were encouraged by persons other than Lord Beaverbrook; many of the others were nominated before the Carlton Club Meeting, that is, before Beaverbrook's efforts began.
12 *Doncaster Gazette*, 3 November 1922. By running in one seat against a Lloyd George Liberal while he supported a Lloyd George Liberal in the neighbouring constituency, the Conservative candidate may have hoped to maintain cordial relations with both groups. In 1923 he was made a peer. Earlier in 1922, the candidate had made overtures about a peerage (*Lloyd George Papers*, F 29/4/109)

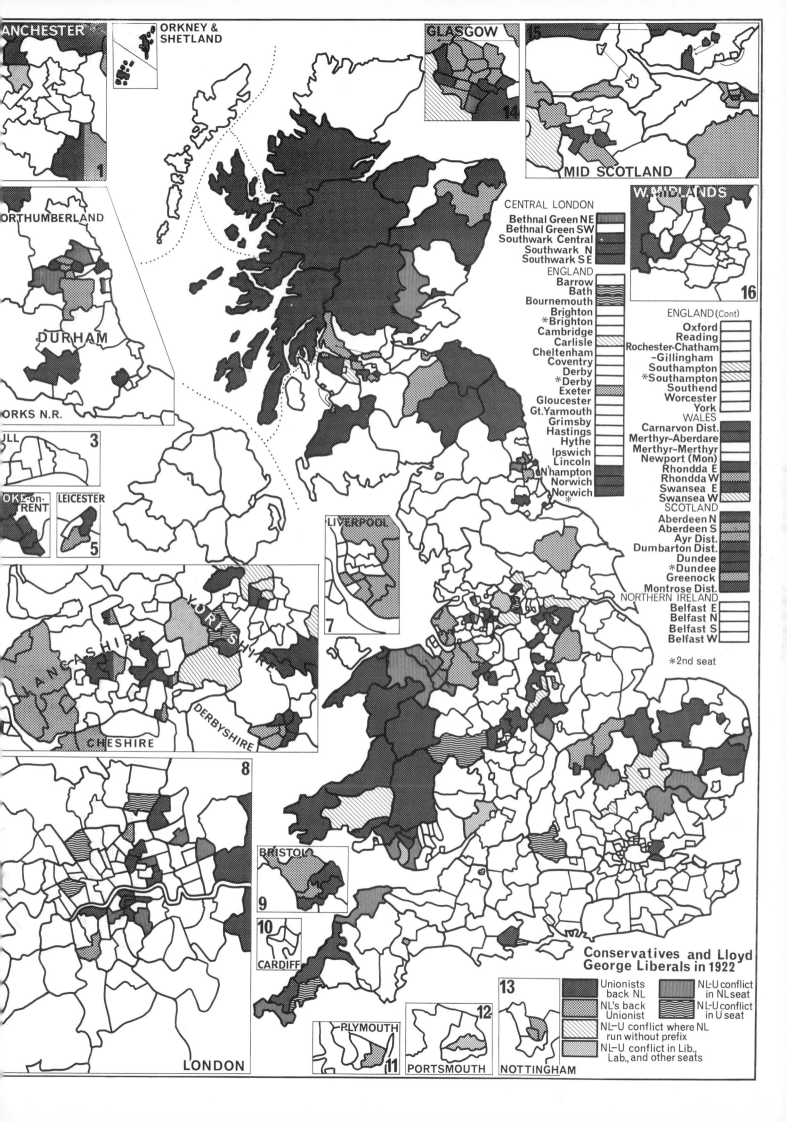

Conservatives and Lloyd George Liberals in 1922

Liberal Unionists 1886-1910

The map shows seats won by Liberal Unionists from 1886 to 1910. It does not necessarily indicate where Liberal Unionist strength was greatest; in some cases it merely reflects the decision of a local Conservative Association to choose a Liberal Unionist candidate instead of a Conservative.[1] For example, in 1906 the safe Conservative seat of Croydon elected H. Arnold-Forster, a Liberal Unionist. It is unlikely that Arnold-Forster's selection as the Unionist candidate signified the presence of a strong body of Liberal Unionist feeling in Croydon. Probably his post of Secretary of State for War was the decisive factor. Most other Liberal Unionist seats in London were basically safe Conservative seats. The location of the Conservative Central Office in London probably gave it greater influence over the choice of candidates than in more distant constituencies. Some other Liberal Unionist seats were also probably basically Conservative: in 1906 a Conservative, J. W. Hills, defeated a Liberal Unionist in Durham City. In both elections of 1910 Hills ran as a Liberal Unionist. Probably Hills' conversion to Liberal Unionism did not represent a change in political views but a desire to reconcile the local wings of the Unionist coalition. In Northern Ireland the Liberal Unionists probably provided a relatively small proportion of the Unionist total in the constituencies they contested, but this was sufficient to make the difference between Nationalist and Unionist wins in 2 constituencies during most of the period 1886 to December 1910.[2]

The areas which elected most Liberal Unionists were the West Midlands, Devon and Cornwall, and Scotland. East Lancashire also had some Liberal Unionist M.P.s, mainly between 1886 and 1892. All these were areas of relative Coalition strength at the Carlton Club Meeting in October 1922.[3] This indicates a probable difference in the attitude of Unionist organisations in places with many Unionist M.P.s, and places with few of them. Possibly Unionist constituencies in the Liberal Unionist districts tended to be more marginal than those in some other parts of the country, so that local Conservative Associations were more willing to make deals with semi-Liberals in order to win what they might otherwise lose.[4]

The map shows that the Liberal Unionists were rarely elected in several areas: Wales, the South-east, the East Midlands and nearly all seats in England north of a line drawn from Barrow to Hull. These were either safe Conservative districts, where local Conservative associations did not feel the need to nominate Liberal Unionists to win elections, or else safe Liberal or Labour areas, where Liberal Unionists had little chance of being elected even if they were nominated. Most Liberal Unionist seats were in marginal districts, and because of this the Liberal Unionist base in Parliament was much shakier than that of the other main parties. The rapid decline of the Liberal Unionists after 1892 may largely be attributed to this.

1 It may in some cases also reflect the presence of a Liberal Unionist candidate with a strong personal following. See map, General Election of 1886, p. 19
2 In Londonderry County South and Tyrone County South

3 See map, Carlton Club Meeting, p. 105
4 The only exceptions were a few agricultural seats in the West Midlands and most seats in Birmingham. In both places Liberalism was very weak after the break in 1886

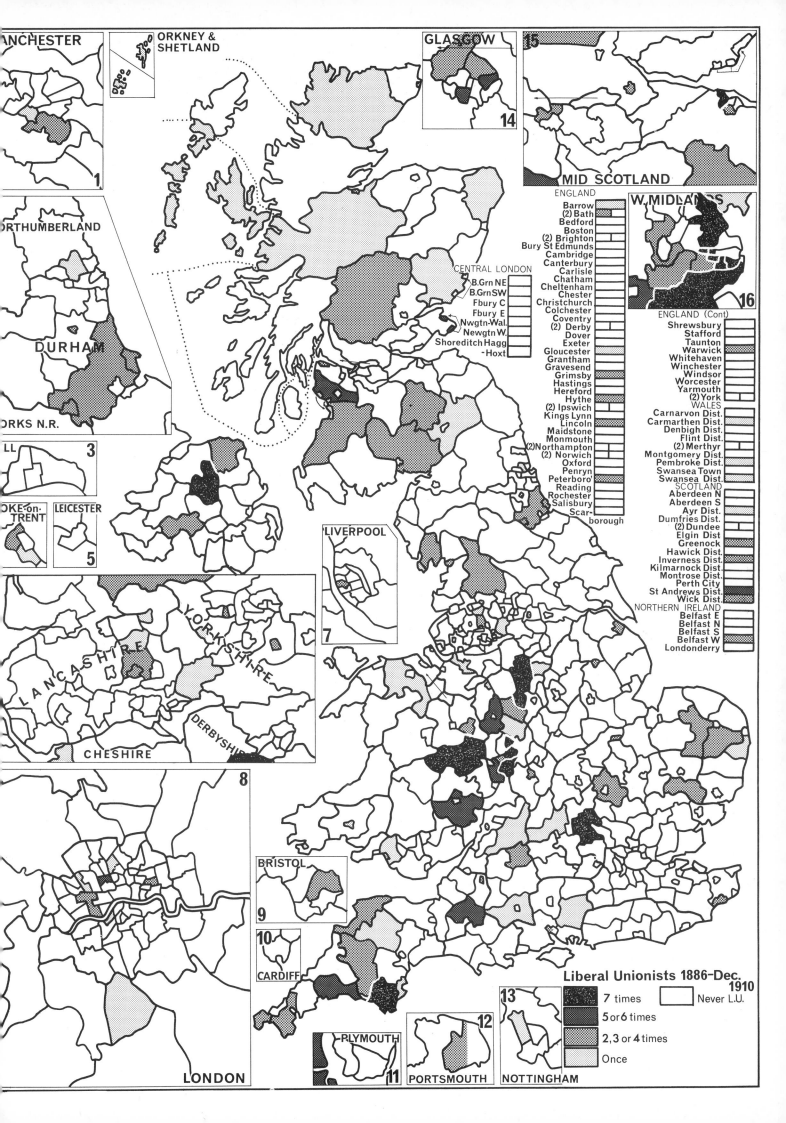

Unionist Free Traders in 1904

Between 1900 and 1940 there were 3 major splits within the Conservative or Unionist Party: all involved the Chamberlain family. In 1903-6 the Unionists were divided over tariff reform and Joseph Chamberlain; in 1920-22 they were divided over the Coalition and Austen Chamberlain; and in 1937-40 they were divided over appeasement, and Neville Chamberlain. In the case of tariff reform and the Coalition the Unionist rebels won; in the case of appeasement they did not.[1]

An early 'census' of Unionist Free Trade M.P.s was taken some time in 1903 or 1904[2] by Herbert Gladstone, for the use of the Liberal Party. This 'census' indicated that there were 51 probable Unionist Free Traders in Parliament. From the time he resigned from Balfour's Cabinet in 1903 until he was incapacitated by illness in mid-1906, Joseph Chamberlain waged a bitter struggle with the Unionist Party on behalf of tariffs. Shortly before the 1906 election only 27 Unionist M.P.s openly supported Free Trade; 10 former Unionist Free Traders had by that time joined the Liberals.[3] The number of Unionist Free Trade M.P.s was further reduced to 16 by the 1906 election;[4] and by 1922 there were only 22 Unionist Free Traders in Parliament. At each interval examined, the proportion of Unionist Free Trade M.P.s declined.[5]

Gladstone's 'census' of 1904 had estimated that there were 51 Unionist Free Traders in Parliament. However, an amendment of 15 February 1904 showed that only 24 on Gladstone's list actually voted for Free Trade, while 8 abstained and 21 voted against it. It should not be assumed that all those who voted against this Free Trade amendment were in favour of Tariff Reform: immediately before the vote was taken, the Government announced that it did not intend to place a tariff on food or raw materials. This meant that some Unionist Free Traders could conscientiously vote against the amendment and still remain Free Traders.

The map shows how Unionist M.P.s on Gladstone's list voted on this division. It indicates that there were 4 general areas of Unionist Free Trade strength: London, the Glasgow district, Lancashire and the agricultural seats in the South of England. In none of these areas did the Free Traders form a majority of Unionist M.P.s, but in all they formed an appreciable proportion. The views of the Unionist M.P.s need not have been those of their constituents, but it is interesting to note that the only place where a majority of the Free Traders voted for the Free Trade amendment was Lancashire.[6] This could indicate that the M.P.s from Lancashire felt that support of the amendment would help them in their

constituencies. It is notable also that 12 of the 21 Unionist Free Traders elected in 1922 came from Lancashire and 2 more came from seats bordering on Lancashire.[7]

In the 1906 election 6 Unionist Free Traders were opposed by other Unionists, and all but one lost.[8] In the 5 territorial seats the Free Traders won by over 60% of the total Unionist vote, indicating that a slight majority of the Unionist voters either supported Free Trade, or that they resented Independent Unionist candidatures. Five of the 6 Tariff Reform candidates later became M.P.s, and 4 were at the Carlton Club Meeting which overthrew the Coalition. All voted against the Coalition.[9]

APPENDIX I

Gladstone's estimate of Unionist Free Trade strength 1904

Sources: B.M.Add. MSS 46106 ff. 147-150, for Herbert Gladstone.s estimate. 4 H.C.Deb., CXXIX, 1445-1452, for vote of 15 February 1904.

Ayes: Those voting for Free Trade amendment; Nays: those voting against it; Non-voters: abstainers, absentees, etc.

name	constituency	result of 1906 election
Ayes		
Bowles, T.	Kings Lynn	Ran as Ind. Cons.; lost to a Lib.
Cavendish, R.	North Lonsdale	Ran as Lib.; lost to a Unionist
Cecil, Ld. H.	Greenwich	Ran as Unionist; lost to a Lib.
Churchill, W.	Oldham	Won Manchester N.-w. as a Lib.
Corbett, A.	Glasgow –Tradeston	Re-elected as Unionist
Dickson-Poynder, J.	Chippenham	Ran as Lib. and won
Elliott, A.	Durham City	Ran as Lib. Unionist; lost to Cons.
Foster, M.	London Univ.	Ran as Lib.; lost to Lib. Unionist
Gorst, J.	Cambridge Univ.	Ran as Cons.; lost to another Cons.
Goschen, G. J.	East Grinstead	Lost in Bolton as a Cons.
Greville, R.	Bradford East	Retired
Guest, I. C.	Plymouth	Won Cardiff as a Lib.
Hain, E.	St. Ives	Retired after becoming a Lib.
Hamilton, Ld. G.	Ealing	Retired
Kemp, G.	Heywood	Retired after becoming a Lib.
Lambton, F.	Durham S.-E.	Re-elected as Unionist
Ritchie, C.	Croydon	Retired
Russell, T. W.	Tyrone South	Re-elected as Lib.
Seeley, C.	Lincoln	Defeated by Lib.; opposed by Unionist
Seeley, J.	Isle of Wight	Won Abercromby as a Lib.
Simeon, J.	Southampton	Retired
Smith, A.	Hertford	Re-elected as Unionist
Taylor, A.	East Toxteth	Re-elected as Unionist; joined Libs.
Wood, J.	Down East	Ran as Lib.; lost to Unionist

1 In the division which brought about the fall of Neville Chamberlain in 1940, his Government had a majority of 81 over all other parties

2 This 'census' is given in Appendix I to this map. The original typescript is undated but it refers to J. Johnstone, who died in 1904, and to A. Taylor, elected in November 1902. This information is based on Dr. A. Russell's thesis on the 1906 election, p. 564

3 Also listed in Appendix I

4 According to P. Fraser, 'Unionism and Tariff Reform', *Historical Journal,* 1962, 155. Only 10 of those on Gladstone's list were re-elected as Unionists, and one more (A. Taylor) as a Unionist-Liberal. Of the 11, 6 had voted against the Free Trade amendment of 15 February 1904

5 The proportion of Unionist Free Traders varied as follows: 1904–12%; 1907–10%; 1922–6% of all Unionist M.P.s

6 Four of the 6 Unionist Free Traders from Lancashire voted for the amendment; one of the 4 from Glasgow; 3 of the 10 from London; and 4 of the 10 agricultural seats in the South of England voted for it

7 Indicated in Appendix II by an asterisk (*)

8 Listed in Appendix I

9 See map, The Carlton Club Meeting, p. 105. The M.P.s involved were H. Page Croft, J. Hills, A. H. Burgoyne and J. F. Rawlinson. I. H. Benn was also an M.P. by 1922, but he was absent from the Carlton Club Meeting. The only Tariff Reformer who failed to be elected was A. Rosenthal, the candidate in Glasgow – Tradeston

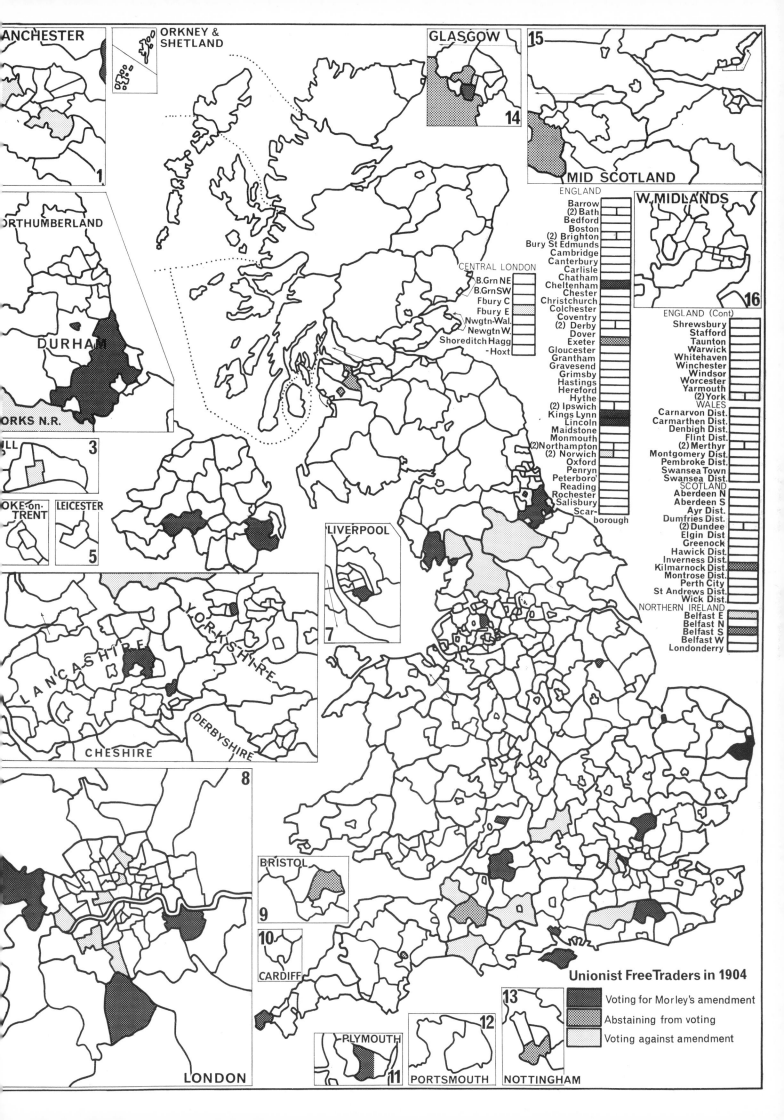

name	constituency	result of 1906 election

Non-voters

Bentinck, Ld. H.	Nottingham South	Defeated by Lab.
Denny, J.	Kilmarnock Burghs	Retired
Hobhouse, H.	Somerset East	Retired
Shaw-Stewart, M.	Renfrew East	Defeated by Lib.
Sloan, T.	Belfast South	Re-elected as Unionist
Stirling-Maxwell, J.	Glasgow–College	Defeated by Lib.
Vincent, E.	Exeter	Defeated by Lib.
Wills, F.	Bristol North	Retired

Nays

Bagot, J.	Kendal	Defeated by Lib.
Baird, J.	Glasgow–Central	Defeated by Lib.
Campbell, J.	Glasgow Univ.	Retired
Cohen, B.	Islington East	Defeated by Lib.
Dickinson, R.	Wells	Defeated by Lib.
Fisher, T.	Fulham	Defeated by Lib.
Hartland, F. D-	Uxbridge	Re-elected as Unionist
Hoare, S.	Norwich	Retired
Hutton, J.	Richmond (Yorks)	Retired
Johnstone, J.	Horsham	Died in 1904
King, H.	Hull Central	Re-elected as Unionist
Knowles, L.	Salford West	Defeated by Lib.
Morrell, G.	Woodstock	Defeated by Lib.
Peel, W.	Manchester South	Defeated by Lib. in Harrow
Richards, H.	Finsbury East	Died in 1905
Smith, W.	Strand	Re-elected as Unionist
Thornton, P.	Clapham	Re-elected as Unionist
Tritton, C.	Norwood	Retired
Williams, R.	Dorset West	Re-elected as Unionist
Wolff, G.	Belfast East	Re-elected as Unionist

The following Unionist Free Traders ran as Unionists in 1906, and were opposed by other Unionists:

Free Trader	Tariff Reformer	Free Trade % of Unionist vote	Tariff Reform % of Unionist vote
Bowles, T.	Burgoyne, A.	60·1	39·9
Cecil, Ld. H.	Benn, I.	39·8	60·2
Corbett, A.	Rosenthal, A.	94·7	5·3
Elliott, A.	Hills, J.	40·1	59·9
Seeley, C.	Page Croft, H.	76·2	23·8
Gorst, J.	Rawlinson, J.	—	—

The average % won by Free Traders in 5 seats was 62·2%
The average % won by Tariff Reformers in 5 seats was 37·8%
It is not possible to calculate the percentages in Gorst's constituency of Cambridge University, as there were 3 Unionist candidates
The following Unionist Free Traders joined the Liberals between 1904 and 1906: Cavendish, Churchill, Dickson-Poynder, Foster, Guest, Hain, Kemp, Russell, Seeley (J.), Taylor and Wood

APPENDIX II

Unionist Free Traders elected in 1922

M.P.s from Lancashire marked *

name	constituency	reference
*Ainsworth, C.	Bury	Bury Guardian, 11 Nov. 1922
*Brass, W.	Clitheroe	Clitheroe Advertiser and Times, 3 Nov. 1922
*Briggs, W.	Blackley	Yorkshire Post, 6 Nov. 1922
Bentinck, Ld. H. C.	Nottingham S.	Appendix I
Cecil, Ld. Hugh	Oxford Univ.	Appendix I
Cecil, Ld. Robert	Hitchin	Cecil, R, All the Way, 124
*Cohen, J. B. B.	Fairfield	Liverpool Post, 9 Nov. 1922
Colvin, Gen. R.	Epping	West Essex Gazette, 11 Nov. 1922
*de Frece, W.	Ashton-u-Lyne	Ashton-under-Lyne Herald, 28 Oct. 1922
Fawkes, F.	Pudsey and Otley	Pudsey and Stanningley News, 10 Nov. 1922
*Halstead, D.	Rossendale	Bacup Times, 4 Nov. 1922
*Henn, S.	Blackburn	Blackburn Weekly Telegraph, 28 Oct. 1922
James, C.	Bromley	Beckenham Journal, 11 Nov. 1922
Manville, E.	Coventry	Coventry Herald, 10 Nov. 1922
Roundell, R.	Skipton	Westmorland Gazette, 4 Nov. 1922
*Russell, W.	Bolton	Bolton Evening News, 11 Nov. 1922
*Singleton, J.	Lancaster	Yorkshire Post, 25 Sept. 1922
*Stockton, E.	Manchester–Exchange	Manchester Evening News, 27 Oct. 1922
Stewart, G.	Wirral	Birkenhead and Cheshire Advertiser, 11 Nov. 1922
*Watts, T.	Withington	Gee, New Parliament, 162
*White, G.	Southport	Southport Journal, 11 Nov. 1922

Several other Unionists elected in 1922 supported a modified version of Free Trade: F. Astbury (Salford West) was a Free Trader except for the dye industry[1]; D. Brown (Hexham) opposed tariffs but supported protection for 'key industries'[2]; and E. Wallace (Rugby) opposed tariffs but supported anti-dumping rules[3]. There may have been a few more Free Traders elected in 1922, but an extensive survey of local newspapers has failed to reveal any

1 Gleanings and Memoranda, January 1923, 49
2 Hexham Herald, 4 November 1922
3 Rugby Observer, 10 November 1922

The Conservatives fought the 1923 election ostensibly on the issue of tariffs and protection. However, a small number of Conservative candidates expressed opposition to the Baldwin government's policies. Two junior members of the government, W. Brass and A. Buckley, resigned their posts over the issue. Brass was kept on as candidate by his local party, but Buckley was denied renomination.[1]

Sir Allan Smith was also denied renomination in Croydon South, while H. S. Dutton was dismissed as candidate because of their free trade views. In Bolton, W. Russell resigned as candidate rather than run as a protectionist, while G. D. White expressed similar views. Sir Robert Newman, though he supported anti-dumping legislation, ran as an overall supporter of free trade. (In 1929, Newman was denied renomination by his local Conservative Party, but he won as an Independent.)[2]

The table lists 16 Unionist/Conservative MPs and candidates who supported free trade openly during the 1923 election. There were probably several others who preferred to keep their counsel; but even if one doubles the number in the table, it would be only 32, which would still have been under 5% of the total of Conservative/Unionist candidates. This was a smaller proportion than in either 1923 or 1904, and it was a clear indication that protection had carried the day, at least on the Unionist side.

In fact, not all of those listed in this appendix came out resolutely in favour of free trade; many fudged the issue. For instance, Sir Edwin Stockton, perhaps the leading Unionist Free Trader in this election, said that he would vote against the government on tariffs, but 'not to put the socialists in.'[3] Lord Hartington described himself as a 'temporary protectionist', who hoped to have free trade again soon. Marshall Stevens labelled himself a 'Cobdenite Free Trader'. Stevens explained that in Cobdenite Free Trade one could have protective tariffs. Similarly, F. Blindell supported both tariffs and free trade, 'up to a point'; while F. Astbury would support free trade only if other countries adopted it too. G. B. Hurst supported protection, but not 'tariff walls', which on first glance would seem to be the same things. Thus of the 16 'free traders' listed here, only about half were untrammelled.[4]

Only 6 of the 16 Conservatives in this list were successful in 1923; there were doubtless a few other Unionist Free Traders who won, but who did not make as public an issue of their views.

APPENDIX III
Unionist Free Trade candidates in 1923

candidates elected marked E
candidates in Lancashire marked *

name	constituency	reference
*Astbury, F.	Salford W.	17 Nov., 1923
E*Blindell, F.	Ormskirk	22 Nov., 1923
E*Brass, W.	Clitheroe	19 Nov., 1923
Brown, D. C.	Hexham	24 Nov., 1923
Falcon, M.	Norfolk E.	*Swaffam Journal* 1 Dec., 1923
*Finburg, S.	Salford N.	22 Nov., 1923
*Flanagan, W.	Manch–Clayton	26 Nov., 1923
E Gould, J. C.	Cardiff Central	17 Nov., 1923
E Hartington, Ld	Derbyshire W.	28 Nov., 1923
*Hurst, G.B.	Manch–Moss Side	22 Nov., 1923
*Metcalf, H.	Leigh	*Bolton Evening News*, 20 Nov., 1923
Preston, W.	Mile End	24 Nov., 1923
E*Rankin, J. S.	Liv–E. Toxteth	24 Nov., 1923
Smith, A.	Croydon S/Partick	15 Nov., 1923
*Stevens, M.	Eccles	28 Nov., 1923
E*Stockton, E.	Manch–Exchange	26 Nov., 1923

All references are to the *Manchester Guardian* except where indicated.

---

1 *Manchester Guardian*, 19 & 20 Nov., 1923; also cited in C. P. Cook, *The Age of Alignment*, 137-139, which is the best study available of the 1923 and 1924 elections.
2 *Manchester Guardian*, 15, 19 & 20 Nov., 1923. Smith was renominated in a new constituency, Glasgow-Partick, as a Unionist Free Trader.
3 On 21 January, 1924, on a Labour motion referring to tariffs, the Baldwin government fell. No Conservative or Unionist voted with the Liberal and Labour Parties; ten Liberals and one independent supported Baldwin.
4 *Manchester Guardian*, 22, 28, & 30 Nov., 1923.

The Carlton Club Meeting 19 October 1922[1]

The M.P.s who voted to reject the Lloyd George Coalition in 1922 did so according to a fairly clear pattern: most Conservative M.P.s who sat for old Liberal or Liberal Unionist areas voted in favour of the Coalition, while most who sat for safe Conservative seats voted against it. There were exceptions to this but they were in a fairly small minority. The chief areas of Coalition strength were Scotland, East Lancashire, the South-west of England and East–Central England. In each place a majority of Conservative M.P.s voted to retain the Coalition. As Conservative M.P.s in the South-west and East–Central districts were few, they did not affect the result very much. However, Conservative M.P.s for Scotland and East Lancashire provided the backbone of support for the Lloyd George administration. In some places the Coalition was stronger than the map indicates. For example, in Yorkshire the Conservative M.P.s voted by 11 to 3 against the Coalition, but the Yorkshire Division of the National Unionist Association had decided by only 'a small majority' to break with the Coalition.[2] In East Anglia most Conservative M.P.s voted in favour of the Coalition but, as most seats in the area were represented by Lloyd George Liberals, the possible pro-Coalition vote there among Conservatives was much reduced.

Generally, M.P.s opposing the Coalition came from safe Conservative seats, mainly in the South of England, and in scattered safe seats elsewhere. The 'Diehards' came from all parts of the country, whether they sat for safe seats such as Bournemouth or Eastbourne, or highly marginal ones such as Shettleston, St. Rollox, East Fife or Walsall. The notion that the 'Diehards' came only from safe seats is inaccurate, as is the impression that retiring M.P.s as a group supported the Coalition.[3] The 'Diehards' were mostly men who would not change their minds merely because they happened to sit for marginal constituencies. Other Conservative M.P.s, however, seemed to be more influenced by the previous political alignments of their constituencies.

1 The overall vote was 187 against the Coalition and 87 in favour, with many abstentions
2 *Yorkshire Evening Press,* 22 July 1922

3 According to Lord Beaverbrook, 'some Welsh Members and . . . several Scottish Members, most of whom intended to retire' provided most of the backbench support for the Coalition (Beaverbrook, *Decline . . . of Lloyd George,* 202). The voting list in Austen Chamberlain's papers does not bear this out

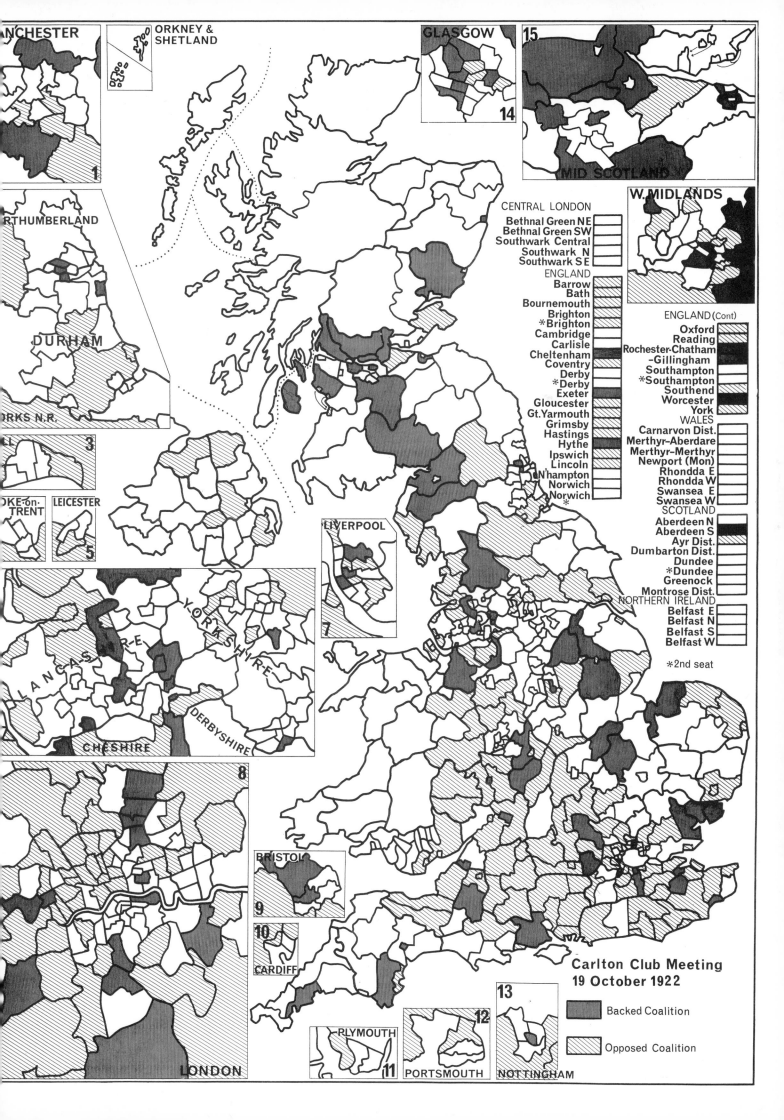

Conservative Seats 1918-29

Between 1918 and 1929 the Conservatives won 1,582 out of a possible 3,010 times in Great Britain.[1] This represented 52·5% of the possible wins. To a considerable degree the pattern of Conservative success after 1918 resembled that before 1918. The chief exceptions were that they lost some ground in Birmingham, Liverpool and English agricultural districts, while they gained some in rural Scotland. They remained weak in most industrial areas, including all mining districts, the West Yorkshire textile district, Central Scotland, East London and most industrial sections of large cities. All these areas gave the Conservatives little support prior to 1918, and the fact that they were unable to win many seats in them after 1918 indicates that the Conservatives did not substantially broaden the basis of their support in the early 1920s. This may be contrasted with frequent Liberal and Labour wins in wide varieties of seats. Fortunately for the Conservatives, the redistribution of 1918 favoured them, because it added many seats in the suburbs of large cities. Most of the new seats remained faithfully Conservative in elections from 1918 to 1929: 23 new seats voted Conservative in every election, and many other new seats voted Conservative in a majority of elections.

The Conservatives lost ground in 2 large cities, Liverpool and Birmingham. Between 1886 and December 1910 Liverpool had elected Conservatives at all times in most of its constituencies, while Birmingham had elected Conservatives or their allies in every constituency. After 1918 the Liberals and Labour broke this Conservative dominance. The Liberals won 5 seats in Liverpool and suburbs in 1923; and although they lost all of them in 1924, the Labour Party picked up several, and in 1929 won 6 in the same general areas. Liberals won no seats in Birmingham in the 1920s, but Labour won one in 1924, and expanded their hold to 6 out of 12 in 1929. The net result was that the Conservatives won only 4 of the 11 Liverpool seats, and only 5 of the 12 Birmingham seats in all elections of the 1920s. While the Conservatives still dominated the 2 cities electorally, they could no longer count on overwhelming victories even in bad years, as they had been able to do before 1918. Moreover, they lost some seats, such as Wirral and Wavertree, which they retained even in 1964 and 1966, when there were strong local tides against the Conservatives.[2] Probably the reason for the Conservative loss of grip on Liverpool and Birmingham was the increasing irrelevance of some pre-1918 political issues such as Home Rule, which had tended to split the anti-Conservative vote.

Another group of seats showing a slight drift away from Conservatism were the agricultural seats of England. Before 1918 the Conservatives had held 5 agricultural districts with hardly any breaks: the areas were around Worcester, York, Exeter and Lincoln, and in the extreme South-east. Between 1918 and 1929 they retained solid control only of the districts around Worcester and York. In the others, Liberals won several seats, especially in the election of 1923. This suggests that the English agricultural seats were slightly more marginal than they had been before 1918. This may have hurt the Liberals more than it hurt the Conservatives, because the Liberals had so few areas of consistent strength in agricultural England before 1918, that they could ill afford to lose what they had. On the other hand, the Conservatives could lose a few formerly safe seats and still have enough in hand to do well.

In Scotland the Conservatives penetrated nearly all the rural seats which had evaded them between 1885 and December 1910. In 1918 and 1922 they won few seats in rural Scotland, but they gained slightly in 1923 and substantially in 1924. There was no noticeable division between Eastern and Western Scotland, as there had been before 1918, and the only significant division was between urban and rural seats. The only rural area the Conservatives failed to penetrate was the group of Gaelic-speaking seats in the extreme North-west. Before 1918 several of these seats had voted Conservative in at least one election.

The chief area of Conservative strength remained the South-east, especially the area South of the Thames. North of the Thames, the Conservatives lost some heavily middle-class seats such as Finchley and Harrow; but South of the river, they won nearly every seat which had more than 30% middle class.[3] Seats with a high proportion of middle-class voters in other parts of the country provided most other safe Conservative seats in this period.

1 Northern Ireland is excluded; for a table of Conservative wins, see map on p. 84
2 See maps on pp. 67 and 69, and also on p. 79
3 The 2 exceptions were Lambeth North and Lambeth-Kennington. The middle-class percentage for Lambeth as a whole was 30·7. It is possible that the percentage was higher in the 2 Southern seats for Lambeth, Brixton and Norwood, than in the 2 Northern ones

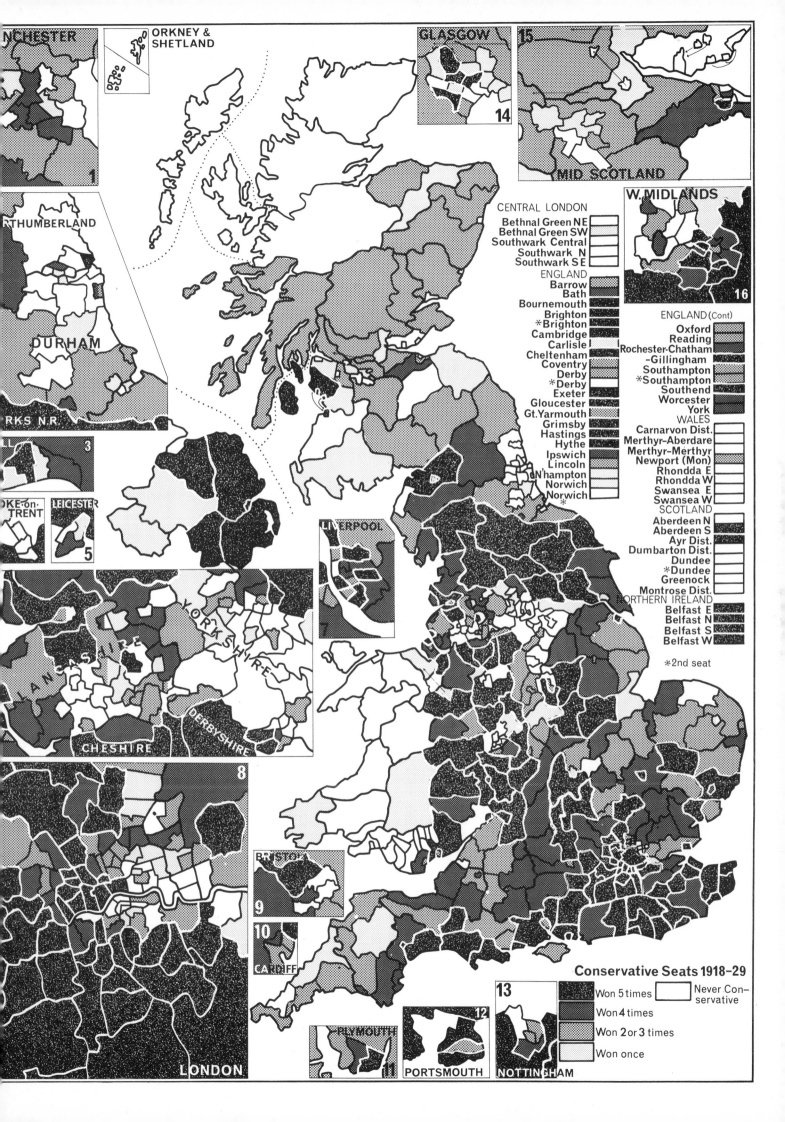

MANCHESTER 1

ORKNEY & SHETLAND

GLASGOW 14

15

MID SCOTLAND

W. MIDLANDS 16

RTHUMBERLAND

DURHAM

RKS N.R.

3

OKE-on-TRENT

LEICESTER 5

YORKSHIRE

LANCASHIRE

CHESHIRE

DERBYSHIRE

LIVERPOOL

8

BRISTOL 9

CARDIFF 10

LONDON

PLYMOUTH 11

PORTSMOUTH 12

NOTTINGHAM 13

CENTRAL LONDON
Bethnal Green NE
Bethnal Green SW
Southwark Central
Southwark N
Southwark S E
ENGLAND
Barrow
Bath
Bournemouth
Brighton
*Brighton
Cambridge
Carlisle
Cheltenham
Coventry
Derby
*Derby
Exeter
Gloucester
Gt. Yarmouth
Grimsby
Hastings
Hythe
Ipswich
Lincoln
N'hampton
Norwich
Norwich
*

ENGLAND (Cont)
Oxford
Reading
Rochester-Chatham
-Gillingham
Southampton
*Southampton
Southend
Worcester
York
WALES
Carnarvon Dist.
Merthyr-Aberdare
Merthyr-Merthyr
Newport (Mon)
Rhondda E
Rhondda W
Swansea E
Swansea W
SCOTLAND
Aberdeen N
Aberdeen S
Ayr Dist.
Dumbarton Dist.
Dundee
*Dundee
Greenock
Montrose Dist.
ORTHERN IRELAND
Belfast E
Belfast N
Belfast S
Belfast W

*2nd seat

Conservative Seats 1918–29

Won 5 times   Never Con-servative

Won 4 times

Won 2 or 3 times

Won once

Divisional Labour Parties 1918-24

The following table lists all constituencies in England and Wales which did not have Divisional Labour Parties (DLPs) by the time of the 1922 Annual Conference. It also lists the type of Labour Organisation in the constituency, and the probable reason for the lack of a DLP. The table is based on the 1922 Conference Report, pp. 133-66.

The sign * indicates that the probable reason for the lack of a DLP was electoral weakness. BLP indicates that a Borough Labour Party took responsibility for several constituency organisations. TC indicates that a Trades Council took the responsibility. C and ILP indicate that the probable reason for the lack of a DLP was the strength of the Communists or of the ILP in the constituency.

constituency	Local Labour organisation	Probable reason for no DLP	Date DLP set up if 1922-1924
1 London Boroughs			
Battersea North	BLP	C	—
Battersea South	BLP	C	—
Bermondsey West	—	ILP	1923
Bethnal Green North-east	BLP	C	—
Bethnal Green South-west	BLP	C	—
City of London (2)	—	*	—
Hammersmith North	BLP	Right-wing candidate	1923
Hammersmith South	BLP	C	1923
Lewisham West	BLP	C	1923
Paddington North	BLP	Conflict with HQ	—
Paddington South	BLP	Conflict with HQ	—
Westminster – Abbey	BLP	C	—
Westminster – St. George's	BLP	C	—
Woolwich East	—	Right-wing MP	—
Woolwich West	—	Right-wing MP	—
2 English Boroughs			
Ashton-under-Lyne	TC	1920 candidate–TUC Pres.	—
Birkenhead East	BLP	Co-operated with Libs.	—
Birkenhead West	BLP	Co-operated with Libs.	—
Birmingham – Deritend	BLP	ILP-Lab. candidate, 1922	1923
Birmingham – Edgbaston	BLP	*	1924
Birmingham – Handsworth	BLP	*	1924
Birmingham – Kings Norton	BLP	Co-op. cand., 1918; ILP-Lab., 1922	1923
Birmingham – Moseley	BLP	C	1924
Bradford Central	BLP	ILP	—
Bristol Central	BLP	Right-wing candidates, 1918 and 1922	1924
Burnley	TC	S.D.F. MP	—
Halifax	TC	Speaker's seat	—
Hastings	TC	*	1923
Huddersfield	TC	ILP	1924
Leigh	TC	Miners' MP	—
Liverpool – East Toxteth	BLP	Lib. and Lab. backed Ind., 1922	1923
Liverpool – Exchange	BLP	Lib. and Lab. backed Nat., 1885-1929	—
Manchester – Exchange	BLP	*	1923
Manchester – Gorton	TC	Right-wing MP; SDF opposition	—
Middlesbrough East	BLP	Co-operated with Libs.	—
Middlesbrough West	BLP	Co-operated with Libs.	—
Newcastle on Tyne North	BLP	Co-operated with Libs., 1922	1923
Newcastle on Tyne West	BLP		—
Nottingham Central	BLP	*	1924
Nottingham East	BLP	ILP, 1918; Co-op., 1922	1924
Oldham (2)	TC		—
Plymouth – Drake	BLP	ILP	1923

constituency	Local Labour organisation	Probable reason for no DLP	Date DLP set up if 1922-1924
Plymouth – Sutton	BLP		1923
Rochester – Chatham	TC	Co-operated with Libs.	—
Rochester – Gillingham	—	Co-operated with Libs.	1924
St. Helens	TC	Right-wing MP	—
Salford South	BLP	As in Plymouth – Drake (same candidate)	1923
Sheffield Central	—	*	1924
Smethwick	TC	Right-wing MP	—
Stockton	TC		—
Tottenham North	BLP		1923
West Ham – Plaistow	BLP	Right-wing MP; ILP	1924
West Ham – Silverton	BLP	Right-wing MP; ILP	1924
West Ham – Stratford	BLP	ILP	1923
West Ham – Upton	BLP	ILP	1923
3 English Counties			
Beds – Mid	—	*	1924
Berks – Windsor	—	*	1924
Cheshire – Eddisbury	—	*	1924
Cornwall – Bodmin	—	*	1924
Cumberland North	—	*	1924
Cumberland – Penrith	TC	*	1924
Derbyshire West	—	*	1924
Devon – Honiton	—	*	1924
Devon – Tavistock	—	*	1924
Devon – Totnes	—	*	1924
Dorset North	—	*	—
Essex – Romford	—	ILP	1923
Hants – Aldershot	—	*	1924
Hereford – Hereford	County LP	*	—
Hereford – Leominster	County LP	*	—
Herts – Hertford	—	*	1924
Kent – Chislehurst	—	*	1924
Lancs – Darwen	TC		—
Lancs – Fylde	—		1923
Lincs – Horncastle	—	*	1923
Oxon – Henley	—	*	1924
Suffolk – Sudbury	—	*	1923
Sussex – Rye	—	*	—
Westmorland	—	*	1924
Worcs – Evesham	—	*	1924
East Yorkshire – Buckrose	—	*	1924
East Yorkshire – Holderness	—	*	1924
East Yorkshire – Howden	—	*	1924
North Yorkshire – Richmond	—	*	—
West Yorkshire – Ripon	—	*	1923
4 Welsh Boroughs			
Carnarvon District	—	*	1924
5 Welsh Counties			
Anglesey	—	* and Ind. Lab. MP	1924
Cardigan	—	*	1923
Carmarthen – Carmarthen	—	*	1923
Denbigh – Denbigh	—	*	1924
Merioneth	—	*	1923

In June 1920 the National Agent of the Labour Party stated that 'today there are not six constituencies out of the 602 in England, Scotland and Wales where some form of Labour organisation does not exist'.[1] At that time, 297, or nearly half, were without Divisional Labour Parties(D.L.P.s). In some places Trades Councils acted as substitutes; in most, there was no Labour organisation worth speaking of. However, in some English borough seats,

1 *Report of the Annual Conference of the Labour Party* (hereafter *R.A.C.L.P.*) 1920, 8

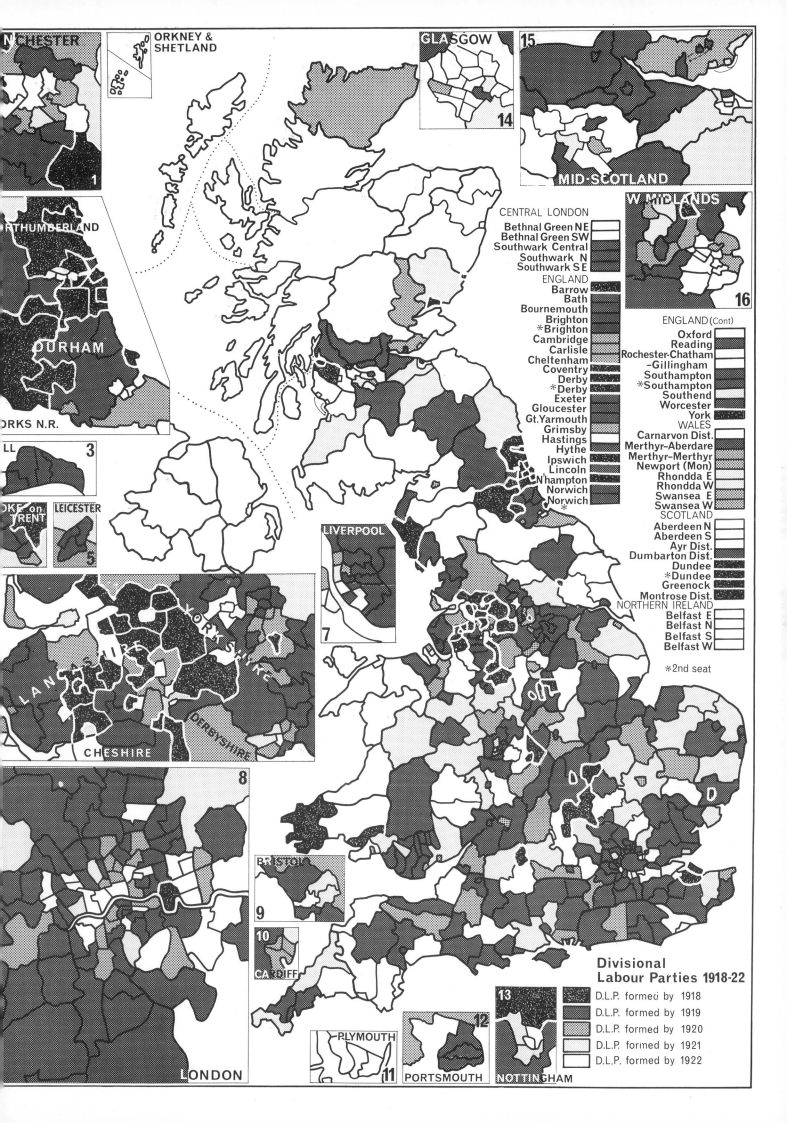

MANCHESTER 1

ORKNEY & SHETLAND

NORTHUMBERLAND

DURHAM

YORKS N.R.

HULL 3

STOKE on TRENT   **LEICESTER** 5

GLASGOW 14

MID·SCOTLAND 15

W MIDLANDS 16

CENTRAL LONDON
Bethnal Green NE
Bethnal Green SW
Southwark Central
Southwark N
Southwark SE
ENGLAND
Barrow
Bath
Bournemouth
Brighton
*Brighton
Cambridge
Carlisle
Cheltenham
Coventry
Derby
*Derby
Exeter
Gloucester
Gt. Yarmouth
Grimsby
Hastings
Hythe
Ipswich
Lincoln
N'hampton
Norwich
Norwich
*

ENGLAND (Cont)
Oxford
Reading
Rochester-Chatham
 -Gillingham
Southampton
*Southampton
Southend
Worcester
York
WALES
Carnarvon Dist.
Merthyr–Aberdare
Merthyr–Merthyr
Newport (Mon)
Rhondda E
Rhondda W
Swansea E
Swansea W
SCOTLAND
Aberdeen N
Aberdeen S
Ayr Dist.
Dumbarton Dist.
Dundee
*Dundee
Greenock
Montrose Dist.
NORTHERN IRELAND
Belfast E
Belfast N
Belfast S
Belfast W

*2nd seat

LIVERPOOL 7

LANCASHIRE   **YORKSHIRE**

CHESHIRE   **DERBYSHIRE**

8

BRISTOL 9

10

CARDIFF

13

LONDON

PLYMOUTH 11

PORTSMOUTH 12

NOTTINGHAM

Divisional Labour Parties 1918-22

D.L.P. formed by 1918
D.L.P. formed by 1919
D.L.P. formed by 1920
D.L.P. formed by 1921
D.L.P. formed by 1922

D.L.P.s were not set up because of factional quarrels within the Labour Party.

One type of factional quarrel was over support for the First World War. In 1918 at least 5 constituency Labour groups attempted to unseat pro-War Labour M.P.s. In Norwich the Trades Council denounced G. H. Roberts as 'more reactionary than the worst Tories',[1] and asked for a replacement Labour candidate without even hearing Roberts' side. Roberts then ran as a 'Coalition Labour' candidate, supporting Lloyd George. In Gorton a self-styled 'Selection Committee' attempted without reference to the national party to repudiate their M.P., John Hodge; this also happened in Barrow.[2] In West Ham I.L.P. supporters attempted to turn the local Labour Party against two sitting Labour M.P.s, Jack Jones and Will Thorne. Jones and Thorne managed to retain official recognition as Labour candidates, so the I.L.P. put up two 'socialists' against them. The I.L.P. gained control of the West Ham Borough Labour Party, and elected one of the 2 'socialist' candidates of 1918 as Secretary.[3] Perhaps the I.L.P. hoped that in this way they could apply pressure on Jones and Thorne. At any rate, they did not allow the Borough Labour Party to be subdivided into four D.L.P.s, one for each constituency, until 1923. Many Labour M.P.s had good reason to believe that the establishment of D.L.P.s in their constituencies would weaken their personal hold, and they did not wish to encourage the establishment of bodies which might turn against them. This was more common with right-wing M.P.s such as Hodge, than with left-wing ones. Fifteen seats with Labour M.P.s did not have D.L.P.s in their constituencies by the time of the 1920 Conference. Eleven of them had been strongly pro-War,[4] one was a member of the Social Democratic Federation,[5] one was a strong supporter of the I.L.P.,[6] and one was a Labour M.P. with self-styled 'independent' views.[7]

A second type of factional quarrel was that between Communists and other groups in the Labour Party. In several divided London boroughs, Communists dominated the borough Labour Party. Subdivision of such Labour Parties into 2 or more D.L.P.s would have made continued Communist control more difficult, and the result was that the parties often remained undivided. For instance, the Borough Labour Party in Bethnal Green was controlled by Communists, who monopolised Labour candidatures in the 2 constituencies of Bethnal Green during the elections of the early 1920s. In 1922 they sponsored J. J. Vaughan as an 'independent' Labour candidate in Bethnal Green South-west, while W. Windsor ran openly as a Communist in North-east.[8] Probably this Communist predominance in the Bethnal Green Labour Party helped make Bethnal Green the last stronghold of Liberalism in London.[9] The I.L.P. also acted as a hindrance to the formation of D.L.P.s in many places. In Bradford, F. W. Jowett of the I.L.P. and the leading Labour politician in the city, preserved I.L.P. dominance in the local Labour organisation for many years after D.L.P.s had been set up in neighbouring constituencies. I.L.P. strength in Mid-Scotland also hindered the spread of D.L.P.s, and it was not until after the Labour sweep in the area in 1922 that D.L.P.s were established in most working-class seats in Central Scotland.

In some places the Labour Party made local pacts with the Liberals, and the maintenance of undivided Borough Labour Parties facilitated such pacts. For instance, in 1922 and 1923 a Labour candidate ran in Birkenhead West while a Liberal ran in Birkenhead East. The parties did not acknowledge the deal openly, but it was certainly made: when the Labour candidate received his party's nomination in 1922, he absent-mindedly thanked his followers for the Liberal nomination. When it was pointed out that he was nominated by the Labour Party, he said there was no real difference in policy, anyway. The I.L.P. in Birkenhead East wished to run a candidate against the Liberal but decided 'after some discussion' not to do so. Perhaps if they had had the support of a D.L.P. in their constituency, they would have opposed the Liberal.[10]

A final type of internal quarrel was over individuals. At the 1919 Conference, H. Roberts, the delegate from Paddington Borough Labour Party, complained that Arthur Henderson had attempted to interfere in local affairs.[11] Roberts made similar statements in later years, and it is likely that he did not wish to see his local power split by dividing the Paddington party into two D.L.P.s.

Despite the quarrels which prevented the growth of D.L.P.s in certain areas, local Labour Parties spread rapidly. In 1918 there were only 49; by 1923 there were 506. Most of the increase came in 1919, when 235 D.L.P.s were formed. This rapid expansion indicates that many Labour voters in the country wished to take advantage of individual membership in the party, which had not been available before 1919. The first areas with many D.L.P.s were the textile districts of West Yorkshire and North-east Lancashire, and the mining districts of West Lancashire and Durham. The last major area in England to be organised was London. It is unlikely that the headquarters of the Labour Party wished to hinder the spread of D.L.P.s in London, although the National Organiser had gone so far as to sign the nomination papers of the Liberal candidate in North Croydon in 1918.[12] A few Labour candidates in London made abortive arrangements with local Liberals, but these, too, were not extensive.[13] Consequently, the relatively slow growth of D.L.P.s in London was probably caused mainly by the penetration of several London Borough Labour Parties by Communists.[14]

1 *R.A.C.L.P.*, 1918, 108
2 *R.A.C.L.P.*, 1918, 5
3 *R.A.C.L.P.*, 1921, 111
4 Pro-War M.P.s sat for Gorton, Platting, Salford North, St. Helens, Smethwick, Rhondda East and West, Gower, Plaistow, Silvertown, Woolwich East
5 The M.P. for Burnley
6 The M.P. for Govan
7 The M.P. for Aberdeen City North. See F. Rose, *Our Industrial Jungle*, for his views
8 Both were members of the Communist Party (*The Communist*, 14 and 25 November 1922)
9 The Liberals attributed their success to their ownership of the largest drinking club in the constituency (*New York Times*, Magazine Section, 1 April 1923)
10 *Birkenhead Advertiser*, 28 October 1922
11 Roberts said that Henderson first tried to get the B.L.P. to support a Conservative, then that he had pressure on Paddington to get their chosen candidate to retire, and finally that he had put in a 'black leg' friend of Henderson himself (*R.A.C.L.P.*, 1919, 124)

12 *R.A.C.L.P.*, 1919, 124-5
13 C. G. Ammon raised the possibility of a London pact between Liberals and Labour at a meeting of the National Executive of the Labour Party in 1922, but according to Hugh Dalton, 'there was a look of disgust all around the table. It was unanimously decided to take no action,' (*Dalton Papers*, Diary, 9 January 1922). Viscount Gladstone, the Liberal organiser, thought the scheme 'very sensible and profitable'; and Dalton himself contemplated 'friendly co-operation' between the Liberals and Labour in his own constituency only a few months later. (*Viscount Gladstone Papers*, Add. MSS 46085 f. 5, Gladstone to E. Hatch, 25 January 1922; and *Dalton Papers*, Diary, 22 May 1922)
14 In 1926, 1927 and 1928 the Labour Party expelled local organisations from the following London boroughs because of Communist influence in them: Battersea B.L.P., Bethnal Green B.L.P., Camberwell B.L.P., Chelsea D.L.P., East Ham B.L.P., East Ham – Stratford D.L.P., Hackney B.L.P., Holborn D.L.P., Islington North D.L.P., Lewisham B.L.P., Lewisham East D.L.P., and Poplar B.L.P. (*R.A.C.L.P.*, 1926, 19; 1927, 15; 1928, 19)

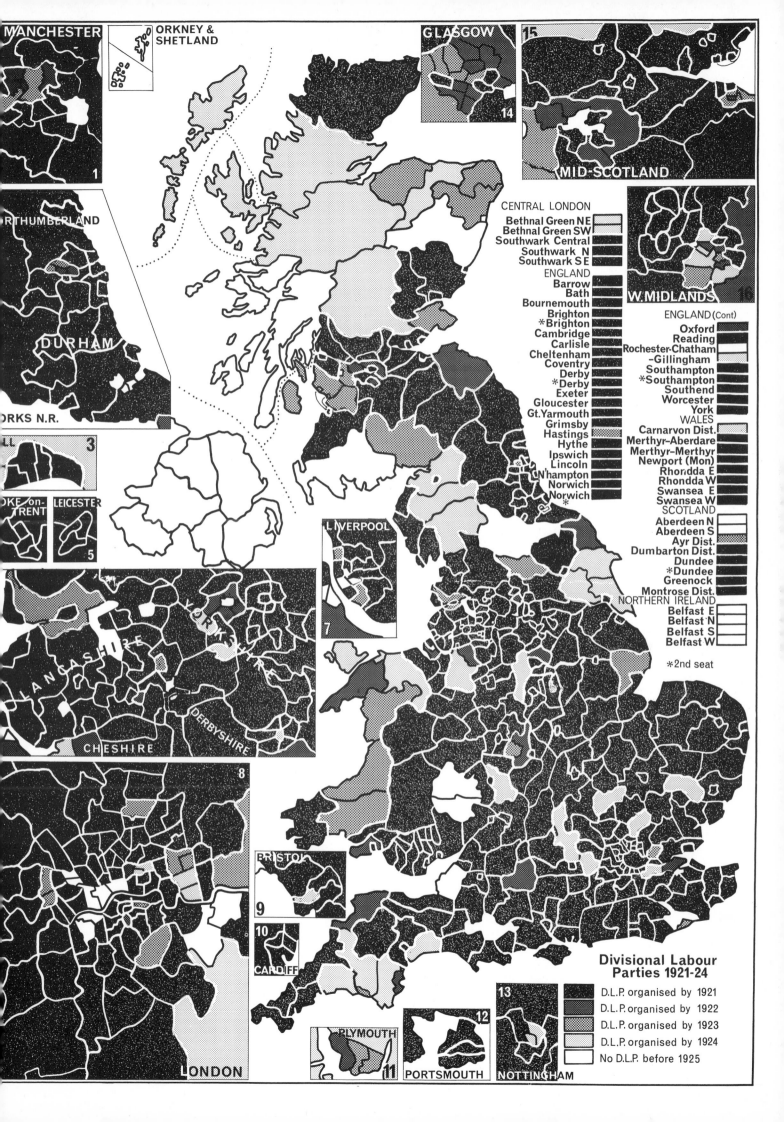

MANCHESTER

ORKNEY & SHETLAND

GLASGOW

15

MID-SCOTLAND

14

NORTHUMBERLAND

DURHAM

YORKS N.R.

3

STOKE on-TRENT

LEICESTER

5

LANCASHIRE

CHESHIRE

DERBYSHIRE

YORKSHIRE

LIVERPOOL

7

8

BRISTOL

9

CARDIFF

10

13

PLYMOUTH

11

PORTSMOUTH

12

NOTTINGHAM

CENTRAL LONDON
Bethnal Green NE
Bethnal Green SW
Southwark Central
Southwark N
Southwark SE
ENGLAND
Barrow
Bath
Bournemouth
Brighton
*Brighton
Cambridge
Carlisle
Cheltenham
Coventry
Derby
*Derby
Exeter
Gloucester
Gt.Yarmouth
Grimsby
Hastings
Hythe
Ipswich
Lincoln
N'hampton
Norwich
Norwich
*

W.MIDLANDS
16

ENGLAND (Cont)
Oxford
Reading
Rochester–Chatham
–Gillingham
Southampton
*Southampton
Southend
Worcester
York
WALES
Carnarvon Dist.
Merthyr–Aberdare
Merthyr–Merthyr
Newport (Mon)
Rhondda E
Rhondda W
Swansea E
Swansea W
SCOTLAND
Aberdeen N
Aberdeen S
Ayr Dist.
Dumbarton Dist.
Dundee
*Dundee
Greenock
Montrose Dist.
NORTHERN IRELAND
Belfast E
Belfast N
Belfast S
Belfast W

*2nd seat

LONDON

Divisional Labour Parties 1921-24

D.L.P. organised by 1921
D.L.P. organised by 1922
D.L.P. organised by 1923
D.L.P. organised by 1924
No D.L.P. before 1925

Labour Seats 1918-29

During the 1920s few places other than mining seats consistently voted Labour. In other industrial seats the Liberals had a substantial following at least until 1924.[1] The Liberals did well in the textile districts of West Yorkshire and East Lancashire, and also in slums of large cities. In these places the Liberals maintained the support which they had built up before 1918. Because of Liberal strength in most industrial areas, it was not until 1935 that something like the post-Second World War political pattern was established. The Labour Party had considerable difficulty even in retaining such urban seats as Bermondsey West or Bethnal Green South-west. In some places Labour did not attempt to displace the Liberals entirely, but co-operated with them;[2] elsewhere, Labour did not co-operate with the Liberals, but until 1924 it remained unable to eliminate the Liberals, either.

Possibly Labour failed to win solid support in most non-mining industrial areas because pre-war Liberal strength in them had built up voting habits which were hard to break. This explanation is insufficient, however, because at most only a third of the electorate could have voted in any election before 1914.[3] Habitual allegiance therefore could not account for the failure of Labour to win solid support more rapidly than it did, in industrial areas. Some observers felt that the Liberals remained strong because they had perverted the electorate in some manner: in Bethnal Green, because they had a large political drinking club; in Bermondsey West, because the Liberal candidate distributed 3,628 turkeys just before the election of 1923.[4] This explanation, too, may be regarded as insufficient.

A more likely view is that many working-class voters considered Liberal policies relevant to their needs. At least until 1924 it was possible to regard the Liberal Party as a partial ally of Labour; it was only the fall of the Labour Government which really shattered this illusion. A further explanation of Liberal strength in industrial districts is that some Labour candidates were on the extreme left of their party; in constituencies which nominated them, many Labour supporters may have felt that the Liberal candidate expressed their views more closely than did the Labour candidate. Perhaps the industrial seats in question would eventually have gone Labour, but the adoption of left-wing candidates probably delayed the shift. It is notable that in several industrial areas where Labour won relatively few elections before 1924, there was a strong left-wing element in the local Labour Party. London and Birmingham were examples of this. Liberal strength in London and Conservative strength in Birmingham may have weakened the moderate element in the Labour Parties there in the early 1920s, and this may have been why the left-wing element was relatively stronger in local Labour groups in the two cities.[5]

The election of 1924 ended Liberal strength in most urban seats, thus clearing the way for Labour expansion in subsequent elections. In the election of 1929 Labour took many former Liberal seats, especially in London and West Yorkshire, and former Conservative seats, especially in Liverpool and Birmingham. However, no persistent Labour pattern was established in these places until the election of 1935.

---

1 See map, Liberal Seats, 1918-1929, p. 85
2 In Willesden and Birkenhead, for example
3 The electorate rose from 7,006,815 in 1910 to 20,554,875 in 1922, in Great Britain. It may be assumed that a large proportion of the 1910 electors had died by 1922, so that only a third, at most, of the 1922 electors could have voted in 1910, even if there had been 100% turnout in 1910

4 See map on p. 109 and F. Brockway, *Bermondsey Story,* 118. Kedward, the Liberal candidate in Bermondsey West in 1923, acted for the Wesleyan Mission in the constituency when he distributed the turkeys. However, the turkeys were issued 'with Mr Kedward's compliments'
5 Between 1926 and 1929 numerous local Labour groups were expelled from the Labour Party for left-wing views. Most were in London or Birmingham. See maps, Divisional Labour Parties, 1918-1924, pp. 109 and 111

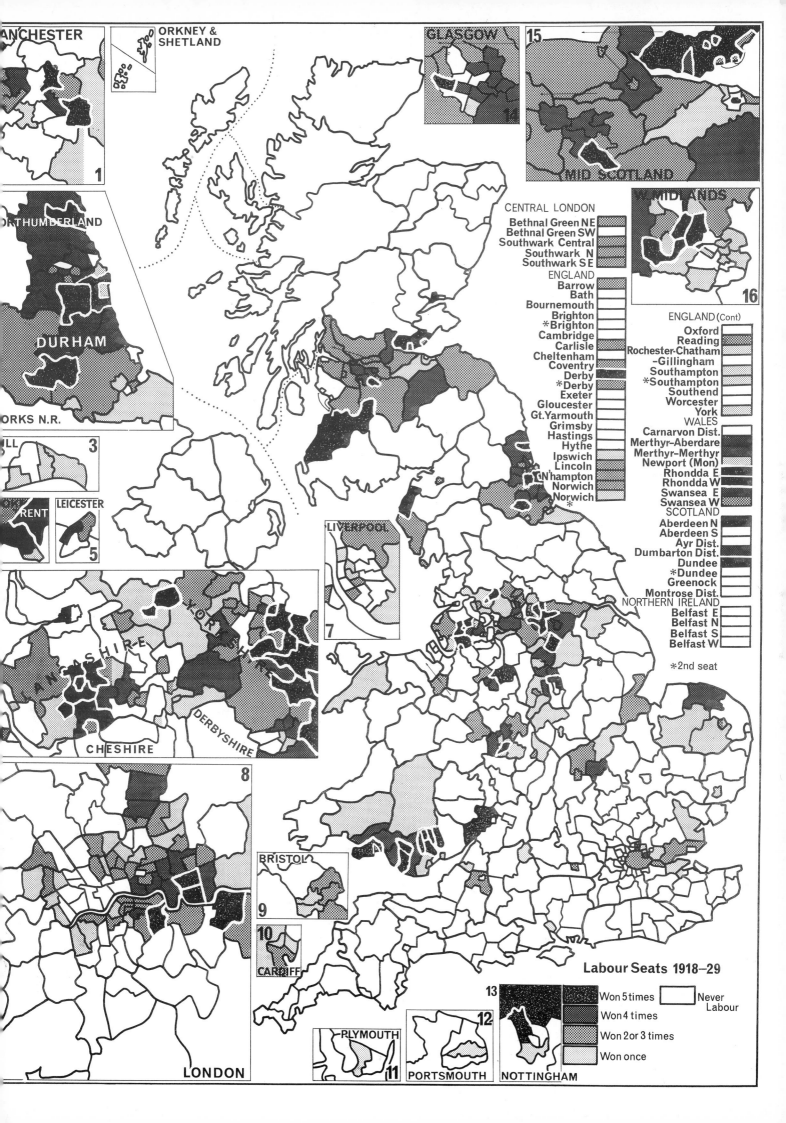

MANCHESTER

ORKNEY & SHETLAND

1

NORTHUMBERLAND

DURHAM

YORKS N.R.

3

HULL

TRENT

LEICESTER

5

GLASGOW

14

15

MID SCOTLAND

W. MIDLANDS

16

LIVERPOOL

7

YORK

LANCASHIRE

DERBYSHIRE

CHESHIRE

8

BRISTOL

9

10

CARDIFF

13

PLYMOUTH

11

12

PORTSMOUTH

NOTTINGHAM

LONDON

CENTRAL LONDON
Bethnal Green NE
Bethnal Green SW
Southwark Central
Southwark N
Southwark S E
ENGLAND
Barrow
Bath
Bournemouth
Brighton
*Brighton
Cambridge
Carlisle
Cheltenham
Coventry
Derby
*Derby
Exeter
Gloucester
Gt.Yarmouth
Grimsby
Hastings
Hythe
Ipswich
Lincoln
N'hampton
Norwich
Norwich
*

ENGLAND (Cont)
Oxford
Reading
Rochester-Chatham
-Gillingham
Southampton
*Southampton
Southend
Worcester
York
WALES
Carnarvon Dist.
Merthyr–Aberdare
Merthyr–Merthyr
Newport (Mon)
Rhondda E
Rhondda W
Swansea E
Swansea W
SCOTLAND
Aberdeen N
Aberdeen S
Ayr Dist.
Dumbarton Dist.
Dundee
*Dundee
Greenock
Montrose Dist.
NORTHERN IRELAND
Belfast E
Belfast N
Belfast S
Belfast W

*2nd seat

Labour Seats 1918–29

Won 5 times   Never Labour
Won 4 times
Won 2 or 3 times
Won once

Labour Seats 1955-66

A 'marginal seat' is often considered to be one with a small majority, because such a seat is more likely to change hands than one with a large majority. Generally, this is the case, but it is not invariably so. Many seats with quite small majorities have not changed when they were expected to do so, while other seats with much larger majorities have changed. For instance, in 1966 Labour failed to gain either Norfolk South-west or Dorset South, despite the fact that the Conservative majorities in 1964 had been only 123 and 935 respectively. It begs the question to say that the 2 seats mentioned failed to change because of local conditions. Similar examples can be found in all other elections between 1955 and 1964. A seat is effectively marginal when it changes hands frequently, whether majorities in it are large or small; and it is not effectively marginal if it does not change hands. The map shows seats which were effectively marginal between 1955 and 1966. It indicates that they were located in 2 main areas, the textile districts of West Lancashire and East Yorkshire, and the fringes of London, especially the Southern fringes. In addition to these two main areas, scattered seats throughout the country changed hands in at least one of the elections in question. Not all of these changes were short-term. In rural Wales the Labour gains represented a long-term shift from the Liberals to Labour which had been in progress since the end of the Second World War. Most other Labour gains were the result of short-term trends.

Generally, the map of pre-1945 Labour wins (p. 113) was similar to that of the period 1955-66, except that Labour filled in many gaps which had previously existed. Also, Labour had solid control of the core seats in most large cities, and the marginal seats were on the fringes. Probably this represented population movements away from the slums in the centre of large cities, towards the outskirts. Labour retained nearly all its strongholds in mining constituencies, and as between 1918 and 1923, the industrial area with the largest number of effectively marginal seats was the textile district. This may have reflected a continued Liberal presence in textile seats,[1] which weakened the Labour vote there.

Very few agricultural seats changed hands in the 1950s and 1960s, primarily because the Labour base in them was much weaker than the Liberal base had been in the early 1920s. The most notable feature of the map is probably that Labour appears very strong in a few areas, and weak in most others. To some extent, the map exaggerates this, because the Labour vote very rarely was below 25% of the total; but in such places no substantial Labour support is indicated. One must remember in looking at a map of this sort that the clusters of Labour areas indicate only that Labour won those areas, not that it won 100% of the votes in them, and 0% in others.

1 See map, The Liberal Vote in 1964, p. 87

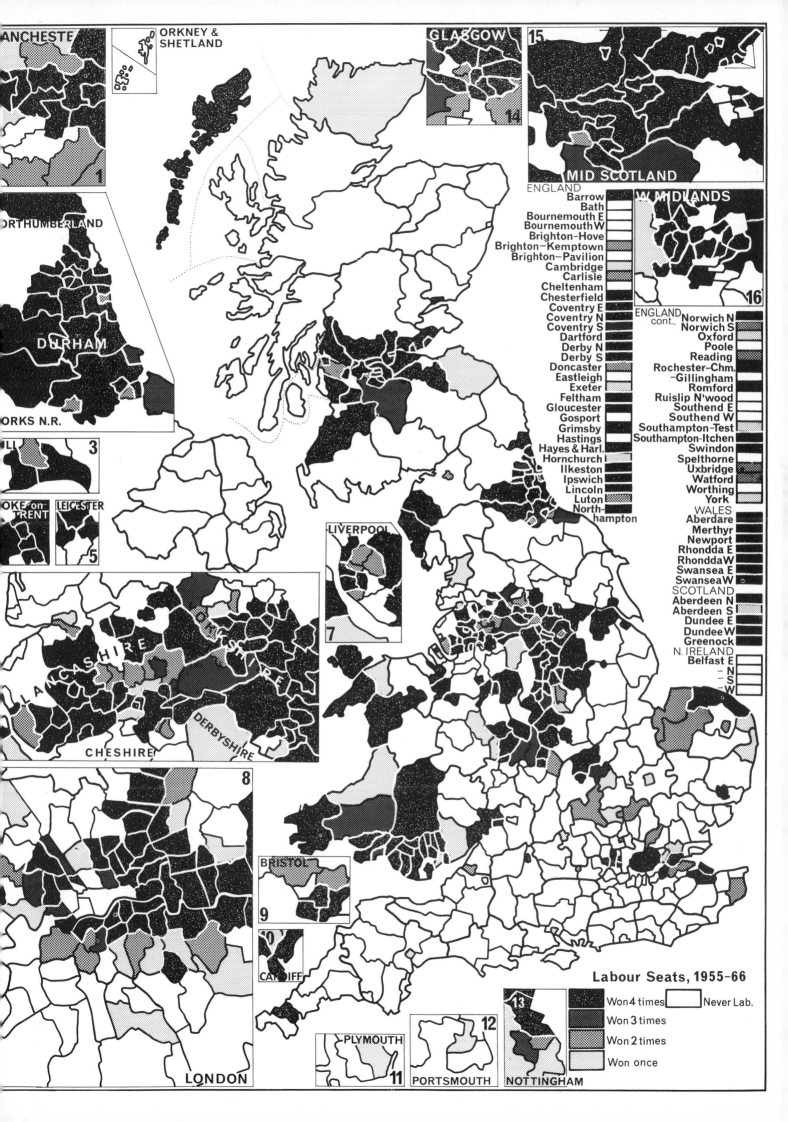

The Mining Vote in 1921

Constituencies with more than 20% of their occupied male population over the age of 12 engaged in mining are listed in the following table, which is based on the county volumes of the *Census of 1921*.

constituency	% miners
1 London Boroughs	
None	
2 English Boroughs	
Barnsley	43·7
Leigh	46·9
Morpeth	58·2
Newcastle-under-Lyme	37·3
Rotherham	23·9
St. Helens	30·6
South Shields	23·6
Stoke-on-Trent (3 seats)	22·2
Wallsend	28·1
Wigan	42·3
3 English Counties	
Cumberland – Whitehaven	37·9
Workington	27·5
Derbyshire – Belper	34·8
Chesterfield	33·2
Clay Cross	62·3
Ilkeston	51·4
North-east	54·6
Durham – Barnard Castle	44·6
Bishop Auckland	50·7
Blaydon	53·6
Chester-le-Street	56·6
Consett	55·4
Durham	58·5
Houghton-le-Spring	53·6
Seaham	71·4
Sedgefield	33·7

constituency	% miners
Spennymoor	62·2
Gloucester – Forest of Dean	33·6
Lancashire – Farnworth	34·2
Ince	57·8
Newton	30·3
Westhoughton	43·3
Leicestershire – Bosworth	33·2
Northumberland – Hexham	27·3
Wansbeck	45·3
Nottinghamshire – Bassetlaw	25·8
Broxtowe	52·9
Mansfield	56·3
Somerset – Frome	27·6
Staffordshire – Cannock	45·2
Leek	30·1
Lichfield	30·1
Warwickshire – Nuneaton	40·3
West Yorkshire – Doncaster	28·5
Don Valley	41·8
Hemsworth	65·4
Normanton	62·7
Penistone	23·0
Pontefract	23·6
Rother Valley	56·1
Rothwell	45·8
Wentworth	66·5
4 Welsh Boroughs	
Merthyr Tydfil (2 seats)	61·2
Rhondda (2 seats)	74·4

constituency	% miners
5 Welsh Counties	
Brecon and Radnor	23·7
Carmarthen – Carmarthen	22·5
Llanelly	27·8
Carnarvonshire	21·7
Denbigh – Wrexham	42·6
Glamorgan – Aberavon	26·8
Caerphilly	65·6
Gower	33·1
Neath	44·6
Ogmore	63·6
Pontypridd	55·1
Monmouth – Abertillery	73·0
Bedwellty	67·0
Ebbw Vale	55·6
Pontypool	47·5
6 Scottish Burghs	
Dunfermline District	32·3
Kirkcaldy District	26·4
7 Scottish Counties	
Ayrshire South	40·2
Fife West	51·9
Lanark – Bothwell	48·2
Hamilton	46·0
Lanark	36·8
Northern	37·3
Rutherglen	32·9
Linlithgow	36·4
Midlothian – North	31·7
South and Peebles	29·0
Stirling – East	23·8
West	30·1

The Census of 1921 did not give occupational statistics by constituency, but by rural and urban districts. Generally, the borders of constituencies coincided with those of the rural districts, but not always. In such cases the population of the rural districts has been apportioned between the constituencies involved in the ratio of the distribution of parishes. Thus if a rural district had 10 parishes, 6 of them in one constituency and 4 in another, the population of the rural district as a whole has been divided in the ratio of 6:4. This assumes that all the villages were of the same size and that they were all similar in occupational make-up. While this assumption may be slightly in error, there is no other way of estimating the distribution. In any case, such calculations were unnecessary in most constituencies.

The Labour Party won many mining seats in every election from 1918 to 1935. However, there was a noticeable difference in the behaviour of the 5 most important mining districts in the election of 1931. In 1931 Welsh and West Yorkshire mining seats[1] remained faithful to Labour, while mining seats in Durham, Derbyshire and Mid-Scotland voted for the National Government. This difference in behaviour bore only a slight relation to the percentage of miners in the seats involved, and the decisive factor seemed to be the proportion of middle-class voters. The following tables illustrate this:

% miners	Labour, 1931	National, 1931
70 or over	3	1
60-69·9	10	—
50-59·9	7	8
40-49·9	8	8
30-39·9	2	18
20-29·9	4	17
	34	**52**

% middle-class	Labour, 1931	National, 1931
Over 10%	9	42
Under 10	25	10
	34	**52**

West Fife is excluded from both tables, because the Labour and Communist vote combined was 57·1% but because of the Labour – Communist split, the National Government candidate won

1 Defined here as seats with over 20% miners in 1921

116

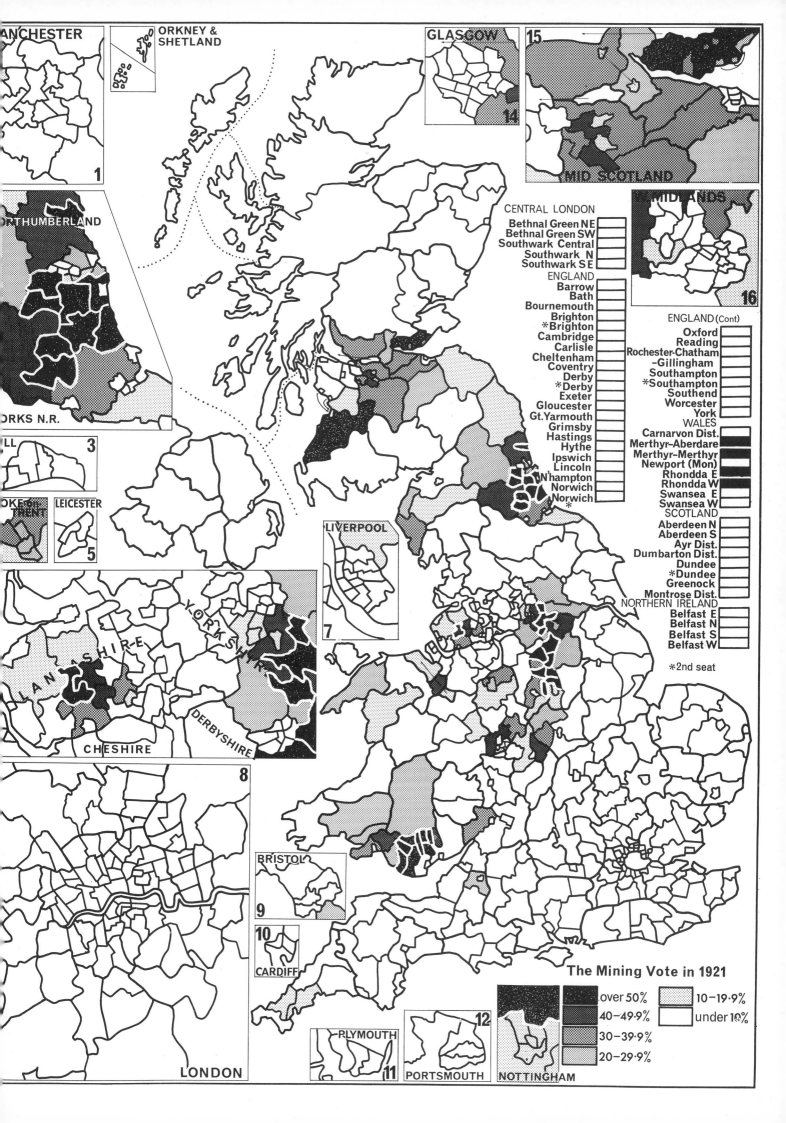

The Mining Vote in 1921

over 50%		10–19·9%
40–49·9%		under 10%
30–39·9%		
20–29·9%		

CENTRAL LONDON
Bethnal Green NE
Bethnal Green SW
Southwark Central
Southwark N
Southwark S E
ENGLAND
Barrow
Bath
Bournemouth
Brighton
*Brighton
Cambridge
Carlisle
Cheltenham
Coventry
Derby
*Derby
Exeter
Gloucester
Gt.Yarmouth
Grimsby
Hastings
Hythe
Ipswich
Lincoln
N'hampton
Norwich
Norwich
*

ENGLAND (Cont)
Oxford
Reading
Rochester-Chatham
 -Gillingham
Southampton
*Southampton
Southend
Worcester
York
WALES
Carnarvon Dist.
Merthyr–Aberdare
Merthyr–Merthyr
Newport (Mon)
Rhondda E
Rhondda W
Swansea E
Swansea W
SCOTLAND
Aberdeen N
Aberdeen S
Ayr Dist.
Dumbarton Dist.
Dundee
*Dundee
Greenock
Montrose Dist.
NORTHERN IRELAND
Belfast E
Belfast N
Belfast S
Belfast W

*2nd seat

In addition to the proportion of middle-class voters, other factors probably influenced the outcome in several mining districts. In Durham Ramsay Macdonald's candidature probably influenced the outcome in his own constituency, Seaham. In 3 other Durham seats, Consett, Houghton and Barnard Castle, there was an above-average number of Nonconformists and the Liberals had done well in the election of 1929. The Liberal vote was probably decisive in winning these 3 seats for the National Government. In Derbyshire the Liberals maintained connections with the Labour movement during the 1920s. In Chesterfield the Liberal, Barnet Kenyon, received the support of the miners in the elections of 1918 and 1922.[1] Even in 1923 and 1924 Kenyon defeated Labour candidates. A Liberal had won North-east Derbyshire in 1918, and the Liberals remained strong there in other elections in the 1920s. In Derbyshire, as in Durham, several National Government victories in mining seats were probably due to vestigial Liberal support among miners. The Liberals were weak in the Scottish mining seats, and the National Government victories there were probably caused by the combination of the presence of some extreme Left-wing Labour and Communist candidates, and continuing feuds in some places between Protestant and Roman Catholic voters.[2] There were also more middle-class voters in Scottish mining seats than in English or Welsh ones. In normal elections these factors would have been insufficient to make the Scottish mining districts leave Labour, but 1931 was not a normal election. Because of this, splits in working-class ranks were sufficient to cause numerous Labour defeats in Scottish mining seats.

Two major mining areas remaining faithful to Labour in 1931 were South Wales and West Yorkshire. In both places the Labour movement had shown considerable political strength before the First World War. In the smaller mining district of West Lancashire, Labour had also won numerous victories before the War, and the Liberals had been consequently weakened. Because of this, there was not much Liberal support for the National Government to carry these mining districts.

---

1 See J. E. Williams, *The Derbyshire Miners,* 806-34; and Kinnear, *The Fall of Lloyd George,* Appendix 2

2 In 1918 and 1922 H. Ferguson ran in Motherwell as an 'Orange and Protestant' candidate. He got 10·7% in 1918 and 29·1% in 1922 *(Lloyd George Liberal Magazine,* June 1922)

3 Gregory, *The Miners and British Politics, 1906–14,* 192–201, calculates the proportion of miners in each constituency before 1914. Gregory's figures are based on the location of collieries, rather than directly on the census figures as in this book. Gregory also estimates the number of miners in each seat who could vote. The figures in this book refer only to the post-1918 period, when all adult males were eligible to vote, rather than prior to 1914, when only 59% had that right. Considerable allowances must be made for using the Gregory figures, which are, however, of some use.

The Agricultural Vote in 1921

Constituencies with more than 20% of their occupied male population over the age of 12 engaged in agriculture are listed in the following table, which is based on the county volumes of the *Census of 1921*.

constituency	% agriculturists
1 London	
None	
2 English Boroughs	
None	
3 English Counties	
Beds – Mid	40·5
Berks – Abingdon	35·6
Newbury	31·5
Bucks – Aylesbury	22·3
Buckingham	31·3
Cambridgeshire	56·9
Cheshire – Eddisbury	27·5
Knutsford	21·3
Cornwall – Bodmin	31·6
Camborne	24·4
Northern	39·3
St. Ives	27·7
Cumberland – Northern	45·8
Penrith and Cockermouth	29·3
Derbyshire – West	27·1
Devon – Barnstaple	25·3
Honiton	35·2
S. Molton	54·1
Tavistock	38·4
Totnes	34·1
Tiverton	41·6
Dorset – North	45·1
West	39·6
Essex – Chelmsford	28·8
Colchester	20·7
Harwich	20·0
Maldon	35·0
Saffron Walden	50·2
Gloucestershire – Cirencester	46·8
Stroud	21·8
Thornbury	22·3
Hants – Basingstoke	32·7
New Forest	30·7
Petersfield	37·1
Hereford – Hereford	33·1
Leominster	55·5
Herts – Hemel Hempstead	22·0
Hertford	28·7
Hitchin	27·8
Huntingdonshire	43·3
Isle of Ely	54·7

constituency	% agriculturists
Kent – Ashford	36·9
Canterbury	23·8
Chislehurst	22·0
Maidstone	28·1
Sevenoaks	31·8
Lancashire – Fylde	20·5
Lonsdale	21·5
Ormskirk	29·9
Leicestershire – Harborough	21·1
Melton	28·6
Lincolnshire – Brigg	21·1
Gainsborough	37·5
Grantham	35·9
Holland	54·6
Horncastle	50·9
Louth	49·1
Rutland and Stamford	41·5
Norfolk – Eastern	52·9
Kings Lynn	42·2
Northern	44·1
Southern	53·3
South-western	56·3
Northants – Daventry	37·1
Peterborough	21·0
Northumberland – Berwick	26·9
Hexham	22·7
Nottinghamshire – Bassetlaw	21·9
Newark	32·4
Oxford – Banbury	37·7
Henley	38·0
Salop – Ludlow	42·6
Oswestry	36·8
Shrewsbury	23·9
Somerset – Bridgwater	28·5
Taunton	29·6
Wells	34·4
Weston-super-Mare	25·8
Yeovil	31·2
Staffordshire – Stone	27·1
Suffolk – Bury St. Edmunds	37·5
Eye	50·2
Sudbury	47·2
Woodbridge	38·6
Surrey – Guildford	20·6
Reigate	23·4
East	20·8
Sussex – Chichester	32·4
East Grinstead	33·0
Horsham and Worthing	26·7
Lewes	23·6
Rye	37·6
Warwickshire – Rugby	24·6
Tamworth	20·1
Warwick	20·1

constituency	% agriculturists
Westmorland	32·1
Wiltshire – Chippenham	38·7
Devizes	40·1
Salisbury	25·1
Westbury	27·1
Worcestershire – Bewdley	39·8
Evesham	45·5
Yorkshire, East – Buckrose	38·4
Holderness	38·5
Howdenshire	43·6
Yorkshire, North – Richmond	40·4
Scarborough and Whitby	20·6
Thirsk and Malton	48·9
Yorkshire, West – Barkston Ash	25·9
Ripon	21·3
Skipton	22·0
4 Welsh Boroughs	
None	
5 Welsh Counties	
Anglesey	37·2
Brecon and Radnor	30·3
Cardigan	40·5
Carmarthen – Carmarthen	35·1
Carnarvon County	29·1
Denbigh – Denbigh	36·1
Merioneth	32·7
Monmouth – Monmouth	27·6
Montgomery	48·0
Pembroke	28·0
6 Scottish Burghs	
None	
7 Scottish Counties	
Aberdeenshire – Central	50·4
East	37·5
West and Kincardineshire	46·3
Argyll	27·5
Ayrshire – South	23·2
Banff	33·3
Berwick and Haddington	33·3
Caithness and Sutherland	41·0
Dumfries	31·1
Fife – East	41·9
Forfar	43·8
Galloway	43·3
Inverness – Inverness	34·0
Ross and Comarty	38·3
Western Isles	39·5
Moray and Nairn	33·6
Orkney and Shetland	43·2
Perth – East	22·7
West and Kinross	42·9
Roxburgh and Selkirk	25·6

In 1921 only 12 seats had more than 50% engaged in agriculture. Nine of them were in East Anglia; no other part of the country had more than one seat with over 50% agriculturists. However, the agricultural vote was politically significant in the 141 seats with over 20% engaged in agriculture. Though it is sometimes stated that the agricultural vote favoured the Conservatives strongly,[1] this was probably not the case in the inter-war period. The most heavily agricultural seats showed less support for the Conservatives than the partly agricultural seats, as the following table indicates. The table was calculated by finding the number of times seats in a given category went Conservative in the 7 elections from 1918 to 1935, and comparing it with the possible number of times they could have gone Conservative. For example, there were 12 seats with more than 50% agriculturists, so that the Conservatives could have won a maximum of 12 seats 7 times in the 7 elections, or 84 wins all told. In fact, the Conservatives won only 47 times, so that their percentage of possible wins was 56·0%.

1 For example, by E. Kriebehl, 'Geographic influences in British Elections', *Geographical Review*, 1916, 422-9

119

% of agriculturists	% of possible wins actually won by Cons.	Number of seats
Over 50%	56·0	12
40–49·9	64·9	26
30–39·9	69·1	48
20–29·9	76·6	55

Northern Ireland is excluded, because seats were redistributed there in 1922

The general rule which can be deduced from this table is that the higher the proportion of persons engaged in agriculture, the lower was the proportion of the Conservative vote. The difference between the most agricultural seats, and those with only 20 to 29% agriculturists, was very marked, and it cannot be dismissed as being due to regional differences. That is, the most highly agricultural districts were not all highly Nonconformist, or Welsh or Scottish; within a given area, the more agricultural a seat was, the more likely it was to vote against the Conservatives. In Kent, for instance, the only seats to vote Liberal in the period 1918-1935 were Sevenoaks and Ashford.[1] These were the only constituencies in Kent which had more than 30% agriculturists. In Essex the only seats to vote Liberal in the same period were Saffron Walden, Harwich and Chelmsford, all of which had over 20% agriculturists. In the only other Essex constituencies with more than 20% agriculturists, Labour won Maldon in 1923, with Liberal support; and the Conservative in Colchester was a well-known supporter of co-operation between Liberals and Conservatives.[2]

Although the Conservatives were weakest in the agricultural seats prior to 1924, they remained relatively weaker there than in the rest of the country in subsequent elections. The agricultural districts continued after 1924 to elect more Liberals than most other types of constituency, as the following table shows:

Seats with more than 30% agriculturists (total 86)

party	1918	1922	1923	1924	1929	1931	1935
Conservatives	54	48	38	74	55	64	64
Liberal	29	35	43	11	26	22	19
Labour	1	2	5	1	5	—	2
Other	2	1	—	—	—	—	1

The only elections in which the Conservatives won more than half the seats with over 50% agriculturists were those of 1924, 1931 and 1935. In each of these elections there was a Conservative landslide in the country as a whole, so that Conservative victories in these agricultural seats were not surprising. The most notable feature of elections in the agricultural seats was the great turnover. In the 86 seats with more than 30% agriculturists, only 33 remained with the same party in every election from 1918 to 1935, 25 of them Conservative and 8 Liberal. More than half these seats staying Conservative in all 7 elections had either a middle-class vote of over 20%, or no Liberal candidate in 1923, or both.[3] The degree of turnover can be seen by examining only Liberal–Conservative changes in only 3 elections, those of 1922, 1923 and 1924:

	Lib. gains from Cons.	Cons. gains from Lib.[4]	Net gains
1922	15	13	2 Lib.
1923	15	8	7 Lib.
1924	—	31	31 Cons.

In these 3 elections there were also 11 other changes, making a total of 81 changes in 86 seats, so that on average a third of the agricultural seats changed hands in each of the 3 elections. This is only partly explained by the small majorities in some agricultural seats. In many agricultural seats majorities were large in some elections, yet there was a turnover. For instance, the results in Hereford were:

year	Cons.	Lib.	Lab.	majority	swing to Cons.
1923	55·3%	40·0%	4·7%	15·3% Cons.	—
1924	60·6	39·4	—	21·2 Cons.	3·0%
1929	44·8	48·7	6·5	3·9 Lib.	−12·6

In some elections the farm vote did not behave in the same manner in all parts of the country. The 1922 election is a good example of this, because in 1922 some agricultural districts moved away from the Conservative government, while others moved towards the Conservatives. This was probably caused in part by variations in the prosperity of the agricultural seats involved. It is possible to estimate the prosperity of the farm voters by examining the production of wheat and barley in each county, and by comparing it with the average production in the previous 10 years in the same county. It is reasonable to assume that agricultural districts would show greater tendencies to support the Government where production stayed firm than where it declined. In 1922 this was further complicated by the fact that the Lloyd George Liberals had formed part of the Government until a few weeks before the election. Consequently, Conservative candidates running against Lloyd George Liberals in agricultural seats could have expected to win much of the agricultural protest vote, if there was such a vote. In seats held by the Conservatives before 1922, the Asquith Liberals could have expected to gain most of the protest vote. Because of this complication a distinction should be made between sitting Conservatives and Lloyd George Liberals on the one hand, and sitting Asquith Liberals and prospective Conservative candidates on the other. In English counties where wheat production in 1922 was below 95% of the previous 10-year average, and where there were several agricultural seats, the Conservative percentage of the vote went down in 8, stood steady in one, and rose in 2 counties.[5] Ten of the 15 Liberal gains in agricultural seats in 1922 were in counties with below-average wheat production, and 5 of the remaining 6 Liberal gains were in counties with below-average barley production in 1922.

A further factor in determining the political allegiance of the agricultural seats was the proportion of Nonconformists. In most elections from 1885 to 1935, the Liberals did best in the agricultural seats with over 7½% Nonconformists.[7] Agricultural districts with fewer Nonconformists than 7½% rarely voted Liberal. Examples of this were the seats around Exeter and Worcester, and in the South-east. The chief exceptions were seats in Norfolk, with relatively few Nonconformists, but which voted strongly for the Liberals from 1885 to 1910. Part of the explanation may be that Norfolk had more than the national average proportion of farm labourers per farm.[8] Liberal strength before 1918 was probably due in part to rural radicalism. This was confirmed by the election of Labour candidates in 1922, 1923, 1924 and 1929, in agricultural constituencies in Norfolk.

1 Dartford, an industrial seat in Kent, also voted Liberal: it was a suburb of London, and the Liberal won with Conservative backing
2 See Kinnear, *Fall of Lloyd George*, Appendix 2
3 1923 was the year of the greatest number of Liberal wins in the agricultural seats
4 Six of the 8 Conservative gains in 1923 were in seats which had had no Conservative candidates in 1922
5 Counties with below-average wheat production and swings against the Conservatives in agricultural seats were: Cornwall, Devon, Dorset, Hants., Norfolk, Salop, Surrey, Wilts.; there was no significant change in West Sussex; and the

Conservatives gained in Gloucestershire and Herefordshire. In Gloucestershire, the Conservative percentage gain in Cirencester was probably caused by the fact that the Independent candidate of 1918 ran in 1922 for Labour
6 See *Agricultural Statistics 1922*, LVII, i, 82, for county reports of wheat and barley yields in 1922 compared with the 1912–1921 average
7 In 1922. See map, Nonconformists in 1922, p. 127
8 Norfolk had 2·54 labourers per farm in 1921; the average for England as a whole was 1·70 (*Agricultural Statistics 1921*, 42–4)

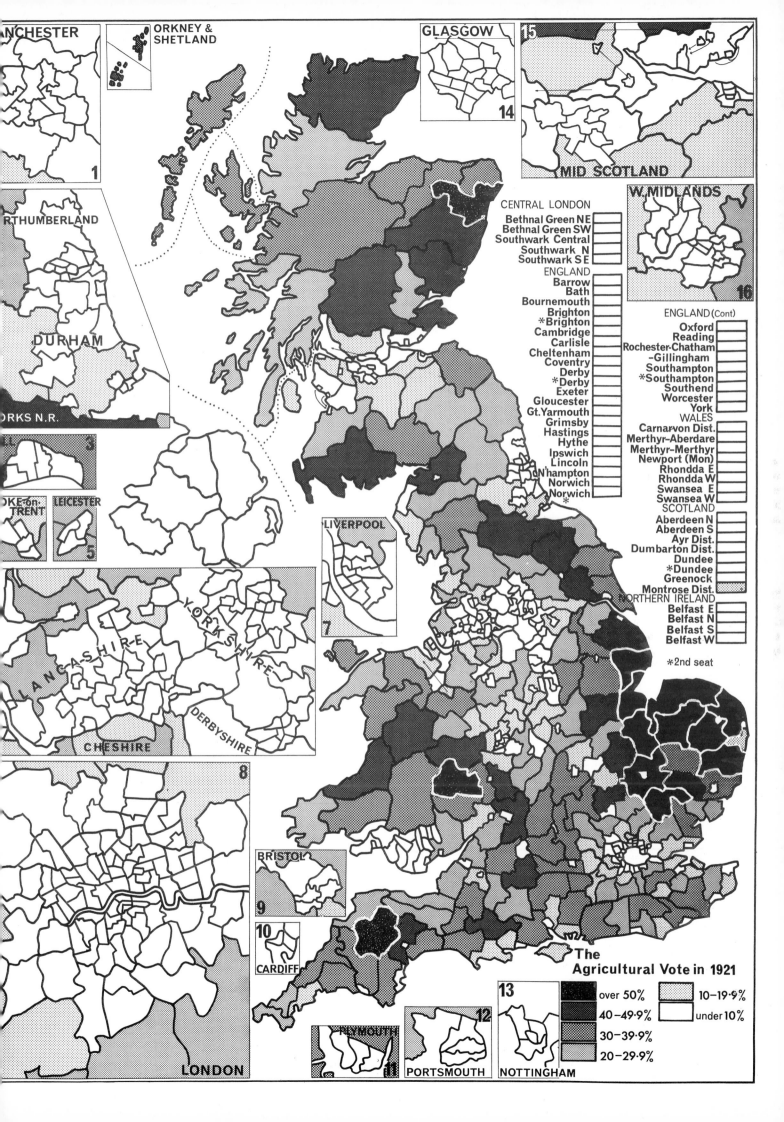

The
Agricultural Vote in 1921

███ over 50%	░░░ 10-19·9%		
███ 40-49·9%	☐ under 10%		
▓▓▓ 30-39·9%			
▒▒▒ 20-29·9%			

CENTRAL LONDON
Bethnal Green NE
Bethnal Green SW
Southwark Central
Southwark N
Southwark S E
ENGLAND
Barrow
Bath
Bournemouth
Brighton
*Brighton
Cambridge
Carlisle
Cheltenham
Coventry
Derby
*Derby
Exeter
Gloucester
Gt.Yarmouth
Grimsby
Hastings
Hythe
Ipswich
Lincoln
N'hampton
Norwich
*Norwich

ENGLAND (Cont)
Oxford
Reading
Rochester-Chatham
-Gillingham
Southampton
*Southampton
Southend
Worcester
York
WALES
Carnarvon Dist.
Merthyr-Aberdare
Merthyr-Merthyr
Newport (Mon)
Rhondda E
Rhondda W
Swansea E
Swansea W
SCOTLAND
Aberdeen N
Aberdeen S
Ayr Dist.
Dumbarton Dist.
Dundee
*Dundee
Greenock
Montrose Dist.
NORTHERN IRELAND
Belfast E
Belfast N
Belfast S
Belfast W

*2nd seat

GLASGOW
15
MID SCOTLAND
14

W.MIDLANDS
16

MANCHESTER
1
ORKNEY &
SHETLAND

NORTHUMBERLAND
DURHAM
YORKS N.R.

3
STOKE-on-
TRENT
LEICESTER
5

LANCASHIRE E
YORKSHIRE
DERBYSHIRE
CHESHIRE
8

LIVERPOOL
7

BRISTOL
9

CARDIFF
10

LONDON

PLYMOUTH
11
PORTSMOUTH
12
NOTTINGHAM
13

The Middle-Class Vote in 1921

Constituencies with more than 20% of their occupied male population over the age of 12 in census categories 23, 24, 25 and 28 are listed in the following table, which is based on the county volumes of the *Census of 1921*.

constituency	% middle class
1 London	
Battersea (2)	26·7
Camberwell (4)	28·6
Chelsea	31·1
City of London (2) (residents)	34·3*
Deptford	23·6
Fulham (2)	29·6
Greenwich	22·7
Hackney (3)	28·1
Hammersmith (2)	26·2
Hampstead	48·6
Holborn	35·9
Islington (4)	25·7
Kensington (2)	36·1
Lambeth (4)	30·7
Lewisham (2)	42·7
Paddington (2)	33·4
St. Marylebone	31·3
St. Pancras (3)	25·9
Stoke Newington	37·2
Wandsworth (5)	40·0
Westminster (2)	36·6
Woolwich (2)	29·2
*Probably over 75% if outvoters counted.	
2 English Boroughs	
Bath	25·4
Blackpool	32·2
Bournemouth	34·1
Brighton (2)	32·0
Bristol (5)	23·1
Bromley	39·9
Cambridge	30·6
Carlisle	20·8
Cheltenham	25·7
Croydon (2)	38·1
Ealing	45·1
East Ham (2)	26·1
Eccles	20·3
Exeter	31·8
Gloucester	21·1
Great Yarmouth	24·5
Hastings	32·1
Hornsey	53·7
Hythe	35·5
Ilford	49·1
Ipswich	21·1
Kingston-on-Thames	36·5
Leyton (2)	32·4
Manchester (10)	23·3
Newcastle-on-Tyne (4)	20·3
Norwich (2)	22·4
Oxford	30·6
Plymouth (3)	40·8
Portsmouth (3)	42·8
Preston (2)	20·2
Reading	24·7
Richmond (Surrey)	42·2
Rochester (2)	36·3
Southampton (2)	20·4
Southend	47·4
Southport	33·3
Stockport (2)	22·0
Tottenham (2)	26·3
Wallasey	39·2
Walthamstow (2)	25·3
Willesden (2)	28·9
Wimbledon	37·1
Worcester	21·3
York	38·6
3 English Counties	
Berkshire–Abingdon	30·2
Windsor	27·1
Buckinghamshire–Aylesbury	25·5
Cheshire–Altrincham	30·3
Chester	24·7
Knutsford	21·7
Wirral	23·2
Cornwall–Bodmin	24·8
Devon–Barnstaple	20·1
Torquay	31·8
Dorset–West	23·1
South	39·2
Essex–Colchester	23·5
Epping	36·6
Harwich	24·7
Romford	23·1
South-eastern	20·1
Hampshire–Aldershot	54·3
Fareham	26·3
Petersfield	22·6
Winchester	24·0
Hertfordshire–Hemel Hempstead	21·1
St. Albans	27·3
Watford	29·1
Isle of Wight	26·7
Kent–Canterbury	26·2
Chislehurst	23·7
Dover	28·0
Faversham	22·3
Isle of Thanet	34·9
Tonbridge	23·2
Lancashire–Farnworth	20·4
Lancaster	20·9
Stretford	29·7
Waterloo	29·7
Lincolnshire–Holland	21·0
Middlesex–Acton	29·8
Brentford and Chiswick	31·9
Enfield	23·1
Finchley	45·3
Harrow	37·1
Hendon	40·7
Spelthorne	26·7
Twickenham	36·7
Uxbridge	27·5
Wood Green	46·8
Nottinghamshire–Rushcliffe	20·6
Shropshire–Shrewsbury	21·7
Somerset–Weston-super-Mare	23·1
Suffolk–Woodbridge	24·0
Surrey–Chertsey	25·7
Eastern	37·9
Epsom	32·7
Farnham	32·5
Guildford	26·3
Mitcham	31·2
Reigate	23·6
Sussex–Chichester	20·4
Eastbourne	28·7
East Grinstead	24·9
Horsham and Worthing	22·9
Lewes	20·6
Wiltshire–Salisbury	33·4
Yorkshire, East–Buckrose	20·1
Holderness	20·2
Yorkshire, North–Scarborough	24·8
Yorkshire, West–Pudsey	21·1
Ripon	23·5
4 Welsh Boroughs	
Carnarvon District	32·3
Newport	20·0
Cardiff (3)	23·2
5 Welsh Counties	
None	
6 Scottish Burghs	
Ayr District	22·1
7 Scottish Counties	
Bute and North Ayr	20·1
East Perth	20·1

The following census categories have been arbitrarily defined as constituting the 'middle class' in 1921:

23 Commerce and Finance, excluding clerks
24 Public Administration, including military
25 Professional
28 Clerks, including company secretaries, registrars and office managers

The Census of 1921 did not break down census groups according to income, nor did it usually state what proportion of a given census group was managerial. For example, it did not state, except in the case of large boroughs, whether persons in category 24 were higher civil servants, or clerks. To estimate the middle-class vote, on the same basis for every constituency, it has been necessary to include all the persons in the above 4 categories. Some clerks of non-managerial grades have therefore been included, and some

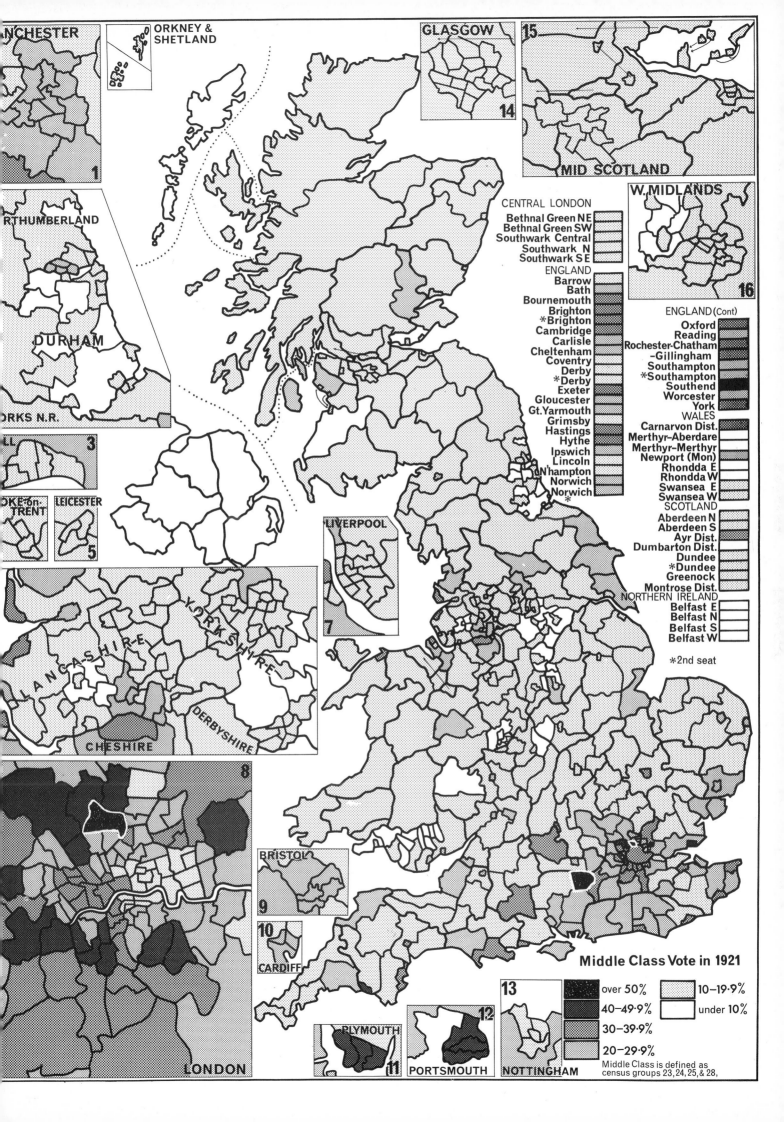

managerial persons in other census categories have been excluded. For example, managers of metal works were counted in the metal workers' category, and managers of transport works in the transport category. Usually the managers in categories other than 23, 24, 25 and 28 more than outnumbered the non-managerial clerks. In the city of Oxford, where full statistics were available, there were 5,240 managerial and professional persons in all 31 census categories, while there were 4,905 persons in the 4 census categories chosen.[1] In most other places the census groups 23, 24, 25 and 28 can be considered a good guide to the number of managerial and professional persons. The only significant exceptions were the 17 constituencies with large military establishments.

The middle class as defined above was substantial in all parts of the country. Except in the mining districts of South Wales, West Yorkshire and Durham, the middle class formed at least 10% of the occupied male population. In the Conservative strongholds of the South-east, the middle-class voters formed over 20% in nearly every constituency. The middle-class electorate was also relatively strong in suburban seats adjacent to several large boroughs.[2] The middle class formed over 50% of the occupied male population in only 2 constituencies, Hornsey and Aldershot, most of the 'middle-class' population of Aldershot consisting of military personnel. The middle class formed between 40 and 49% in 22 constituencies, 15 of them suburban seats in London, one in Southend, and 6 in the naval bases of Plymouth and Portsmouth.

The Census of 1921 did not break down the occupational tables by constituencies in large boroughs; consequently, only one figure is available for boroughs such as Manchester, though certain seats within Manchester were slums while others were not. Such seats are listed here as having a 'middle-class' vote of more than 20% because the average figure for the whole borough was over 20%. Despite the probable presence of some slums in the group of seats with more than 20% middle class, the group as a whole voted overwhelmingly Conservative between 1918 and 1935, as the following tables show:

party	1918	1922	1923	1924	1929	1931	1935
Conservative	165	158	119	169	131	185	165
Liberal	28	20	46	7	12	10	10
Labour	6	19	34	22	57	5	25
Other	1	3	1	2	—	—	—

% middle class	% of possible wins actually won by Conservatives	number of seats
Over 50	100	2
40–49·9	93·3	21
30–39·9	90·1	52
20–29·9	70·0	125
Under 20	47·5	402 [3]

The middle-class vote apparently provided the basis of Conservative support during the inter-war period, and it was more faithful to Conservatism than was the agricultural vote. In addition, the middle-class seats shifted to the Conservatives more rapidly than did the agricultural seats. Between 1918 and 1935 the Liberals lost 64·2% of their middle-class seats, while they lost only 34·7% of their agricultural seats, to the Conservatives. [4]

The military vote was important in 17 constituencies. In 12 of them, the naval vote, and in 4 the army vote, predominated. The army and navy were roughly equal in one seat, South Dorset. The Conservatives won nearly all contests in the army constituencies from 1885 to 1935. They lost in 2 of them in 1885, Hythe and Petersfield. However, there was a Conservative split in Petersfield, while there was no Conservative candidate in Hythe in 1885. Therefore, the only clear case of a Conservative loss in a seat with a substantial army vote was in Salisbury in 1923.[5] Excluding Hythe and Petersfield in 1885, the Conservatives won 56 times out of a possible 57, or 98·2% of the time. Seats with a large navy vote did not support the Conservatives as strongly as those with a large army vote. Between 1885 and 1910 the navy seats voted Conservative only 68·8% of the time, while from 1918 to 1935 they voted Conservative 83·3% of the time.

seat	% military voters 1921	
Aldershot	41·3	Army
Gillingham	30·0	Navy
Portsmouth (3 seats)	27·4	Navy
Plymouth (3 seats)	27·4	Navy
South Dorset	24·6	Army and Navy
Fareham	21·8	Navy
Salisbury	20·6	Army
Bodmin	12·9	Navy
Woodbridge	11·2	Navy
Hythe	10·6	Army
Chatham	10·4	Navy
Faversham	10·0	Navy
Petersfield	10·0	Army

1 Only occupied males over 12 are considered
2 Altrincham, Pudsey, Wallasey, Weston-super-Mare, Waterloo, Stretford, Eccles and Farnworth are examples. Farnworth also had a large mining electorate
3 Excluding Northern Ireland
4 The figures were, in seats with over 20% agriculturists, that the Liberals had 42 seats in 1918, and 26 in 1935; while in seats with over 20% middle-class, the Liberals had 28 in 1918 and 10 in 1935
5 The Conservative candidate in Salisbury in 1923 was a local landowner with no military experience; the Liberal who defeated him by 665 votes was a Major and had won the M.C.

Distribution of Nonconformists in England in 1922

The following table lists the number of Wesleyan, Primitive and United Methodists, Congregationalists, Baptists and Presbyterians in each constituency or group of borough constituencies in England in 1922. Nonconformists in Wales are examined in the map on p. 135.

Constituency	Methodist Wesleyan	U.M.	Primitive	Congreg.	Baptist	Presbyt.	Total	%
Accrington	1653	240	255	650	1652	—	4450	10·6
Ashton under Lyne	746	1320	255	1165	149	—	3635	10·5
Barrow	770	463	312	266	219	580	2610	7·3
Bath	694	263	205	487	1347	122	3118	9·4
Batley and Morley	1534	966	975	1174	406	—	5055	13·3
Barnsley	1294	1563	865	316	329	—	4367	12·4
Birkenhead	1380	—	864	1345	762	2160	6511	10·4
Birmingham	7932	1565	1840	6246	6712	638	24933	5·7
Blackburn	1300	486	645	2152	499	572	5654	8·7
Blackpool	1987	658	406	1580	712	—	5343	11·5
Bolton	4367	782	772	1997	676	380	8974	10·6
Bootle	1434	—	282	992	525	685	3918	11·8
Bournemouth	922	—	496	2547	757	319	5041	13·4
Bradford	6150	1156	2033	4255	2789	337	16730	10·6
Brighton	979	377	300	1880	1106	282	4924	6·1
Bristol	5011	3161	1171	4943	7091	371	21748	11·6
Bromley	711	—	240	122	1235	223	3631	7·9
Burnley	1329	954	810	840	2103	—	6036	12·0
Bury	663	847	461	722	383	—	3076	9·5
Cambridge	721	—	342	657	1131	245	2096	7·4
Carlisle	1089	208	380	507	78	1047	3309	13·5
Cheltenham	546	83	152	329	792	101	2003	9·3
Coventry	961	—	380	1637	1653	—	4631	7·6
Croydon	804	291	335	1335	1483	492	4740	5·0
Darlington	1446	425	641	284	388	374	3558	11·7
Derby	1703	586	1275	1252	1528	234	6578	10·6
Dewsbury	981	653	352	933	161	—	3080	10·9
Dudley	547	704	320	526	314	69	2480	9·6
Ealing	581	—	290	325	717	623	2536	7·8
East Ham	1164	762	—	838	440	606	3810	5·6
Eccles	791	—	—	470	28	93	1382	3·9
Edmonton	—	—	—	368	335	—	703	2·4
Exeter	1213	—	—	664	382	—	2259	7·7
Gateshead	1917	845	1402	250	323	1306	6043	11·0
Gloucester	756	105	152	384	563	203	2163	8·4
Great Yarmouth	471	320	570	492	420	—	2273	8·4
Grimsby	2049	177	1938	334	490	183	5171	9·9
Halifax	1991	1840	664	2380	1145	—	8020	15·8
Hartlepools	700	665	690	554	478	767	3854	9·4
Hastings	1071	65	88	792	438	245	2699	9·4
Hornsey	—	—	243	832	1398	—	2473	5·5
Huddersfield	3273	2851	402	1406	1346	175	9453	16·8
Hythe	620	—	141	515	530	—	2806	13·6
Ilford	1203	—	—	1634	1605	387	4829	10·7
Ipswich	1351	—	328	1391	1562	191	4823	12·4
Kingston-upon-Hull	5942	725	3742	832	863	833	12937	9·4
Kingston-on-Thames	462	—	215	653	52	140	1522	4·9
Leeds	8103	3442	3074	3429	2459	619	21126	9·4
Leicester	3253	499	2390	1666	4892	310	13010	11·6
Leigh	982	315	500	98	514	133	2542	6·9
Leyton	—	—	259	1145	1454	228	3086	4·9
Lincoln	2157	851	834	538	303	—	4683	15·0
Liverpool	6150	1177	1256	5962	3845	5879	24269	6·7
Manchester-Salford	12206	4517	3255	8175	4165	3041	35359	7·9
Middlesbrough	1879	663	853	422	418	435	4670	7·3
Morpeth	1009	608	1425	187	17	1203	4449	10·3
Nelson and Colne	1486	—	794	745	772	—	3797	8·7
Newcastle-under-Lyme	1089	627	629	380	52	—	2777	9·2
Newcastle-upon-Tyne	4433	2122	1535	1045	861	4767	14763	11·1
Northampton	855	—	757	1283	1673	—	4568	10·2
Norwich	464	843	919	1509	1308	236	5279	8·8
Nottingham	4278	2105	—	2034	2708	463	11588	9·3
Oldham	2214	1164	1608	2138	698	111	7933	11·2
Oxford	1547	334	195	364	809	—	3249	12·9
Plymouth	3398	1691	317	1031	1550	132	8119	7·7
Portsmouth	2042	545	450	1132	2405	150	6724	6·0
Preston	1956	559	674	772	214	200	4375	7·6
Reading	1074	—	694	998	1522	295	4583	10·2
Richmond-Surrey	380	—	162	440	52	175	1209	3·5
Rochdale	925	2152	276	760	857	193	5163	11·1
Rochester	910	557	401	812	758	216	3654	6·0
Rossendale	2028	674	712	348	3544	—	7306	20·5
Rotherham	1658	—	876	999	74	—	3607	8·8
St. Helens	1242	—	340	1340	294	301	3517	8·0
Sheffield	7243	5704	2861	3890	1921	413	22032	9·5
Smethwick	691	—	—	225	381	62	1359	4·0
Southampton	861	379	490	1643	966	384	4723	6·3
Southend	1062	—	305	2094	1351	208	5020	11·8
Southport	1742	589	1127	1124	496	210	5388	15·9
South Shields	590	770	900	237	539	1401	4437	8·5
Stockton	1641	105	805	326	856	573	4306	11·3
Stockport	3350	982	825	1319	369	—	6845	10·9
Stoke	3253	3377	1655	1104	528	116	19333	9·8
Sunderland	2250	2088	1278	1355	276	1607	8854	12·0
Tottenham	1060	—	225	661	808	76	2830	4·0
Tynemouth	1223	564	700	265	221	906	3879	13·8
Wakefield	810	866	632	528	115	—	2951	12·3
Wallasey	1200	—	—	983	485	2184	4852	12·2
Wallsend	—	—	—	259	37	1128	1424	3·8
Walsall	1339	—	605	505	568	137	3154	7·1
Walthamstow	497	855	170	626	1389	215	3752	6·2
Warrington	1143	—	146	411	95	182	1977	5·8
Wednesbury	974	172	626	231	210	—	2213	5·9
West Bromwich	1114	—	580	507	228	—	2429	7·4
West Ham	1755	1524	510	1113	1830	441	7173	5·4
Wigan	1286	486	161	414	432	216	2995	7·5
Willesden	—	381	325	345	646	1024	2721	3·4
Wimbledon	—	—	—	624	611	414	1649	4·4
Wolverhampton	2144	454	922	1702	864	134	6220	6·1
Worcester	309	—	210	287	444	78	1328	5·6
York	2231	318	689	207	125	689	3836	9·7

County Constituencies (not including Middlesex)

Constituency	Methodist Wesleyan	U.M.	Primitive	Congreg.	Baptist	Presbyt.	Total	%
Bedfordshire								
Bedford	1157	—	370	683	1164	—	3374	10·0
Luton	2768	—	1097	792	1688	—	6345	16·8
Mid-Beds	1708	—	275	177	1013	—	3173	10·6
Berkshire								
Abingdon	—	—	327	219	396	39	981	3·7
Newbury	653	—	762	541	460	—	2416	7·8
Windsor	963	—	318	459	411	—	2151	5·7
Buckinghamshire								
Aylesbury	465	—	340	613	1804	—	3222	8·8
Buckingham	796	—	474	1105	710	—	3085	8·5
Wycombe	622	—	668	564	1127	—	3071	6·8
Cambridgeshire and Ely								
Cambridgeshire	284	—	159	1795	1732	—	3970	10·8
Isle of Ely	1021	—	1047	492	1154	—	3714	10·1

Constituency	Methodist Wesleyan	U.M.	Primitive	Congreg.	Baptist	Presbyt.	Total	%
Cheshire								
Altrincham	1028	—	562	1605	389	380	3964	8·8
Chester	615	—	984	882	240	209	2930	10·8
Crewe	1378	423	1936	518	470	168	4893	13·2
Eddisbury	1621	374	550	334	137	—	3016	13·4
Knutsford	258	257	—	639	75	—	1229	3·5
Macclesfield	1473	935	1076	762	324	—	4570	12·0
Northwich	1393	988	724	514	318	168	4105	10·3
Stalybridge & Hyde	427	539	212	869	400	—	2447	5·7
Wirral	369	—	170	374	—	1336	2249	6·6
Cornwall								
Bodmin	3128	1978	73	270	94	—	5543	16·7
Camborne	4938	2459	489	—	39	—	7925	23·2
Northern	3641	4000	—	265	177	—	8083	28·0
Penryn & F'mouth	3087	1523	279	345	415	—	5649	15·1
St. Ives	3113	1146	332	124	184	—	4919	16·8
Cumberland								
Northern	277	—	458	184	—	280	1199	5·5
Penrith & C'mouth	1583	—	759	353	—	208	2903	13·8
Whitehaven	892	444	452	205	45	428	2466	9·0
Workington	965	—	654	254	271	513	2657	8·4
Derbyshire								
Belper	351	389	663	304	459	—	2166	6·7
Chesterfield	1480	493	1037	532	157	—	3699	10·7
Clay Cross	—	470	542	60	56	—	1128	3·5
High Peak	1627	689	694	921	—	—	3931	11·5
Ilkeston	1663	1813	810	383	601	—	5270	17·1
North-eastern	759	—	629	289	102	—	1779	5·0
Southern	636	692	1078	149	777	—	3332	7·7
Western	620	204	1189	596	164	—	2773	9·2
Devonshire								
Barnstaple	1800	1206	—	850	878	—	4734	14·3
Honiton	286	56	152	760	414	—	1668	5·6
South Molton	816	2588	—	730	460	—	4594	16·1
Tiverton	258	1131	—	365	630	—	2384	8·7
Torquay	1286	428	405	811	760	76	3766	10·5
Totnes	774	85	—	777	543	—	2179	5·4
Tavistock	1280	400	—	342	235	—	2257	8·2
Dorset								
East	1010	—	210	717	420	—	2357	7·4
Northern	1321	—	719	547	116	—	2703	11·0
Southern	798	122	298	359	219	—	1796	6·4
Western	849	—	—	995	307	—	2151	9·0
Durham								
Barnard Castle	1485	200	1545	172	384	—	3786	18·2
Bishop Auckland	1215	—	2075	56	60	107	3513	10·1
Blaydon	—	—	444	299	—	—	743	2·1
Chester-le-Street	1062	—	790	80	—	—	1932	5·0
Consett	774	489	990	—	242	368	2863	7·6
Durham	1123	486	1710	72	—	149	3540	11·4
Houghton-le-Steet	720	—	620	80	—	—	1420	4·0
Jarrow	443	—	640	260	103	965	2411	6·2
Seaham	695	375	1396	—	—	120	2586	6·3
Sedgefield	—	—	—	25	—	106	131	0·3
Spennymoor	1803	516	2512	—	129	460	5420	16·1
Essex								
Chemlsford	382	—	198	1497	545	—	2622	7·5
Colchester	609	—	370	985	406	—	2370	8·0
Epping	526	24	—	1889	954	—	3393	8·4
Harwich	1195	—	427	425	441	—	2488	8·7
Maldon	—	—	334	1903	376	—	2613	8·9
Romford	—	—	83	689	607	—	1379	3·4
Saffron Walden	244	—	220	1524	653	—	2641	8·3
South-eastern	292	—	82	915	596	—	1885	4·5
Gloucestershire								
Cirencester	913	106	266	471	663	—	2419	6·7
Forest of Dean	1109	283	532	547	583	—	3324	11·6
Stroud	619	—	164	1257	1334	—	3374	9·4
Thornbury	267	1392	—	1240	398	—	3297	9·5
Hampshire								
Aldershot	299	31	275	101	205	128	1039	4·1
Basingstoke	638	—	679	597	286	—	2200	6·6
Fareham	719	—	—	929	621	—	2269	6·6
Isle of Wight	1477	1637	334	973	688	—	5745	11·5
New Forest	791	—	230	1044	692	—	2757	7·5
Petersfield	434	66	329	420	—	96	1345	4·5
Winchester	—	181	402	202	394	—	1179	3·5
Herefordshire								
Hereford	440	—	304	228	832	—	1804	6·5
Leominster	347	—	651	267	261	—	1526	5·8

Constituency	Methodist Wesleyan	U.M.	Primitive	Congreg.	Baptist	Presbyt.	Total	%
Hertfordshire								
Hemel Hempstead	—	—	170	447	1358	—	1975	7·4
Hertford	—	—	—	1571	427	—	1998	6·0
Hitchin	577	—	—	623	923	—	2123	6·6
St. Albans	791	—	—	1536	492	324	3143	8·9
Watford	854	—	370	445	1444	135	3248	9·9
Huntingdonshire	835	272	217	—*	1155	—	2479	8·8

*Baptists and Congregationalists had joint or Union chapels in Huntingdonshire

Constituency	Methodist Wesleyan	U.M.	Primitive	Congreg.	Baptist	Presbyt.	Total	%
Kent								
Ashford	76	143	—	283	683	—	1485	4·1
Canterbury	673	45	188	622	559	97	2184	6·3
Chislehurst	367	—	—	443	669	—	1479	5·2
Dartford	407	—	130	1000	806	86	2429	5·2
Dover	789	—	141	432	936	—	2298	6·1
Faversham	886	214	153	974	459	—	2686	6·7
Gravesend	408	—	84	503	392	101	1488	4·7
Isle of Thanet	1088	—	232	694	791	—	2805	7·3
Maidstone	513	—	125	477	528	—	1643	5·0
Sevenoaks	400	18	—	300	569	62	1349	4·3
Tonbridge	903	19	95	866	742	—	2625	6·8
Lancashire								
Chorley	686	238	518	536	—	—	1978	5·5
Clitheroe	976	761	110	481	481	108	2917	8·7
Darwen	522	296	340	1846	122	—	3126	10·0
Farnworth	940	—	725	1368	—	—	3033	8·8
Fylde	704	—	275	686	125	—	1790	4·7
Heywood and Radcliffe	751	416	208	1108	446	43	2972	7·3
Ince	—	—	—	286	42	—	328	1·0
Lancaster	1553	522	448	1184	357	164	4228	11·7
Lonsdale	548	—	120	378	127	—	1173	4·2
Middleton & P'wic	—	—	310	753	224	—	1287	3·5
Mossley	372	869	—	1487	—	—	2728	6·7
Newton	—	—	467	327	168	29	991	3·9
Ormskirk	699	—	140	267	73	76	1255	4·2
Royton	300	304	150	712	579	—	2045	5·6
Stretford	309	—	—	237	285	—	831	2·1
Waterloo	685	—	—	720	131	895	2431	8·8
Westhoughton	—	—	280	458	11	—	749	2·4
Widnes	512	134	174	599	96	—	1515	4·8
Leicestershire								
Bosworth	681	—	865	654	1580	—	3780	11·1
Harborough	285	—	—	1272	1016	—	2573	9·0
Loughborough	1960	258	757	168	1976	—	5119	15·9
Melton	1009	—	642	277	474	—	2402	7·7
Lincolnshire								
Brigg	1842	42	1620	172	65	—	3741	12·2
Gainsborough	1772	—	1715	142	58	—	3687	13·6
Grantham	1777	184	441	232	133	—	2767	7·8
Holland-with Boston	1444	848	762	422	605	—	4081	9·8
Horncastle	2729	28	593	90	151	—	3591	14·7
Louth	1975	1063	818	22	208	—	4086	14·4
Rutland & Stamford	755	—	106	334	304	—	1499	5·5
Norfolk								
Eastern	481	—	1275	146	278	—	2180	6·8
Kings Lynn	850	175	886	172	339	—	2422	6·9
Northern	288	348	1064	209	240	—	2149	7·0
Southern	664	113	998	338	487	—	2600	8·0
South-western	933	3541	1794	223	356	—	3660	11·3
Northamptonshire								
Daventry	744	—	—	809	887	—	2440	8·0
Kettering	727	—	155	1138	1492	182	3694	10·6
Peterborough	872	431	840	487	1059	—	3689	10·4
Wellingborough	1795	—	190	893	1044	—	3922	12·0
Northumberland								
Berwick-on-Tweed	337	76	947	484	198	6273	8315	28·5
Hexham	2410	873	1783	221	75	1343	6705	25·4
Wansbeck	—	173	938	247	164	1167	2689	5·8
Nottinghamshire								
Bassetlaw	1699	459	360	331	38	—	2887	9·2
Broxtowe	31	814	682	475	1222	—	3224	8·4
Mansfield	1511	667	1305	380	585	—	4448	10·6
Newark	1785	—	199	175	269	—	2428	8·2
Rushcliffe	—	328	—	37	515	—	880	2·4
Oxfordshire								
Banbury	2020	—	655	198	585	—	3458	9·8
Henley	—	—	180	583	40	—	803	2·6

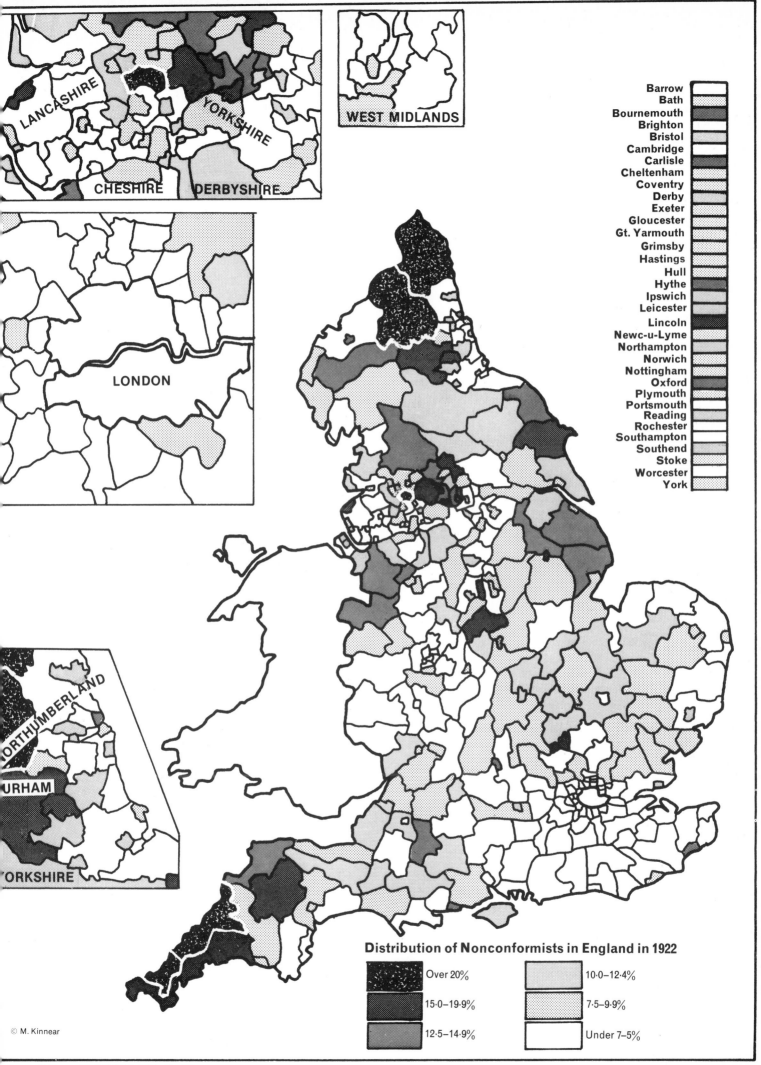

WEST MIDLANDS

LANCASHIRE   YORKSHIRE

CHESHIRE   DERBYSHIRE

LONDON

NORTHUMBERLAND

DURHAM

YORKSHIRE

Barrow
Bath
Bournemouth
Brighton
Bristol
Cambridge
Carlisle
Cheltenham
Coventry
Derby
Exeter
Gloucester
Gt. Yarmouth
Grimsby
Hastings
Hull
Hythe
Ipswich
Leicester
Lincoln
Newc-u-Lyme
Northampton
Norwich
Nottingham
Oxford
Plymouth
Portsmouth
Reading
Rochester
Southampton
Southend
Stoke
Worcester
York

Distribution of Nonconformists in England in 1922

Over 20%   10·0–12·4%

15·0–19·9%   7·5–9·9%

12·5–14·9%   Under 7–5%

© M. Kinnear

Source: M. Kinnear, *The British Voter* [1981 ed], p. 127

Constituency	Methodist Wesleyan	U.M.	Primitive	Congreg.	Baptist	Presbyt.	Total	%
Shropshire								
Ludlow	421	—	974	239	156	—	1790	7·2
Oswestry	748	—	2038	1380	269	—	4435	13·9
Shrewsbury	516	155	577	860	245	97	2450	9·5
Wrekin	1274	121	908	187	223	—	2713	8·3
Somerset								
Bridgwater	1190	130	—	712	784	—	2816	9·2
Frome	1413	527	885	484	733	—	4042	11·3
Taunton	952	396	—	761	1106	—	3225	10·9
Wells	883	—	145	637	225	—	1890	6·9
Weston-super-Mare	1437	524	88	845	1210	—	4104	11·3
Yeovil	1574	308	196	1014	792	—	3884	11·3
Staffordshire								
Burton	1103	1094	567	307	526	112	3709	10·6
Cannock	555	465	300	131	63	—	1514	3·8
Kingswinford	—	287	1155	122	144	—	1708	4·3
Leek	860	—	1105	312	4	—	2281	6·2
Lichfield	110	—	600	306	—	—	1016	3·2
Stafford	429	80	380	238	219	107	1453	6·0
Stone	374	—	520	343	—	—	1237	4·4
Suffolk								
Eye	—	142	256	887	864	—	2149	6·6
Lowestoft	929	175	314	837	326	—	2581	7·4
Woodbridge	—	—	—	469	904	100	1473	4·7
Bury St. Edmunds	782	—	711	356	671	—	2520	8·2
Sudbury	—	—	437	1283	546	—	2266	8·7
Surrey								
Chertsey	502	—	173	597	253	—	1525	3·5
Eastern	—	—	—	667	56	—	723	2·9
Epsom	699	—	—	599	353	—	1651	4·7
Farnham	573	—	—	502	358	—	1433	4·1
Guildford	439	—	99	1221	390	—	2149	5·5
Mitcham	—	—	—	132	—	292	424	1·3
Reigate	330	—	100	893	415	344	2082	6·2
Sussex								
Eastbourne	598	—	65	674	288	616	2241	7·2
East Grinstead	78	—	—	1038	204	—	1320	3·4
Lewes	78	—	—	414	280	70	842	3·3
Rye	785	—	90	724	217	73	1889	6·4
Chichester	403	—	—	658	181	—	1242	2·7
Horsham & W'thg	1016	—	243	690	692	—	2641	5·9
Warwickshire								
Nuneaton	553	—	201	596	678	—	2028	4·2
Rugby	854	—	177	440	340	—	1811	5·6

Constituency	Methodist Wesleyan	U.M.	Primitive	Congreg.	Baptist	Presbyt.	Total	%
Tamworth	110	529	181	650	229	—	1699	4·6
Warwick and Leamington	777	—	282	698	831	—	2588	6·0
Westmorland	1124	132	627	598	49	143	2673	8·8
Wiltshire								
Chippenham	164	—	1303	385	345	—	2197	7·9
Devizes	460	—	—	227	147	—	834	3·3
Salisbury	1119	340	735	391	540	—	3125	10·8
Swindon	1282	—	1005	351	743	174	3555	10·8
Westbury	760	—	176	1319	1671	—	3926	13·4
Worcestershire								
Bewdley	375	—	—	268	271	—	914	3·5
Evesham	378	—	—	53	482	—	913	3·1
Kidderminster	1157	166	680	737	1081	—	3821	9·3
Stourbridge	1215	1087	922	596	265	—	4075	8·8
East Yorkshire								
Buckrose	1685	161	2020	257	141	—	4264	15·0
Holderness	1119	—	1123	385	145	—	2772	10·1
Howdenshire	1215	—	591	334	—	—	2140	8·6
North Yorkshire								
Cleveland	1098	—	1196	368	209	226	3097	7·2
Richmond	2613	—	485	337	59	—	3494	11·3
Scarborough	2280	97	1809	734	322	67	5309	13·7
Thirsk & Malton	2250	—	600	137	137	—	3124	11·2
West Yorkshire								
Barkston Ash	1715	—	332	25	207	—	2279	6·7
Colne Valley	1192	148	725	693	1114	—	3872	9·5
Doncaster	2021	—	460	91	223	222	3017	8·1
Don Valley	—	—	580	184	51	—	815	2·5
Elland	441	1568	810	1486	905	—	5210	14·8
Hemsworth	—	—	160	150	—	—	310	1·1
Keighley	1787	624	1036	528	1236	—	5211	14·1
Normanton	598	606	872	180	80	—	2336	7·3
Penistone	573	351	—	503	71	—	1498	4·4
Pontefract	1436	140	999	314	—	—	2889	9·1
Pudsey and Otley	1248	1287	800	817	899	—	5051	15·5
Ripon	1921	367	795	463	213	170	3929	11·0
Rother Valley	—	—	400	218	9	—	627	1·8
Rothwell	661	—	299	167	10	—	1137	3·1
Shipley	1572	—	571	630	773	—	3546	9·6
Skipton	2117	165	678	735	1023	—	4718	12·7
Sowerby	1525	1237	528	658	2509	—	6451	18·4
Spen Valley	1065	1027	698	2759	328	—	5877	14·7
Wentworth	1196	—	475	226	—	—	1897	4·6

The preceding table has been prepared by determining the constituency in which each chapel or circuit was located in 1922, for each of the Nonconformist groups examined. It has been assumed that the members of each chapel were voters in the constituency in which the chapel was located. The table lists only the overall figure for multi-membered boroughs, as many members of chapels in such boroughs may have crossed constituency lines to attend chapels. In the country divisions, and in single-membered boroughs, this was probably a negligible factor. There might have been members of chapels under voting age, but they probably did not amount to a high proportion of the total chapel membership. Moreover, they were roughly the same proportion throughout the country. There are two drawbacks to the tables. The first is that they do not list all Nonconformists; the second is that the Methodist figures are for circuits, not chapels.

There was no religious Census of England except that of 1851. Excluding the Welsh Calvinist Methodists, nearly all of whom were in Wales, the groups examined made up 88·1% of the total Nonconformist population.[1] Only Nonconformist groups with over 50,000 members are listed. The remaining Nonconformists belonged to numerous smaller sects. Although it is possible that these small sects were concentrated in a few constituencies, it is not possible to identify all of them. Moreover, even if it were possible to identify all of them, it would be misleading to assume that they were voters in the constituency which contained their chapel. Members of the large Nonconformist groups had several thousand chapels to attend, and it is reasonable to assume that they attended the nearest. However, members of small Nonconformist groups had only a few chapels, and many members of such chapels may have had to travel long distances to attend them.

A more important drawback to the tables is that the Primitive and Wesleyan Methodist statistics refer to circuits, not to chapels. In some cases, circuits covered several constituencies, so that Methodist figures may show many members in one constituency, and few in nearby ones. This was significant mainly in places where there were very few Methodists. Where there were several circuits to each constituency, it is fair to assume that nearly all the Methodists in each circuit were in the constituency concerned.

Because there was no religious census except that of 1851, it is difficult to verify the accuracy of all the statistics in the first table. However, the National Council of Evangelical Free Churches published a summary of the denominational membership of 199 local and county councils in 1904.[2] A comparison of this summary with the estimated percentage of Nonconformists in 1922 shows

1 In 1922 the Baptist figures included those of the Countess of Huntingdon's Connexion, and some small Baptist groups; the Presbyterian figures included several Presbyterian groups. In the 1851 Census these were all listed separately

2 The Education Act at Work: A Handbook for Free Church Workers, London, Thomas Law

a strong relation between the two. This indicates that the 1922 table is generally correct in its estimate of the distribution of Nonconformists. Where the Nonconformists are estimated to have comprised over 10% of the population in 1922, they won proportionately more council seats in 1904 than where they are estimated to have been under 10%.[1] The following table shows the relation between the estimated percentage of Nonconformists in 1922 and the ratio of Nonconformist to Anglican councillors in 1904:

% est. Nonconf. 1922	number of Nonconf. councillors per Anglican councillor in 1904
Over 15	2·0
12·5-14·9	1·3
10·0-12·4	0·9
7·5-9·9	0·6
Under 7·5	0·6

In 1922 Nonconformity was strongest in small- and medium-sized boroughs and in most agricultural districts. It was weakest in large boroughs and in 6 areas of England. These areas comprised the South-east, West Lancashire, mining seats in Yorkshire, an agricultural area around Exeter, the West Midlands and much of the coast of East Anglia. Before 1918 the East Anglian coast and the mining districts of West Yorkshire[2] were strongly Liberal, while the other districts were strongly Unionist. Between 1918 and 1935 the former 2 districts rapidly shifted away from the Liberals. Consequently, between the wars the map of Nonconformity bore

more resemblance to the map of Liberal strength than it had done before 1918.

There was no seat in England where the Nonconformists were even a third of the electorate, although they did form over 10% of the electorate in 123 of the 413 seats in England.[3] If other factors determining the outcome of elections were roughly balanced, the presence of a large number of Nonconformists in a constituency was probably decisive.

For instance, the above-average swings to the Liberals in 1922 and 1923 in Oxford and Southend may be attributed to the large Nonconformist vote in both places.[4] In post-1918 elections, such issues as church schools and Welsh disestablishment were not often raised.[5] Consequently, the tie between the Liberals and the Nonconformists was probably the result of habit. The following tables indicate that this tie still existed during the inter-war period, and also that it seemed to be relatively more important to the Liberals at the end than at the beginning of the period. This may account for the greater overlapping of Nonconformist and Liberal areas after 1918 than before.

% Nonconformist 1922	% of possible wins actually won by Liberals, 1918-1935 [6]	number of seats
Over 20	40·0	5
15·0–15·9	33·9	16
12·5-14·9	19·3	20
10·0-12·4	17·4	82
7·5–9·9	13·3	117
5·0–7·4	8·8	111
0–4·9	5·3	62

1 The only area of the country where the Nonconformists are estimated to have been weak, and where they nevertheless did well in the council elections, was in the Birmingham district. This is probably because in the Birmingham district, both Anglicans and Nonconformists were weak, and there was a relative Nonconformist majority. The diocese of Birmingham had only 4·1% Anglican communicants in Easter 1923. This was the lowest percentage in England except for the diocese of Sheffield with 3·8% (Official Year Book of the Church of England, 1925, 442-3). The estimated percentages of Nonconformists in Birmingham, Wolverhampton, Wednesbury and West Bromwich in 1922 were 5·3%, 5·4%, 7·4% and 5·7%
2 In West Yorkshire the woollen district was strongly Nonconformist, while the

mining district was very weakly Nonconformist. This may partially explain the political division in the area in 1923, when the Nonconformist woollen district voted Liberal and the mining district voted Labour. The weak Nonconformity of mining districts in West Yorkshire contrasts with the strong Nonconformity in some mining seats in Durham. In Durham the basis of Nonconformity was Primitive Methodism
3 Excluding London, Middlesex county divisions and University seats
4 Oxford and Southend were among the most Nonconformist seats in the South of England, with 11·5% and 11·8% respectively
5 See Kinnear, Fall of Lloyd George, ch. 7
6 Excluding London, Middlesex county divisions and University seats

Scotland

Distribution of Roman Catholics in Scotland, 1900 and 1922 (Maps A and B)

1900 constituency	% R.C.	1922 constituency	% R.C.
Aberdeen City	2·8	Aberdeen City	3·5
Ayr District	9·4	Ayr District	12·9
Dumfries District	12·2	Dumbarton District	27·9
Dundee	13·6	Dundee	16·5
		Dunfermline District	11·2
Edinburgh and Leith District	7·2	Edinburgh and Leith	7·9
Elgin District	3·7		
Falkirk District	15·8		
Glasgow, Govan, Partick	17·8	Glasgow	22·5
Greenock	17·6	Greenock	28·1
Hawick District	3·0		
Inverness District	3·6		
Kilmarnock District	18·0		
Kirkcaldy District	2·9	Kirkcaldy	5·9
Montrose District	—	Montrose District	1·1
Paisley	14·3	Paisley	19·2
Perth City	4·4		
St. Andrews District	—		
Stirling District	8·4	Stirling District	10·6
Wick District	—		
Aberdeenshire East and West	—	Aberdeenshire – Central	—
		East	—
		West and Kincardine	—
Argyll	2·5	Argyll	4·2
Ayrshire – North	6·2	Ayr – Bute and North Ayr	6·7
South	3·9	Kilmarnock	6·6
		South Ayrshire	3·9
Banff	5·5	Banff	4·6
Berwick	—	Berwick and Haddington	6·7
Bute	10·7		
Caithness	—	Caithness and Sutherland	—
Clackmannan and Kinross	2·0		
Dumbartonshire	13·2	Dumbartonshire	17·3
Dumfriesshire	—	Dumfries	3·7
Elgin and Nairn	—		
Fife – East	—	Fife – East	—
West	1·3	West	3·2
Forfar	5·8	Forfarshire	—
Haddington	3·3	Galloway	3·6
Inverness	12·1	Inverness – Inverness	4·5
		Ross and Cromarty	—
		Western Isles	11·4
Kincardineshire	—		
Kirkcudbright	1·7		
Lanark – North-west	25·1	Lanark – Bothwell	16·7
North-east	17·9	Coatbridge	34·8
Mid	20·7	Hamilton	22·5
South	—	Lanark	3·8
		Motherwell	20·5
		North	21·3
		Rutherglen	30·8
Linlithgow	11·0	Linlithgow	7·5
Midlothian	6·9	Midlothian North	9·5
		Moray and Nairn	2·4
Orkney and Shetland	—	Orkney and Shetland	—
Peebles and Selkirk	1·4	Peebles and South Midlothian	2·6
		Perth and Kincardine – West	4·4
Perthshire East and West	1·6	Perth	1·1
Renfrew East	4·6	Renfrew – East	10·9
West	6·4	West	27·0
Ross and Cromarty	—		
Roxburgh	—	Roxburgh and Selkirk	1·5
Stirlingshire	6·7	Stirling – East and Clackmannan	3·5
Sutherland	—	West	11·6
Wigtown	6·5		

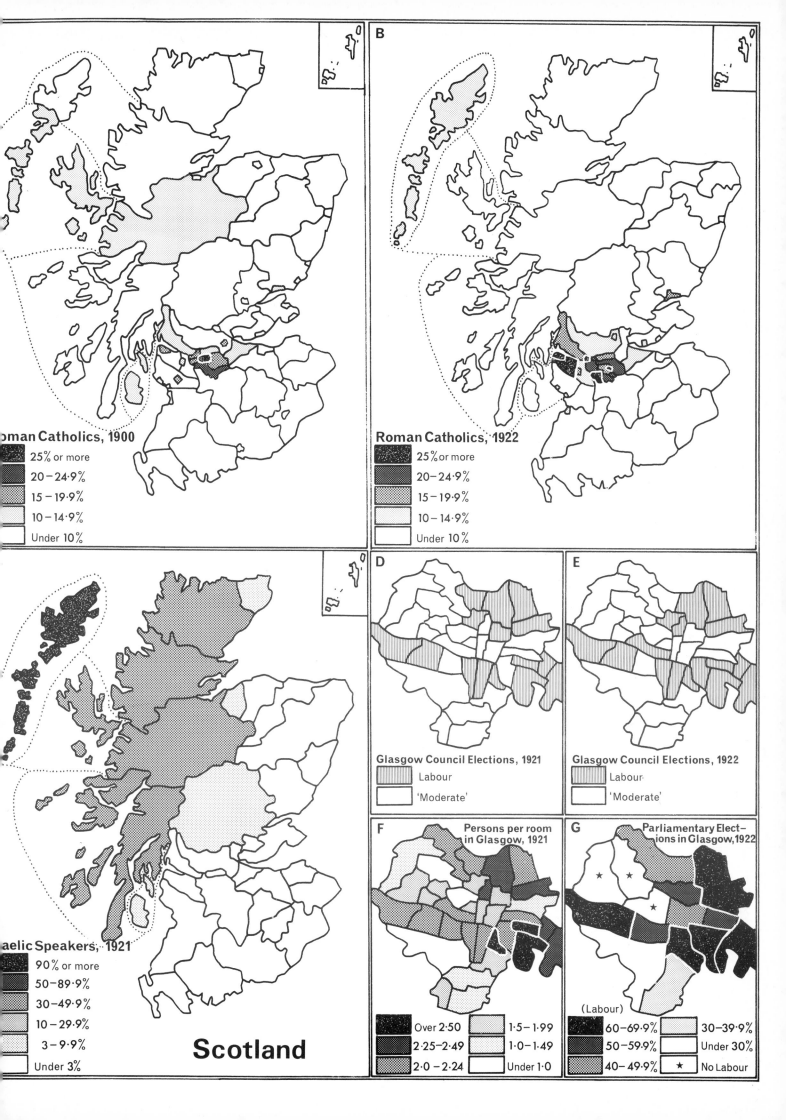

Roman Catholics, 1900

- 25% or more
- 20 – 24·9%
- 15 – 19·9%
- 10 – 14·9%
- Under 10%

Roman Catholics, 1922

- 25% or more
- 20 – 24·9%
- 15 – 19·9%
- 10 – 14·9%
- Under 10%

Gaelic Speakers, 1921

- 90% or more
- 50 – 89·9%
- 30 – 49·9%
- 10 – 29·9%
- 3 – 9·9%
- Under 3%

Scotland

Glasgow Council Elections, 1921

- Labour
- 'Moderate'

Glasgow Council Elections, 1922

- Labour
- 'Moderate'

Persons per room in Glasgow, 1921

- Over 2·50
- 2·25 – 2·49
- 2·0 – 2·24
- 1·5 – 1·99
- 1·0 – 1·49
- Under 1·0

Parliamentary Elections in Glasgow, 1922

(Labour)

- 60 – 69·9%
- 50 – 59·9%
- 40 – 49·9%
- 30 – 39·9%
- Under 30%
- ★ No Labour

The preceding tables are based on information obtained from *The Catholic Directory for the Clergy and Laity in Scotland* for the relevant years. The English *Catholic Directory* did not publish sufficient information for tables to be made showing the distribution of Roman Catholics by constituency in England or Wales. The calculations for 1900 are based on average figures of baptisms in 1899-1901, and those for 1922 on average figures in 1921-3. This reduces errors in estimates of the Catholic population caused by unusual numbers of births in any one constituency in any one year.

Figures were not published of the number of Roman Catholics in each constituency in 1900 or in 1922; however, estimates of the total Roman Catholic population of each diocese were published, as were precise figures of baptisms by church or chapel. By combining the 2 figures it is possible to estimate the number of Roman Catholics in each constituency. These estimates are obtained as follows. First, one divides the estimated number of Roman Catholics in a diocese by the number of baptisms in the diocese. This gives a factor which is the average number of Roman Catholics for every baptism in a given constituency,[1] to arrive at the estimated number of Roman Catholics in that constituency. For example, in 1922 there were an estimated 450,000 Roman Catholics in the diocese of Glasgow. The average number of baptisms in that diocese in the period 1921-1923 was 15,237, so that there were, on average, 29·5 Roman Catholics for every baptism. The average number of baptisms in those years in the Dumbarton District of Burghs was 615; by multiplying 615 by the factor of 29·5, one arrives at the estimated Roman Catholic population of 18,163, which was 27·9% of the total population. Using similar calculations it is possible to estimate the number and percentage of Roman Catholics in other Scottish constituencies. In the case of large burghs it is possible to obtain only the estimated Roman Catholic population for the entire burgh, since many Roman Catholics possibly crossed constituency boundaries to have baptisms. In country districts it is improbable that many would travel long distances, as there were numerous local churches or chapels to serve them.

The Roman Catholic population cannot be estimated precisely, because the figures from which the estimates are calculated are themselves estimates of the total Roman Catholic population in each diocese. Probably the original estimates were fairly accurate, but it is unlikely that they were precise. Consequently, the estimated percentages of Roman Catholics may be off by as much as 2 or 3 percentage points. Larger errors are improbable. The 'multiplying factor' for 5 of the 6 dioceses in 1922 was between 23·8 and 29·5 Roman Catholics for each baptism. This differs substantially from the figure of 44·3 persons per baptism in Scotland in 1922,[2] but this can be accounted for by the fact that most of the Catholic population were fairly young Irish immigrants. In the only place with an indigenous Roman Catholic population, the diocese of Argyll and the Isles, the 'multiplying factor' was 43·1. This was practically the same as the Scottish average for 1922.

In 1900 Roman Catholicism was numerically significant only in the industrialised Central Lowlands and in the southern islands of the Outer Hebrides. To a large extent, the areas where Roman Catholics were numerous were also areas where Liberals fared

worst in Scotland between 1885 and 1910. In the most strongly Roman Catholic seats, however, the Liberals did well in this period, indicating that the Roman Catholic votes offset what the Liberals lost through Protestant reaction. The religious issue, however, could not explain some Scottish results: there were several seats with few Roman Catholics, but where the Liberals did badly after 1885. Roxburgh and Wick District are examples of this. The religious divisions of Scotland were therefore probably only one of several important factors deciding political alignments in Scotland before 1914.

In only 2 places were Roman Catholics a majority in Scotland; both were in the Outer Hebrides. South Uist county district had 52% Roman Catholics in 1900, while Barra County District had no fewer than 99·9% Roman Catholics.[3] Both were in the constituency of Inverness, and brought the average of the constituency up from practically nil to 12·1%. Other county districts in the Outer Hebrides had virtually no Roman Catholics.

By 1922 the Roman Catholics were much more numerous in Scotland, partly because of immigration, but mainly because the high birth rate of previous Roman Catholics had been much higher than that of Scotland as a whole. Much of this 'high' birthrate can be ascribed to the fact that many of the Roman Catholics were immigrants of childbearing age.[4] The areas of Roman Catholics were much the same as in 1900, with expansion in the areas already most strongly Roman Catholic. The Roman Catholic islands in the Outer Hebrides had been detached from Inverness by the redistribution of 1918, and joined to the other islands in the Outer Hebrides to form the constituency of the Western Isles. The Western Isles stayed Liberal until 1935, when Labour won them. In 1935 this was the only primarily agricultural seat Labour won, possibly because the seat had a different social tradition from most other rural Scottish constituencies.[5]

Gaelic-speakers in 1921

Gaelic-speakers in Scotland, Census of 1921

county	no. speaking Gaelic	total pop.	% Gaelic
Aberdeenshire	405	153,392	—
Argyll	25,188	76,862	32·7
Ayrshire	1,399	299,273	—
Banff	258	57,298	—
Berwick	65	28,246	—
Bute	1,453	33,711	4·3
Caithness	1,003	28,285	3·5
Clackmannan	157	32,542	—
Dumbartonshire	2,033	150,861	1·3
Dumfries	160	75,370	—
Fife	893	292,925	—
Forfarshire	323	102,737	—
Haddington	264	47,487	—
Inverness	25,421	66,656	38·1
Kincardineshire	15	30,440	—
Kinross	64	7,963	—
Kircudbright	99	37,155	—
Lanark	1,685	505,268	—
Linlithgow	178	83,962	—
Midlothian	234	86,113	—
Moray	812	41,558	2·0
Nairn	537	8,790	6·1
Orkney	61	24,111	—
Peebles	55	15,332	—
Perth	6,270	125,503	5·0

1 This figure is obtained by placing all Roman Catholic churches or chapels in Scotland in their appropriate constituencies and counting the number of baptisms in those churches or chapels
2 Mitchell and Deane, *British Historical Statistics*, 32
3 The figures are derived from baptisms. It is possible that some Roman Catholics from northern islands in the Outer Hebrides travelled to Barra or South Uist for baptisms, but it is not likely. *The Catholic Directory . . . Scotland 1885*, 129, stated that Oriskay had 'about 450' Roman Catholics, or about 99% of the population of the whole island. The same source did not state the Roman Catholic population of Barra or South Uist, but it did say that the church in Barra, which accommodated

500, did not give 'more than half the accommodation which the congregation would require'
4 In 1891, 88·32% of Irish immigrants to Scotland were over 20. See map, p. 000. Only 49·02% of the whole Scottish population were over 20 in 1891 (*Census of Scotland, 1891*, 280)
5 'Agricultural seats' are here defined as those seats where more than 20% of the occupied male population over 12 was engaged in agriculture. Labour won 2 other seats in 1935 which fell in this category, Bassetlaw and Carmarthen. However, both those seats were also partly mining.   See maps on pp. 121 and 117

Gaelic-speakers in Scotland, Census of 1921

county	no. speaking Gaelic	total pop.	% Gaelic
Renfrew	3,655	298,904	1·2
Ross and Cromarty	15,003	42,440	35·4
Roxburgh	101	44,989	—
Selkirk	44	22,607	—
Shetland	107	25,520	—
Stirling	1,233	161,719	—
Sutherland	8,867	17,802	49·8
Western Isles	39,807	44,177	90·1
Wigtown	100	30,783	—
Scotland	**138,009**	**4,882,479**	**2·8**

In 1921 Gaelic-speakers were a majority in only one constituency, the Western Isles. There, they formed over 90% of the population.[1] However, in almost every mainland civil parish on the West Coast of Scotland north of Kilbrandon in central Argyll, Gaelic-speakers were a majority. In the same area Gaelic-speakers did not form a majority in most inland parishes. The following table[2] illustrates this:

	over 50% Gaelic-speaking	under 50% Gaelic-speaking
Inland parishes	2	48
Coastal parishes	21	2

Gaelic-speaking seemed to hold out most in places where it was strongest. Where the vast majority of the population had spoken Gaelic in 1881, most continued to speak Gaelic in 1921; but where under 60% had spoken Gaelic in 1881, the decline of Gaelic-speaking in the subsequent 40 years was at a more rapid rate. Apparently Gaelic was kept alive only where it was spoken by an overwhelming proportion of the population, as the following table[3] illustrates:

Gaelic-speakers	average % 1881	average % 1921	% change 1881-1921	proportional % 1881-1921	number of parishes
90-100%	94	84	−10	−10	27
80-89%	86	64	−22	−25	26
60-79%	70	36	−34	−49	33
35-59%	47	22	−25	−51	20
0-34%	17	8	−9	−53	9

The Liberals were supposed to have depended on the 'Celtic fringe' for most of their support in the period 1885-1910,[4] but this appears to have been the case only in Wales. In Wales there was a close relation between areas of Welsh-speaking and areas of Liberalism, but in Scotland there was no close relation between areas speaking Gaelic and areas voting Liberal. Of the 6 constituencies where over 4% of the population spoke Gaelic in 1921, only one, Ross and Cromarty, voted Liberal consistently from 1885 to 1910. Two, Bute and West Perth, hardly ever voted Liberal, while a third, Argyll, voted Liberal only 5 times out of a possible 8.[5] The Liberal strongholds in the Scottish Highlands were not the Gaelic-speaking areas, but those in the North-east, where Gaelic was hardly spoken at all. Of the 10 Highland seats which always went Liberal from 1885 to 1910, only one, Ross and Cromarty, had an appreciable number of Gaelic-speakers in 1921.[6] The others were all in the North-east except for Caithness. Caithness differed markedly from the other seats in the North-west in its very low proportion of Gaelic-speakers.[7] The Liberal hold on the 'Celtic fringe' in Scotland became apparent only after 1924, when Liberals tended to do better there than in other parts of the Scottish Highlands.[8] This can be seen in the maps showing the results of elections from 1924 to 1935.

Glasgow (Maps D. E. F and G)

Glasgow housing, and municipal election results, 1921 and 1922

ward	persons per 100 rooms[9]	1921 result[10]	1922 result[11]
Dalmarnock	272	Lab.	Lab.
Mile-End	264	Lab.	Lab.
Hutchesontown	252	Lab.	Lab.
Provan	243	Lab.	Lab.
Parkhead	235	Lab.	Lab.
Shettleston–Tollcross	233	Lab.	Lab.
Cowcaddens	230	M.*	Lab.
Cowlairs	226	Lab.	Lab.
Calton	224	M.	Lab.
Springburn	219	Lab.	Lab.
Govan	217	Lab.	Lab.
Fairfield	217	Lab.	Lab.
Maryhill	217	M.	M.
Ruchill	216	Lab.	M.
Anderston	213	M.	Lab.
Whitevale	212	M.	M.
Gorbals	207	Lab.	Lab.
Kingston	207	Lab.	Lab.
Kinning Park	202	M.	M.
Woodside	197	Lab.	Lab.
Exchange	192	M.	M.
Townhead	188	Lab.	M.
Govanhill	173	M.	M.
Partick West	162	M.	M.
Sandyford	158	M.	M.
Partick East	156	M.	M.
Blythswood	151	M.	M.
Whiteinch	151	M.	M.
Pollokshaws	150	M.	M.
North Kelvin	149	M.	M.
Dennistoun	139	M.	M.
Cathcart	105	M.	M.
Camphill	109	M.	M.
Langside	104	M.	M.
Park	95	M.	M.
Pollokshields	82	M.	M.
Kelvinside	68	M.	M.

* M.– 'Moderate'

The local elections in Glasgow in 1921 and 1922 indicate the high degree of class-consciousness in that city. An accurate measure of the social composition of an area is the degree of overcrowding. In Glasgow the degree of overcrowding was published, by ward, in the Census of 1921. Nearly all the Labour victories in the 1921 and 1922 local elections occurred in places where there were more than 1·97 persons per room; in such places Labour won almost every seat both times in the two elections. The only exceptions were Cowcaddens and Calton. There were 2 other apparent exceptions, Ruchill and Maryhill, but in each, the census figures were misleading. Maryhill had a large barracks and Ruchill a large hospital, both of which inflated the figure for the average number of persons per room.

Glasgow turned to the Labour Party more rapidly than did London, probably because the Liberals in Glasgow were more right-wing than those in London. In Glasgow nearly every active constituency Liberal Association backed the Coalition of 1919-22.[12] There was consequently no strong Liberal element among the Glasgow working class to impede the growth of the Labour Party. In London, on the other hand, the Liberals had much stronger support in working-class seats, and it was not until 1935 that London split along class lines as closely as Glasgow had done in 1921 and 1922.[13]

1 The two places with the highest proportion of the population who could speak Gaelic only were Barra (18·9%) and South Uist (23·6%). These were also the only 2 places in Scotland where over 50% of the population was Roman Catholic in 1900 or in 1922.
2 This table considers all mainland civil parishes in Argyll north of Kilbrandon, and all mainland civil parishes in Inverness, Ross and Cromarty, and Sutherland
3 Based on county reports for 1921 in Argyll, Inverness, Ross and Cromarty, and Sutherland
4 Ensor, England 1870-1914, 207
5 Including portions of the Outer Hebrides which were later detached.

6 The others were Banff, Aberdeenshire West, Aberdeen City (2 seats), Montrose District, Elgin District, Kincardineshire, East Perth and Caithness
7 Caithness had 3·5% Gaelic-speakers in 1921, compared with 49·8% in Sutherland and 57·0% in Ross and Cromarty
8 See maps on pp. 47, 49, 51, 53 and 87.
9 Census of Scotland 1921, 'Glasgow', 54-6
10 Glasgow Herald, 2 October 1922
11 Glasgow Herald, 8 November 1922
12 See map on p. 89
13 See maps from pp. 39 to 53

Wales

Distribution of Nonconformists and Anglicans in Wales 1905 (Maps A and B)

county	% Nonconformist	% Anglican	Nonconformist/ Anglican
Anglesey	42·0	9·5	4·4
Brecon	25·7	12·0	2·1
Cardigan	46·6	15·2	3·1
Carmarthen	43·9	13·8	3·2
Carnarvon	42·5	10·5	4·0
Denbigh	27·2	13·1	2·1
Flint	17·2	14·2	1·2
Glamorgan	23·6	7·1	3·3
Merioneth	50·4	8·3	6·1
Monmouth	17·0	7·8	2·2
Montgomery	29·2	14·1	2·1
Pembroke	29·5	13·0	2·3
Radnor	20·9	16·7	1·3
Welsh Average	**27·4**	**9·6**	**2·9**

Source: K. O. Morgan, *Wales in British Politics*, 313

Nonconformity in 1905

Statistics for 1905 represent the most complete picture of Nonconformity in Wales available for a recent period: the only other full religious census of Wales was taken in 1851. These figures for 1905 are fuller than those given for England on p. 127, as the latter refer only to the 5 largest Nonconformist groups. The figures for 1905 probably exaggerate slightly the real strength of Welsh Nonconformity, because the years 1903-5 witnessed a revival of Nonconformist strength, which soon tapered off. This Nonconformist revival took place at the same time as the controversy over the Education Act of 1902. Probably many lukewarm Nonconformists returned to their chapels for the duration of that controversy. This is confirmed by the fact that soon after, the numbers of Nonconformists declined.

year	number of Nonconformists	change from previous figure
1903	465,794	—
1904	512,023	+46,229
1905	549,123	+37,100
1910	528,131	−20,992
1913	523,277	−4,854

Source: Morgan, *Wales in British Politics*, 314

The 5 counties with more than 40% Nonconformists all voted Liberal in every election from 1885 to 1910; and they all voted Liberal in nearly every election from 1918 to 1945. However, there was not a complete overlapping of Liberal and Nonconformist strongholds in Wales. For instance, the only seat the Liberals won in every election from 1885 to 1966 was Montgomeryshire, which had only 29·6% Nonconformists in 1905. Several other seats had more Nonconformists but did not have an unbroken Liberal representation. Merioneth, the only seat with over 50% Nonconformists, went Liberal in only one election after 1945; while Car-

narvonshire, with 42·5% Nonconformists, did not go Liberal at all in the post-1945 period. The relationships between Nonconformity, opposition to Sunday opening in 1961, and the degree of Welsh-speaking, are all much closer than that between Nonconformity and Liberalism. A comparison of maps A, C and G indicates that the greater the degree of Nonconformity in 1905, the greater the opposition to Sunday opening in 1961, and the greater the degree of Welsh-speaking in 1921.

Anglicanism in 1905

The Anglican church in 1905 was a small but growing minority in Wales. According to the religious census of 1851, the ratio of Nonconformists to Anglicans had been 3·6 Nonconformists to each Anglican.[1] By 1905 the ratio was only 2·9 Nonconformists to every Anglican.[2] Much of this Anglican gain came from the expansion of the Anglican proportion of the population following 1886; this expansion reached a peak in 1905, and thereafter declined. Since the Anglican peak came in the same year as the Nonconformist peak, the two were probably connected; and the subsequent decline of each group appears to confirm this. The following table[3] indicates the proportion of Anglicans in the general population:

year	Anglican Easter Communicants as % of total population
1886	4·9
1893	6·3
1905	9·6
1923	6·5

Anglicans were strongest in Cardigan, Radnor and Flint, in 1905. In Radnor and Flint there were almost as many Anglicans as Nonconformists but this had different political effects in the 2 counties. Flint was Liberal in every election from 1885 to 1910, while Radnor was Liberal in only half of them. Flint had many more Welsh-speakers than anglicised Radnor, which may account for the greater influence of Liberalism in Flint. Apart from Flint and Radnor, the ratio of Nonconformists to Anglicans was high; this meant that the Anglicans had little effect on the outcome of elections in most Welsh seats.

Welsh-speakers in 1921 (Map C)

county or borough	% Welsh-speakers 1911	1921	1931	change 1911-1931
Anglesey	88·7	84·9	87·4	−1·3
Brecon	41·5	37·2	37·3	−4·2
Cardigan	89·6	82·1	87·1	−2·5
Carmarthen	84·9	82·4	82·3	−2·6
Carnarvon	85·6	75·0	79·2	−6·4
Denbigh	56·7	48·4	48·5	−8·2
Flint	42·2	32·7	31·7	−10·5
Glamorgan	38·1	31·6	30·5	−7·6

1 *Religious Census of 1851*, Table N, ccc
2 Morgan, *Wales in British Politics*, 313

3 Based on Morgan, *Wales in British Politics*, 61, 83 and 313; and on *Official Year Book of the Church of England 1925*, 442-3

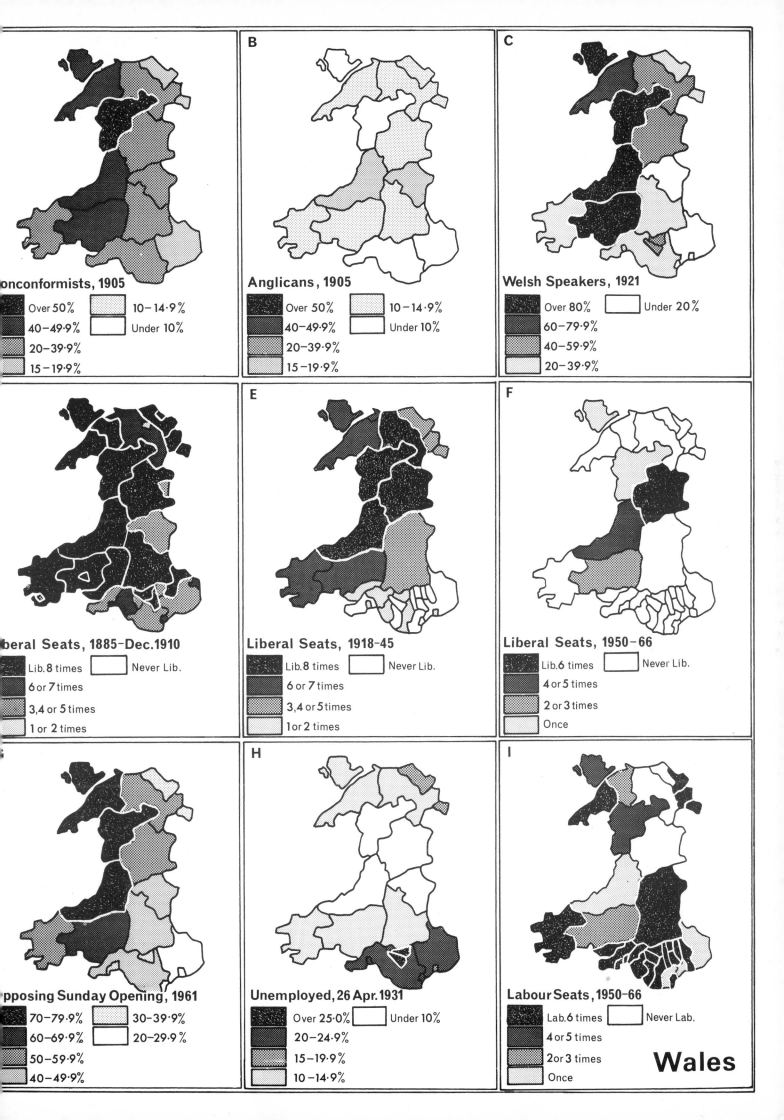

A

onconformists, 1905

- Over 50%
- 40–49·9%
- 20–39·9%
- 15–19·9%
- 10–14·9%
- Under 10%

B

Anglicans, 1905

- Over 50%
- 40–49·9%
- 20–39·9%
- 15–19·9%
- 10–14·9%
- Under 10%

C

Welsh Speakers, 1921

- Over 80%
- 60–79·9%
- 40–59·9%
- 20–39·9%
- Under 20%

D

beral Seats, 1885–Dec.1910

- Lib. 8 times
- 6 or 7 times
- 3,4 or 5 times
- 1 or 2 times
- Never Lib.

E

Liberal Seats, 1918–45

- Lib. 8 times
- 6 or 7 times
- 3,4 or 5 times
- 1 or 2 times
- Never Lib.

F

Liberal Seats, 1950–66

- Lib. 6 times
- 4 or 5 times
- 2 or 3 times
- Once
- Never Lib.

G

pposing Sunday Opening, 1961

- 70–79·9%
- 60–69·9%
- 50–59·9%
- 40–49·9%
- 30–39·9%
- 20–29·9%

H

Unemployed, 26 Apr. 1931

- Over 25·0%
- 20–24·9%
- 15–19·9%
- 10–14·9%
- Under 10%

I

Labour Seats, 1950–66

- Lab. 6 times
- 4 or 5 times
- 2 or 3 times
- Once
- Never Lab.

Wales

| county or borough | % Welsh-speakers | | | change |
	1911	1921	1931	1911-1931
Merioneth	92·3	84·7	86·1	−6·2
Monmouth	9·6	6·4	6·0	−3·6
Montgomery	44·8	42·3	40·7	−4·1
Pembroke	32·4	30·3	30·6	−1·8
Radnor	5·4	6·3	4·7	−0·7
Cardiff	6·7	5·0	5·1	−1·7
Merthyr Tydfil	50·2	41·4	39·8	−10·4
Newport (Mon.)	2·6	2·1	2·1	−0·5
Rhondda	55·2	45·5	46·5	−8·7
Swansea	27·1	28·5	27·3	+0·2
Welsh Average	**43·5**	**37·1**	**36·8**	**−6·7**

Source: for 1921 and 1911 figures, *Census of 1921*, county series, table xx for each county; for 1931 figures, *Census of 1931*, General Report, 184-5. Persons below 3 years of age not included

The greatest decline in Welsh-speaking in the period 1911-1931 did not occur in places where the overwhelming majority spoke Welsh. In most such places, the decline was small in both relative and absolute terms. The only place where many spoke Welsh in 1911, and where there was a significant decline by 1931, was Carnarvonshire. However, in Carnarvonshire most of the decline occurred in boroughs where the proportion of Welsh-speakers was low even in 1911.[1] The places which had the greatest drops in the proportion of Welsh-speakers were ones where between 35% and 60% had spoken Welsh in 1911.[2] This indicates that Welsh was most on the defensive where it was not spoken by the overwhelming majority of the population. In Scotland, Gaelic was also most on the defensive where Gaelic-speakers were not an overwhelming majority; where Gaelic-speakers were such a majority, the language held its ground very well.

In 1921 Welsh was a majority language in only 4 counties, Anglesey, Cardigan, Carmarthen and Carnarvon. Although these were for a long time Liberal strongholds, 3 of them elected Labour candidates in the 1920s who campaigned as left-wing Liberals rather than as socialists.

Liberal seats 1885-1910 (Map D)

no. of times Liberal	no. of seats
8	16
6 or 7	8
3, 4 or 5	9
1 or 2	1
never	—
	34

In the period 1885-1910, the Liberals won all Welsh seats with over 40% Nonconformists; they also won all but one of the seats with over 20% Nonconformists,[3] the exception being Denbigh. Denbigh was, however, an area of relative Anglican strength in comparison with the rest of Wales. The groupings of small boroughs were areas of relative Unionist strength between 1885 and 1910: only the Flint District of boroughs acted in the same way as its county, by voting consistently Liberal; Monmouth District was more Liberal than its Unionist hinterland. Apparently Wales was split politically along rural/urban lines, perhaps because of the greater anglicisation of the urban constituencies. In addition, since the rural areas contained nearly all the single-school districts with Anglican schools, a more militant variety of Nonconformity probably developed in the country than in the towns. This in turn could account for the greater Liberal strength in the country than in the towns.

1 *Census of 1921*, Carnarvonshire County Report, xxxviii
2 The 5 places experiencing the greatest drops were Denbigh, Flint, Glamorgan, Merthyr Tydfil and Rhondda. All had between 35% and 60% Welsh-speakers in 1911
3 Excluding Glamorgan seats, several of which had Liberal-Labour M.P.s
4 This map is not the Welsh section of the map on p. 85 which deal with Liberal seats in the period 1918-29

Liberal seats 1918-45[4] (Map E)

no. of times Liberal	no. of seats
8	4
6 or 7	5
3, 4 or 5	4
1 or 2	9
never	13
	35

This map illustrates the great decline in Liberal strength between the wars. In 1918 the Liberals won most seats in Wales, with 21 out of 35. In 1922 they were cut to 10, with Labour making the heaviest gains, mainly in mining constituencies. The Liberals did not regain a single mining constituency in South Wales in any election from 1922 to 1966, and they won very few in the seaports of the South Coast. After 1922 Welsh Liberalism was virtually confined to rural seats, and even there the Labour Party made inroads. In the inter-war period, more than in the pre-1914 period, Welsh Liberalism seemed to coincide with Welsh Nonconformity: the Liberals won all constituencies with over a quarter Nonconformists in at least half the inter-war elections; in the seats with under a quarter Nonconformists they rarely won.

Liberal seats 1950-66 (Map F)

no. of times Liberal	no. of seats
6	1
4 or 5	1
2 or 3	1
1	2
never	31
	36

The great reduction of Liberal seats shown in this map was a continuation of earlier trends, the most notable being Labour victories in rural Nonconformist strongholds with relatively little industry. In 1945 Liberals or National Liberals held 7 Welsh seats; but in 1950 Labour gained one of these, Pembroke; in 1951 it gained Anglesey and Merioneth; in 1959 Carmarthen; and in 1966 Cardigan. It is difficult to avoid the conclusion that in the period 1945-66, the Labour Party captured most of the old Welsh Nonconformist radical vote, whether that vote was middle-class, working-class or agricultural. The political relevance of Nonconformity was small even in the inter-war period, as the Anglican church had been disestablished in 1920, and that had been one of the chief remaining grievances of Welsh Nonconformists; so it was to be expected that the old Liberal voters would turn to the other two parties; what was not necessarily predictable was that most of them would turn to Labour.

Welsh Sunday Opening Referendum, 8 November 1961 (Map G)

county or borough	% against Sunday opening of public houses[1]
Anglesey	72·3
Brecon	46·6
Cardigan	73·7
Carmarthen	67·3
Carnarvon	70·6
Denbigh	52·5
Flint	39·3
Glamorgan	40·5
Merioneth	75·8
Monmouth	28·9
Montgomery	57·0
Pembroke	58·0
Radnor	41·9
Cardiff	27·1
Newport	27·1
Merthyr	33·6
Swansea	38·4
Wales	**46·2**

Source: *The Times*, 18 November 1961

A poll held throughout Wales on 8 November 1961 on the issue of Sunday opening of public houses led to the defeat of the proposal in 8 rural counties, and its acceptance in the other 5, as well as in 4 boroughs. The vote was almost exactly along the lines of the distribution of Nonconformists in 1905: the counties which had had the most Nonconformists (Merioneth and Cardigan) rejected it by the greatest margins, while the counties which had had the fewest Nonconformists (Flint and Monmouth) accepted it with the widest margin.[1] This is a strong indication that the relative distribution of Nonconformists in Wales did not change much between 1905 and 1961, and by implication, that the relative distribution of Nonconformists in England did not change much either, at any rate in rural areas.[2]

Unemployment in 1931 (Map H)

county or borough	% unemployed on 26 April 1931 (Census Day), males only
Anglesey	13·7
Brecon	14·8
Cardigan	9·0
Carmarthen	12·9
Carnarvon	11·1
Denbigh	11·8
Flint	19·7
Glamorgan	21·7
Merioneth	8·2
Monmouth	20·7
Montgomery	7·5
Pembroke	12·9
Radnor	5·3
Cardiff	20·1
Merthyr Tydfil	35·8
Newport	18·7
Rhondda U.D.	25·9
Swansea	24·1
Average for England and Wales	**12·7**

Source: Census of 1931, General Report, 162

The rate of 35·8% unemployment in Merthyr Tydfil was the third highest in the country,[3] while that of industrial South Wales generally was exceeded only by the North-east. Welsh unemployment was concentrated in the industrial areas while that in rural areas was low. Only 6 places[4] had a lower degree of unemployment than Cardigan, all but one of them being middle-class districts. The map shows how the depression of the 1920s and 1930s hit industrial South Wales. These areas voted Labour in 1931, when the rest of Wales supported the Liberals or Conservatives.

Labour seats 1950-66 (Map I)

no. of times Labour	no. of seats
6	27
4 or 5	1
2 or 3	2
1	3
never	3
	36

Apart from the rural constituencies of Denbigh and Montgomery, and the partly suburban seat of West Flint, the Labour Party won every seat in Wales at least once between 1950 and 1966. Their victories included several rural constituencies where the working-class vote could not alone account for their wins. In 1918 and 1922 Labour candidates won in Anglesey and Carnarvonshire. It would be misleading to attribute these victories to the presence of a large rural proletariat, since the proportion of agricultural labourers to farmers in these counties was the smallest of any county in England and Wales.[5] Much of the Labour vote could therefore be attributed to Nonconformist middle-class and farming voters who considered themselves radicals. Otherwise, the Labour wins in Cardigan or Merioneth would be difficult to explain. By 1966 the Labour Party had apparently captured much of the Liberal vote, and the Liberals' old position as the dominant party in Wales.

1 Boroughs are excluded, as figures for the percentage of Nonconformists were not available for units smaller than counties
2 Assuming, as is probable, that the Nonconformists provided most anti-Opening votes
3 South Shields had 35·9% and Sunderland had 36·6% unemployed on Census Day, 1931 (Census of 1931, General Report, 162)
4 Luton, City of London, Cambridge City, Oxford City, Finchley, Westmorland
5 The average number of agricultural labourers per farm in 1921 was 0·71 in Anglesey and 0·60 in Carnarvon. The average for England and Wales was 1·70 (Agricultural Statistics, 1921, 42, 44)

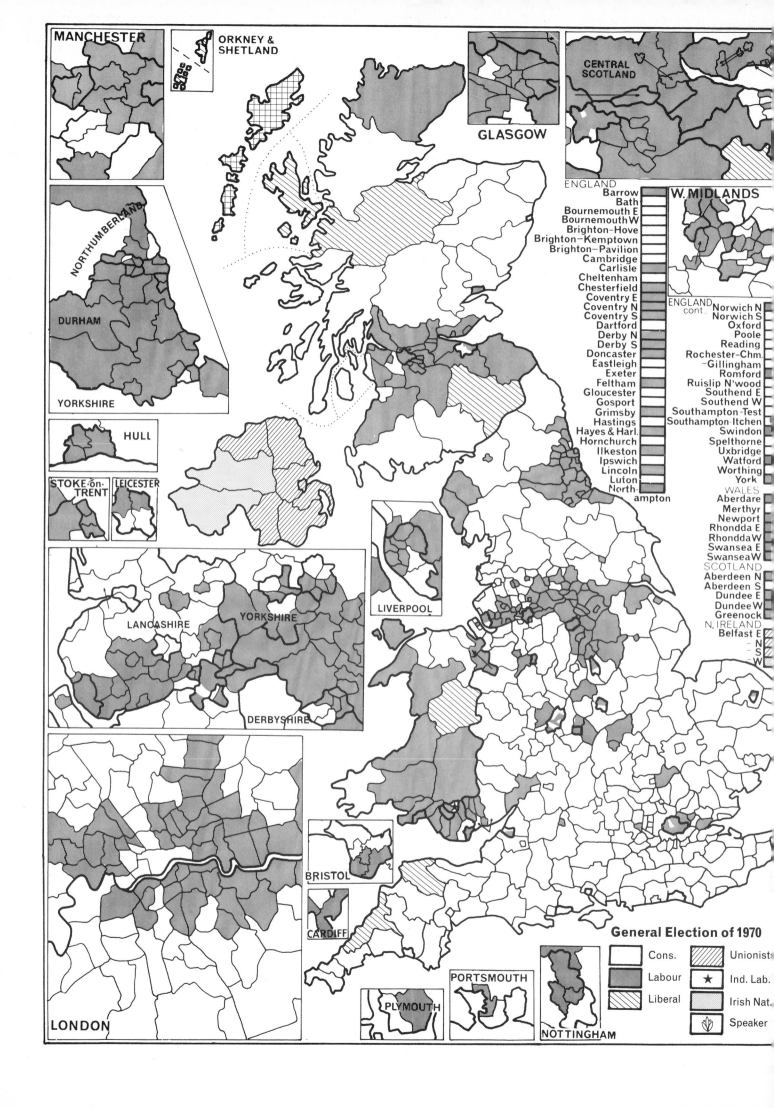

MANCHESTER

ORKNEY & SHETLAND

GLASGOW

CENTRAL SCOTLAND

NORTHUMBERLAND

DURHAM

YORKSHIRE

HULL

STOKE-on-TRENT

LEICESTER

LANCASHIRE

YORKSHIRE

DERBYSHIRE

LIVERPOOL

W. MIDLANDS

ENGLAND

Barrow
Bath
Bournemouth E
Bournemouth W
Brighton–Hove
Brighton–Kemptown
Brighton–Pavilion
Cambridge
Carlisle
Cheltenham
Chesterfield
Coventry E
Coventry N
Coventry S
Dartford
Derby N
Derby S
Doncaster
Eastleigh
Exeter
Feltham
Gloucester
Gosport
Grimsby
Hastings
Hayes & Harl.
Hornchurch
Ilkeston
Ipswich
Lincoln
Luton
North-ampton

ENGLAND cont..

Norwich N
Norwich S
Oxford
Poole
Reading
Rochester–Chm.
–Gillingham
Romford
Ruislip N'wood
Southend E
Southend W
Southampton-Test
Southampton-Itchen
Swindon
Spelthorne
Uxbridge
Watford
Worthing
York

WALES

Aberdare
Merthyr
Newport
Rhondda E
Rhondda W
Swansea E
Swansea W

SCOTLAND

Aberdeen N
Aberdeen S
Dundee E
Dundee W
Greenock

N. IRELAND

Belfast E
–N
–S
–W

BRISTOL

CARDIFF

LONDON

PLYMOUTH

PORTSMOUTH

NOTTINGHAM

General Election of 1970

Cons.		Unionist
Labour	★	Ind. Lab.
Liberal		Irish Nat.
	Speaker	

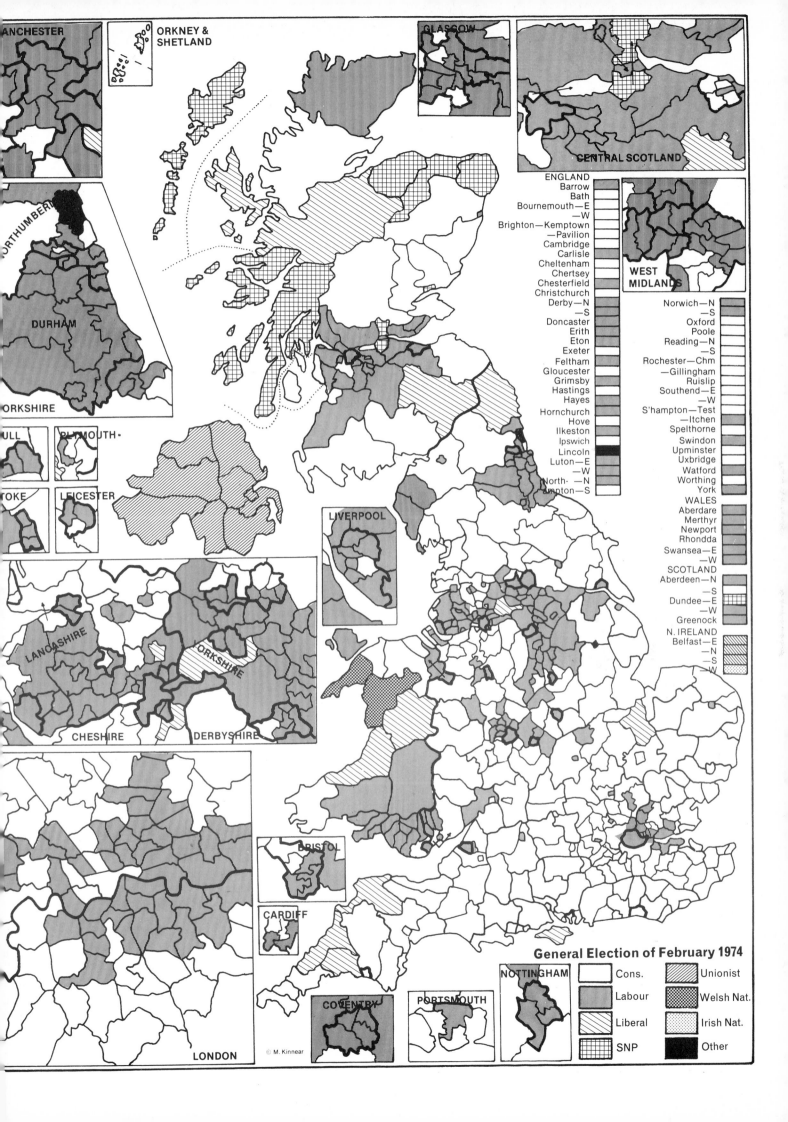

MANCHESTER

ORKNEY &
SHETLAND

GLASGOW

NORTHUMBERLAND

DURHAM

YORKSHIRE

HULL   PLYMOUTH

STOKE   LEICESTER

LANCASHIRE

YORKSHIRE

CHESHIRE   DERBYSHIRE

CENTRAL SCOTLAND

WEST
MIDLANDS

LIVERPOOL

BRISTOL

CARDIFF

NOTTINGHAM

COVENTRY   PORTSMOUTH

LONDON

© M. Kinnear

General Election of February 1974

ENGLAND
Barrow
Bath
Bournemouth—E
—W
Brighton—Kemptown
—Pavilion
Cambridge
Carlisle
Cheltenham
Chertsey
Chesterfield
Christchurch
Derby—N
—S
Doncaster
Erith
Eton
Exeter
Feltham
Gloucester
Grimsby
Hastings
Hayes
Hornchurch
Hove
Ilkeston
Ipswich
Lincoln
Luton—E
—W
North- —N
ampton—S

Norwich—N
—S
Oxford
Poole
Reading—N
—S
Rochester—Chm
—Gillingham
Ruislip
Southend—E
—W
S'hampton—Test
—Itchen
Spelthorne
Swindon
Upminster
Uxbridge
Watford
Worthing
York
WALES
Aberdare
Merthyr
Newport
Rhondda
Swansea—E
—W
SCOTLAND
Aberdeen—N
—S
Dundee—E
—W
Greenock
N. IRELAND
Belfast—E
—N
—S
—W

	Cons.		Unionist
	Labour		Welsh Nat.
	Liberal		Irish Nat.
	SNP		Other

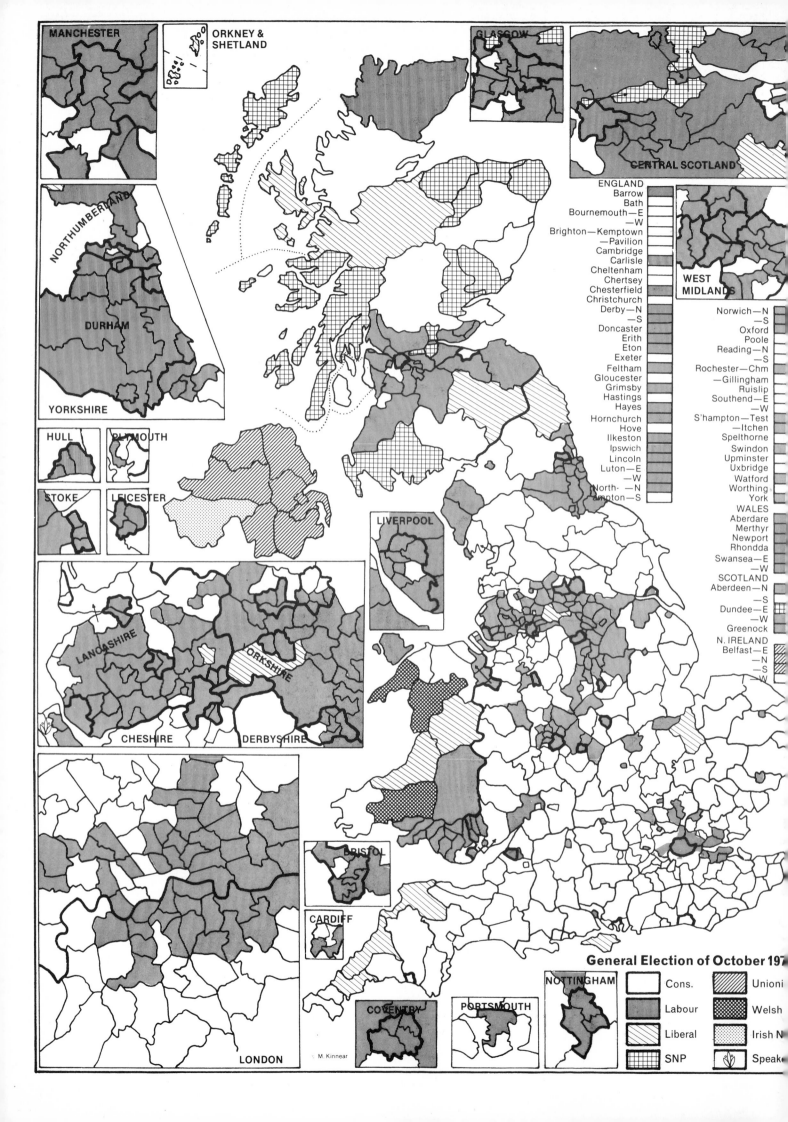

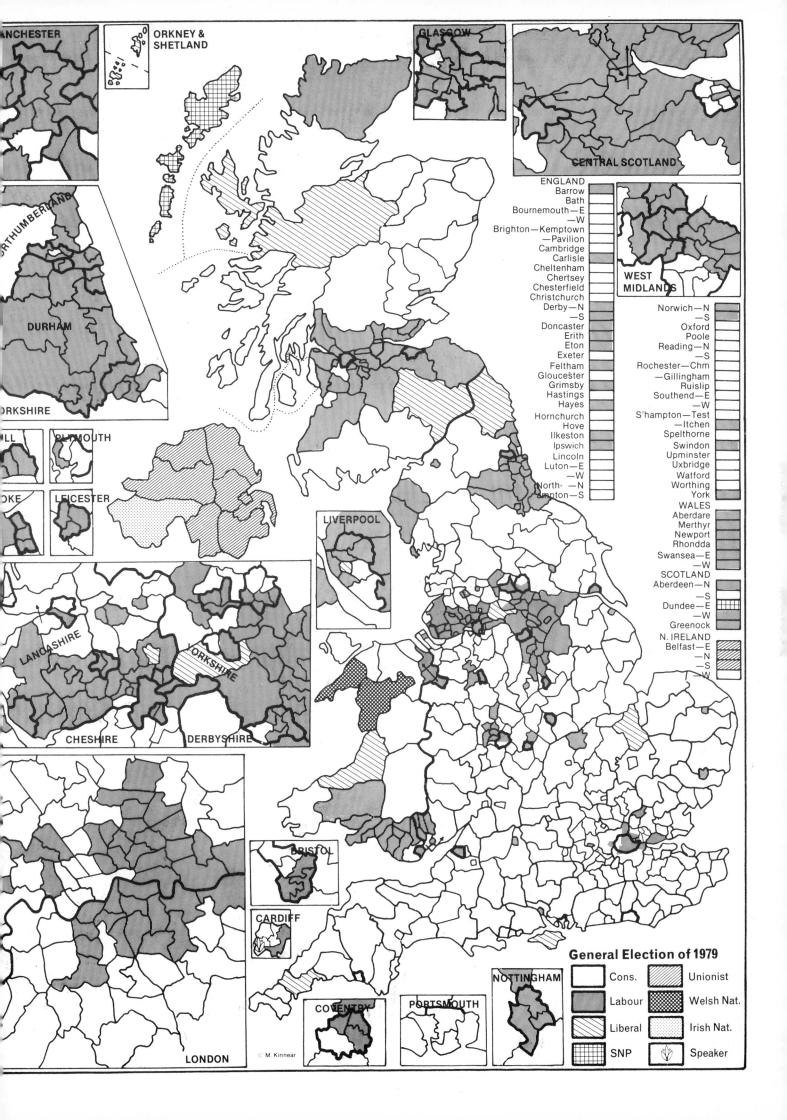

MANCHESTER

ORKNEY & SHETLAND

GLASGOW

CENTRAL SCOTLAND

ENGLAND
Barrow
Bath
Bournemouth—E
—W
Brighton—Kemptown
—Pavilion
Cambridge
Carlisle
Cheltenham
Chertsey
Chesterfield
Christchurch
Derby—N
—S
Doncaster
Erith
Eton
Exeter
Feltham
Gloucester
Grimsby
Hastings
Hayes
Hornchurch
Hove
Ilkeston
Ipswich
Lincoln
Luton—E
—W
North- —N
ampton—S

WEST MIDLANDS

Norwich—N
—S
Oxford
Poole
Reading—N
—S
Rochester—Chm
—Gillingham
Ruislip
Southend—E
—W
S'hampton—Test
—Itchen
Spelthorne
Swindon
Upminster
Uxbridge
Watford
Worthing
York
WALES
Aberdare
Merthyr
Newport
Rhondda
Swansea—E
—W
SCOTLAND
Aberdeen—N
—S
Dundee—E
—W
Greenock
N. IRELAND
Belfast—E
—N
—S
—W

NORTHUMBERLAND

DURHAM

YORKSHIRE

HULL

PLYMOUTH

OKE

LEICESTER

LIVERPOOL

LANCASHIRE

YORKSHIRE

CHESHIRE

DERBYSHIRE

BRISTOL

CARDIFF

LONDON

© M. Kinnear

COVENTRY

PORTSMOUTH

NOTTINGHAM

General Election of 1979

	Cons.		Unionist
	Labour		Welsh Nat.
	Liberal		Irish Nat.
	SNP		Speaker

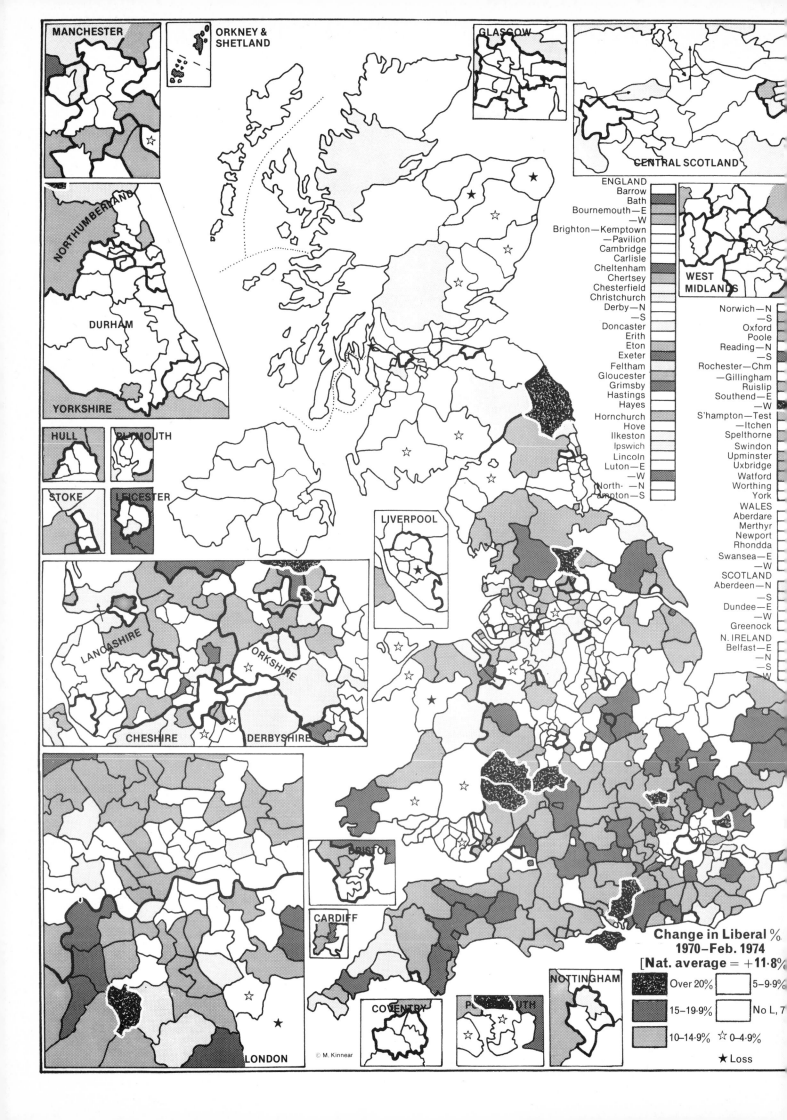

Change in Liberal % 1970–Feb. 1974 [Nat. average = +11·8%]

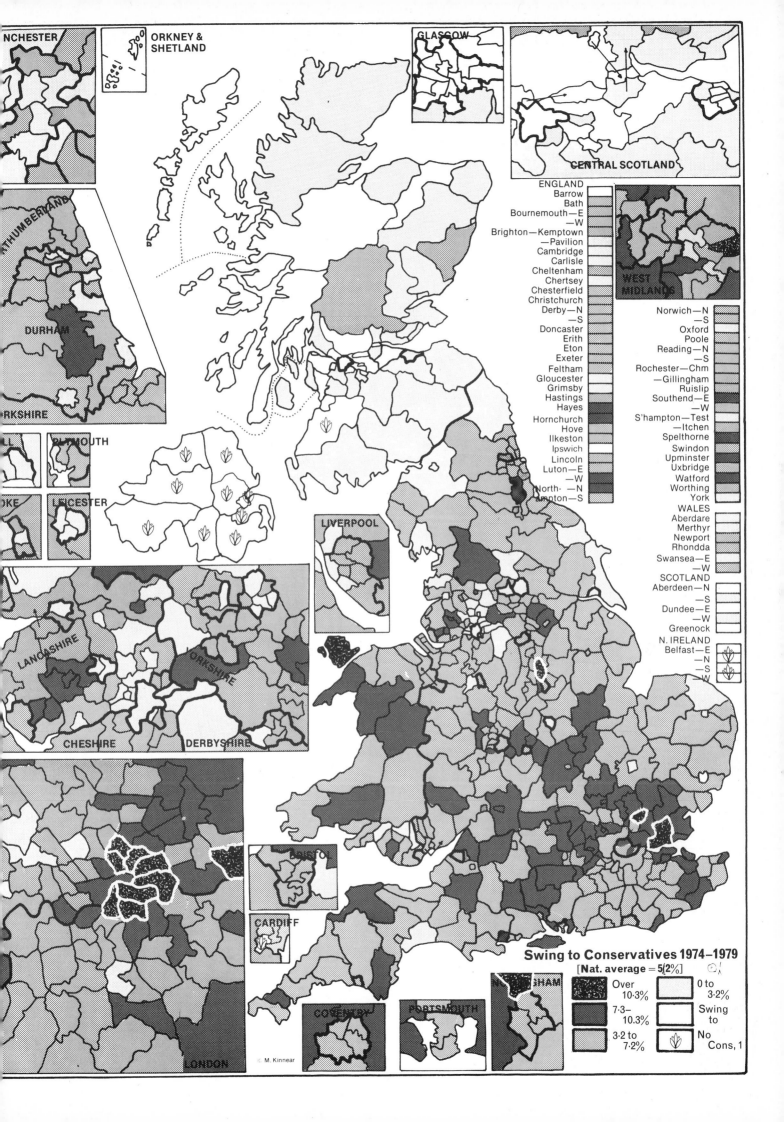

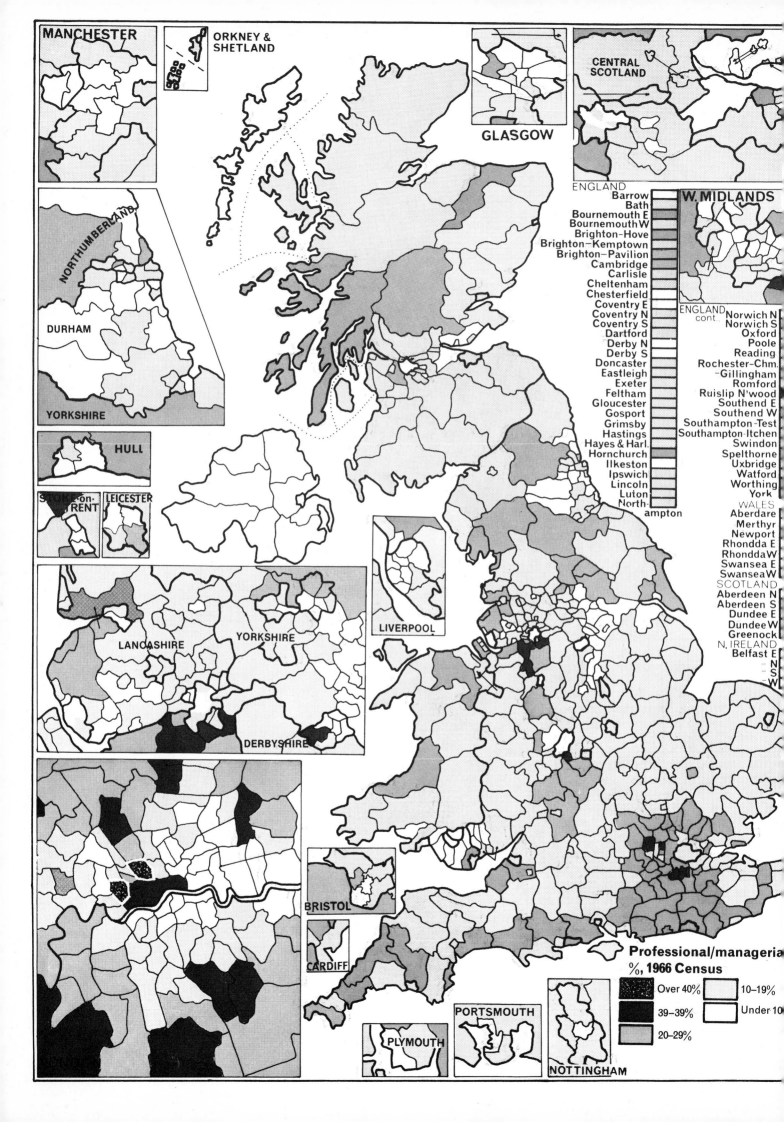

MANCHESTER

ORKNEY & SHETLAND

GLASGOW

CENTRAL SCOTLAND

NORTHUMBERLAND

DURHAM

YORKSHIRE

HULL

STOKE-on-TRENT

LEICESTER

LANCASHIRE

YORKSHIRE

LIVERPOOL

DERBYSHIRE

BRISTOL

CARDIFF

PORTSMOUTH

PLYMOUTH

NOTTINGHAM

ENGLAND
Barrow
Bath
Bournemouth E
Bournemouth W
Brighton-Hove
Brighton-Kemptown
Brighton-Pavilion
Cambridge
Carlisle
Cheltenham
Chesterfield
Coventry E
Coventry N
Coventry S
Dartford
Derby N
Derby S
Doncaster
Eastleigh
Exeter
Feltham
Gloucester
Gosport
Grimsby
Hastings
Hayes & Harl.
Hornchurch
Ilkeston
Ipswich
Lincoln
Luton
North-ampton

W. MIDLANDS

ENGLAND cont..
Norwich N
Norwich S
Oxford
Poole
Reading
Rochester-Chm.
-Gillingham
Romford
Ruislip N'wood
Southend E
Southend W
Southampton-Test
Southampton-Itchen
Swindon
Spelthorne
Uxbridge
Watford
Worthing
York
WALES
Aberdare
Merthyr
Newport
Rhondda E
Rhondda W
Swansea E
Swansea W
SCOTLAND
Aberdeen N
Aberdeen S
Dundee E
Dundee W
Greenock
N. IRELAND
Belfast E
— N
— S
W

Professional/managerial %, 1966 Census

- Over 40%
- 39–39%
- 20–29%
- 10–19%
- Under 10

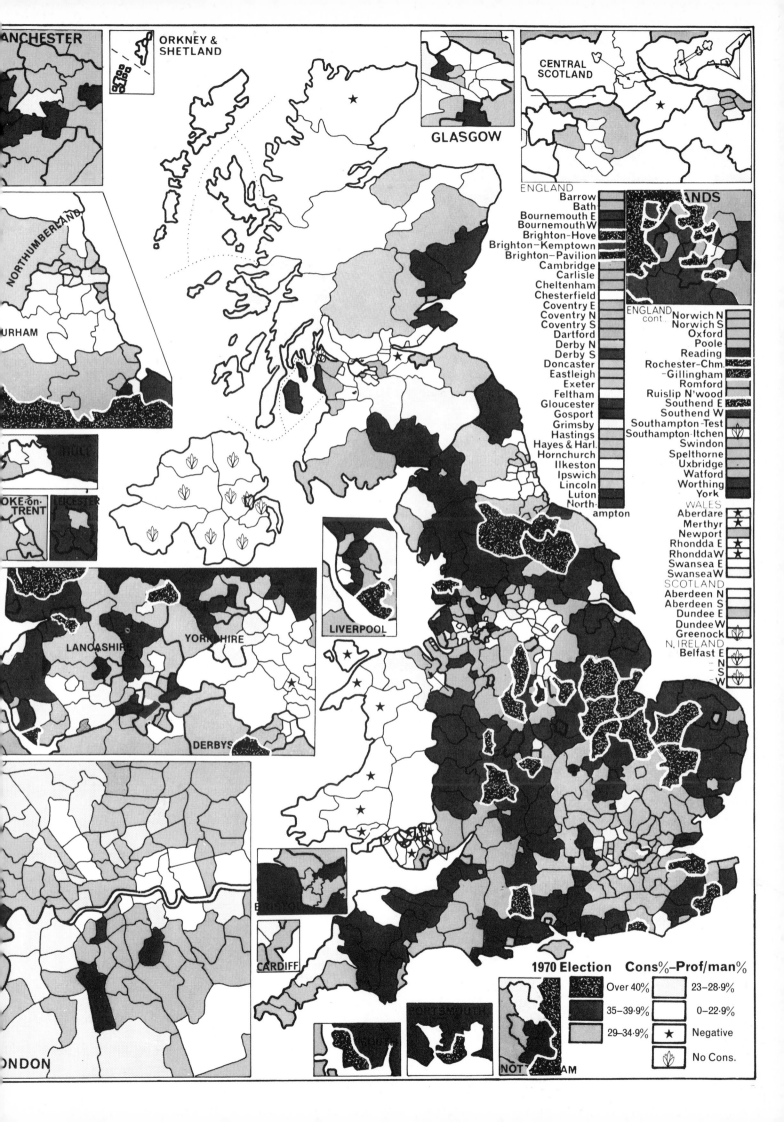

ORKNEY & SHETLAND

ANCHESTER

GLASGOW

CENTRAL SCOTLAND

NORTHUMBERLAND

URHAM

HULL

OKE-on-TRENT

LEICESTER

ENGLAND
Barrow
Bath
Bournemouth E
Bournemouth W
Brighton-Hove
Brighton-Kemptown
Brighton-Pavilion
Cambridge
Carlisle
Cheltenham
Chesterfield
Coventry E
Coventry N
Coventry S
Dartford
Derby N
Derby S
Doncaster
Eastleigh
Exeter
Feltham
Gloucester
Gosport
Grimsby
Hastings
Hayes & Harl.
Hornchurch
Ilkeston
Ipswich
Lincoln
Luton
North-
ampton

ANDS

ENGLAND cont.
Norwich N
Norwich S
Oxford
Poole
Reading
Rochester-Chm.
-Gillingham
Romford
Ruislip N'wood
Southend E
Southend W
Southampton-Test
Southampton-Itchen
Swindon
Spelthorne
Uxbridge
Watford
Worthing
York

WALES
Aberdare ★
Merthyr ★
Newport
Rhondda E ★
Rhondda W ★
Swansea E
Swansea W

SCOTLAND
Aberdeen N
Aberdeen S
Dundee E
Dundee W
Greenock

N. IRELAND
Belfast E
-N
-S
-W

LANCASHIRE
YORKSHIRE

LIVERPOOL

DERBYS

LONDON

BRISTOL

CARDIFF

ORTSMOUTH

NOT   AM

1970 Election   Cons%—Prof/man%

Over 40%   23–28·9%

35–39·9%   0–22·9%

29–34·9%   ★ Negative

                 No Cons.

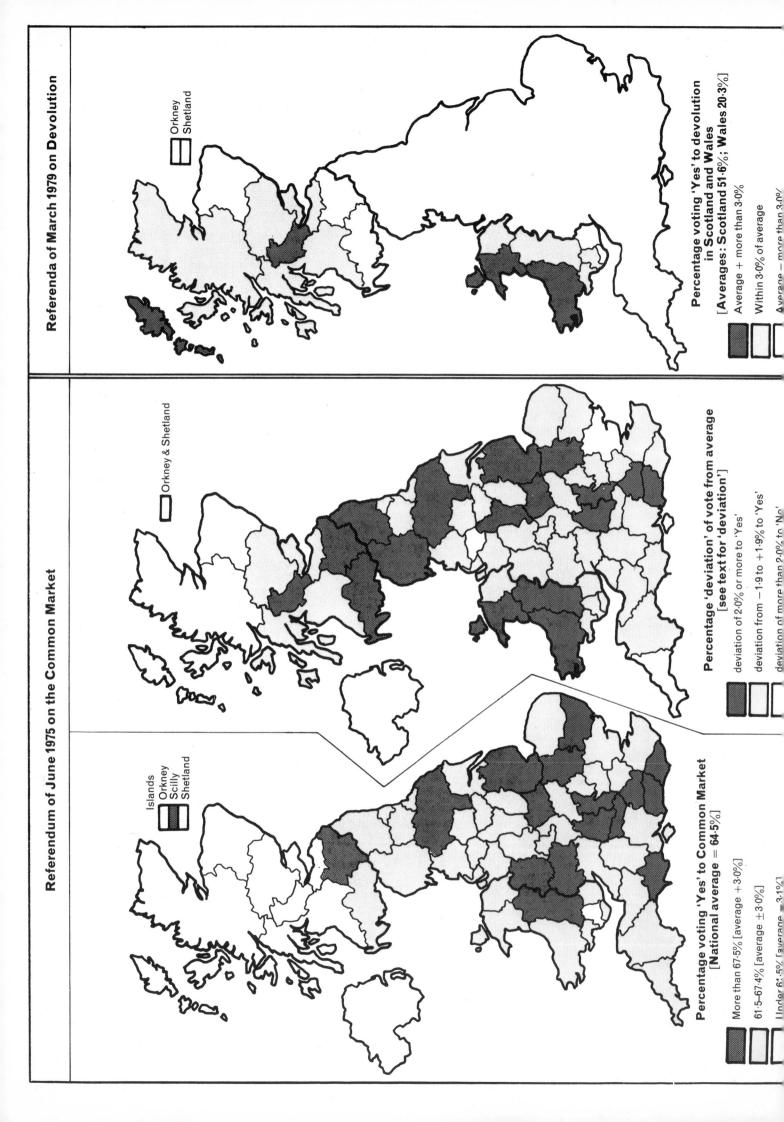

Referenda of March 1979 on Devolution

Orkney
Shetland

**Percentage voting 'Yes' to devolution
in Scotland and Wales**
[Averages: Scotland 51·6%; Wales 20·3%]

Average + more than 3·0%

Within 3·0% of average

Average − more than 3·0%

Referendum of June 1975 on the Common Market

Orkney & Shetland

Percentage 'deviation' of vote from average
[see text for 'deviation']

deviation of 2·0% or more to 'Yes'

deviation from −1·9 to +1·9% to 'Yes'

deviation of more than 2·0% to 'No'

Islands
Orkney
Scilly
Shetland

Percentage voting 'Yes' to Common Market
[National average = 64·5%]

More than 67·5% [average +3·0%]

61·5–67·4% [average ±3·0%]

Under 61·5% [average −3·1%]

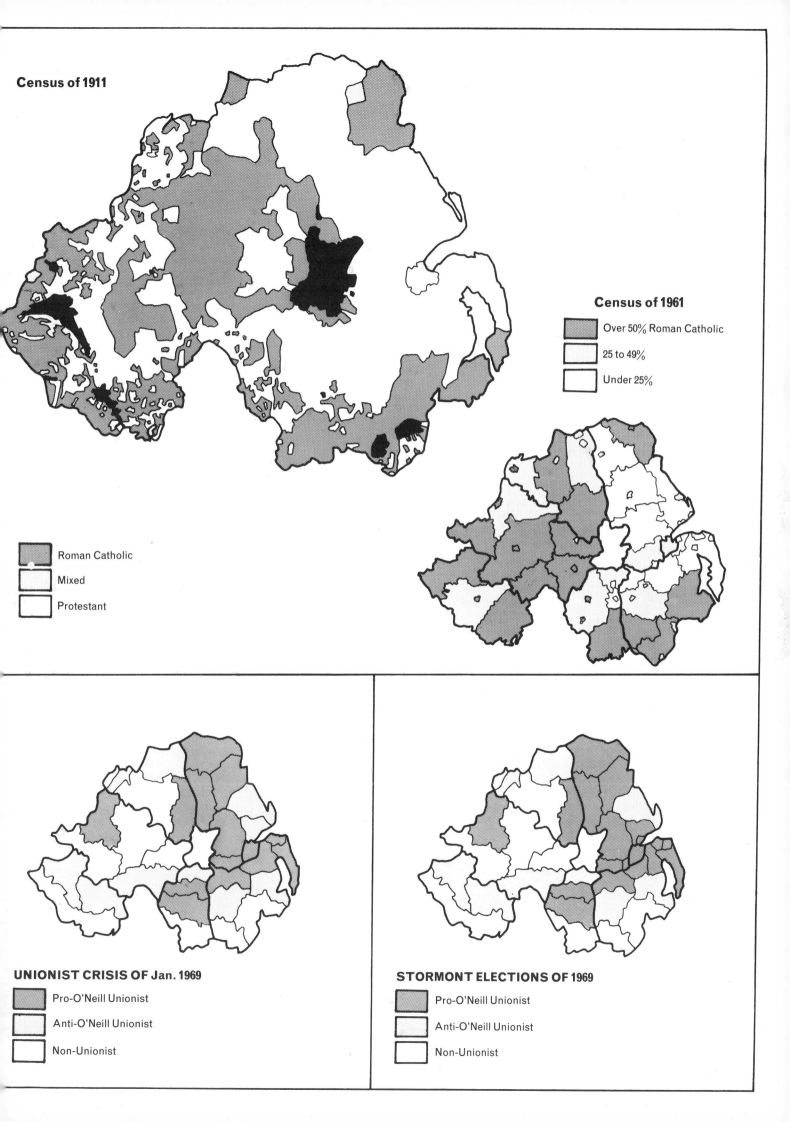

Census of 1911

Census of 1961

Over 50% Roman Catholic

25 to 49%

Under 25%

Roman Catholic

Mixed

Protestant

UNIONIST CRISIS OF Jan. 1969

Pro-O'Neill Unionist

Anti-O'Neill Unionist

Non-Unionist

STORMONT ELECTIONS OF 1969

Pro-O'Neill Unionist

Anti-O'Neill Unionist

Non-Unionist

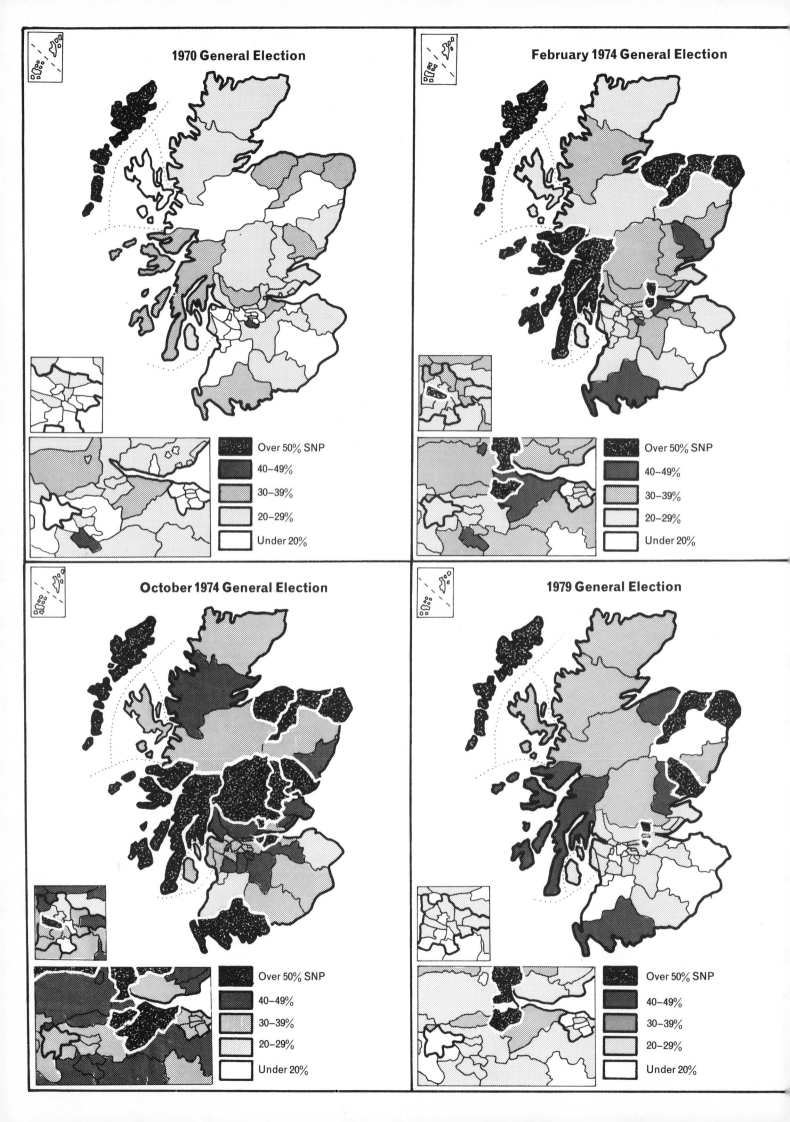

1970 General Election

Over 50% SNP
40–49%
30–39%
20–29%
Under 20%

February 1974 General Election

Over 50% SNP
40–49%
30–39%
20–29%
Under 20%

October 1974 General Election

Over 50% SNP
40–49%
30–39%
20–29%
Under 20%

1979 General Election

Over 50% SNP
40–49%
30–39%
20–29%
Under 20%

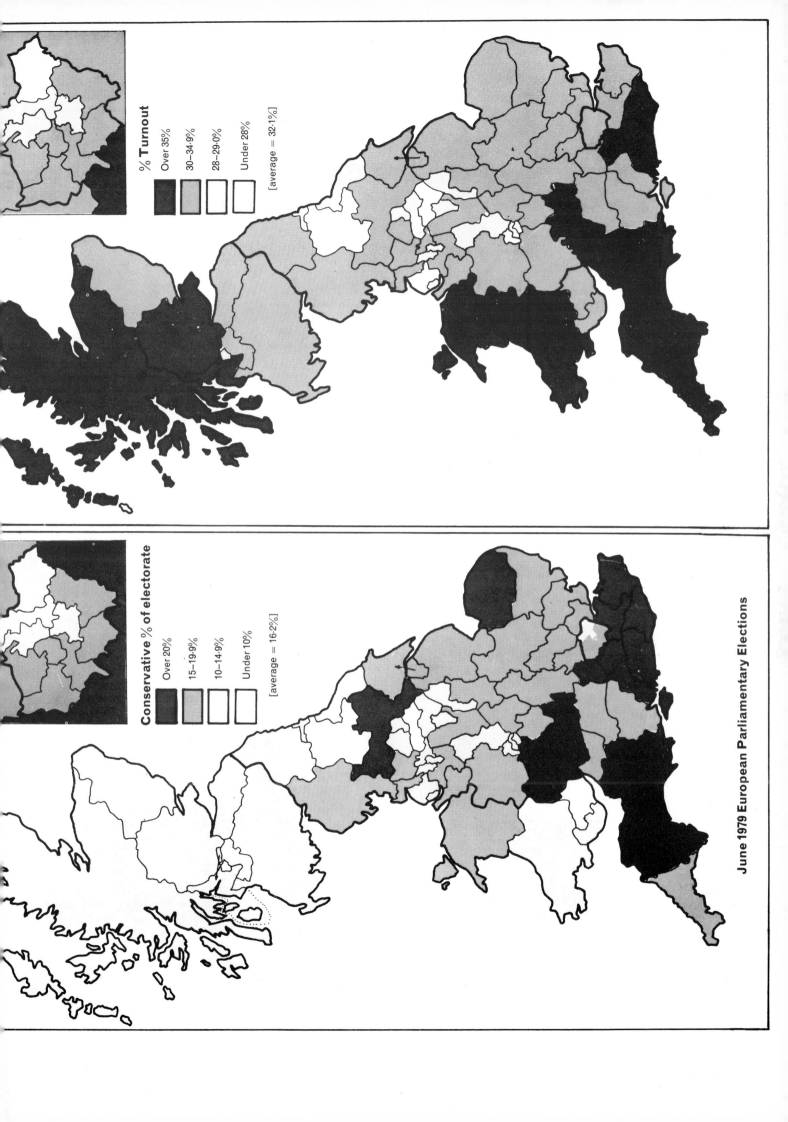

% **Turnout**

Over 35%

30–34.9%

28–29.0%

Under 28%

[average = 32.1%]

Conservative % of electorate

Over 20%

15–19.9%

10–14.9%

Under 10%

[average = 16.2%]

June 1979 European Parliamentary Elections

General Elections of 1970 to 1979

Overall results

	1970 total vote	%	February 1974 total vote	%	October 1974 total vote	%	1979 total vote	%
Great Britain								
Conservative	12,723,082	44·9	11,868,906	37·9	10,464,675	35·9	13,697,753	43·9
Labour	12,081,147	42·6	11,639,243	37·1	11,456,597	39·3	11,506,741	36·9
Liberal	2,105,003	7·4	6,063,470	19·4	5,346,800	18·3	4,305,324	13·8
Scottish National	306,802	1·1	632,032	2·0	839,628	2·9	504,259	1·6
Welsh National	175,016	0·6	171,364	0·6	166,321	0·6	132,544	0·4
National Front	11,449	*	76,736	0·2	113,843	0·4	191,706	0·6
Communist	37,970	*	32,741	*	17,426	*	16,858	*
Speaker (a)	29,417	*	——		——		27,035	*
Others	95,772		131,148		81,222		171,205	
total in G.B.	27,565,685		30,615,640		28,486,512		30,526,390	
Northern Ireland								
Official Unionist (b)	422,041		94,301		——		254,578	
Paisley Unionist (c)	35,303		41,282		——		70,975	
United UU Council	——		297,564		407,778		——	
Other Unionist	17,787		27,817		28,126		84,866	
Total Unionist	**475,131**	1·7	**460,964**	1·5	**435,904**	1·5	**410,419**	1·3
Unity/Ind Unity	140,954		17,593		——		——	
NILab/Ind NILab	98,194		17,284		11,539		4,411	
Republican Labour	30,649							
Soc. Dem. and Labour	——		160,437		154,193		137,110	
Republican Clubs	——		15,152		21,633		12,100	
Liberal	11,805		——		——			
Alliance	——		22,660		44,644		82,892	
Other non-unionist	22,204		23,496		34,361		48,957	
Total non-Unionist	**303,805**	1·1	**256,622**	0·8	**266,370**	0·9	**285,470**	0·9
total in N. Ireland	778,937		717,586		702,274		695,889	
total in U.K.	28,344,807		31,333,226		29,188,786		31,222,279	

* = under 0·1%.
a = In both 1974 elections, the Speaker had Labour and Liberal opponents; his vote is counted as Conservative.
(b)= Unionists in 1970; supporters of the Sunningdale Agreement in February 1974; Official Ulster Unionists in 1979.
(c)= Protestant Unionists in 1970; Democratic Unionists in February 1974 and in 1979.

Source: based on constituency results published in *The Times Guides to the House of Commons, 1970, February 1974, October 1974, and 1979*. The overall vote totals differ in several cases from those shown in *The Times Guides*.

Seats won by area

1970

area	Cons.	Lab.	Lib.	Other	total
England	292	216	2	1	511
Wales	7	27	1	1	36
Scotland	23	44	3	1	71
N. Ireland	—	—	—	12	12
Total	**322**	**287**	**6**	**15**	**630**

'others':
Unionist	8
Prot. Unionist (Paisley)	1
Republican Labour (Fitt)	1
Ind. Unity (Devlin)	1
Unity (McManus)	1
Scots National	1
Indep. Labour (Davies)	1
Speaker	1

(N. Ireland: 9 Unionists, 3 non-Unionist)

October 1974

area	Cons.	Lab.	Lib.	Other	total
England	253	255	8	—	516
Wales	8	23	2	3	36
Scotland	16	41	3	11	71
N. Ireland	—	—	—	12	12
Total	**277**	**319**	**13**	**26**	**635**

'others':
Unionist Council	11
Scots National	11
Welsh National	3
Soc. Dem. (Fitt)	1

(Speaker counted as Conservative)

(N. Ireland: 11 Unionists, 1 non-Unionist)

February 1974

area	Cons.	Lab.	Lib.	Other	total
England	268	237	9	2	516
Wales	8	24	2	2	36
Scotland	21	40	3	7	71
N. Ireland	—	—	—	12	12
Total	**297**	**301**	**14**	**23**	**635**

'others':
Unionist Council	11
Social Dem. & L. (Fitt)	1
Social Dem. (Taverne)	1
Scots National	7
Welsh National	2
Indep. Labour (Milne)	1

(Speaker counted as Conservative)

(N. Ireland: 11 Unionists, 1 non-Unionist)

1979

area	Cons.	Lab.	Lib.	Other	total
England	306	203	7	—	516
Wales	11	21	1	1	36
Scotland	22	44	3	2	71
N. Ireland	—	—	—	12	12
Total	**339**	**268**	**11**	**17**	**635**

'others':
Official Unionist	5
Democratic Unionist (Paisley)	3
United Ulster U. (Dunlop)	1
Ulster Unionist (Kilfedder)	1
Scots National	2
Welsh National	2
Soc. Dem. (Fitt)	1
Independent (Maguire)	1
Speaker	1

(N. Ireland: 10 Unionists, 2 non-Unionists)

Commentaries on the 1970–1979 elections

General comments on 1970–79

When the first edition of this book appeared in 1968, the average number of elections per decade between 1885 and 1966 was 3·7; in the ten years 1970-79, counting referenda, and the elections to the European parliament, there have been seven direct tests of the electorate. There have been four general elections, the European election, and two referenda, one on the Common Market, and one pair on devolution. This unusually large number of elections alone made the decade an interesting one for the psephologist.

However, there have also been three major changes in political and electoral alignments. The old Unionist coalition, which dominated Ulster politics since the beginning of the period covered by this book, began its decline in 1969, and disappeared almost completely in February 1974, with the overwhelming defeat of those Unionists who supported the Heath's government's proposals for power-sharing. In both Scotland and Wales, the rise of local nationalist parties broke the hegemony of the British political parties, which had been virtually unchallenged hitherto. But perhaps the most important change during the decade was the rise of the Liberal vote from 7% in 1970 to just under 20% in both 1974 elections. This vote declined once more in 1979, but only to 14%. The chief loser from this shift to the Liberals in England was the Labour Party. It is still too soon to say whether the Liberals will recapture much of the decisive middle ground of politics which they lost to Labour in the 1920s, or whether the defection of Shirley Williams and Roy Jenkins will have a lasting effect. But the groundwork for a Liberal revival exists, particularly if one notes that the previous recent Liberal revivals (1962–63 and 1972–73) took place during Conservative governments.

With so many topics for examination during 1970-79, it is almost inevitable that some interesting ones have to be excluded. However, those included cover most of the main subjects: each election (including the referenda), Ireland, Scottish Nationalism, the Liberal vote, and the distribution of social classes in the 1960s. The bibliography has also been enlarged to include books published since 1968.

General Election of June, 1970

One feature of the 1970 election was its low turnout, 72·0%, compared with an average turnout of 78·0% for the other elections held between 1950 and 1979. It is tempting to view this low turnout in 1970 (the lowest since 1935) as an early indication of the dissatisfaction of the electorate with both major parties. This voter dissatisfaction became much more evident in February 1974, when turnout rose to 78·7%, accompanied by a doubling of the minor party votes from 12·5 to 25·0%. Mere apathy had developed into positive antipathy to the two major parties.

The vote for the Liberals and other minor parties was much the same in 1970 as it had been in 1966. Indeed, the Liberal percentage was down slightly, from 8·5 to 7·4. In this election, as in every other one from 1951 to 1979, whenever the Labour Party was in power, the Liberal percentage dropped; while whenever the Conservatives were in power, the Liberal percentage rose.

The Nationalist vote was still small, and the Nationalists dropped the two by-election gains they had made from Labour, in Hamilton and Carmarthen. The Welsh Nationalists, or Plaid Cymru, would increase their seats to an average of 2 in each of the following elections, but their vote never achieved the peak of 1970; in fact, it declined in each election after 1970. On the other hand, the Scots Nationalists were to increase both their seats and votes dramatically in each election up to 1979.

The 1970 election was fought on the same boundaries as that of 1955; and the net swing to the Conservatives in Britain was very small over the 15-year period, only 0·3%. But the small net swing concealed numerous regional variations.

Between 1955 and 1970, the Conservative vote rose dramatically in the Black Country, ranging around 8% in 9 constituencies. In another 15 in the area bounded by eastern Birmingham, Leicester, and Derby, the Conservatives benefited by about 4%; there was also a pro-Conservative swing of 4% in 9 seats around Bristol; and of the same magnitude in half a dozen in East Anglia. Some, but by no means all, of these seats trending towards the Conservatives had a high proportion of immigrants. That does not seem to have been decisive in more than about half of them, though, since the others included a number of agricultural seats where long-term trends away from rural radicalism (eg, SW Norfolk, W. Gloucestershire) counted for as much, if not more, of the swing.

There were also several regions where the long-term trends favoured Labour. Glasgow, Manchester, and Liverpool contained 33 seats, which swung to Labour an average of 8·5%, 6·5%, and 5·7% respectively. Hull, Tees-side, and Newcastle also had swings to Labour of 6% to 9% during the years 1955-70. Virtually all these seats with big swings to Labour were in industrial cities with stagnant economies. In addition, 29 seats in the southern and western suburbs of London had swings to Labour in the region of 3% to 8%. Most of this was due to movement of Labour voters from the city centre to the suburbs; as could be seen by the increased Tory vote in half a dozen inner-city ex-slums.

The election of 1970 was the last, for several years at any rate, in which the basic swing was a straight Conservative-Labour shift. During the election itself, according to public opinion surveys, about 3% of the voters shifted from Labour to Conservative. Movement to and from the Liberals was of much smaller significance.[1]

General Election of February 1974

Beginning in October 1972, with a Liberal gain in Rochdale, half the by-elections held resulted in gains for the Liberals or another minor party. One of the most striking changes occurred in

---

1 Butler and King, *The British General Election of 1970*, 185 and n.

Lincoln, where Dick Taverne resigned as the Labour MP, and ran successfully as a Democratic Labour candidate.

The February 1974 general election showed that these by-election changes were not merely temporary electoral hiccoughs, but symptoms of deeper changes. The Liberals won more than 6 million votes in this election, the highest figure in their history, and their highest percentage since 1929. The Scottish Nationalists doubled their vote, and won 7 seats.

During the election campaign, which was fought in an atmosphere of industrial crisis, all the major polling organisations published surveys which, without exception, showed shifts from the Conservatives to the Liberals. These polls differed over changes in the Labour vote. Since their figures for the Conservatives and Liberal changes also differed, clearly not all the surveys were correct. However, if one averages all the surveys together, there seems to have been a shift of 5·8% from Conservative to Liberal during the campaign itself.[1] This shift would have been more than sufficient to have kept the Conservatives in office, had it not taken place. It may or may not be significant, but if one takes this 5·8% from the Liberal total in February 1974, and adds it to the Conservative poll, the adjusted figures then come within 0·2% of the actual 1979 results for all three major parties.[2]

Another major result of the February 1974 election was the elimination of the old Unionist party in Northern Ireland. In 1974, the party was split between supporters and opponents of the Sunningdale power-sharing agreement. The supporters were the followers of the party leader, Mr Faulkner, and of the Conservatives. They took only a fifth of the overall Unionist total, and did not contest the October 1974 or the 1979 elections. Thus from this election onwards, the Unionist MPs at Westminster could no longer be regarded as just another branch of the Conservative Party, but would have to be considered effectively as a separate force.

For the first time, a significant number of Nationalist MPs was elected, 9 in all. Four maps show the rise and fall of the Scottish Nationalist vote. In February 1974, the SNP obtained 22% of the vote in Scotland; on the other hand, the Plaid Cymru took only 11% of the Welsh vote.

The Plaid Cymru obtained more than 20% in only 8 of the 36 Welsh constituencies, and it got under 5% in 13. Four of the 8 seats where it did well were in predominantly Welsh-speaking areas; the remaining 4 consisted of 3 where there was no Liberal candidate, and 1 where there was a split in the local Labour Party. Thus it is probably not unrealistic to categorise the Plaid Cymru as a linguistic-nationalist force rather than as a regional one based on economic and political grievances such as the SNP. Since only 24·8% of the population in Wales spoke Welsh in 1961, it is not surprising that the Plaid Cymru has made so little headway.

Another feature of this election was the defection of Enoch Powell from the Conservatives. He advised his supporters to vote Labour, and in the 16 seats around his former constituency, there was an average swing of 7·5% to Labour, compared with a swing

of only 2–3% in comparable seats elsewhere. It seems probable that most of this swing was caused by returning Labour supporters who had swung in above-average numbers to the Conservatives in 1970.[1]

The Labour Party with 37·1% won 4 more seats than the Conservatives, who had 37·9%; the indecisive result led to the shortest Parliament since 1681.

1 Butler and Kavanagh, *British General Election of February 1974*, 105n and 331.

General Election of October 1974

The election of October 1974 resulted in a narrow overall majority of 3 seats for Labour, based on only 39% of the vote. Never before had a party won a majority of seats with under 40% of the vote.[1] Labour strength rose most in major urban centres (by 4·9%) less in smaller cities, (by 3·8%) and least in rural ones (by 2·0%).[2] The total Labour vote remained remarkably stable during the 1970s, varying only by a few hundred thousand from the peak in 1970 to the trough in October 1974. This may be contrasted with the vote for the Conservatives, Liberals and Scottish Nationalists, all of which moved much more dramatically between elections.

The Liberal vote dropped by 1·1%. However, their decline was really greater, since the Liberals contested 102 more seats than in February. Without the new candidacies, the Liberals would have had over a million votes less than they got, and would have had just over 14% of the national total. This was not far off their actual result in 1979.

Most of the drop in the Conservative vote seems to have come from the Liberal interventions. In seats contested by all three parties in February, the Conservative vote dropped by only 0·3%. However, in the seats where the Liberals intervened in October, the Conservative drop was 9%, compared with a drop of only 5% for Labour. This was despite the fact that Labour had much more to lose in these seats, since most of the interventions were in Labour strongholds.

The Conservative decline was particularly noticeable in industrial areas, but at the same time, opinion surveys revealed that this decline was spread evenly among the social classes. The Liberal vote dropped more in the upper economic brackets than it did at the bottom end of the social scale.[3]

The Scottish Nationalists increased their share of the vote in Scotland from 22 to 30·4%, and emerged as the second party in Scotland in terms of votes, though the Conservatives took 5 more seats. The SNP came second in 42 seats, and within 5% of winning in 8 of them. If the SNP had taken the 11 seats where they were within 10% of the Labour winners, the October election would have had as indecisive a result as that of February.

The Plaid Cymru and the Ulster Unionists both lost some support. In the case of the Plaid Cymru, this was offset by a gain in one seat, Carmarthen, which they had lost in February by only 3 votes. They did come second in 6 mining seats where Labour held overwhelming majorities, but they were nowhere close to winning any of the 6, nor were they close in other seats in Wales.

---

1 *The Times Guide to the House of Commons, February 1974*, 32, lists the polls published during the election by the six major survey firms. These showed Conservative losses of 2·3, 3·9, 5·0, 5·8, 8·5, or 8·9% during the campaign, or an average loss of 5·7%. The Liberal gain was, depending on the poll, 4·0, 4·1, 5·1, 6·2, 8·5, or 11·1%, for an average gain during the campaign of 5·8%
2 Conservative: 37·9% in Feb. 1974 + 5·8% = 43·7%, as compared with the 1979 result of 43·9%
Liberal: 19·4% in Feb. 1974 – 5·8% = 13·6%, as compared with the 1979 result of 13·8%
Labour: 37·1%, as compared with 36·9% in 1979

1 In 1922, the Conservatives obtained 38·5% and a majority of seats; but this election was not really comparable, since the Conservatives did not contest 132 of the 615 seats, and 43 Conservatives were elected without opposition, so had no votes cast for them. If there had been contests in all seats, and Conservative candidates in each, the Tory percentage would have been considerably higher than 38·5%. In October 1974, Labour contested all 623 seats outside Ulster.
2 cf. table in Steed, 'The Results Analysed', Butler & Kavanagh, *British General Election of October 1974*, 335.
3 *Ibid.*, 278; and *British General Election of February 1974*, 263 have tables showing the distribution of support by social class

General Election of June 1979

The Conservatives gained 8·0% in this election, which was the biggest change up or down for either of the two main parties in any postwar election. However, it was marked by major regional variations in swing, as the map on page 143 shows. Many observers have commented on the apparent difference in swing between England north and south of the Trent, with the latter having a much larger swing. However, as the map shows, the big swings took place in a group of semi-rural seats north and west of London, and in a handful of central London seats, rather than in southern England as a whole.

The swing to the Conservatives was less marked in industrial areas, and this had a significant impact on Conservative wins. This can be seen by comparing the map of the 1979 election with that of 1959. There was a similar Conservative lead in each election, 5·6% in 1959 and 7·0% in 1979. Yet in 1959, the Conservatives won 95 more seats than Labour,[1] while in 1979, with a bigger gap in percentages, they won only 71 more seats. The difference was primarily in 13 industrial cities, where the number of Conservative seats fell from 43 to 14.[2] There were also Labour gains in some other industrial centres, but these were offset by a few Conservative gains in rural areas of Wales and in Norfolk.

The minor parties all lost ground in this election, both the Liberals and the SNP heavily; and both the Plaid Cymru and Ulster Unionists more modestly. However, the Plaid Cymru and Unionist declines represented long-term trends based on population changes, while the Liberal and SNP declines could be seen as short-term swings of the sort which characterise nearly every election. Of all these changes, the most important is probably that affecting the Ulster Unionists. In 1979, as in the other three elections of the 1970s, there was a uniform drop in the Unionist total vote. The non-Unionist vote has risen slightly in each of the elections held since 1970. If, as seems likely, the change results from a narrowing of the population gap between Protestants and Roman Catholics, then one might expect even greater tensions during the 1980s than during the 1970s, since the Unionists would no longer feel as secure in their numerical predominance in the six counties.

The two-party system did not reappear in 1979 in the full-blown form which had existed during the 1950s and much of the 1960s. The number of third-party MPs outside Ulster dropped from 27 to 14, but their percentage of the vote declined less steeply, from 23% to 17·4%. The Liberals, despite their loss of a million votes, still got a higher percentage than in any other election (apart from 1974) since 1929. The SNP, which lost 9 of its 11 seats, still got 17·3% of the Scottish vote. This, with the Liberal vote in Scotland, came to 25·2% of the total Scottish vote.

The Labour Party did not benefit from the decline of third-party voters, and its percentage, 36·9, was its poorest performance since the disaster of 1931. Labour held as many seats as it did because of its relatively good long-term performance in urban industrial seats. However, the strengthening hold of Labour on its safe seats, and its apparent lack of appeal elsewhere could be regarded as a sign of incipient fossilisation. Yet it is too soon to count the Labour Party out of the race, despite its internal difficulties and mediocre electoral performance; just as it was too soon after October 1974 to count out the Conservatives, as many observers did.[3] All three major parties, even the Liberals, have shown remarkable ability to recover from seemingly adverse circumstances.

The Liberal Vote in February 1974

The continued existence and periodic revival of the Liberal Party is one of the chief curiosities of current British politics. Since the early 1920s, it has been clear even to Liberals that the party was booked on a one-way journey to the electoral wilderness. Voters in most constituencies have realised that the Liberal candidates have had little chance of winning, and the electoral system has been biassed heavily against the Liberals.[4]

Despite the many factors operating against them, the Liberals have revived three times since the war: in 1958, in 1962–63, and most recently in 1972–74. Each revival came during periods of Conservative government; only the revival of 1972–74 went right up to a general election.

There is little reason to publish here the map showing the Liberal percentage in February 1974, since in almost every respect it is similar to that on page 87 showing the Liberal percentage in 1964. The major changes were that in 1974, the Liberals did fairly well in Liverpool and Birmingham, using strong local candidates; and their overall percentage throughout the country was somewhat higher in 1974 than ten years earlier. Otherwise, the two maps show remarkable stability in the potential Liberal vote in both these periods of revival. The Liberal appeal to voters on the basis of social class also shows considerable stability.[5]

The map on page 142, showing changes in Liberal support between 1970 and February 1974, is more instructive than one which shows only the party percentage in one election. It shows that the Liberals made their biggest gains outside the industrial areas. In central London, western Lancashire, all mining districts, and most areas of heavy industry, the Liberals did poorly in 1974, and also picked up proportionally less between 1970 and February 1974 than they did in the country as a whole.

The Liberals improved their performance most in the commuter seats north and east of London; and next-best in a large number of constituencies in the southern half of England outside the major urban centres. It was in many of these same constituencies that the Conservatives picked up the most ground in 1979. All these influences tend to confirm the emergence of a group of voters who switch from Liberal to Conservative, with the Labour party retaining a fairly steady, perhaps diminishing, proportion of the electorate as a whole.

Swing to the Conservatives, October 1974–June 1979

The map on page 115 shows that the seats which changed hands

---

1 Excluding the 12 Unionists elected from Northern Ireland.
2 The cities, with the number of Conservative losses compared with 1959 in brackets were: Birmingham (4), Bolton (2), Bradford (2), Bristol (1), Glasgow (4), Hull (1), Leicester (1), Liverpool (4), Manchester (3), Newcastle (1), Nottingham (3), Preston (1), and Stockport (2).
3 On 26 March 1981, 14 MPs (13 Labour and 1 Conservative) formed the Social Democratic Party.

4 Steed, 'The Results Analysed', in Butler & Kavanagh, *British General Election of February 1974*, 329, estimates the potential number of Liberal MPs at 123 to 131 in February 1974, if varying forms of proportional representation had been available; instead of the mere 14 the party actually won.
5 The post-election NOP polls for 1964 and February 1974 indicated the following support for the Liberals by social class:

	AB	C1	C2	DE
1964	15	14	11	9
1974	20	25	20	17
Change	+5	+9	+8	+8

in 1955-1966 were concentrated in five areas: south-central London, the Pennine district between Yorkshire and Lancashire, Bristol, Nottingham, and Glasgow. In the 1979 election, every one of these areas, except for south-central London, had abnormally low swings to the Conservatives. The only other part of Britain with such low swings in 1979 was rural Scotland, where the large SNP vote makes it misleading to calculate a two-party swing.

These areas of low swing to the Conservatives (or of actual swings to Labour, as in Glasgow and central Scotland generally) indicates a continuing trend to Labour in industrial seats, a trend which was hardly interrupted even in such a poor year for Labour as 1979. But Labour has advanced in many of these cities as far as it can, since there are no Conservative seats left in many of them.[1]

While Labour kept practically all its strength in its traditional areas, the Conservatives picked up substantial ground in rural Wales. In the 5 Welsh rural seats concerned, there had been a long Liberal tradition based on Nonconformity. As the last becomes less and less a political factor, the Conservatives seem likely to strengthen support in these seats; unless some unforeseen factor intervenes.

Conservatives and the Professional-managerial vote

In every recent election, the Conservatives have obtained the overwhelming support of the professional and managerial voters. This ranged from a high of 85% in 1955 to a low of only 63% in October 1974. In 1970, the Conservatives obtained a middling 79%. Although the professional and managerial voters (PM's) were only 15·3% of the total electorate in 1970, they provided more than a quarter of the total Tory vote.

The two maps on pages 144 and 145 are not intended to replace the valuable multiple regression analysis performed by Crewe and Payne on the data,[2] but to supplement it and to indicate some regional variations.

The first map, showing the distribution of P/M voters, may be compared with that on page 123, showing the Middle Class voters in 1921. There were some differences in methods of calculation: the 1921 map includes all the military, and most office workers. The 1966 map excludes most military (a smaller proportion of the total electorate anyway, than in 1921), and many office workers at the lower levels. Even so, the two maps have many similarities. The most obvious is that the P/M voters are spread all over the country, with scattered strong-points, particularly in the outer London suburbs. Only a handful of seats, mostly mining ones, had under 10% P/M voters in either election.

On the other hand, there was no group of overwhelmingly P/M or middle-class voters, though 134 seats in 1970 had more than 20%. If the Conservatives were to get 80% of the P/M vote in these seats, they would need only a third of the remaining non-PMs to ensure 45% of the total vote. In most cases, 45% would be sufficient to win; and in 1970, the Tories won 132 of the 134 seats in question.[3]

The 134 seats would not give the Conservatives a majority in any election; but they have provided a secure base which has allowed the party to bring back able, but defeated candidates. The Liberals have lacked a secure base of this sort ever since 1918, and the credibility of their Parliamentary party has frequently suffered because of it.

The map on page 145 shows the 1970 Conservative vote minus the P/M percentage in the constituency. This indicates how much of an appeal the Conservatives had to non-professional voters in the constituency: the average figure was 29·6%, so that the two shadings of 23·0 to 34·9% indicate the average plus or minus 6%.

The point of this map is that it eliminates the middle-class component of the Conservative vote, and shows, for example, that the southern Home Counties were somewhat less Tory than the seats north and west of London. The map also shows that the Conservatives retained considerable strength in northern Lancashire and NW Yorkshire, as well as in Liverpool and the West Midlands. In the latter, the very high figures for Tory support among non-P/M voters may have been due to Powell and to anti-immigrant feeling.

Agricultural areas provided a number of seats with high Conservative non-professional percentages, particularly in North Yorkshire, East Anglia and Lincolnshire. Elsewhere, the impact of agricultural voters on the map had less significance.

The Referenda of June 1975 on the EEC and of March 1979 on Devolution

In 1972, after 11 years of negotiations, the EEC admitted Britain to membership. The final vote in the Commons on July 13, 1972, was only 301 to 284 in favour, with 69 Labour MPs supporting the Heath government. Throughout the period 1967-73, opinion polls had generally showed a majority against joining the EEC, and it was only in 1975 that a substantial majority began to back it. According to the Gallup polls, Labour voters were the most divided: on the eve of the referendum, they split 35% to 28% in favour, with 37% undecided.

Several Labour leaders opposed joining the EEC, and when the Labour Party took office, Mr Wilson decided to put the question to a national referendum, the first one ever held. The only notable Conservative to support the 'Nos' was Enoch Powell, no in a new guise as an Ulster Unionist; no Liberal MP opposed the EEC, but many prominent Labour leaders did, among them Douglas Jay, Barbara Castle and Michael Foot. Ian Paisley also opposed it, and announced that 'The Virgin Mary is the Madonna of the Common Market'.

The referendum resulted in a clear victory for the EEC supporters. In an article in *The Economist*, Michael Steed calculated that Conservatives voted 'Yes' by 85 to 15; Liberals by 70 to 30; and Labour by 52·5 to 47·5. Steed also calculated the 'deviation' of each county from a norm, assuming that the 1974

---

1 There were in 1979 no Conservative seats in Bolton, Hull, Leicester, Nottingham, Stockport, and Tees-side; and only 1 each in Coventry, Glasgow, Manchester, and Newcastle. In the 1950s and 1960s, these cities had from 1 to 7 marginal seats each.
2 Crewe and Payne, "Analysing the census data", in Butler and Pinto-Duschinsky,

British General Election of 1970, 416–436.
3 The other 2 seats were Cornwall N (a Liberal win), and Cardigan (Labour, with the vote split 4 ways).

election results were to be applied, using these figures. The deviations are shown in the central map on page 146.[1]

As can be seen, the areas voting in favour of the EEC were predominantly the Conservative ones, as shown in the left-hand map. Even when one takes the 'deviations' into account, as in the central map, one notes that the favourable deviations took place mostly in Conservative regions, particularly where agriculture played an important role in the economy. There is little if any relationship of the map of deviance with the 1974 or 1979 results, and it would appear more likely that the satisfaction of agricultural voters with the Common Agricultural Policy produced the above-average proportion of 'Yes' votes.

The success of the 1975 referendum in partially defusing conflicts inside the Labour Party may have decided Mr Callaghan to call the second set of referenda on devolution in 1979. The results were very different from those of 1975.

In Wales, only 20·3% of the electors voted 'Yes', on a low turnout. The support for Plaid Cymru in general elections had been declining for some years, and its failure to reach out beyond its own narrow base could not have been more apparent. The 'Yes' voters were concentrated in the less populous counties of northern Wales. Assuming that virtually all the Plaid Cymru voters turned out and voted 'Yes', there remained only 70,000 or so others who voted 'Yes', as against just under a million who voted 'No'. Nationalism in Wales seems unlikely to grow much further until it obtains economic and social planks to give its appeal significance to the vast majority of Welshmen who do not speak the Welsh language.

On the other hand, Scottish nationalism proved much stronger, probably because it was based primarily on economic and political aspirations rather than cultural ones. Just over half (51·6%) of the voters supported devolution. But because 40% of the registered electorate (including dead voters who were still on the lists) had to support it, devolution was also voted down. The figure of 51·6%, though it may have given heart to the SNP, was misleading to them, since in the general election immediately afterwards, their poll dropped by two-fifths. The 1·2 million Scots who voted 'Yes' contrast with the mere 410,419 who voted for the SNP just three months later.

Religions in Ulster and the 1969 Unionist Crisis

From the middle 1920s until 1969, Ulster was rarely in the minds of British voters, except perhaps as one of many rural Tory strongholds. But starting in January 1969, this changed dramatically. Prime Minister Terence O'Neill for the first time made genuine overtures to conciliate the Roman Catholic minority. Although these overtures were by no means revolutionary,[2] they might have been the beginning of a settlement between the religious groups. Opinion polls published in the Sunday Times indicated that two-thirds of the voters supported O'Neill's initiatives, and that he had majority backing from both religious groups. However, the overtures were highly alarming to some of O'Neill's own supporters, and 15 of his provincial MPs rebelled against his leadership. Virtually all his opponents came from

isolated Protestant enclaves in the south and west, or from mixed areas of Belfast. His supporters came more from the solidly Protestant regions.

The two upper maps on page 147 show the distribution of religions in Ulster in 1911 and 1961. The 1911 map shows the many small and isolated enclaves of Roman Catholics and Protestants. It has often been observed that religious extremism is most common in areas with a highly mixed population, and Ulster is no exception.[3]

Following this internal party crisis, O'Neill called a general election for March 1969. This was marked by two innovations. First, a large number of moderate Unionist candidates supporting O'Neill ran against his opponents. Secondly, an opinion poll taken during the election showed that O'Neill had the support of an overwhelming majority of Protestants, and even more surprisingly of a majority of Roman Catholics. 61% backed him against only 31% for his sectarian opponents combined, and 9% for the Labour Party. The figures were:

	R.C.	Prot.	All voters[4]
Pro-O'Neill U	45	69	61
Anti-O'Neill U	1	15	11
Paisleyite	—	7	5
Nationalist	20	—	6
N. Ireland Labour	20	4	9
Other/don't know	14	5	8

But the 1969 election turned on selection committees rather than on opinion polls. 23 of the Ulster seats had more than one Unionist candidate, and for the time being, the views of the local party officials carried the most weight. The same opinion poll showed that 71% of the Unionist supporters regarded their party's unity as 'very important', and the Unionist winner were almost always those with official local Unionist backing, regardless of their attitude to O'Neill. It was probably unrealistic for O'Neill to hope to depose many of the dissident MPs at nomination meetings, since most of them had strong local ties. And the independent Unionists who supported him had only a few weeks to defeat the entrenched local Unionist machinery. Even so, the election changed the overall position in the Unionist caucus from 15 to 21 for O'Neill to 12 to 26 in his favour.[5] He did not regard this improvement as sufficient, and resigned two months after the election. From that point, the political situation in Ulster deteriorated rapidly.

Ironically, the Unionist Party which had done so much to restrain O'Neill's victory in 1969, began to disintegrate soon after into several splinter groups; and no subsequent Ulster leader could command such widespread support as O'Neill had done.

The Scottish Nationalist vote, 1970-1979

The SNP came from virtually nowhere in 1966 to a close second place in October 1974. In the election of 1979, it lost 9 of its 11 seats, and 2/5 of its vote. The overall voting figures for Scotland were:

---

1 cf. Steed, 'The perfect result', The Economist, 14 June, 1975, p. 18
2 Richard Rose, in Governing Without Consensus, 100, notes that even O'Neill appointed a few Roman Catholics to prominent positions
3 cf. de Mayer, et al., Verkiezingen in de landen van de Europese Germeenschappen en in het Verenigd Koninkrijk, 304–311. De Meyer shows that the extreme Protestant Calvanist Political League did best in areas bordering Roman Catholic sections of the south, rather than in the solidly Protestant parts of northern Holland.
4 Sunday Times, 1 Feb., 1969
5 Counting the unofficial pro-O'Neill Unionists

election	Labour	Cons.	SNP	Liberal
1966	49·9%	37·6%	5·0%	6·8%
1970	44·5	38·0	11·4	5·5
1974F	36·7	32·9	21·9	7·9
1974O	36·3	24·7	30·4	8·3
1979	41·5	31·4	17·3	8·7

The overall figures indicate that the SNP gained from Labour in 1970; in February 1974 from both Conservatives and Labour; and in October 1974 mostly from the Conservatives. In 1979, it lost support to both main parties in about equal numbers.

In England, the pattern of third party voting has been that of an increase during periods of Conservative rule, and of a decrease following a Labour government. The SNP vote has risen and fallen in a more complex manner. Its first big jump came in 1970, after a Labour government; but its biggest drop also came after a Labour government, in 1979. The 1974 elections saw a large drop in the vote for both major parties. Much of the drop in those elections appears to have been 'tactical' voting by Conservative and Labour supporters in seats where the SNP seemed to have had the best chance for defeating the other major party.

The distribution of the SNP vote was roughly similar in all four elections illustrated in the maps on page 148. It was weak in almost all the Glasgow seats, in Edinburgh, and in the mining and industrial areas of central Scotland. It did have occasional successes in these seats, and in October 1974, a swing of 2·5% from Labour to SNP would have given the latter five industrial seats.[1] Otherwise, these maps show many similarities to those of Liberal strength in the 1920s and in 1964.[2] This suggests that the SNP vote of the 1970s is not entirely a new thing, but rather the expression of a long-term lingering antagonism to the two main English parties, an antagonism which until recently has expressed itself via the Liberals.

EEC elections, June 1979

The first direct elections to the European Assembly could have been regarded as the beginning of a new era. Instead, the voters evidently regarded it as irrelevant, since less than a third (31·5%) turned out to vote. Turnout in British elections is generally lower than in continental countries, but the gap was wider than ever this time.[3]

Because the Labour Party in effect ignored these elections, the map shows the Conservative percentage of the electorate, rather than the percentage of those who turned out. Not unexpectedly, the left-hand map shows a strong correlation with that of the 1979 general election, held a month previously. If the EEC election had followed the 1979 results precisely, then the Conservatives would have taken 49 seats, and Labour 29.[4] This is because the Conservatives would have won virtually all the seats with a mixed urban and rural background, while Labour would have been restricted to the solidly-Labour seats in industrial areas.

The very low turnout deprived Labour of almost half its 'expected' seats, the result being 60 Conservatives, 17 Labour, one SNP, and in Ulster, 2 Unionists and one SDLP. The low turnout makes it somewhat misleading to calculate swing, but there was a small shift to Mrs Castle in Manchester North in comparison with the general election, and unusually high shifts to the Conservatives in the Midlands.[5]

Turnout was relatively high (compared with the other areas) in the semi-rural seats north of Leeds, in rural Wales, central Scotland, the southwest, and the southern Home Counties. All except the last had high turnout in May. On the other hand, the seats in line from Huddersfield to Northampton also had a high turnout in May, and a low turnout in June, probably because of the higher Labour percentage in these seats in May, and above-average Labour abstentions in June.

Proportional representation would have produced about 36 Conservative seats, 30 Labour, and 15 others; but the system of extremely large single-member constituencies adopted for this election was weighted heavily in favour of the Conservatives. This fact went a long way to explain the low turnout, since many Labour voters knew that their ballots would not count. All the other EEC countries used some form of proportional representation in this election, and had a much higher turnout. One may speculate therefore whether a future Labour government would retain the current EEC electoral system.

---

1 W. Stirlingshire, Lanark, Stirling, W. Lothian, and W. Dunbartonshire
2 cf. pages 84-87
3 The following table shows the differences:

Country	EEC election turnout	Previous general election turnout	EEC turnout as a % of gen. el. turnout
Italy	85·9	89·9	95·5
Luxembourg	85·6	90·0	95·1
Belgium	82·0	92·0	89·1
Ireland	58·0	76·0	76·3
France	61·2	85·0	72·0
Germany	65·9	91·6	71·9
Denmark	47·0	70·0	67·1
Holland	57·8	88·0	65·7
U.K.	31·3	76·0	41·2

(Based on tables in *Le Monde*, 12 June, 1979; and on *Die Welt*, 12 June, 1979 and *il Giornale*, 5 June, 1979)

4 Estimated by the *Evening Standard*, 4 June, 1979
5 cf. Decornoy et al., *les premières élections européennes* (1979), 106

Bibliography

I Statistics

a. Census figures

County volumes issued after each census show the distribution of occupational groups in each urban and rural district in England and Wales, and in the larger districts in Scotland. They also show the birthplaces of the inhabitants. The county volumes for Scotland and Wales show the distribution of linguistic minorities, as do the general volumes for some censuses. The general volume for the 1931 census shows the distribution of unemployed in many parts of the country, and the county volumes for the same census show the distribution of unemployed on a more detailed level. Since 1966, census figures have been available by Parliamentary constituency.

b. Election results

1885-1910: *The Constitutional Yearbook, 1919*, shows results by constituencies. McCalmont, F. H., *Parliamentary Poll Book of All Elections*, new ed. by J. Vincent (1971) is an invaluable compilation, with much useful material not in the original edition.

1918-1929: *The Constitutional Yearbook, 1925*, shows results by constituencies; however, only editions of this book prior to 1924 show the 1918 results in Ireland. *The Times Guide to the House of Commons, 1929*, gives the results of the 1929 election. M. Kinnear, *The British General Election of 1922* (D.Phil. thesis, 1965) and Rowe, E. A., *The British General Election of 1929* (B.Litt. thesis, 1959) have the percentage figures by constituency for 1918, 1922, 1924 and 1929.

1931-1979: *The Times Guides to the House of Commons*, issued shortly after each election, give the results in each constituency, and brief biographies of the candidates. The volumes after 1935 have maps showing the national results; and those after 1959 calculate the party percentages by constituency.

Mitchell, B. R., and Boehm, K., *British Parliamentary Results, 1950-1964* (1966), and Cook, C. P. and McKie, D., *The Guardian/Quartet Election Guide* (1970, 1974, and 1979) contain results by constituency for 1950-64, and 1970-74, as do two works by Craig, F., *Britain Votes I & II* (1980).

c. Economic statistics

The *Ministry of Labour Gazette* (monthly) shows the number of unemployed or on relief in the larger areas of the country. It also shows monthly price changes. The *Agricultural Statistics* (annual) for England, Scotland and Wales show the price and production of agricultural goods, as well as the average number of farm workers per holding, in each county.

The most accessible source of economic statistics is Mitchell, B. R., and Deane, P., *Abstract of British Historical Statistics* (1962). This valuable work is especially helpful for the late nineteenth and early twentieth centuries. It lists many figures on trade, employment, prices, and so on.

d. Religious statistics

No official religious census has been taken in England since 1851, although one was taken in Wales in 1905. The 1851 religious census lists the number of people attending Anglican, Nonconformist and other services on Sunday 30 March 1851. Its reliability is discussed in Thompson, D. M., 'The 1851 Religious Census: Problems and Possibilities', *Victorian Studies,* 1967. Numerous unofficial surveys were made in the late nineteenth century by religious and social groups, but, as they were made by interested parties, their accuracy is open to question. *The Education Act at Work: A Handbook for Free Church Workers* (n.d.) shows the proportion of Anglican, Nonconformist, Roman Catholic, and other denominations on a large number of local councils and education authorities in 1904.

Figures showing the membership of religious groups are of varying utility. Anglican and Roman Catholic figures are generally available only at the diocesan level, although there are scattered exceptions. The Anglican figures, given in the annual *Official Year Book of the Church of England,* show the number of each communicants in each diocese on Easter Sunday 2 years before the date of issue. The annual *Catholic Directory* shows the estimated number of baptised Roman Catholics in each diocese in England and Wales. The *Catholic Directory for the Clergy and Laity in Scotland* shows the estimated number of Roman Catholics for each diocese, and the number of baptisms in individual churches. It is possible from this to estimate the approximate number of Roman Catholics in each constituency. Some late nineteenth-century issues of this book also state the number of Roman Catholics in particular towns.

Nonconformist yearbooks show the number of chapel members and Sunday scholars in individual chapels or circuits. The *Baptist Hand Book,* and the *Congregational Yearbook* both give figures for individual chapels, as does the *Blwyddiadur neu Lyfr Swyddogol y Methodistiaid Calfinaidd* (Welsh Presbyterian Yearbook). However as this book often refers to towns as 'Bethel', 'Moriah', 'Horeb', and so on, it is difficult to determine the location of the chapels. The *Minutes of the General Assembly of the Presbyterian Church of England* shows the membership of individual presbyteries in the year preceeding the date of issue.

The *Primitive Methodist Year Book* and the *Minutes of the Wesleyan Methodist Conference* both show the number of members of each circuit before the reunion of the 2 churches in 1932. Very often, circuits covered more than one constituency, and these books do not therefore show the precise number of Methodists in individual constituencies. However, in areas of Methodist strength, there were usually 2 or more circuits in each constituency. This makes it possible to estimate more accurately the number of Methodists in such constituencies.

II Surveys of elections

a. General

Allen, A. J., *The English Voter* (1964) examines census and other material, with an emphasis on 78 selected constituencies. Although it deals primarily with the 1959 results, it has historical sections.

Blewett, N., 'The Franchise in the United Kingdom, 1885-1918', *Past and Present,* 1965, estimates the significance of the lodger and plural voting, and other related matters.

Butler, D. E., *The Electoral System in Britain, 1918-1951* (1953) examines parliamentary debates over franchise reform. An appendix diagnoses the detailed working of the electoral system.

Dunbabin, J. P. D., 'Parliamentary Elections in Great Britain, 1868-1900: A Psephological Note', *English Historical Review,* 1966, lists results of by-elections and estimates the year-to-year trend in elections.

Krehbiel, E., 'Geographic Influences in British Elections', *Geographic Review,* 1916, examines election results from 1885 to 1910. Its statistics are less helpful than the maps, which show the location of coalfields and areas of Liberal strength.

Madge, C., ed., *Pilot Guide to the General Election* (1945) has some material on interwar elections.

Pelling, H., *The Social Geography of British Elections, 1885-1910* (1967) is interesting but gossipy.

b. Individual elections

1880 Lloyd, T., *The General Election of 1880* (1968) analyses party organisation and votes cast.

1886 Savage, D. C., *The General Election of 1886 in Great Britain and Ireland* (London Ph.D. thesis, 1958).

1906 Rempel, R., *Unionists Divided* (1972) examines conflicts in the Unionist ranks over Free Trade during this election.

Russell, A., *Liberal Landslide* (1973) is a Nuffield-type study of the election of 1906.

1910 Blewett, N., *The Peers, The Parties and The People: The general elections of 1910* (1972) is a full account of both elections and of the constitutional conference of 1910.

1918 McEwen, J. M., 'The Coupon Election of 1918 and Unionist Members of Parliament', *Journal of Modern History,* 1962, estimates the significance of changes in the background of MPs.

Wilson, T., 'The Coupon and the British General Election of 1918', *Journal of Modern History,* 1964, considers the distribution of coupons.

Kinnear, M., *The Fall of Lloyd George* (1973) also looks at the 1918 election and at coupons.

1922 Kinnear, M., *The British General Election of 1922* (Oxford D.Phil. thesis, 1965), has electoral and economic statistics for 1910-22.

1923 and 1924 Cook, C. P., *The Age of Alignment: Electoral politics in Britain, 1922–1929* (1975) deals primarily with the 1923 and 1924 elections, and is an invaluable source.

1929 Rowe, E. A., *The British General Election of 1929* (Oxford B.Litt. thesis, 1959) has the 1924 and 1929 results by constituency.

1935 Stannage, T., *Baldwin Thwarts the Opposition: The British General Election of 1935* war announced but not yet published when this book was written.

1945 McCallum, R. B., and Readman, A., *The British General Election of 1945* (1947, republished in 1964) was the first extensive study of a British election, and set the pattern for others. It has a section on the relation of seats to votes.

1950 Chrimes, S. B. ed., *The General Election in Glasgow, February, 1950* (1950) examines the campaign at a local level, and has useful maps of Glasgow.

Nicholas, H. G., *The British General Election of 1950* (1951) has an extensive survey of the press during the election.

1951 Butler, D. E., *The British General Election of 1951* (1952).

1955 Butler, D. E., *The British General Election of 1955* (1955).

1959 Butler, D. E., and Rose, R., *The British General Election of 1959* (1960).

Cadart, J., 'Les Elections Générales du 8 Octobre 1959 en Grande-Bretagne et la Crise du Parti Travailliste', *Revue Française de Science Politique,* 1959.

1964 Berrington, H., 'The General Election of 1964', *Journal of the Royal Statistical Society,* Series A, 1965. A detailed examination of the election results.

Butler, D. E., and King, A., *The British General Election of 1964* (1965).

Cadart, J., and Mabileau, A., 'Les Elections Britanniques de 1964: les Partis en face d'une Nouvelle Société', *Revue Française de Science Politique,* 1964.

Howard, A., and West, R., *The Making of the Prime Minister 1964* (1965).

Rose, R., *Influencing Voters* (1967) considers the effect of publicity in the 1964 election.

1966 Beloff, M., 'Reflections on the British General Election of 1966', *Government and Opposition,* 1966.

Butler, D. E., and King, A., *The British General Election of 1966* (1966).

1970 Butler, D. E., and Pinto-Duschinsky, M., *The British General Election of 1970* (1971) is noteworthy for an analysis by Crewe and Payne of the census data.

1974(F) Butler, D. E., and Kavanagh, *The British General Election of February 1974* (1974) and *The British General Election of October 1974* (1975) and of 1979 (1980) by the same authors have extended statistical analyses by Michael Steed.

1979 Taylor, P. J., 'The changing geography of representation in Britain', *Professional Geographer, II, 4, 1979 (289-294) discusses changes in the electoral geography of Britain from 1966 to 1979.*

III Regional and Constituency Studies

a. Regions

Few regional studies exist, but the following are helpful.

Clarke, P. F., *Lancashire and the New Liberalism* (1971) deals with Lancashire before 1914.

Morgan, K. O., *Wales in British Politics, 1868-1922* (1963) discusses the origins of the Welsh Parliamentary Party, and other aspects of Welsh politics. It has statistical tables showing the distribution of Nonconformists in 1905, and an extensive bibliography on Welsh affairs.

Thompson, P., *Socialists, Liberals and Labour: The struggle for London, 1885-1914* (1967) has 30 maps of London politics, showing occupational groups, religions, and political adherence in the period.

—— —— , 'Liberals, Radicals and Labour in London', *Past and Present,* 1964, also has maps of London politics before 1914.

b. Constituencies

Bealey, F., Blondel, J., and McCann, W. P., *Constituency Politics: a Study of Newcastle-under-Lyme* (1965) is the most detailed study yet made of a single constituency. It examines the structure of the local political parties, the allegiance of voters, and local council elections.

Benney, M., Gray, A. P., and Pear, R. H., *How People Vote* (1956) studies voting behaviour in Greenwich in the 1950s, and has detailed tables.

Benney, M., and Pear, R. H., 'Voting Behaviour in Droylesden in October 1951', *Manchester School of Economic and Social Studies,* 1952.

Benney, M., and Geiss, P., 'Social Class and Politics in Greenwich', *British Journal of Sociology,* 1950, has several tables referring to sample surveys.

Birch, A. H., et al., *Small Town Politics: A Study of Political Life in Glossop* (1959) examines in detail a small town in northern Derbyshire.

Blondel, J., *The Political Structure of Reading* (Oxford B.Litt. thesis, 1955) has a useful map showing the distribution of jurors by streets.

Budge, I., and Urwin, D. W., *Scottish Political Behaviour* (1966) is primarily about Glasgow politics in the 1960s.

Campbell, P., and Birch, A. H., 'Voting Behaviour in a Lancashire Constituency', *British Journal of Sociology*, 1950, has sample surveys of Stretford.

Campbell, P., and Birch, A. H., 'Politics in the North-West', *Manchester School of Economic and Social Studies*, 1950.

Milne, H. S., and Mackenzie, H. C., *Straight Fight* (1954) is a study of voting behaviour in Bristol Northeast in 1951, based on sample surveys.

Milne, H. S., and Mackenzie, H. C., *Marginal Seat* (1958) continues the examination of Bristol Northeast on the same basis as *Straight Fight*.

Rowntree, B. S., *Poverty: A Study in Town Life* (1901) examines social and economic conditions in York in 1899, and relies extensively on interviews. It gives sample weekly budgets of families, and many other statistics of considerable historical interest.

— — , *Poverty and Progress: A Second Social Survey of York* (1941) compares conditions in 1899 with those in 1936.

— — , *Poverty and the Welfare State* (1951), the third social survey of York, deals with 1950.

IV Other topics

a. Agriculture and politics

Benyon, V. H., and Harrison, J. E., *The Political Significance of the British Agricultural Vote* (University of Exeter, Department of Agricultural Economics, 1962) is an examination of the 1959 election results, to determine seats where the agricultural vote was decisive.

Hunt, K. E., *Changes in British Agriculture* (1952) comments on the agricultural statistics in detail.

Self, P., and Storing, H. J., *The State and the Farmer* (1962) studies the National Farmers' Union, and the changing electoral significance of agriculture.

b. Immigration, race, and politics

Collins, S., 'Social Processes Integrating Coloured People in Britain', *British Journal of Sociology*, 1952, compares 'Moslem' and 'Negro' immigrants on Tyneside.

Crewe, I., *British Political Sociology Yearbook 2: The politics of race* (1975) has an extensive bibliography on the subject.

Deakin, N., ed., *Colour and the British Electorate, 1964* (1965) surveys 6 constituencies in the 1964 election.

Foot, P., *Immigration and Race in British Politics* (1965) deals with the historical development of racial problems in Britain, and in particular with Smethwick in the early 1960s.

Jackson, J. A., *The Irish in Britain* (1963) has maps showing the distribution of Irish-born in 1841, 1861, 1891 and 1951.

Rex, J., and Moore, R., *Race, Community and Conflict* (1967) deals with immigrant groups in the Birmingham constituency of Sparkbrook in the 1960s.

Spiers, M., and le Lohé, M. J., 'Pakistanis in the Bradford Municipal Election of 1963', *Political Studies*, 1964, has sample surveys of immigrants in 2 wards.

c. Local elections and by-elections

Bealey, F., and Bartholomew, D. J., 'The Local Elections in Newcastle-under-Lyme, May 1958', *Political Studies*, 1962, 2 articles.

Charlot, M., 'Les Elections dans "Le Grand Londres" (9 Avril 1964)', *Revue Française de Science Politique*, 1964, examines the Greater London Council elections. It has a map of the results which may be compared with the map showing the 1967 results in *The Times*, May 1967.

Mabileau, A., 'Le Renouveau du Parti Libéral et les Elections Partielles en Grande-Bretagne,' *Revue Française de Science Politique*, 1962, examines the position of the Liberals after 1945, and by-election results between 1959 and 1962.

Sharpe, L. J., *A Metropolis Votes* (1962).

d. Social class and politics

Abrams, M., 'Class Distinctions in Britain', in *Future of the Welfare State* (1958) is a convenient introduction.

— — , 'Social Class and British Politics', *Public Opinion Quarterly*, 1961.

— — , 'Social Trends and Electoral Behaviour,' *British Journal of Sociology*, 1962, discusses differential turnout and other aspects of voting behaviour in 1959.

Bonham, J., *The Middle Class Vote* (1954) surveys voting patterns in the early 1950s, based on a large survey.

Martin, F. M., 'Social Status and Electoral Choice in two Constituencies', *British Journal of Sociology*, 1952, considers Greenwich and Hertford.

e. Other books and articles

Beer, S., *Modern British Politics* (1965).

Blondel, J., *Voters, Parties and Leaders* (1963).

Dogan, M., and Rokkan, S., *Social Ecology* (1969 and 1974). On electoral theory.

Harman, N., 'Minor Political Parties in Britain', *Political Studies*, 1962, lists fringe groups operating in the 1960s.

Highet, J., 'Scottish Religious Adherence', *British Journal of Sociology*, 1953, has several tables showing denominational strength in Scotland in 1950.

Kendall, M. G., and Stuart, A., 'Cubic Proportion in Election Results', *British Journal of Sociology*, 1950.

Lambert, G., and Schwartz, J., 'The voting behaviour of British Conservative Backbenchers', in Patterson, S. C., and Wahlke, J., *Comparative Legislative Behaviour* (1972).

Milne, R. S., and Mackenzie H. C., 'The Floating Vote,' *Political Studies*, 1955, has several tables.

Nordlinger, E. A., *The Working Class Tories* (1967) deals with the 'deferential' voter.

Pulzer, P., *Political Representation and Elections in Britain* (1967).

Rasmussen, J., *Retrenchment and Revival: A Study of the Contemporary British Liberal Party* (1964) has 3 maps showing Liberal strength in 1959.

— — , 'The Disutility of the Concept of Swing in British Psephology', *Parliamentary Affairs*, 1965.

Rose, R., *Politics in England* (1963).

Rose, R., ed. *Electoral Behaviour* (1974) is an excellent comparitive study.

Taylor, P. J., and Johnston, R. J., *Geography of Elections* (1979) is a general analysis of factors affecting elections in Britain, the USA and elsewhere. A useful and handy reference.

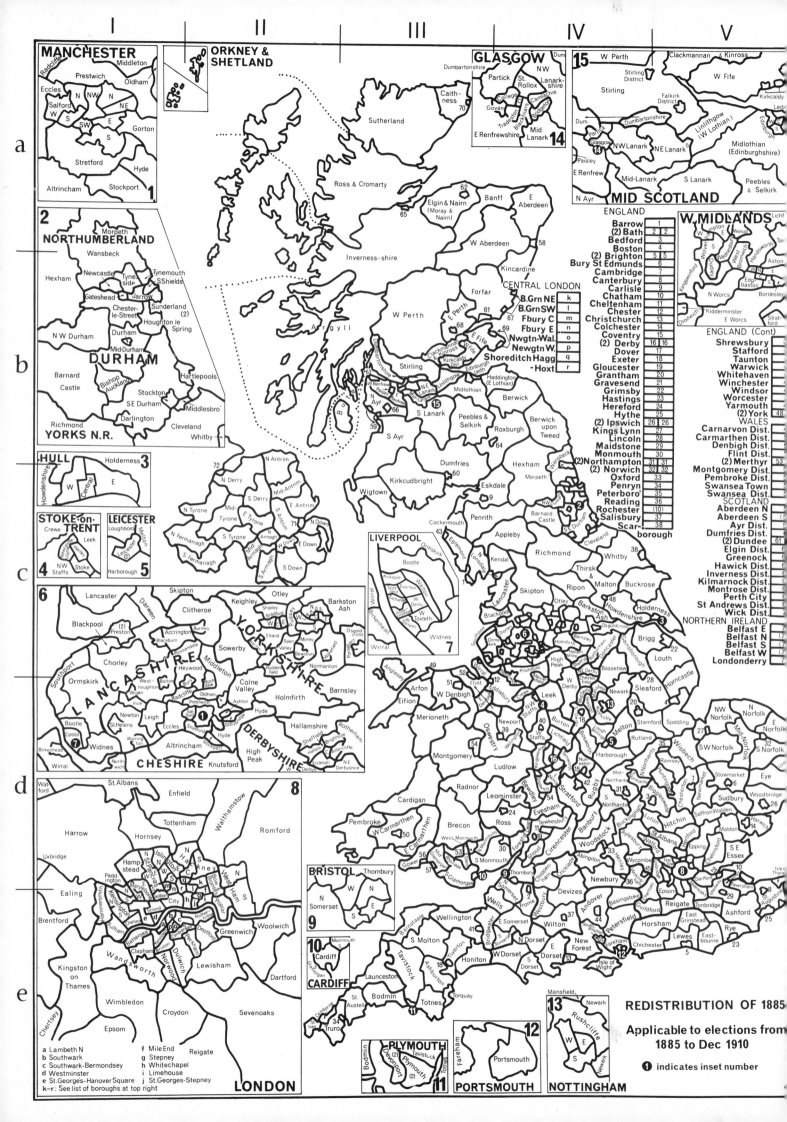

REDISTRIBUTION OF 1885

Applicable to elections from 1885 to Dec 1910

● indicates inset number

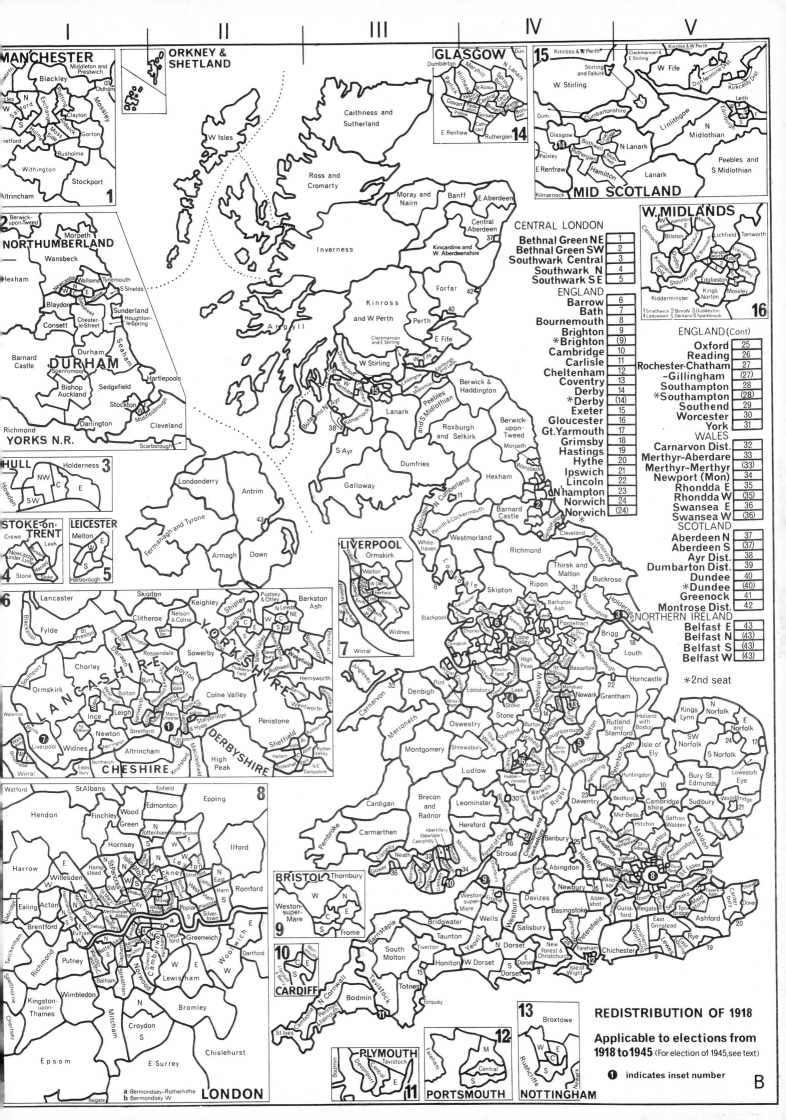

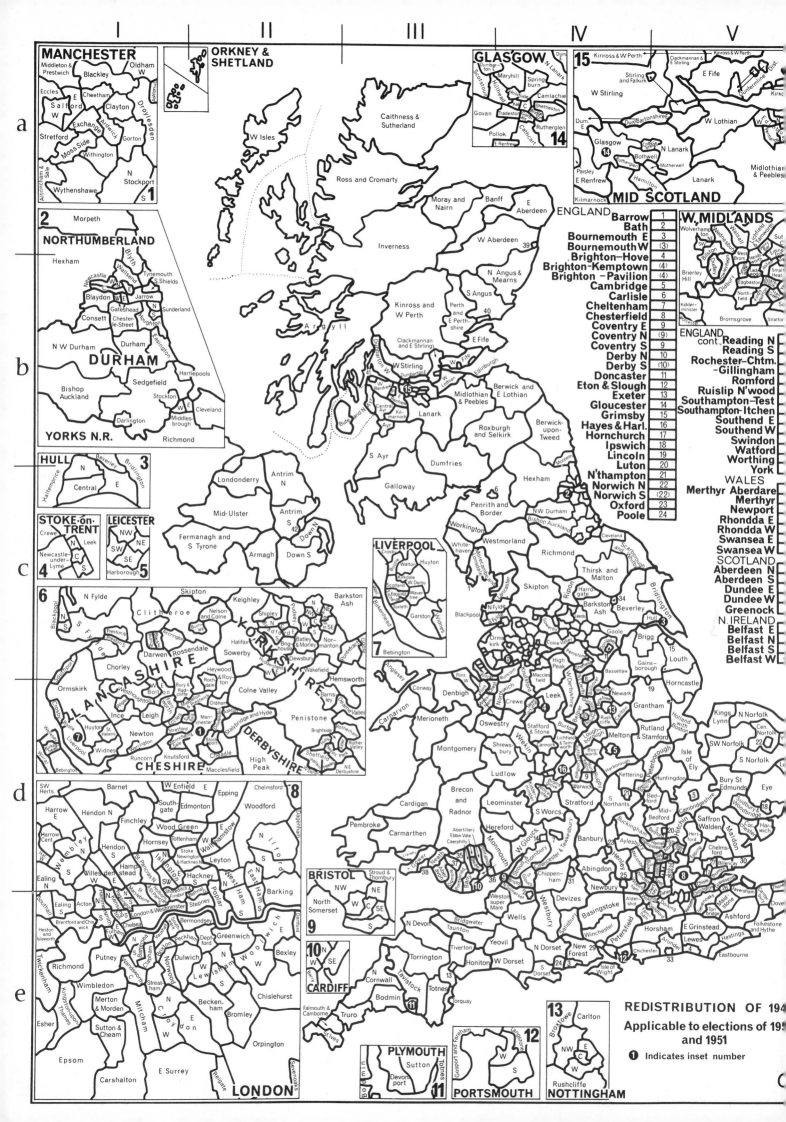

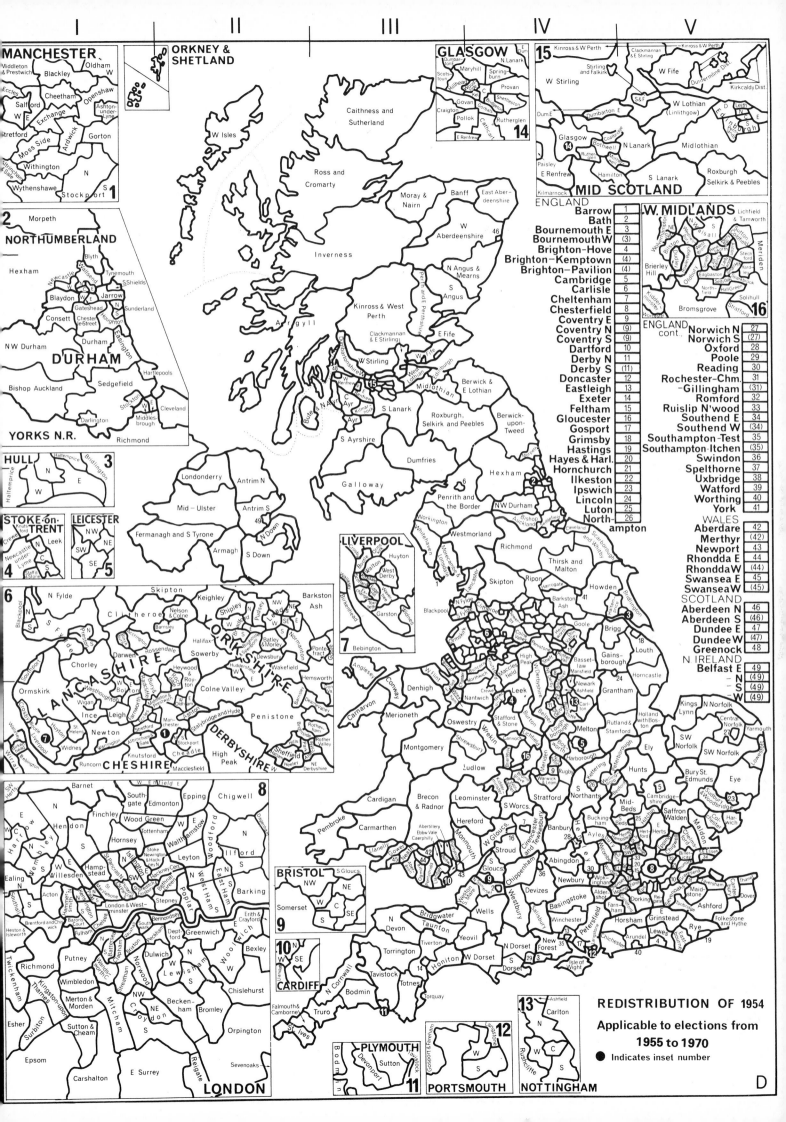

REDISTRIBUTION OF 1954

Applicable to elections from 1955 to 1970

● Indicates inset number

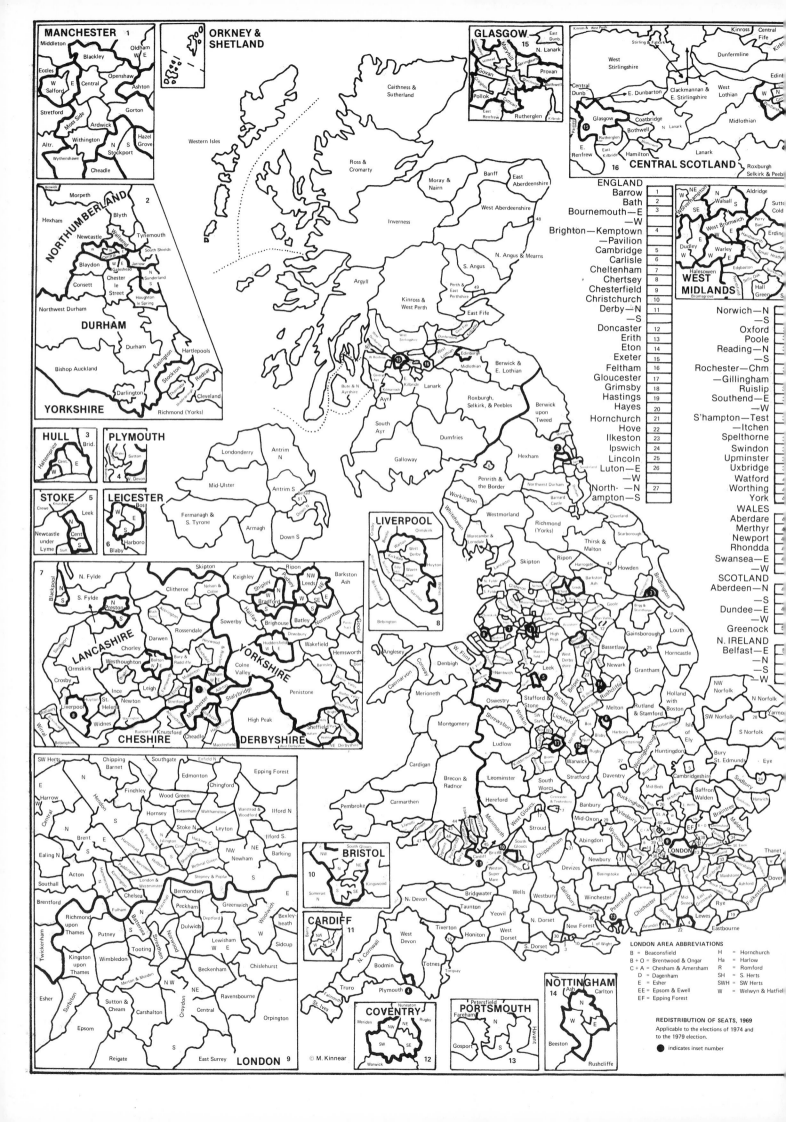

REDISTRIBUTION OF SEATS, 1969
Applicable to the elections of 1974 and to the 1979 election.
● indicates inset number

LONDON AREA ABBREVIATIONS

B	= Beaconsfield	H	= Hornchurch
B + O	= Brentwood & Ongar	Ha	= Harlow
C + A	= Chesham & Amersham	R	= Romford
D	= Dagenham	SH	= S. Herts
E	= Esher	SWH	= SW Herts
EE	= Epsom & Ewell	W	= Welwyn & Hatfield
EF	= Epping Forest		

© M. Kinnear

ENGLAND

Barrow	1
Bath	2
Bournemouth—E	3
—W	
Brighton—Kemptown	4
—Pavilion	
Cambridge	5
Carlisle	6
Cheltenham	7
Chertsey	8
Chesterfield	9
Christchurch	10
Derby—N	11
—S	
Doncaster	12
Erith	13
Eton	14
Exeter	15
Feltham	16
Gloucester	17
Grimsby	18
Hastings	19
Hayes	20
Hornchurch	21
Hove	22
Ilkeston	23
Ipswich	24
Lincoln	25
Luton—E	26
—W	
North-—N	27
ampton—S	

Norwich—N	
—S	
Oxford	
Poole	
Reading—N	
—S	
Rochester—Chm	
—Gillingham	
Ruislip	
Southend—E	
—W	
S'hampton—Test	
—Itchen	
Spelthorne	
Swindon	
Upminster	
Uxbridge	
Watford	
Worthing	
York	

WALES

Aberdare	
Merthyr	
Newport	
Rhondda	
Swansea—E	
—W	

SCOTLAND

Aberdeen—N	
—S	
Dundee—E	
—W	
Greenock	

N. IRELAND

Belfast—E	
—N	
—S	
—W	

Index of Constituencies

*The letters A, B, C, D and E refer to the 5 preceding maps, which cover the Redistributions of 1885, 1918, 1948, 1954 and 1969. Constituencies which were set up specially for the Elections of 1918 or 1945 are indicated by the signs * and † respectively.*

Constituency	maps	ref.	Constituency	maps	ref.	Constituency	maps	ref.
Aberavon	BCDE	IIId	Battersea North (London)	BCDE	Ie	Bow & Bromley (London)	AB	IId
Abercrombie (Liverpool)	A	IIIc	Battersea South (London)	BCDE	Ie	Bradford Central	ABC	IIc
Aberdare	BCDE	IIId	Beaconsfield	E	IVd	Bradford East	ABCD	IIc
Aberdeen City North	ABCDE	IVa	Bebington	CD	Id	Bradford North	BCDE	IIc
Aberdeen City South	ABCDE	IVa	Bebington & Ellesmere	E	Id	Bradford South	BCDE	IIc
Aberdeenshire Central	B	IVa	Beckenham	CDE	IIe	Bradford West	A DE	IIc
Aberdeenshire East	ABCDE	IVa	Bedford	ABCDE	IVd	Braintree	E	Vd
Aberdeenshire West	A CDE	IVa	Bedfordshire Mid	BCDE	IVd	Brecon (Brecknock)	A	IIId
Aberdeenshire West & Kincardine	B	IVa	Bedfordshire South	CDE	IVd	Brecon & Radnor	BCDE	IIId
Abertillery	BCDE	IIId	Bedwellty	BCDE	IVd	Brent East	E	Id
Abingdon	ABCDE	IVd	Beeston	E	IVe	Brent North	E	Id
Accrington	ABCDE	Ic	Belfast East	ABCDE	IIc	Brent South	E	Id
Acocks Green (Birmingham)	†	Vb	Belfast North	ABCDE	IIc	Brentford	A	Ie
Acton	BCDE	Ie	Belfast South	ABCDE	IIc	Brentford & Chiswick	BCD	Ie
Aldershot	BCDE	IVe	Belfast West	ABCDE	IIc	Brentford & Isleworth	E	Ia
Aldridge-Brownhills	E	Va	Belfast: Cromac, Duncairn, Falls,			Brentwood & Ongar	E	Vd
All Saints (Birmingham)	D	Vb	Ormeau, Pottinger, St. Annes,			Bridgeton (Glasgow)	ABCD	IVa
Altrincham	AB	Id	Shankhill, Victoria & Woodwale	*	IIc	Bridgwater	ABCDE	IIIe
Altrincham & Sale	CDE	Id	Belper	BCDE	IVd	Bridlington	E	Vc
Andover	A	IVe	Bermondsey (London)	A CDE	Ie	Brierley Hill	CD	Va
Anglesey	ABCDE	IIIc	Bermondsey West (London)	B	Ie	Brigg	ABCD	IVc
Angus North & Mearns	CDE	IVb	Berwickshire	A	IVb	Brigg & Scunthorpe	E	IVc
Angus South	CDE	IIIb	Berwick & Haddington (E. Lothian)	BCDE	IVb	Brighouse & Spenborough	CDE	IIc
Antrim	B	IIc	Berwick-upon-Tweed	ABCDE	IVb	Brighton	AB	Ve
Antrim East	A*	IIc	Bethnal Green (London)	CD	IId	Brightside (Sheffield)	ABCDE	IId
Antrim Mid	A*	IIc	Bethnal Green North-east	AB	IId	Bristol Central	BCD	IIIe
Antrim North	A* CDE	IIc	Bethnal Green South-west	AB	IId	Bristol East	AB	IIIe
Antrim South	A* CDE	IIc	Bethnal Green & Bow	E	Ie	Bristol North	AB	IIIe
Appleby	A	IVc	Beverley	C	IVc	Bristol North-east	CDE	IIIe
Ardwick (Manchester)	BCDE	Ia	Bewdley	AB	IVd	Bristol North-west	CDE	IVd
Arfon	A	IIId	Bexley	†CD	IIe	Bristol South	ABCDE	IIIe
Argyll	ABCDE	IIb	Bexleyheath	E	IIe	Bristol South-east	CDE	IIIe
Armagh	BCDE	IIc	Biggleswade	A	Vd	Bristol West	ABCDE	IIIe
Armagh Mid	A*	IIc	Billericay	CD	Vd	Brixton (London)	ABCD	Ie
Armagh North	A*	IIc	Bilston	BCD	Va	Bromley	BCDE	IIe
Armagh South	A*	IIc	Birkenhead	A CDE	Id	Bromsgrove	CDE	Vb
Arundel & Shoreham	CD	Ve	Birkenhead East	B	Id	Bromwich West—see West		
Arundel	E	Ve	Birkenhead West	B	Id	Bromwich		
Ashburton	A	IIIe	Birmingham Central	A	Vb	Broxtowe	BC	IVd
Ashfield	DE	IVd	Birmingham East	A	Vb	Buckingham	ABCDE	IVd
Ashford	ABCDE	Ve	Birmingham North	A	Vb	Buckinghamshire South	CD	IVd
Ashton-under-Lyne	ABCDE	IId	Birmingham South	A	Vb	Bucklow	†	Id
Aston (Birmingham)	ABCD	Va	Birmingham West	AB	Vb	Buckrose	AB	IVc
Attercliffe (Sheffield)	ABCDE	IId	Bishop Auckland	ABCDE	Ib	Burnley	ABCDE	IIc
Aylesbury	ABCDE	IVd	Blaby	E	IVd	Burslem (Stoke-on-Trent)	B	Ic
Ayr	CDE	IIIb	Blackburn	AB DE	Ic	Burton	ABCDE	IVd
Ayr District	AB	IIIb	Blackburn East	C	Ic	Bury	AB	Ic
Ayrshire Central	CDE	IIIb	Blackburn West	C	Ic	Bury & Radcliffe	CDE	Ic
Ayrshire North	A	IIIb	Blackfriars & Hutchestontown			Bury St. Edmunds	ABCDE	Vd
Ayrshire North & Buteshire	BCDE	IIIb	(Glasgow)	A	IVa	Bute	A	IIIb
Ayrshire South	ABCDE	IIIb	Blackley (Manchester)	BCDE	Ia	Caerphilly	BCDE	IIId
			Blackpool	AB	Ic	Caithnesshire	A	IIIa
Balham & Tooting (London)	B	Ie	Blackpool North	†CDE	Ic	Caithness & Sutherland	BCDE	IIIa
Banbury	ABCDE	IVd	Blackpool South	†CDE	Ic	Camberwell North (London)	AB	Ie
Banff	ABCDE	IIIa	Blaydon	BCDE	Ib	Camberwell North-west (London)	B	Ie
Barking	†CDE	IIe	Blyth	CDE	Ia	Camborne	AB	IIe
Barkston Ash	ABCDE	IVc	Bodmin	ABCDE	IIIe	Cambridge	ABCDE	Vd
Barnard Castle	AB	IVc	Bolsover	CDE	IVd	Cambridgeshire	BCDE	Vd
Barnet	†CD	Id	Bolton	AB	Id	Camlachie (Glasgow)	ABC	IVa
Barnsley	ABCDE	IId	Bolton East	CDE	Id	Cannock	BCDE	IVd
Barnstaple	AB	IIIe	Bolton West	CDE	Id	Canterbury	ABCDE	Ve
Barons Court (London)	D	Ie	Bootle	ABCDE	IIIc	Cardiff District	A	IIe
Barrow-in-Furness	ABCDE	IIIc	Bordesley (Birmingham)	A	Vb	Cardiff Central	B	IIe
Barry	CDE	IIId	Boston	A	Vd	Cardiff East	B	IIe
Basildon	E	Vd	Bosworth	ABCDE	IVd	Cardiff North	CDE	IIe
Basingstoke	ABCDE	IVe	Bothwell	BCDE	IVa	Cardiff North-west	E	IIe
Bassetlaw	ABCDE	IVc	Bournemouth	B	IVe	Cardiff South	B	IIe
Bath	ABCDE	IVd	Bournemouth East	E	IVe	Cardiff South-east	CDE	IIe
Batley & Morley	BCDE	Ie	Bournemouth East & Christchurch	CD	IVe	Cardiff West	CDE	IIe
Battersea (London)	A	Ie	Bournemouth West	CDE	IVe	Cardiganshire	ABCDE	IIId

Constituency	maps	ref.
Carlisle	ABCDE	IIIc
Carlton	CDE	IVd
Carmarthen District	A	IIId
Carmarthen	BCDE	IIId
Carmarthenshire East	A	IIId
Carmarthenshire West	A	IIId
Carnarvon (Caernarvon)	BCDE	IIId
Carnarvon District	AB	IIId
Carshalton	† CDE	Ie
Cathcart (Glasgow)	BCDE	IVa
Chatham (Rochester)	AB	Vd
Cheadle	CDE	IId
Cheetham (Manchester)	CD	Ia
Chelmsford	ABCDE	Vd
Chelsea (London)	ABCDE	Ie
Cheltenham	ABCDE	IVd
Chertsey	ABCDE	Vd
Chesham & Amersham	E	IVd
Chester City	ABCDE	IIId
Chesterfield	ABCDE	IVd
Chester-le-Street	ABCDE	IIb
Chesterton	A	Vd
Chichester	ABCDE	IVe
Chigwell	D	IId
Chingford	E	IId
Chippenham	ABCDE	IVd
Chipping Barnet	E	Id
Chislehurst	BCDE	IIe
Chorley	ABCDE	Ic
Christchurch	A	IVe
Christchurch & Lymington	E	IVe
Cirencester	A	IVd
Cirencester & Tewkesbury	BCDE	IVd
City of London	AB	Ie
Cities of London & Westminster	CDE	Ie
Clackmannan & Kinross	A	Va
Clackmannan & East Stirlingshire	BCDE	Va
Clapham (London)	ABCD	Ie
Clay Cross	B	IVd
Clayton (Manchester)	BC	Ia
Cleveland	ABCD	Ib
Cleveland & Whitby	E	IVe
Clitheroe	ABCDE	IIc
Coatbridge	BCDE	Va
Cockermouth	A	IIIc
Colchester	ABCDE	Vd
College (Glasgow)	A	IVa
Colne Valley	ABCDE	IId
Consett	BCDE	Ib
Conway	CDE	IId
Cornwall North	CDE	IIIe
Coventry	AB	IVd
Coventry East	† CD	IVd
Coventry North	CD	IVd
Coventry North-east	E	IIId
Coventry North-west	E	IIId
Coventry South	CD	IVd
Coventry South-east	E	IIId
Coventry South-west	E	IIId
Coventry West	†	IVd
Craigton (Glasgow)	DE	IIIa
Crewe	ABCDE	IVd
Cricklade	A	IVd
Crosby	CDE	Id
Croydon	A	Ie
Croydon Central	E	Ie
Croydon East	C	IIe
Croydon North	BC	Ie
Croydon North-east	DE	IIe
Croydon North-west	DE	Ie
Croydon South	B DE	Ie
Croydon West	C	Ie
Cumberland North	B	IIIc
Dagenham	† CDE	IId
Darlington	ABCDE	Ib
Dartford	ABCDE	IIe
Darwen	ABCDE	Ic
Daventry	B E	IVd
Dearne Valley	CDE	IId
Denbigh	BCDE	IIId
Denbigh District	A	IIId
Denbigh East	A	IIId
Denbigh West	A	IIId
Deptford (London)	ABCDE	IIe

Constituency	maps	ref.
Derby	AB	IVd
Derby North	CDE	IVd
Derby South	CDE	IVd
Derby West (Liverpool)—see West Derby		
Derbyshire Mid	A	IVd
Derbyshire North-east	ABCDE	IVc
Derbyshire South	AB	IVd
Derbyshire South-east	CD	IVd
Derbyshire West	ABCDE	IVd
Deritend (Birmingham)	B	Vb
Devizes	ABCDE	IVd
Devonport (Plymouth)	ABCDE	IVe
Devon North	CDE	IIIe
Devon West	E	IIIe
Dewsbury	ABCDE	IIc
Doncaster	ABCDE	IVc
Don Valley	BCDE	IVc
Dorking	CDE	Ve
Dorset East	AB	IVe
Dorset North	ABCDE	IVe
Dorset South	ABCDE	IVe
Dorset West	ABCDE	IVe
Dover	ABCD	Ve
Dover & Deal	E	Ve
Down	B	IIc
Down East	A*	IIc
Down Mid	*	IIc
Down North	A* CDE	IIc
Down South	A* CDE	IIc
Down West	A*	IIc
Drake (Plymouth)	B E	IIIe
Droylsden	C	Ia
Duddeston (Birmingham)	B	Vb
Dudley	ABCD	Vb
Dudley East	E	Va
Dudley West	E	Va
Dulwich (London)	ABCDE	Ie
Dumbarton District	B	IIIb
Dumbartonshire (Dunbartonshire)	AB	IIIb
Dunbartonshire Central	E	IVa
Dunbartonshire East	CDE	IIIb
Dunbartonshire West	CDE	IIIb
Dumfries District	A	IIIc
Dumfriesshire	ABCDE	IIIb
Dundee	AB	IIIb
Dundee East	CDE	IIIb
Dundee West	CDE	IIIb
Dunfermline	E	Va
Dunfermline District	BCD	Va
Durham	ABCDE	Ib
Durham Mid	A	Ib
Durham North-west	A CDE	Ib
Durham South-east	A	Ib
Ealing	AB	Ie
Ealing East	†	Ie
Ealing North	CDE	Ie
Ealing South	CD	Ie
Ealing West	†	Ie
Easington	CDE	Ib
Eastbourne	ABCDE	Ve
East Grinstead	ABCDE	Ve
East Ham North	BCD	IId
East Ham South	BCD	IIe
East Kilbride	E	IVa
Eastleigh	DE	IVe
Ebbw Vale	BCDE	IIId
Eccles	ABCDE	Id
Ecclesall (Sheffield)	AB	IId
Eddisbury	AB	IVd
Edgbaston (Birmingham)	ABCDE	Vb
Edge Hill (Liverpool)	BCDE	IIIc
Edinburgh Central	ABCDE	Va
Edinburgh East	ABCDE	Va
Edinburgh North	BCDE	Va
Edinburgh South	ABCDE	Va
Edinburgh West	ABCDE	Va
Edmonton	BCDE	Id
Egremont	A	IIIc
Eifion	A	IIId
Elgin District	A	IIIa
Elgin & Nairn (Moray & Nairn)	ABCDE	IIIa
Elland	AB	IIc

Constituency	maps	ref.
Ely, Isle of (Wisbech)	ABCDE	Vd
Enfield	AB	IId
Enfield East	CD	IId
Enfield North	E	Id
Enfield West	CD	Id
Epping	ABCDE	Vd
Epsom	ABCDE	Ie
Erdington (Birmingham)	BC E	Va
Erith & Crayford	DE	IIe
Esher	CDE	Vd
Eskdale	A	IIIc
Essex South-east	AB DE	Vd
Eton & Slough	† CDE	IVd
Everton (Liverpool)	AB	IIIc
Evesham	AB	IVd
Exchange (Liverpool)	ABCD	IIIc
Exchange (Manchester)	BCD	Ia
Exeter	ABCDE	IIIe
Eye	ABCDE	Vd
Fairfield (Liverpool)	B	IIIc
Falkirk	A	Va
Falmouth & Camborne	CDE	IIe
Fareham	AB E	IVe
Farnham	BCDE	IVd
Farnworth	BCDE	Id
Faversham	ABCDE	Ve
Feltham	DE	Vd
Fermanagh North	A*	IIc
Fermanagh South	A*	IIc
Fermanagh & South Tyrone	CDE	IIc
Fermanagh & Tyrone	B	IIc
Fife Central	E	Va
Fife East	ABCDE	IIIb
Fife West	ABCD	IIIb
Finchley	BCDE	Id
Finsbury (London)	B	Id
Finsbury Central (London)	A	Id
Finsbury East (London)	A	Id
Flint District	A	IIIc
Flintshire	AB	IIIc
Flintshire East	CDE	IIIc
Flintshire West	CDE	IIId
Folkestone & Hythe	CDE	Ve
Forest of Dean	AB	IVd
Forfar	AB	IIIb
Frome	AB	IVe
Fulham (London)	A DE	Ie
Fulham East (London)	BC	Ie
Fulham West (London)	BC	Ie
Fylde	B	Ic
Fylde North	CDE	Ic
Fylde South	CDE	Ic
Gainsborough	ABCDE	IVc
Galloway	BCDE	IIIc
Garscadden (Glasgow)	E	IIIa
Garston (Liverpool)	CDE	IIIc
Gateshead	AB	Ib
Gateshead East	CDE	Ib
Gateshead West	CDE	Ib
Gillingham (Rochester)	BCDE	Vd
Glamorgan East	A	IIId
Glamorgan Mid	A	IIId
Glamorgan South	A	IIId
Glasgow Central	ABCDE	IVa
Gloucester	ABCDE	IVd
Gloucestershire South	CDE	IVd
Gloucestershire West	CDE	IVd
Goole	CDE	IVc
Gorbals (Glasgow)	BCD	IVa
Gorton (Manchester)	ABCDE	Ia
Gosport & Fareham	CDE	IVe
Govan (Glasgow)	ABCDE	IVa
Gower	ABCDE	IIId
Grantham	ABCDE	IVc
Gravesend	ABCDE	Vd
Greenock	ABCDE	IIIb
Greenwich (London)	ABCDE	IIe
Grimsby	ABCDE	IVc
Grinstead East—see East Grinstead		
Guildford	ABCDE	Ve
Hackney Central (London)	AB DE	IId
Hackney North (London)	AB	IId

Constituency	maps	ref.
Hackney South (London)	ABC	Id
Hackney South & Shoreditch	E	IId
Haddingtonshire	A	IIIb
Haggerston (London)	A	Id
Halesowen & Stourbridge	E	Vb
Halifax	ABCDE	IIc
Hallam (Sheffield)	ABCDE	IIc
Hallamshire	A	IId
Hall Green (Birmingham)	CDE	Vb
Haltemprice	CDE	Ic
Ham—see East Ham and West Ham		
Hamilton	BCDE	IVa
Hammersmith	A	Ie
Hammersmith North	BCDE	Ie
Hammersmith South	BC	Ie
Hampstead	ABCDE	Id
Handsworth (Birmingham)	ABCDE	Va
Hanley	AB	Ic
Harborough	ABCDE	IVd
Harlow	E	Vd
Harrogate	CDE	IVc
Harrow	AB	Id
Harrow Central	CDE	Id
Harrow East	† CDE	Id
Harrow West	† CDE	Id
Hartlepools (Hartlepool)	ABCDE	Ib
Harwich	ABCDE	Vd
Hastings	ABCDE	Ve
Havant & Waterloo	E	IVe
Hawick District	A	IIIb
Hayes & Harlington	CDE	Vd
Hazel Grove	E	Ia
Heeley (Sheffield)	CDE	IId
Hemel Hempstead	BCDE	IVd
Hemsworth	BCDE	IIc
Hendon	B	Id
Hendon North	† CDE	Id
Hendon South	† CDE	Id
Henley	ABCDE	IVd
Hereford	ABCDE	IVd
Hertford	ABCD	Vd
Hertford & Stevenage	E	IVd
Hertfordshire East	DE	Vd
Hertfordshire South	E	IVd
Hertfordshire South-west	CDE	Ie
Heston & Isleworth	† CD	Ie
Hexham	ABCDE	IVb
Heywood	A	IIc
Heywood & Radcliffe	B	IIc
Heywood & Royton	CDE	Ie
High Peak	ABCDE	IVc
Hillhead (Glasgow)	BCDE	IVa
Hillsborough (Sheffield)	BCDE	IVa
Hitchin	ABCDE	Vd
Holborn (London)	AB	Ie
Holborn & St. Pancras South (London)	CDE	Ie
Holderness	AB	Vc
Holland (Spalding)	A	Vc
Holland-with-Boston	BCDE	Vd
Holmfirth	A	IId
Honiton	ABCDE	IIIe
Horncastle	ABCDE	Vd
Hornchurch	† CDE	Vd
Hornsey	ABCDE	Id
Horsham	A† CD	Ve
Horsham & Crawley	E	Ve
Horsham & Worthing	B	Ve
Houghton-le-Spring	ABCDE	Ib
Hove	CDE	Ve
Hoxton (London)	A	Id
Howdenshire (Howden)	AB DE	IVc
Huddersfield	AB	IIc
Huddersfield East	CDE	IIc
Huddersfield West	CDE	IIc
Hull—see Kingston-upon-Hull		
Hulme (Manchester)	B	Ia
Huntingdon	ABCDE	Vd
Huyton	CDE	Id
Hyde	A	IId
Hythe	AB	Ve
Ilford	B	IId
Ilford North	† CDE	IId
Ilford South	† CDE	IId

Constituency	maps	ref.
Ilkeston	ABCDE	IVd
Ince	ABCDE	Id
Inverness	ABCDE	IIIa
Inverness District	A	IIIa
Ipswich	ABCDE	IVd
Islington Central	E	Id
Islington East	ABCD	Id
Islington North	ABCDE	Id
Islington South	AB	Id
Islington South & Finsbury	E	Ie
Islington South-west	CD	Id
Islington West	AB	Id
Itchen (Southampton)	CDE	IVe
Jarrow	ABCDE	Ib
Keighley	ABCDE	IIc
Kelvingrove (Glasgow)	BCDE	IVa
Kendal	A	IVc
Kemptown (Brighton)	CDE	Ve
Kennington (London)	AB	Ie
Kensington (London)	E	Ie
Kensington North (London)	ABCD	Ie
Kensington South (London)	ABCD	Ie
Kettering	BCDE	IVd
Kidderminster	ABCDE	Vb
Kilmarnock	BCDE	IIIb
Kilmarnick District	A	IIIb
Kincardineshire	A	IVb
King's Lynn	ABCD	Vd
King's Norton (Birmingham)	BC	Vb
Kingston-upon-Hull Central	ABC E	Ic
Kingston-upon-Hull·East	ABCDE	Ic
Kingston-upon-Hull North	CD	Ic
Kingston-upon-Hull North-west	B	Ic
Kingston-upon-Hull South-west	B	Ic
Kingston-upon-Hull West	A DE	Ic
Kingston-on-Thames	ABCDE	Ie
Kingswinford	AB	Vb
Kingswood	E	IIIe
Kinross & West Perth	BCDE	IIIb
Kircaldy	E	Va
Kirkaldy District	ABCD	Va
Kirkcudbright	A	IIIc
Kirkdale (Liverpool)	ABCDE	IIIc
Knutsford	ABCDE	IVc
Ladywood (Birmingham)	BCDE	Vb
Lambeth Central (London)	E	Ie
Lambeth North (London)	AB	Ie
Lanark	BCDE	IIIb
Lanark Mid	A	IIIb
Lanark North	BCDE	IIIb
Lanark North-east	A	IIIb
Lanark North-west	A	IIIb
Lanark South	A	IIIb
Lancaster	ABCDE	IIIc
Langstone (Portsmouth)	CD	IVe
Launceston	A	IIIe
Leeds Central	ABC	IIc
Leeds East	A DE	IIc
Leeds North	ABC	IIc
Leeds North-east	BCDE	IIc
Leeds North-west	CDE	IIc
Leeds South	ABCDE	IIc
Leeds South-east	BCDE	IIc
Leeds West	ABCDE	IIc
Leek	ABCDE	IVd
Leicester	A	Ic
Leicester East	B	Ic
Leicester North-east	CD	Ic
Leicester North-west	CD	Ic
Leicester South	B E	Ic
Leicester South-east	CD	Ic
Leicester South-west	CD	Ic
Leicester West	B E	Ic
Leigh	ABCDE	Id
Leith	ABCDE	Va
Leominster	ABCDE	IVd
Lewes	ABCDE	Ve
Lewisham (London)	A	IIe
Lewisham East (London)	B E	IIe
Lewisham North (London)	CD	IIe
Lewisham South (London)	CD	IIe
Lewisham West (London)	BCDE	IIe

Constituency	maps	ref.
Leyton	CDE	IId
Leyton East	B	IId
Leyton West	B	IId
Lichfield	AB	IVd
Lichfield & Tamworth	CDE	IVd
Limehouse (London)	AB	IIe
Lincoln	ABCDE	IVc
Linlithgow (West Lothian)	ABCDE	IIIb
Llandaff & Barry	B	IIId
Llanelly (Llanelli)	BCDE	IIId
London, City of	AB	Ie
Londonderry City	A*	IIc
Londonderry County (Derry)	BCDE	IIc
Londonderry County North	A*	IIc
Lonsdale (North Lonsdale)	AB	IIIc
Loughborough	ABCDE	IVd
Louth	ABCDE	Vc
Lowestoft	ABCDE	Vd
Ludlow	ABCDE	IVd
Luton	ABCD	IVd
Luton East	E	IVd
Luton West	E	IVd
Macclesfield	ABCDE	IVd
Maidstone	ABCDE	Ve
Maldon	ABCDE	Vd
Manchester Central	E	Ia
Manchester East	A	Ia
Manchester North	A	Ia
Manchester North-east	A	Ia
Manchester North-west	A	Ia
Manchester South	A	Ia
Manchester South-west	A	Ia
Mansfield	ABCDE	IVd
Marylebone—see St. Marylebone		
Marylebone East	A	IVd
Marylebone West	A	IVd
Maryhill (Glasgow)	BCDE	IVa
Medway	A	Vd
Melton	ABCDE	IVd
Meriden	DE	Va
Merioneth	ABCDE	IIId
Merthyr	B	IIId
Merthyr Tidfil	A CDE	IIId
Merton & Morden	CD	Ie
Middlesbrough	A E	Ib
Middlesbrough East	BCD	Ib
Middlesbrough West	BCD	Ib
Middleton	A	IId
Middleton & Prestwich	BCDE	IId
Midlothian (Edinburghshire)	A DE	IIIb
Midlothian North	B	IIIb
Midlothian & Peebes	C	IIIb
Mile End (London)	AB	IId
Mitcham	BCD	Ie
Mitcham & Morden	E	Ie
Monmouth	BCDE	IVd
Monmouth District	A	IVd
Monmouthshire North	A	IIId
Monmouthshire South	A	IIId
Monmouthshire West	A	IIId
Montgomery District	A	IUd
Montgomeryshire	ABCDE	IIId
Montrose District	AB	IVb
Moray & Nairn (Elgin & Nairn)	ABCDE	IIIa
Morley	A	IIc
Morecambe & Lonsdale	CDE	IIIc
Morpeth	ABCDE	Ia
Moseley (Birmingham)	B	Vb
Mossley	B	Ia
Moss Side (Manchester)	BCDE	Ia
Motherwell	BCD	IVa
Motherwell & Wishaw	E	IVa
Nantwich	DE	IVd
Neath	BCDE	IIId
Neepsend (Sheffield)	C	IId
Nelson & Colne	BCDE	IIc
Newark	ABCDE	IVd
Newbury	ABCDE	IVd
Newcastle-under-Lyme	ABCDE	Ic
Newcastle-upon-Tyne	A	Ib
Newcastle-upon-Tyne Central	BCDE	Ib
Newcastle-upon-Tyne East	BCDE	Ib
Newcastle-upon-Tyne North	BCDE	Ib

Constituency	maps	ref.
Newcastle-upon-Tyne West	BCDE	Ib
New Forest	ABCDE	IVe
Newham North-east	E	Vd
Newham North-west	E	Vd
Newham South	E	Vd
Newington West (London)	A	Ie
Newmarket	A	Vd
Newport (Monmouthshire)	BCDE	IIId
Newport (Shropshire)	A	IVd
Newton	ABCDE	Id
Norfolk Central	CD	Vd
Norfolk East	AB	Vd
Norfolk Mid	A	Vd
Norfolk North	ABCDE	Vd
Norfolk North-west	A E	Vd
Norfolk South	ABCDE	Vd
Norfolk South-west	ABCDE	Vd
Normanton	ABCDE	IIc
Northampton	ABCD	IVd
Northampton North	E	IVd
Northampton South	E	IVd
Northamptonshire East	A	IVd
Northamptonshire Mid	A	IVd
Northamptonshire North	A	IVd
Northamptonshire South	A CD	IVd
Northfield (Birmingham)	CDE	Vb
Northwich	ABCDE	IVd
Norwich	AB	Vd
Norwich North	CDE	Vd
Norwich South	CDE	Vd
Norwood (London)	ABCDE	Ie
Nottingham Central	BCD	IVe
Nottingham East	ABC E	IVe
Nottingham North	DE	IVe
Nottingham North-west	C	IVe
Nottingham South	AB D	IVe
Nottingham West	ABCDE	IVe
Nuneaton	ABCDE	IVd
Ogmore	BCDE	IIId
Oldbury & Halesowen	CD	Vb
Oldham	AB	Ia
Oldham East	CDE	IId
Oldham West	CDE	IId
Openshaw (Manchester)	DE	Ia
Orkney & Shetland	ABCDE	Ia
Ormskirk	ABCDE	Id
Orpington	CDE	IIe
Osgoldcress	A	IVc
Oswestry	ABCDE	IIId
Otley	A	IIc
Oxford	ABCDE	IVd
Oxon, Mid	E	IVd
Paddington	E	Id
Paddington North (London)	ABCD	Id
Paddington South (London)	ABCD	Id
Paisley	ABCDE	IVa
Park (Sheffield)	BCDE	IId
Partick (Glasgow)	AB	IIIa
Pavilion (Brighton)	CDE	Ve
Peckham (London)	ABCDE	IIe
Peebles & Selkirk	A	IIIb
Peebles & South Midlothian	B	IIIb
Pembroke District	A	IIId
Pembrokeshire (Pembroke)	ABCDE	IIId
Penistone	BCDE	IId
Penrith	A	IIIc
Penrith & The Border	CDE	IIIc
Penrith & Cockermouth	B	IIIc
Penryn & Falmouth	AB	IIIe
Pentlands (Edinburgh)	CDE	Va
Perry Barr (Birmingham)	CDE	Va
Perth City	A	IIIb
Perthshire East	AB	IIIb
Perthshire West	A	IIIb
Perth & East Perthshire	CDE	IIIb
Peterborough	ABCDE	Vd
Petersfield	ABCDE	IVe
Plaistow (West Ham)	B	IIe
Platting (Manchester)	B	Ia
Plymouth	A	IIIe
Pollock (Glasgow)	BCDE	IVa
Pontefract	ABCD	IIIc
Pontefract & Castleford	E	IIc
Pontypool	BCDE	IIId
Pontypridd	BCDE	IIId
Poole	CDE	IVe
Poplar South (London)	B	IIe
Portsmouth	A	IVe
Portsmouth Central	B	IVe
Portsmouth North	B E	IVe
Portsmouth South	BCDE	IVe
Portsmouth West	CD	IVe
Preston	AB	Ic
Preston North	CDE	Ic
Preston South	CDE	Ic
Prestwich	A	IId
Provan (Glasgow)	DE	IVa
Pudsey	A CDE	IIc
Pudsey & Otley	B	IIc
Putney (London)	BCDE	Ie
Queen's Park (Glasgow)	E	IVa
Radcliffe	A	Id
Radnor	A	IIId
Ramsey	A	Vd
Ravensbourne (Bromley)	E	IIe
Reading	AB D	IVd
Reading North	C E	IVd
Reading South	C E	IVd
Redcar	E	Ib
Reigate	ABCDE	Ve
Renfrew East	ABCDE	IIIb
Renfrew West	ABCDE	IIIb
Rhondda	A E	IIId
Rhondda East	BCD	IIId
Rhondda West	BCD	IIId
Richmond (Surrey)	BCDE	Ie
Richmond (Yorkshire)	ABCDE	IVc
Ripon	ABCDE	IVc
Rochdale	ABCDE	IIc
Rochester	A	Ve
Rochester & Chatham	CDE	Ve
Romford	ABCDE	IId
Ross (Herefordshire)	A	IVd
Ross & Cromarty	ABCDE	IIIa
Rossendale	ABCDE	IIc
Rotherham	ABCDE	IId
Rotherhithe (London)	AB	IIe
Rother Valley	BCDE	IIId
Rothwell	B	IIc
Rowley Regis & Tipton	CD	Vb
Roxburgh	A	IIIb
Roxburgh & Selkirk	BC	IIIb
Roxburgh, Selkirk & Peebles	DE	IIId
Royal Tunbridge Wells	E	Ve
Royton	B	IIc
Rugby	ABCDE	IVd
Ruislip-Northwood	CDE	Vd
Runcorn	CDE	IVd
Rushcliffe	ABCDE	IVd
Rusholme (Manchester)	B	Ia
Rutherglen	BCDE	IVa
Rutland	A	IVd
Rutland & Stamford	BCDE	IVd
Rye	AB DE	Ve
Saffron Walden	ABCDE	Vd
St. Albans	ABCDE	Vd
St. Andrews District	A	IIIb
St. Augustine	A	Ve
St. Austell	A	IIIe
St. George's-Stepney (London)	A	IIe
St. George's-Hanover Square (London)	AB	Ie
St. Helens	ABCDE	Id
St. Ives	ABCDE	IIe
St. Marylebone (London)	BCDE	Id
St. Pancras East (London)	A	Id
St. Pancras North (London)	ABCDE	Id
St. Pancras South (London)	A	Id
St. Pancras South-east (London)	B	Id
St. Pancras South-west (London)	B	Id
St. Pancras West (London)	A	Id
St. Rollox (Glasgow)	AB	IVa
Salford East	CDE	Ia
Salford North	AB	Ia
Salford South	AB	Ia
Salford West	ABCDE	Ia
Salisbury	ABCDE	IVe
Scarborough	A E	IVc
Scarborough & Whitby	BCD	IVc
Scotland (Liverpool)	ABCD	IIIc
Scotland Exchange (Liverpool)	E	IIIc
Scotstoun (Glasgow)	CD	IIIa
Seaham	B	Ib
Sedgefield	BCD	Ib
Selly Oak (Birmingham)	DE	Vb
Sevenoaks	ABCDE	Ve
Sheffield Central	AB	IId
Shettleston (Glasgow)	BCDE	IVa
Shipley	ABCDE	IIc
Shoreditch (London)	B	Id
Shoreditch & Finsbury	CD	Id
Shoreham	E	Vd
Shrewsbury	ABCDE	IVd
Sidcup	E	IIe
Silvertown (West Ham)	B	IIe
Skipton	ABCDE	IVc
Sleaford	A	IVd
Small Heath (Birmingham)	CDE	Vb
Smethwick	BCD	Va
Solihull	† CDE	Vb
Somerset East	A	IVe
Somerset North	A CDE	IVe
Somerset South	A	IVe
Southall	† CDE	Ie
Southampton	AB	IVe
Southend	B	Vd
Southend East	CDE	Vd
Southend West	CDE	Vd
Southgate	CDE	Id
South Molton	AB	IIIe
Southport	ABCDE	Ic
South Shields	ABCDE	Ib
Southwark	CD	Ie
Southwark Central	B	Ie
Southwark North	B	Ie
Southwark South-west	B	Ie
Southwark West	A	Ie
Sowerby	ABCDE	IIc
Spalding (Holland)	A	IVd
Sparkbrook (Birmingham)	BCDE	Vb
Spelthorne	BCDE	Vd
Spennymoor	B	Ib
Spen Valley	AB	IIc
Springburn (Glasgow)	BCDE	IVa
Stafford	AB	IVd
Stafford & Stone	CDE	IVd
Staffordshire North-west	A	IVd
Staffordshire South-west	E	IVd
Staffordshire West	A	IVd
Stalybridge	A	IIc
Stalybridge & Hyde	BCDE	IIc
Stamford	A	IVd
Stechford (Birmingham)	CDE	Va
Stepney (London)	A CD	IIe
Stepney & Poplar	E	Ie
Stirling District	A	IVa
Stirling & Falkirk	BCDE	IVa
Stirlingshire	A	IVa
Stirlingshire West	BCDE	IVa
Stockport	AB	Ia
Stockport North	CDE	Ia
Stockport South	CDE	Ia
Stockton-on-Tees	ABCDE	Ib
Stoke Newington (London)	B	Id
Stoke Newington & Hackney North	CDE	Id
Stoke-on-Trent	A	Ic
Stoke-on-Trent Central	CDE	Ic
Stoke-on-Trent North	CDE	Ic
Stoke-on-Trent South	CDE	Ic
Stoke-on-Trent Stoke	B	Ic
Stone	B	IVd
Stourbridge	B	Vb
Stowmarket	A	Vd
Strand (London)	A	Ie
Stratford (Warwickshire)	A CDE	IVd
Stratford (West Ham)	B	IId
Streatham (London)	BCDE	Ie
Stretford	ABCDE	IId
Stroud	AB DE	IVd
Stroud & Thornbury	C	IVd

Constituency	maps	ref.
Sudbury	AB	Vd
Sudbury & Woodbridge	CDE	Vd
Sunderland	AB	Ib
Sunderland North	CDE	Ib
Sunderland South	CDE	Ib
Surbiton	DE	Ie
Surrey East	BCDE	IIe
Surrey North-west	E	IVd
Sussex, Mid	E	Ve
Sutherland	A	IIIa
Sutton (Plymouth)	BCDE	IIIe
Sutton & Cheam	† CDE	Ie
Sutton Coldfield	† CDE	Va
Swansea District	A	IIId
Swansea East	BCDE	IIId
Swansea Town	A	IIId
Swansea West	BCDE	IIId
Swindon	BCDE	IVd
Tamworth	AB	Va
Taunton	ABCDE	IIIe
Tavistock	ABCD	IIIe
Test (Southampton)	CDE	IVe
Tewkesbury	A	IVd
Thanet, Isle of	ABCD	Vd
Thanet East	E	Vd
Thanet West	E	Vd
Thirsk & Malton	ABCDE	IVc
Thornaby	E	Ib
Thornbury	AB	IVd
Thurrock	† CDE	Vd
Tiverton	ABCDE	IIIe
Tonbridge (Tunbridge)	ABCD	Ve
Tonbridge & Malling	E	Ve
Tooting	E	Ie
Torquay (Torbay)	ABCDE	IIIe
Torrington	CD	IIIe
Totnes	ABCDE	IIIe
Tottenham	A CDE	Id
Tottenham North	B	Id
Tottenham South	B	Id
Toxteth (Liverpool)	CDE	IIIc
Toxteth West	AB	IIIc
Toxteth East	AB	IIIc
Tradeston (Glasgow)	ABC	IVa
Truro	A CDE	IIIe
Twickenham	BCDE	Ie
Tynemouth	ABCDE	Ib
Tyneside	A	Ib
Tyrone East	A	IIc
Tyrone Mid	A	IIc
Tyrone North	A	IIc
Tyrone North-east	*	IIc

Constituency	maps	ref.
Tyrone North-west	*	IIc
Tyrone South	A*	IIc
Ulster Mid	CDE	IIc
Upminster	E	Vd
Upton (West Ham)	B	IId
Uxbridge	ABCDE	IVd
Vauxhall (London)	CDE	Ie
Wakefield	ABCDE	IIc
Wallasey	BCDE	Id
Wallsend	BCDE	Ib
Walsall	ABC	Va
Walsall North	DE	Va
Walsall South	DE	Va
Walthamstow	A E	IId
Walthamstow East	BCD	IId
Walthamstow West	BCD	IId
Walton (Liverpool)	ABCDE	IIIc
Walworth (London)	A	Ie
Wandsworth (London)	A	Ie
Wandsworth Central (London)	BCD	Ie
Wansbeck	AB	Ib
Wanstead & Woodford	DE	IId
Warley East	E	Va
Warley West	E	Va
Warrington	ABCDE	Id
Warwick & Leamington	ABCDE	IVd
Waterloo	B	IIIc
Watford	ABCDE	Vd
Wavertree (Liverpool)	BCDE	IIIc
Wednesbury	ABCD	Va
Wellingborough	BCDE	IVd
Wellington (Salop)	A	IVd
Wellington (Somerset)	A	IIIe
Wells	ABCDE	IVe
Welwyn & Hatfield	E	Vd
Wembley North	† CD	Id
Wembley South	† CD	Id
Wentworth	B	IIId
West Bromwich	ABCD	Va
West Bromwich East	E	Va
West Bromwich West	E	Va
Westbury	ABCDE	IVe
West Derby (Liverpool)	ABCDE	IIIc
Western Isles	BCDE	IIIa
West Ham North	A CD	IId
West Ham South	A CD	IIe
Westhoughton	ABCDE	Id
West Lothian (Linlithgow)	ABCDE	IIIb

Constituency	maps	ref.
Westminster Abbey (London)	AB	Ie
Westmorland	BCDE	IVc
Weston-super-Mare	BCDE	IIIe
Whitby	A	IVc
Whitechapel (London)	A	IIe
Whitechapel & St. George's-Stepney	B	IIe
Whitehaven	ABCDE	IIIc
Wick District	A	IIIa
Widnes	ABCDE	IId
Wigan	ABCDE	IId
Wight, Isle of	ABCDE	IVe
Wigtown	A	IIIc
Willesden East	BCD	Id
Willesden West	BCD	Id
Wilton	A	IVe
Wimbledon	ABCDE	Ie
Winchester	ABCDE	IVd
Windsor	ABCD	IVd
Windsor & Maidenhead	E	IVd
Wirral	ABCDE	IIIc
Wisbech (Isle of Ely)	ABCDE	Vd
Withington (Manchester)	BCDE	Ia
Woking	CDE	IVd
Wokingham	A CDE	IVd
Wolverhampton East	AB	Va
Wolverhampton North-east	CDE	Va
Wolverhampton South	A	Va
Wolverhampton South-east	E	Va
Wolverhampton South-west	CDE	Va
Wolverhampton West	AB	Va
Woodbridge	AB	Vd
Woodford	† C	IId
Wood Green	BCDE	Id
Woodside (Glasgow)	CD	IVa
Woodstock	A	IVd
Woolwich (London)	A	IIe
Woolwich East (London)	BCDE	IIe
Woolwich West (London)	BCDE	IIe
Worcester	ABCDE	IVd
Worcestershire East	A	Vb
Worcestershire North	A	Vb
Worcestershire South	CDE	IVd
Workington	BCDE	IIIc
Worthing	CDE	Ve
Wrekin, The	BCDE	IVd
Wrexham	ABCDE	IIId
Wycombe	ABCDE	IVd
Wythenshawe (Manchester)	CDE	Ia
Yardley (Birmingham)	BCDE	Vb
Yarmouth, Great	ABCDE	Vd
Yeovil	BCDE	IIIe
York	ABCDE	IVc

General Index

170